DEWEY'S
ENDURING IMPACT

DEWEY'S
ENDURING IMPACT

ESSAYS ON AMERICA'S PHILOSOPHER

EDITED BY JOHN R. SHOOK
AND PAUL KURTZ

Prometheus Books

59 John Glenn Drive
Amherst, New York 14228–2119

Published 2011 by Prometheus Books

Cover design by Jacqueline Nasso Cooke
Cover image of frame © Photo Disc, Inc.
Painting of John Dewey by Edwin B. Child reproduced from the
Dictionary of American Portraits, published by Dover Publications, Inc., in 1967

Inquiries should be addressed to
Prometheus Books
59 John Glenn Drive
Amherst, New York 14228–2119
VOICE: 716–691–0133
FAX: 716–691–0137
WWW.PROMETHEUSBOOKS.COM

15 14 13 12 11   5 4 3 2 1

Library of Congress Cataloging-in-Publication Data

Dewey's enduring impact : essays on America's philosopher / by John R. Shook and Paul Kurtz (eds.).
    p. cm.
Includes bibliographical references.
ISBN 978–1–61614–229–2 (cloth : alk. paper)
ISBN 978–1–61614–277–4 (ebook)
1. Dewey, John, 1859–1952. I. Shook, John R. II. Kurtz, Paul, 1925–

B94S.D44D4955 2010
191—dc22   2010034355

Printed in the United States of America on acid-free paper

CONTENTS

PART THREE: CULTURE AND VALUES

PART FOUR: LIVED EXPERIENCE

PART FIVE: PRAGMATISM AND POLITICS

PART SIX: EDUCATION AND SOCIETY

PREFACE

John R. Shook and Paul Kurtz

During the first half of the twentieth century, no American philosopher was more prominent or more influential than John Dewey, professor of philosophy at Columbia University. The essays in this volume, most of them revised from presentations at John Dewey's 150th Birthday Celebration: An International Conference on Dewey's Impact on America and the World, which took place at the Center for Inquiry in Amherst, New York, in October 2009, focus on his core philosophical views concerning pragmatism, naturalism, humanism, and secularism. In his pragmatist philosophy, these four isms not only cooperated but also mutually supported each other. Subtract one or two of them, and the rest are fatally weakened. Dewey's vast influence upon these intellectual movements is discussed in many of this volume's essays. Perhaps more important is the issue, also addressed in this volume, of Dewey's continuing relevance to contemporary problems. The world seems to be reaching a new tipping point of social, political, and ecological instability. Can Dewey's philosophy help once again?

Dewey's Enduring Impact: Essays on America's Philosopher is important because the contributors are able to reflect on the philosophical influence of John Dewey's thought a half a century after his death. It often takes many decades for historians of ideas to evaluate the impact of a philosopher on his times. And often we can only determine his enduring influence and future relevance through a more distant lens. For the editors of this volume, Dewey stands out in a real sense as *the* philosopher of American culture; for he was able to capture and define the spirit of America. What we have in mind is the experimental, innovative, daring, and optimistic attitude that pervaded so much of the American outlook and motivated those who came to these shores to break new ground not only geographically but also in social and cultural terms.

America was first developed by waves of European settlers who discovered its vast virgin territories. The open frontiers enticed countless millions from Africa, Asia, and other corners of the globe in subsequent decades to come and make a new life for themselves. This rich continent was ripe for the picking. Although the colonialists brought the attitudes and values from a wide range of countries, this newly discovered land gave them unparalleled opportunities to build a new civilization. But this goal would not have been possible if they were constrained by the old dogmas and habits of the past. They needed to forge new values appropriate to the new conditions that they encountered.

John Dewey urged Americans to think creatively and constructively, to abandon the old habits of thought and practice, and to introduce new ways of solving problems. It was Dewey's emphasis on "indeterminate problematic situations" and the need to introduce daring new hypotheses to account for what they discovered and to test these by their consequences in action that was especially relevant to the American experiment. For only an instrumentalist and pragmatic approach could best cope with new obstacles and opportunities encountered in the environment.

Dewey's unique contribution was that he appreciated the power of science and the methods it used to resolve problematic situations, without being constrained by the customs of the past. Americans soon learned that they needed to invent, innovate, and experiment with new forms of behavior. And this methodology was able to conquer the frontier and advance new ways of living.

But more, Dewey recognized the great diversity of the Americans, representing as they did every racial, religious, and ethnic stock; and so his emphasis on democracy proved to be the appropriate formula for enabling the new Americans to live and work together. Every child needed to be educated, not by inculcating the old ways, but by learning how to think, how to cope with new problems; and they rapidly built a new civilization of bountiful harvests and urban commercial centers, skyscrapers, railroads, automobiles, space travel, new frontiers of scientific inquiry, and an improved standard of living for everyone.

Thus John Dewey represented the key values of the emerging American continent: the future is ours to create and possess, and our horizons are virtually unlimited. Many from the old countries considered this to be a form of naive optimism, without a deep sense of the tragic hardships that they had endured in their mother countries. But this American attitude led the way for others to emulate; and after entering a new millennium, we now see that we are no longer

divided from Europe and Asia by two vast oceans that enabled us to live somewhat in isolation during our formative years; but rather that we now play an
influential role on the world stage. Indeed, the American experience, which
Dewey so eloquently expressed, is now on display for the entire planetary community to learn from. We have moved far beyond our isolated existence and have
become a dominant world power, with all of the obligations and challenges that
that presents.

We submit that it is important to study the writings of John Dewey, who
expressed all of the above. We are pleased to present a wide variety of thinkers to
examine and reflect on the significance of the philosophy of Dewey and its relevance to the planetary civilization that is now emerging.

In part 1 on the centrality of Dewey, three authors supply an estimate of
Dewey's proper place in the philosophical canon and the intellectual world in general. Philip Kitcher writes on the importance of Dewey for philosophy (and for
much else besides), approving of Dewey's reorientation of philosophy toward
social inquiries into social problems. Hilary Putnam's "Reflections on Pragmatism"
locates Dewey's theory of inquiry in the wider context of pragmatist views on
knowledge and ethics. The contribution by Paul Kurtz, "Looking Ahead: What
Are the Prospects for Dewey's Philosophy in the Future?" proposes that pragmatic
humanism is well positioned for a global effort at a truly planetary ethics.

Part 2 on inquiry and knowledge starts with Peter Godfrey-Smith's "Dewey
and the Subject Matter of Science," describing Dewey's approach to the philosophy of science. The next essays recount the significance of Darwinian evolution
for features of Dewey's thought: Jay Schulkin, "Dewey and Darwin on Evolution
and Natural Kinds: A Pragmatist Perspective," and Arthur Efron, "Reclaiming
the Pragmatist Legacy: Evolution and Its Discontents." Randall E. Auxier's essay,
"Two Types of Pragmatism: Dewey and Royce," explains where these two American philosophers agree and disagree on phenomenological, epistemological, and
metaphysical matters.

Part 3 on culture and values brings together essays that all start from
Dewey's naturalism and offer ways to locate culture and values in that natural-
istic worldview. John Peter Anton plans out the work yet to be done for Dewey's
unfinished cultural project, while Nathan Bupp sketches the prospects for
Dewey and the moral resources of humanistic naturalism. James Gouinlock's
"Philosophy and the Conduct of Life: Dewey's New Paradigm" worries that
Dewey, in his atheist rejection of the supernatural, did not encourage us to

respect and remold values from past wisdom traditions. Ruth Anna Putnam recounts the experiential and pragmatic foundations for Dewey's faith. Larry A. Hickman explains how John Dewey's spiritual values amount to a defense of liberal humanism as a noble way of life, far better than supernaturalism's subservience to a dictatorial God.

Part 4 concerns lived experience, so central to pragmatism. Aesthetics has a crucial role in Dewey's thought, so Joseph Margolis guides us through a rereading of Dewey's *Art as Experience*, and Russell Pryba offers a detailed account of Dewey and the ontology of art. In "Narrative Naturalism," Judy Walker emphasizes Dewey's appreciation for the way that we humans construct and convey culture through our narratives for living noble and joyous lives.

Part 5 treats pragmatism and politics. Susan D. Carle supplies a historical review, "John Dewey and the Early NAACP: Developing a Progressive Discourse on Racial Injustice, 1909–1921." Judith M. Green's essay, "Public Reason vs. Democratic Intelligence: Rawls *and* Dewey," compares and contrasts these two giants of political theory. Gregory Fernando Pappas discusses several major contemporary political issues in the course of his essay, "Dewey's Ethical-Political Philosophy as a Present Resource." Eric Thomas Weber's "Deweyan Experimentalism and Leadership" suggests ways that Dewey's approach to social inquiry can offer valuable insights for public leadership.

Part 6 contains essays on education and society. Stephen M. Fishman and Lucille McCarthy outline their classroom experiences, which take advantage of Dewey's impact on education. Maura Striano's "An Educational Theory of Inquiry" organizes the principles of Dewey's pedagogy. Giuseppe Spadafora's *The Sources of a Science of Education* by John Dewey and the Italian Interpretations" and Massimo Vittorio's "The Origins of the Italian Misunderstanding of Dewey's Philosophy" recount many aspects of the Italian reception and absorption of Dewey's thought.

To conclude this prefatory survey of the contemporary significance of Dewey's philosophy, we return to the centrality of naturalism in his system. Outdated caricatures of naturalism, and evolution especially, depict humans as instinctively selfish. These crude distortions again forget that humans have higher intelligence and organized culture. Morality functions well for such a social species as ours, and if we are smart, we can improve our moralities just as we improve any other tools. Changing social tools can be harder than modifying steel tools; ethics is difficult because some people can unyieldingly place themselves at the center of everything. Yet naturalism, as pragmatists emphasize, finds no center to the universe. Again, this could be viewed as an open invitation to embrace materialistic nihilism, but humanism is smarter than that. Precisely because humanity is trying to live in a fragile and contingent world, we must cooperatively think harder than ever before.

What else besides a naturalistic humanism can practically undertake this task? Not the Bronze Age mythologies expecting a magical God-rescuer. Not the escapist mysticisms sending souls into unconscious ecstasies. It is not a question of whether ideal ends will determine the destiny of humanity on this planet. Some ideals or another have brought us to this point, and they will take us forward, perhaps to tragedy. Only we can grab control of our ideals and bend them toward a better planetary destiny. Pragmatic humanism is a call to responsibility, a responsibility for the future of life itself. The prospects of Dewey's philosophy in the future amount to our own prospects in the future.

Abbreviations

References to John Dewey's correspondence are to Larry A. Hickman, ed., *The Correspondence of John Dewey* (Charlottesville, VA: InteLex, 1999–2008): vol. 1, *1871–1918* (1999, rev. eds. 2001, 2005, and 2008); vol. 2, *1919–1939* (2001, rev. eds. 2005 and 2008); vol. 3, *1940–1952* (2005, rev. ed. 2008); and vol. 4, *1953–2007* (2008). Citations normally include accession number, writer, addressee, and date. For example, "(09281) John Dewey to Corinne Chisholm Frost, January 1, 1931."

Standard references to John Dewey's work are to the critical (print) edition, *The Collected Works of John Dewey, 1882–1953*, edited by Jo Ann Boydston (Carbondale: Southern Illinois University Press, 1969–1991), published in three series as *The Early Works* (EW), *The Middle Works* (MW), and *The Later Works* (LW). "LW.5.270," for example, refers to *The Later Works*, volume 5, page 270. In order to ensure uniform citations of the critical edition, the pagination of the print edition has been preserved in *The Collected Works of John Dewey, 1882–1953: The Electronic Edition*, edited by Larry A. Hickman (Charlottesville, VA: InteLex, 1996).

Part One

THE CENTRALITY OF DEWEY

1.

THE IMPORTANCE OF DEWEY FOR PHILOSOPHY (AND FOR MUCH ELSE BESIDES)

Philip Kitcher

1.

From the 1920s until his death in 1952, John Dewey was more influential than any American philosopher has been, either before or since his time. For the last half century, however, Dewey's major works, which were once read and studied by philosophers and the broader public alike, have had little impact on American philosophy or on American intellectual culture. Although he has had prominent champions, Richard Rorty and Hilary Putnam among them, Dewey is absent from the curricula of most American universities and colleges, and, even when he appears, it is most often as an inert fragment of intellectual history, as the expression of attitudes that belong to different times and that have no serious implications for the present.

To see how far Dewey is from the fashions of contemporary philosophy, it is only necessary to consider the account of the subject that he offers in *Democracy and Education*:

> If we are willing to conceive education as the process of forming fundamental dispositions, intellectual and emotional, toward nature and fellow men, philosophy may even be defined *as the general theory of education*.[1]

His proposal reminds us of his pioneering work in setting up the lab school at the University of Chicago, and of his continual willingness to cross West 120th Street to join Columbia University to Teacher's College. For those who have been well brought up in late twentieth-century Anglo-American philosophy, the suggestion is, at best, quaint. Applied philosophy is all very well (although philosophy of education ranks as a very low-budget application), but we know where the center of the discipline lies: in logic, metaphysics, epistemology, philosophy of language, and philosophy of mind—the "core areas" as aficionados typically call them. Contrast Dewey's proposal with the influential historical thesis offered by Michael Dummett. The history of philosophy, Dummett contends, shows three phases, the first (extending from ancient Greece until the seventeenth century) for which metaphysics was the central philosophical subject; the second, initiated by the work of Descartes, that instituted epistemology as the heart of philosophy; and the third, inaugurated by Frege, that identifies the central task of philosophy as the construction of a theory of meaning. When Anglophone philosophers disagree with Dummett about details, they continue to play variations on a central theme.

Dewey wanted to sound a different tune. In the sentence that follows his account of philosophy as the general theory of education, he offers a contrast with rival visions:

> Unless a philosophy is to remain symbolic—or verbal—or a sentimental indulgence for a few, or else mere arbitrary dogma, its auditing of past experience and its program of values must take effect in conduct.[2]

The thought that philosophy should be confined to the few is anathema to Dewey, and he recognizes the danger that it may do so. In the paragraph that precedes the definition, he has drawn attention to the pressures that create a gap between philosophy and the broader culture.

> The fact that philosophical problems arise because of widespread and widely felt difficulties in social practice is disguised because philosophers become a specialized class [that] uses a technical language, unlike the vocabulary in which the direct difficulties are stated.[3]

Using technical formulations is dangerous because continued usage of the esoteric language may incline philosophy to concentrate on the allegedly timeless problems bequeathed by tradition, without returning to the genuine source of philosophical reflection, the social difficulties that arise in different forms in different times and places, thus making the professional practice divorced from and irrelevant to the wider culture. A Deweyan survey of contemporary Anglo-Saxon philosophy, particularly focused on those fields that professionals advertise as the "core areas," would give ample reason to think that the danger has not exactly been avoided. Dewey was no clairvoyant and was thus unable to foresee the scholasticism that prevails in much contemporary metaphysics, epistemology, and theory of language and mind, but he saw the same defects in earlier schools of philosophizing, including those that flourished in Britain and America during the early decades of his life. His call for a reconstruction in philosophy, advocated in the aptly titled *Reconstruction in Philosophy* and in many other writings, was based on precisely that awareness.

2.

To understand more clearly what Dewey wanted from a reform of philosophy, and why he thought of it as regeneration rather than abandonment of the enterprise in favor of something else, it helps to begin with an important formulation of related ideas that occurs in the work of his great fellow pragmatist, William James. In one of the most memorable passages in *Pragmatism*, James restates the principle he ascribes to Charles Sanders Peirce:

> It is astonishing to see how many philosophical disputes collapse into insignificance the moment you subject them to this simple test of tracing a concrete consequence. There can be no difference anywhere that doesn't *make* a difference elsewhere—no difference in abstract truth that doesn't express itself in a difference in concrete fact and in conduct consequent upon that fact, imposed on somebody, somehow, somewhere, and somewhen. The whole function of philosophy ought to be to find out what definite difference it will make to you and me, at definite instants of our life, if this world-formula or that world-formula be the true one.[4]

Unsympathetic readers of this passage, especially those in the grip of the thought that philosophy is centrally focused on issues about the meaning of words or the content of thoughts, interpret James as advocating a verificationist approach to meaning—a Very Bad Answer to the Central Question in philosophy. With some strain, that construction might be imposed on the middle sentence of the paragraph. The flanking sentences make it patent, however, that James is concerned not with "cognitive significance" (or linguistic meaning) but with the *importance* of questions and of answering those questions. Moreover, the questions he has in mind are philosophical questions. Reflecting on the practice of philosophers, he wants to know why anyone should be interested in knowing the answers to the questions they labor to address. The standard for importance is psychological—the answer to an important question changes the psychological lives of those who receive it, freeing them from difficulties they had been confronting. Furthermore, James has a very particular question in mind, for he supposes that philosophy is the search for a "world-formula," and its importance lies in the fact that each of us needs to find the true one.

This apparently mysterious language becomes far less puzzling once we attend to central themes in James's early writings. A concern with the function of philosophy already occupied James in the 1870s, when he wrote an early version of "The Sentiment of Rationality." At the core of that essay, and prominent in other lectures and writings—"Is Life Worth Living?" "The Will to Believe," *The Varieties of Religious Experience*—is the proposal that philosophy should make sense of "that somewhat chaotic view which everyone by nature carries about with him under his hat."[5] James's elaboration of the task leaves no doubt about the stimulus that drove him. He yearns for a reconciliation of the scientific picture of the world, synthesized from the physics of Newton and Maxwell, the evolutionary biology of Darwin, and his own and kindred ventures in human psychology, with some sense of purpose in nature, some way of giving point to the whole and a direction to human existence. Achieving that reconciliation is, for James, *the* philosophical project, one that he pursues with remarkable intensity and considerable integrity. A satisfactory world-formula would acquiesce in the scientific facts without blinking, and yet offer James, and his contemporaries who often felt similar anxieties, a sense of the importance and purposiveness of human life.

Dewey agrees with, and takes over, some of this. He shares with James the central thought that philosophical questions need to be assessed for their significance, and that the assessment turns on the differences that are made to human lives. Unlike James, however, he does not take there to be a single vast philosophical problem, centered on something like the reconciliation of natural science and religion—as we shall see, that will turn out to be one issue for him, but it has neither a monopoly nor any special priority. James might be correct to declare, vaguely, that philosophers ought to make sense of the natural and chaotic views we all carry under our hats, but the character of these views and the difficulties they pose for us are not historically invariant. Indeed, Dewey would surely diagnose the specific question that so occupies James as arising in a very particular historical context, one that has absorbed the new physics and the new biology, one that has turned a scientific critical apparatus on religion, and one in which anthropological inquiries are revealing the diversity of the beliefs about the transcendent that guide the lives of diverse groups of people.

The thought that philosophical problems evolve is evident in Dewey's writings. Chapter 3 of *Reconstruction in Philosophy*, for example, traces the way in which the generic Jamesian task of "responding to the difficulties life presents"[6] assumes different forms, as we learn more about the natural world. From the very first pages of *The Quest for Certainty*, Dewey insists that the impetus to philosophy was present in all human contexts, from the natural and social environments of our Paleolithic ancestors, through the variant forms of society we know from history and anthropology, to the circumstances of the present. His central task is to recognize the appropriate questions that arise for his contemporaries:

> The problem of restoring integration and cooperation between man's beliefs about the world in which he lives and the values and purposes that should direct his conduct is the deepest problem of modern life. It is the problem of any philosophy that is not isolated from that life.[7]

Dewey rejects, however, the Jamesian simplification that reduces the problem to reconciling a monolithic entity, *Science*, with another monolithic entity, *Religion*. His closing pages emphasize the partial, fragmentary, and unsystematic character of all our knowledge. We have, he suggests, specific problems that arise from the conditions of modern life, problems of individual conduct and of social organization:

> Man has never had such a varied body of knowledge in his possession before, and probably never before has he been so uncertain and so perplexed as to what his knowledge means, what it points to in action and in consequences.[8]

Within the general project of systematizing the incomplete and disorganized picture of the world that our various fields of inquiry deliver, there are specific issues, urgent questions for people today, that arise concerning what should be valued and what purposes should be pursued. These questions emerge from the actual conditions of democracy, from the fragmentation of large societies, from the inequalities and conflicts that divide people. In some cases, they may be questions that reformulate some problem framed by earlier philosophers in a very different social-historical context; others may be new, beyond the conceptual horizons bounding previous philosophical thought. Genuine philosophy, philosophy that is not "isolated from life," must start from framing and reformulating its questions, taking seriously, from the beginning, James's criterion of significance.

If this is to be more than a vague gesture at reform, two tasks require attention. First, more needs to be said about what makes questions significant, or, in Dewey's version, what enables philosophy to be connected with life. Second, Dewey's readers can reasonably demand some concrete details about how new, or modified, philosophical questions emerge from the circumstances of contemporary life. As I shall argue shortly, Dewey offered us a series of major books, once widely and enthusiastically read, that amply satisfy the latter demand. On the other hand, he did not do much to articulate the general pragmatist thought that "philosophy should make a difference." So, before trying to reconstruct the Deweyan agenda, I shall attempt to make good the lack.

3.

James's criterion—that answering a philosophical question makes a psychological difference to someone, somewhere, and sometime—looks toothless. For consider the scholastic questioners of any age, those who ask after the number of angels that can dance on a pinhead or wonder if evidence someone does not possess can undermine the person's knowledge. Arriving at answers plainly does make a psychological difference to the medieval disputant or to the contemporary epistemologist: these people gain psychological relief, feel satisfied, elated, disappointed. Nor will it help to add, in a Deweyan vein, that the psychological change must find expression in conduct, for, equipped with their answer, the inquirers now do different things. Moving on to new scholastic questions—perhaps about the form of the dance the angels perform or the accessibility of the evidence that subverts—they read different texts, take different notes, and hold different animated conversations from those they would otherwise have engaged in. The Jamesian slogan sounds good, but it is universally tolerant.

It is not hard to recognize what James and Dewey hope to rule out. They conceive of certain intellectual trends as fossilized and sterile, of the people who are dedicated to continuing these trends as benighted, and of the psychological changes brought about by their fruitless inquiries as not really counting—these alterations don't make a genuine difference. To state their intent so baldly only exposes the fact that general talk of psychological change or change that affects conduct is inadequate as a criterion of genuine difference making. Some extra account is required.

What could that account be? One possibility is to make pragmatism definite by insisting on enhanced abilities to intervene in nature. The trouble with answers to questions about dancing angels or undermining evidence is that they don't result in increased powers to cope with our environment. Recalling the familiar pragmatist metaphor of "cash value," one might require that the answer to a significant question must effect psychological changes in those who adopt it, in such a way as to enable them to act in profitable ways. To pursue this line would call for some elucidation of what exactly counts as an intervention in nature and what makes interventions profitable, but, whether or not the necessary explanations are forthcoming, there is an important objection to so bluntly practical a criterion. Any global disregard for questions of clarification whose resolution yields no new possibilities of action seems crude and Philistine, a negation of philosophy rather than a reconstruction of it. Neither James nor Dewey, as I read them, ever doubted that issues of clarification are important for their own sakes, for both recognized that there are forms of inquiry whose aims are purely explanatory. Simply understanding aspects of nature, for example, the starry heavens above us or the passions that work within, is sometimes significant. The demand that clarification always issue in enhanced facilities of intervention cuts away questions that ought to be retained.

Dewey's emphasis on the partial, incomplete, and selective character of human knowledge supplies a clue to a better elaboration of the desired criterion. We shall never, he contends, arrive at the complete truth about the world, for that is, if not incoherent, at least radically unattainable. The image of some final theory that might yield all the truths about nature is unreal, simply because the set of such truths is too vast to be captured in anything we could appreciate as a system. Even right here and now, there is some large nondenumerable infinity of possible languages, in each of which there are infinitely many truths about what goes on—truths about momentary temperature fluctuations, about spatial relations among various constituent parts, and so on and on and on. Human beings pursue inquiry profitably by selecting issues that matter to them, by considering certain types of order that they can find, or sometimes create, in their natural and social environments—pockets of order like Newtonian or Mendelian systems. Success accrues not by discovering all the truths, but by answering the questions that matter.

To say this is simply to present in a more general frame the point that James and Dewey make about philosophy and philosophical significance. The generalization makes apparent the fact that decisions about the significance of questions arise for all kinds of inquiry, and opens up the possibility of addressing the special case of philosophy as an instance of a more global phenomenon. Philosophy is one field of inquiry among many, part of a constellation that extends from art history through zoology. Human resources as well as human abilities are finite, and inquiry must be selective. How then should we apportion time, energy, and talent among various types of inquiry; and within the diverse areas, what questions ought to command attention?

My formulation slides over a crucial point in its casual invocation of the first person plural—who are "we" for whom particular issues matter and who make decisions about directions for inquiry? The "we" that directs inquiry is a fiction, since the selective course of investigation, broadly conceived, results from an uncoordinated play of individual interests and aspirations, constrained to some extent by the variant wants of broader groups (national "wars on cancer" and the like). The "we" for whom some questions matter, on the other hand, is a serious topic for identification, and Dewey, staunch democrat that he is, has an obvious proposal: the inquiries to be pursued are those that affect all members of the human species. The specialists who undertake inquiry, he tells us, represent all of us:

> . . . these persons represent a social division of labor; and their specialization can be trusted only when such persons are in unobstructed cooperation with other social occupations, sensitive to others' problems and transmitting results to them for wider application in action.[9]

He is acutely aware that the tacit contract that links the work of inquiry to the broad needs of people can be broken. In a passage that parallels the concerns about philosophical isolation I have already cited, he writes:

> [Inquiry] degenerates into sterile specialization, a kind of intellectual busy work carried on by socially absentminded men. Details are heaped up in the name of science, and abstruse dialectical developments of systems occur. Then the occupation is "rationalized" under the lofty name of devotion to truth for its own sake.[10]

Dewey's account of philosophical significance is embedded with a standard for well-ordered inquiry, one that is thoroughly democratic and egalitarian.

I elaborate that standard as follows. Well-ordered inquiry would pursue just those lines of investigation, to the extent and in proportion to their evaluation as significant by a group of deliberators representing all human circumstances and points of view, all thoroughly informed as to the existing state of human knowledge and to the foreseeable prospects for developing it further, and all fully committed to mutual engagement with one another. The conditions that figure in this account are intended to rule out the various ways in which, from a thoroughly democratic point of view, inquiry can go astray. Most evident, as Dewey recognizes so clearly, investigations can give priority to the wishes or to the whimsical interests of the few, at cost to the many: biomedical research can focus, as it so strikingly has in recent decades, on projects that might enhance the lives of an affluent minority, while leaving the life-threatening and incapacitating diseases that afflict vast numbers of poor people, most especially children, radically understudied; more abstract disciplines, like philosophy, can pursue issues that fascinate specialists, while paying scant attention to questions that touch on the lives of many people. To demand that all human circumstances and points of view be represented is a first step toward avoiding this predicament. Genuine democracy, however, cannot be content with an expression of the raw wishes of all individuals, uninformed about the actual state of human inquiry and about how it might be developed. For you to make a decision about how inquiry would promote your interests, you need not only the ability to convey your own perspective—to report on the things about which you are the best expert, your own needs and aspirations—but also an understanding of the ways in which your goals could be promoted, given what is already known and what might now be probed and pursued. Democracy thrives on the combination of expertise, in which the individual's own intimate knowledge of context and preference is shaped by the collective corpus of knowledge. Hence, well-ordered inquiry insists that the research agenda be that chosen by well-informed representatives of all points of view. The final condition is needed to overcome a familiar obstacle of actual deliberations, partial insistence on individual points of view, even when it is clear that they bring problematic consequences for others. By requiring that the deliberators be mutually engaged, the constraints on well-ordered inquiry insist that no group's interests can be sacrificed. The three conditions can be viewed as combating three forms of tyranny: the tyranny of wealth and power, the tyranny of ignorance, and the tyranny of the majority.

Much more could be said about the ideal of well-ordered inquiry that I favor—and that seems implicit in Dewey's own writings. I hope, however, that the picture is clear enough to allow for further elaboration of the Jamesian account of significance. The apparent laxity of that account is corrected not by declaring that certain kinds of psychological changes, those felt by contented scholastics, past or present, who arrive at answers to their own esoteric questions, are counted as not mattering because they have no expression in practical intervention, but rather by arguing that these kinds of changes could not be seen as making a genuine difference by the standards of well-ordered inquiry. We can imagine the dialectic between the scholastic and his pragmatist opponent. At the first stage, the pragmatist challenges the scholastic to show how answers to the questions he pursues would make a difference. In response, the scholastic maintains that these answers provide important clarifications, delivering cognitive benefits that, although not evidently yielding increased powers of intervention in nature, are to be valued for their own sake—Dewey's "lofty devotion to truth." Appealing to the standard of well-ordered inquiry, the pragmatist now asks whether this style of clarification can take priority over other investigations that might matter to people: does the current lack of clarity make itself felt in the lives of nonspecialists, does it interfere with projects that might address issues of concern to many? Here, pragmatism acknowledges that pursuit of technical problems, even problems not readily understood by the vast majority of human beings, can be of enormous value. For solving those problems might advance the enterprise of tackling broader issues, eventually leading to results that would be welcomed by all. Well-ordered inquiry endorses the associated projects precisely because ideal deliberators would be able to appreciate these facts, and would, in consequence, support the investigations.

The James-Dewey criterion of significance thus presents a *challenge* to lines of inquiry, not a simple knock-down argument against anything the vulgar find irrelevant or impractical. It is eminently possible that abstract philosophical questions, even those that carry a whiff of scholasticism about them, might meet the challenge and find pragmatic endorsement. Problems about the character of human perception, highlighted by classical forms of philosophical skepticism or issues about the general conditions under which individuals can know, might be shown to underlie ambiguities that permeate large areas of inquiry. If that is the case, then it is valuable to recognize just why it is so, valuable to see how the pragmatist challenge is met. James and Dewey expect that healthy forms of inquiry, including healthy forms of philosophy, will be alert to the possibility that traditional problems, and the derivative questions they generate, may no longer be in accord with the standards of well-ordered inquiry, and that practitioners will pose the challenge for themselves and their colleagues.

There is, of course, no easy algorithm for testing extant or proposed lines of research against the standards of well-ordered inquiry. Often, it will be hard to decide how an ideally informed and mutually engaged discussion among a fully representative sample of human beings would set priorities. Not always, however. In the biomedical case, for example, even though we may not know the details, we can be confident that no ideal discussion would vindicate the profoundly skewed research agenda that has dominated research. Similarly, in fields whose technical "literature" is read only by a small minority of specialists, whose "progress" is marked by no accumulation of results that supports wider inquiries, whose track record shows no significant reshaping of other forms of investigation, there are grounds for suspicion that the pragmatist challenge cannot be met. Pragmatists from Peirce on have taught us that particular doubt, not global skepticism, should be the spur to inquiry, that we should only scratch where it itches. That maxim can be honored by focusing the challenge on those disciplines where we find cause for suspicion—fields so detached from the broader culture that their "contributions" fade without leaving a trace.

Professional Anglophone philosophy, both in Dewey's time and in ours, has the marks that invite the challenge. That is not yet to condemn it, for further argument might reveal that the challenge can be met. I shall postpone until the very end any further consideration of this point. Serious attention to the state of any branch of inquiry is aided by recognizing alternative versions of its future—and so we return to the second topic I promised above, namely Dewey's proposals about how philosophical problems grow out of the conditions of human life.

4.

Dewey's positive vision of philosophy can be illustrated by a number of detailed examples, of which I shall choose three. The first of these centers on ethics and is elaborated in *Human Nature and Conduct*, as well as in the textbook *Ethics*, which he coauthored with James Tufts (Dewey was responsible for the long middle section). His reflections on ethics start not with some proposed system of ethical truths, nor with problems about the meaning of ethical statements or about our knowledge of ethical principles, but with the moral life as it is lived by his contemporaries. Central to his approach is the denial that there is some complete system of ethical truth that would, if only we knew it, supply answers to all questions about what we should do or be. He writes:

> . . . rigid moral codes that attempt to lay down definite injunctions and prohibitions for every occasion in life turn out in fact loose and slack. Stretch ten commandments or any other number as far as you will by ingenious exegesis, yet acts unprovided for by them will occur. No elaboration of statute law can forestall variant cases and the need of interpretation *ad hoc*.[11]

We are offered a hypothesis about the moral life as we experience it, a claim that all of us constantly find the collection of ethical resources, supplied by our communities, by religious teachers or philosophical system builders, to leave us with ethical work to do. We are also offered an analogy: ethics is akin to law; it has a history and evolves over time; moreover, it is never finished, and there is always further work to be done. There are a number of important points in this approach: first, the emphasis on ethical practice and not on the objective values (laws, reasons) it is often assumed to embody; second, the rejection of any ideal set of ethical axioms, to be specified by the ingenious philosopher, and to be supplied with a complete justification; third, the conception of human life as embedded in an ethical practice inherited from earlier generations and extended in the individual's lifetime. The challenge for each of us is to make appropriate use of what we have received and to do what we can to refine and improve it: "The best we can accomplish for posterity is to transmit unimpaired and with some increment of meaning the environment that makes it possible to maintain the habits of decent and refined life."[12]

The term *habit* here is crucial. Dewey recognizes the size of the class of actions we perform daily, understanding that it would be impossible for us constantly to be deliberating about what should be done. Born into ethical practices, we are trained to respond to recurring situations in particular ways. The habits we acquire—some of them common to all members of our society, others arising from various roles and institutions that the society specifies—give rise to patterns of conduct, and it is frequently apt that people produce these patterns without thinking. In a constantly changing world, however, individuals may find their smooth habitual performances disrupted; they feel the pressure of contrary dispositions. This can occur because of unusual contingencies: travelers on their various missions encounter a suffering stranger at the roadside. Or it can arise out of unprecedented opportunities, as when new forms of technology expand our possibilities. An ability to communicate with distant people and to affect their well-being may create new potential analogues of the suffering stranger at the roadside. Learning that faraway people are in want, we can no longer continue our old routines under the more or less regretful assurance that there is nothing that we can do to help them. Similarly, when biomedical advances make it possible to test before birth or to use parts of early embryos to explore ways of relieving disease and disability, old habits of conduct clash, and there is ethical work to be done.

From Dewey's perspective, classical treatments of ethics, whether supplied by philosophers or religious teachers, tend to two dangerous oversimplifications. They take for granted the existence of an ideal ethical system, to be fathomed by the aspiring ethicist, in light of which all conduct could be finally appraised. They also simplify the psychology of the agent, inventing some special "moral point of view," to which we should all aspire. Dewey wants us to reject both fictions in favor of understanding both the incompleteness of ethical practice and the hodgepodge of considerations that figure in ethical life. Instead of supposing that reason (whatever that is) should overwhelm sentiment and habit or that moral sentiments are the ultimate authority in conduct or (to manufacture an implausible position) that proper moral agents are creatures of the habits they have been taught, Dewey supposes that there are serious ethical questions, for each generation, about the kinds of sentiments that should be developed, the circumstances under which they should be given priority, the forms of reasoning that should be employed and the occasions on which they are appropriate, and the domain under which habit is the appropriate guide to what is done.

I shall illustrate his perspective with a serious example, and a claim that many philosophers find absurd. Giorgio Agamben is only one of several European thinkers who have suggested that Auschwitz is a test of all prior systems of ethics. The quick and obvious response is to declare that the validity of ethical maxims cannot be tested in any such way: the horrors of the Holocaust and the death camps merely reveal the inabilities of those who administered the machinery of annihilation to appreciate those maxims. So blunt an answer is inadequate. For, in the first place, the compromises made by the inmates of the camps, those who inhabited what Primo Levi calls "the grey zone," demand an extension of ideal ethical theory to accommodate levels of allowing for external pressures and human frailties. Second, and more significant, even the most superficial acquaintance with the letters and diaries of those most centrally implicated in the daily work of human annihilation makes it evident that these people firmly believed the maxims that have been central to the major ethical traditions. The problem came in their application of those maxims, and its source lay in the categories and classifications they used. There is no field of human inquiry or practice, neither in ethics nor in any of the sciences, in which principles wear their applications on their faces. The ways in which the world is seen and described are crucial for proper responses to it, and an ethical system, broadly construed as a means of assessing, directing, and reforming human action, is deficient to the extent that it allows for forms of blindness that subvert performance—the blindness so evident in the pious *KZ-Arbeiter*, who could write to their families about their love of their neighbors and their derivative duty to free humanity from the pestilence caused by vermin. Previous ethical systems were tested by the atrocities of the twentieth century because they allowed for certain dreadful forms of blindness.

From a Deweyan perspective, some sorts of failure are inevitable, since an ideal language that would block all potential misapplications of ethical resources is a fantasy. The challenge for philosophy is to understand the character of ethical practice—as developed in the psychology of the ethical agent, the social training that begins an individual's ethical life, and the history of the various ethical traditions that survive today. Based on that kind of analytic understanding, one can undertake a version of the task that traditional philosophy has begun with: a search for precepts and methods of resolving ethical debate. Yet because there is no ideal system—no ideal language, no ideal method—to be found, the quest must be for ethical resources that are pertinent to our context, relevant to the failures of ethical practice we can recognize in the past and the difficulties and disputes that confront us now. Specifically, one part of this is a matter of stabilizing and extending what an analytical account of ethical practice reveals as the achievements of our predecessors: learning from the lessons of the twentieth century; seeking ways of making the value of human lives more vivid and more secure; and working to discover proper ways of using the new opportunities technology has made available.

Beyond that, however, is a more ambitious task. The habits we acquire in our socialization are often embedded in institutions and roles that have a long and intricate history. Some current occasions of ethical difficulty result from the conflict of entrenched habits and cannot be resolved without a serious analysis and reform of our social life. Ethical dilemmas may derive from conflicting maxims that presuppose social institutions—as, for example, some of the commandments presuppose institutions of private property and of marriage. As I read him, Dewey envisages the possibility both of genealogical reconstruction that exposes the multilayered purposes roles and institutions are supposed to achieve and of experimental efforts to make those institutions more adequate to current human needs. In the first part of this, he shows an unexpected kinship with apparently more radical thinkers—with Marx, Nietzsche, and Foucault. In seeing genealogy as the prelude to experimentation, however, Dewey stakes out a unique position, one that regards philosophy not as the disclosure of the One True Path, a path that history has previously deserted or for which it has not yet been ready, but rather as the source of proposals that may be democratically discussed and tested against future human experience. Simultaneously, he withdraws from the classical ambitions of systematizing ethicists and offers a more extensive domain in which philosophers might make their admittedly tentative proposals.

5.

My treatment of two other illustrations of Dewey's philosophical program will be much briefer. As we might expect, his contributions to political philosophy diverge from the foundational topics that are typically the focus of philosophical concern. Instead of starting by asking why the state should have authority over us, he relies on the supposition that some sort of association with others and regulation of life together is an unavoidable feature of the human condition. Born into a particular state, we should treat its authority as we treat the authority of our teachers, appraising the resources we have acquired and trying to correct them where they are found wanting. If there are alternatives available to us, we may even want to move elsewhere. On the other hand, if we remain, the important task is to improve the form of political life into which we have been pitched.

John Stuart Mill, whom William James hailed as a precursor of pragmatism, focused a question that he saw as arising within his own society. Victorian

Britain, Mill claimed, was liable to introduce laws and social pressures that inter-fered with freedom and cramped individuality. Dewey follows Mill in supposing that this is an area in which serious difficulties arise for twentieth-century democracies—most notably, the United States—but he poses the problem dif-ferently. He starts from a distinction between the private and the public, which supposes that *interactions* among individuals are private when the important consequences are confined to the group of individuals concerned; they are public when there are significant consequences for outsiders. By analogy with Mill's principle that legal (or public) intervention into the life of an individual is war-ranted when the individual's actions affect the lives of others, Dewey supposes that a transaction among two or more people becomes a matter of public con-cern when it has adverse effects for those who are not party to it.

This may initially appear to be a minor twist on Mill's seminal claims about political liberty, but the shift is consequential. Whereas the life projects Mill champions, the ability of each of us to pursue his own good in his own way, might take any form, and, indeed, might even be completely solitary (say, a ded-ication to life as a hermit), one of Dewey's central claims about humanity is that our lives, if they are worthwhile, are inevitably social. Conjoint action is essential to us, in that a serious life project without it is deficient. On this basis, Dewey replaces the "thin" conception of democracy, in which free elections are viewed as central (a conception he ascribes to James Mill, John Stuart Mill's father), with something far richer. Placing conjoint action at the center of valuable human lives, he supposes that democracy advances human freedom through its ability to provide individual people with the ability to act together and to play a role in directing the activities of a group. So, "in a generic or social sense," democracy is characterized as follows:

> From the standpoint of the individual, it consists in having a responsible share according to capacity in forming and directing the activities of the groups to which one belongs and in participating according to need in the values which the groups sustain.[13]

The ideal of human freedom introduced here mixes elements of the so-called positive and negative conceptions: Dewey takes over from Mill both the thought that the terms on which people enter in to their patterns of conjoint action should be free from coercion, based on an early education that opens up to them a wide range of possibilities for their lives, and the requirement that these interacting groups should be able to carry on their activities without outside interference, except insofar as they impinge upon other like groups; he also draws from the Republican tradition the idea that our freedom is enhanced through the ability to act with others, by operating as part of groups whose activities we can "form and guide according to our capacities." In recognizing this as a part of democratic freedom, Dewey is surely influenced by Tocqueville, who was so strongly impressed by the "voluntary associations" he found in New England communities.

Times have changed, however. Even from the perspective of the 1920s, it was plain that the United States no longer functioned as a body of overlapping groups, each pursuing its activities in harmony with others. As Dewey sees it, the problem for serious democracy in a large and heterogeneous society, arises from the decomposition of the public:

> ... there are too many publics, for conjoint actions which have indirect, serious and enduring consequences are multitudinous beyond comparison, and each one of them crosses the others and generates its own group of persons especially affected with little to hold these different publics together in an integrated whole.[14]

The great opportunities for freedom in large societies result from this multiplication, but the difficulties of overcoming ignorance about the consequences of their diverse activities, coupled with the "scattering" of the citizens and, derivatively, with their inability to appreciate the worth of the projects pursued by people with whom they have little contact, produces a diminution in the freedom experienced by many. Just as Mill was concerned with the limitations placed on freedom by the intrusions of government (and of social prejudice, which, as he admitted, was both invasive and hard to combat), Dewey sees freedom as threatened by citizens' inabilities to cohere as a great community, one in which the joint projects of groups (the many smaller publics) are sustained to the extent that they are pursued in harmony. Anyone who shares this conception of democratic freedom understands that the mere opportunity to register a vote—even under conditions of public honesty—is inadequate to realize it, and that the promise to let citizens keep a slightly larger percentage of their income, at cost to all the social structures that make joint projects possible, is the most cynical debasement and violation of it.

Dewey's social and political philosophy calls for a sociologically and economically informed analysis of the conditions under which his ideal of freedom might be realized in a heterogeneous society. That issue replaces in his writings the traditional focus on the legitimacy of the democratic state. It does so in accordance with the basic pragmatic approach I have identified. We are born into a state, in our case a more or less flawed realization of democracy, and the analysis of the flaws and proposals for improvement are the urgent questions for our times.

I turn finally to a last Deweyan question, the problem that James elevated as *the* philosophical issue. In the wake not only of Darwinism but also of detailed critical study of the scriptural texts (of Judaism as well as of Christianity), of psychological and anthropological discoveries and historical understanding of the world's major religions, James and many of his contemporaries struggled to find a way beyond what they saw as discredited literalist belief toward something that would preserve the fundamental value they found in religious practice. Characteristically, James focuses on the plight of the individual who has heard all the terrible news: how is this individual to reconcile the scientific picture of the world with any sense of purposiveness for himself and his own life? At times, James views the solution to the problem as requiring some sort of license to believe in a "transcendent" being; at other times, he is content to allow that it can be solved satisfactorily if one can reach a state of "affirming the universe" or "identifying oneself with the ultimate things."

Dewey has also heard the terrible news, and he is convinced that it makes any kind of literalism about supernatural entities impossible. The message of the various inquiries—historical, biological, anthropological, and so forth—is that literal belief in anything transcendent has to be abandoned. On this point, he is blunt: "there is nothing left worth preserving in the notions of unseen powers, controlling human destiny to which obedience, reverence, and worship are due."[15] Yet, he suggests, it is worth reflecting on the ways in which, in some traditions, acts of obedience, reverence, and worship have been valuable to individuals and to societies. Dewey's social emphasis is as characteristic as James's focus on the individual predicament. The religious attitude is important for building a unified self, for each of us needs to see our life as having some point or purpose, but it is realized through collective activities, displayed in "art, science, and good citizenship."[16]

Dewey offers an analysis of traditional religions. They identify particular kinds of experiences and behavior as important for people because the pertinent episodes and actions are supposed to disclose or respond to a transcendent being.

The devout are alleged to receive an "enduring change in attitude" because they have apprehended this being and its (his?) will for them. Focusing on the psychological changes, Dewey inverts the perspective:

> I should like to turn the statement around and say that whenever this change takes place there is a definitely religious attitude. It is not *a* religion that brings it about, but, whenever it occurs, from whatever cause and by whatever means, there is a religious outlook and function.[17]

Dewey is as convinced as Nietzsche that God is dead, and, like Nietzsche, he thinks that there is a philosophical issue about what happens next. Unlike Nietzsche (whose individualism is more akin to James's), Dewey's approach to the problem emphasizes the social conditions under which individual lives gain purpose and meaning.

He offers a diagnosis of the difficulties in achieving a thoroughly secular society. With the fragmentation of the public, it is difficult for people to pursue the types of conjoint actions that are so central to human life. Living in heterogeneous societies that no longer function as any kind of community—let alone a Great Community—their possibilities for the collective projects that elaborate their freedom are narrowed, and it is only within the framework of certain institutions, churches, synagogues, and mosques, that they can find opportunities for becoming unified and whole. The philosophical issue of understanding how finite human lives can obtain point and meaning is not simply a question about individual projects and their significance—although it is that as well, and, in this regard, Dewey thinks that artists, novelists, and dramatists have offered more insights than most philosophers—but also about the social conditions under which the religious attitude can develop. Here his exploration of religion connects closely with the problems of ethics and social philosophy, as he conceives them. It is no accident that his set of lectures on religion is entitled *A Common Faith*.

Writing in the 1930s from the Upper West Side, Dewey thought that literalism and supernaturalism in religion were in a crisis from which they could not recover. Were he to contemplate American society today, he would surely be appalled by the massive ignorance that allows the most grotesque forms of biblical literalism to flourish, and he would probably be grateful to the authors who periodically remind those who read their books of the many-sided arguments constructed from the late eighteenth century to the early twentieth century that precipitated the crisis. Yet he would also protest the vehement negativity of the attacks on religion, their scathing lack of concern for what comes next. Despite Dewey's own efforts to point the way, the decline of literalist faith left a vacuum into which even the crudest forms of supernaturalism could easily reintrude. Without some positive attention to issues of meaning and purpose, social structures that make for genuine community and freedom through conjoint action, the secularist program was doomed to leave central human needs unsatisfied. However eloquent, mere exhortations to brace up and join the great Darwinian party are not enough. Dewey saw very clearly that a fully secular society must take up philosophical questions that arise when literalist faith is abandoned, that secular humanism needs not only to be secular but also to be humane.

6.

My three examples give only a very sketchy and incomplete account of the ways in which Dewey aims to reconstruct the philosophical agenda, but I hope to have shown how the issues on which he concentrates relate to broad concerns about human life and society, the kinds of concerns that would be expected to play a role in decisions about well-ordered inquiry. There are two obvious (and related) objections to my defense of his approach. The first would contend that the proposed inquiries do not count as philosophy because of what they require: so thorough an immersion in other disciplines (psychology, sociology, history, and so forth) that they belong to other practitioners. The second would reach the same conclusion by focusing on what they leave out, to wit any connection with the "central problems" that have figured in the history of philosophy and in the professionalized Anglophone practice that has emerged from that history.

I respond to the first criticism by advancing a different vision of what the history of philosophy has taught us. It is impossible to read the greatest thinkers from ancient times to the early twentieth century without recognizing the extraordinary breadth of their knowledge: the writings of Plato and Aristotle, Hume and Kant, Rousseau and Mill, Hegel and Schopenhauer, testify to the many fields that these authors knew, and to which they often contributed. Peirce, James, and Dewey were similarly able to draw on a range of knowledge, and, in the last half century, the deepest and most influential philosophical work, that of John Rawls, of Hilary Putnam, of Michel Foucault, and of Thomas Kuhn, has been permeated by awareness of many different disciplines. Dewey supposes that there is no pure philosophy that can deliver conclusions independently of substantive prior premises. Instead, he takes the philosophical attitude to consist in analysis of a broad swath of inquiries, and the synthesis of ideas from diverse disciplines in a way that no specialized practitioner of any of those investigations could attain. Philosophy is not a discipline for those who are proud to know nothing but for people who aspire to know something of everything so that they can propose (and the modest word is appropriate here) a broader perspective.

Yet one might reasonably ask about the place, if any, that traditional "core questions" in epistemology or metaphysics (say) will have in a Deweyan approach to philosophy. Some questions about knowledge remain pertinent. Unsettled debates in various particular fields of inquiry sometimes require attention to the standards of evidence that are to be employed, and philosophers can help with such controversies by refining and applying methodological canons they can show to be at work in uncontroversially successful investigations. Philosophical research on aspects of the special sciences, from the pioneering suggestions of Peirce to the present, provides clear examples of this useful work. More generally, traditional philosophical questions about the conditions for individual knowledge, questions that seek, for example, convincing accounts of perception or memory, might contribute to improved understanding and consequent removal of obstacles that currently block forms of inquiry. Dewey would insist, however—and rightly so—that these questions be pursued in light of the best information that can be drawn from contemporary sciences, from physics, biology, and psychology in particular. Even more important are epistemological questions that traditional philosophy has largely neglected, issues in *social* epistemology about the direction, certification, and distribution of knowledge. How ought the agenda for inquiry be set? What standards should be applied to count a proposed result as something "we" know, something on which "we" can now build? How should the vast and heterogeneous corpus of human knowledge be disseminated so that it meets the needs of citizens in democratic societies? Only recently has Anglophone philosophy begun to address these issues, but, as Dewey saw very clearly, they are primary for the success of democracy. Our own democratic difficulties reveal only too evidently that that assessment is correct.

As I noted at the very beginning, Dewey lacks a large body of admirers. Among those who do read him closely, there is an understandable tendency to turn him into a regular guy. Commentators labor to discover in particular works—most notably the late *Logic* and the earlier *Experience and Nature*—a set of metaphysical and epistemological proposals that can rival those of his most celebrated Anglophone successors. We are offered accounts of truth and knowledge in terms that articulate the supposedly fundamental notions of *situation* and *instrumentality*. On my own interpretation, these attempts underrate the radical shift that Dewey intended. His aim was not to replace the large epistemological and metaphysical systems of his predecessors with an alternative system, and his writings do not offer rivals to those that are currently in vogue, but rather to disentangle the pictures of the world and our relation to it that would accord with our best scientific understanding from the excrescences of overambitious philosophy. The concepts and claims of epistemology and metaphysics are tools that should be fashioned to enable inquirers to pursue their primary questions. Epistemology and metaphysics are thus subordinate to the issues in philosophy Dewey takes as primary. They are means to the construction of a "general theory of education."

A provocative analogy may help. The business of chemistry requires investigators to have, or to make, vessels in which they can observe reactions. That demand motivates a derivative practice, the blowing of glass with sufficient clarity to enable the observations and sufficient regularity to make measurement easy. A sensible glassblowing practice concentrates on producing the properties that are pertinent to the chemists. We can easily imagine, however, a group of technicians becoming so infatuated with their own craft that they devote hours to the creation of vessels with special properties that have no bearing on chemical success. Ventures in epistemology and metaphysics, Dewey claims, are often guilty of a similar form of self-absorbed blindness.

So he would judge the contemporary philosophical scene. Dewey would find much to admire in contemporary philosophy, in inquiries into the special sciences, in genuine interaction with art and literature, in the sophisticated historical studies that have provided lucid accounts of older philosophers, in the parts of political philosophy and ethics that pay closest attention to the problems and challenges of contemporary societies, and, perhaps most of all, in the growing attention to issues about race, gender, and class. Yet he could not fail to recognize the ways in which the scholasticism against which he reacted in the early twentieth century has reemerged in the early twenty-first. Confronted with the blizzard of isms, the fiercely technical dissections of minute questions that fill specialized journals and that are seen as the province of "Real" or "Core" philosophy, and the patronizing air with which philosophical discussions of, for example, race, are taken as "Worthy" but not quite the "Real Thing," his verdict would be obvious: the glassblowers have taken over the lab.

7.

I close with a personal memory. Thirty years ago, as an assistant professor at the University of Vermont, I listened to Richard Rorty's John Dewey lecture. It was a newer version of a presentation I had heard before, and it would eventually appear in print under the title "Keeping Philosophy Pure." Building on his influential book, *Philosophy and the Mirror of Nature,* Rorty argued that philosophy was not a special discipline—not a *Fach,* as he put it. My reaction, then, was that Rorty had focused only on part of philosophy, and that his obituary for the subject was premature.

That reaction is preserved here, but with a very different emphasis. Rorty, who already claimed Dewey as an ally, was brilliantly insightful in identifying the poverty of "normal philosophy." His critique of philosophy-as-usual is as necessary today as it was in the 1970s or in the 1920s. I differ from him only in seeing the possibility of renewal, where he envisaged a burial. It is, perhaps, a matter of temperament. Pessimists will suppose that attempts to reconstruct philosophy will invariably succumb to the old diseases, whereas optimists will hope that, with the advantages of hindsight, we can learn to do better. So I side with Dewey, who, with his calls to analyze and reform our practices in the light of "intelligence," was one of the great optimists.

2.

REFLECTIONS ON PRAGMATISM

Hilary Putnam

I want to widen the scope of our reflections and talk about the classical pragmatist movement as a whole. I say the "classical" pragmatists because I shall not attempt to cover the contributions of the many pragmatist thinkers who came after the great triumvirate of Peirce, James, and Dewey.

I shall begin with the first member of the "classical pragmatist" trio, Charles S. Peirce.

1. JAMES AND PEIRCE ON TRUTH

Peirce, whom James famously credits with having invented pragmatism, defined truth as "the opinion [that] is fated to be ultimately agreed to by all who investigate." In spite of the very real differences between James's and Peirce's metaphysical views, and contrary to most accounts (for example, Rorty's or Brandom's)[1] variants of this definition abound in James's writing.

For example, in the concluding paragraph of the very early (1878) "Remarks on Spencer's Definition of Mind as Correspondence," we find James combining the famous Jamesian idea that human beings "help to create" truth with the Peircean idea that the true judgments are those that we are fated to believe, not at any given instant, but in the long run, on the basis of "the total upshot of experience":

> I, for my part, cannot escape the consideration forced upon me at every turn, that the knower is not simply a mirror floating with no foothold anywhere, and passively reflecting an order that he comes upon and finds simply existing. The

knower is an actor, and coefficient of the truth on one side, whilst on the other he registers the truth which he helps to create. Mental interests, hypotheses, postulates, insofar as they are bases for human action—action which to a great extent transforms the world—help to *make* the truth which they declare.[2]

But in what sense exactly do Peirce and James think of our "interests" (our "ultimate aim," in Peirce's case) as determining truth? The answer is complex. First, for both James and Peirce truth is a property of opinions or beliefs, and without thinkers there are no beliefs and opinions to be true or false. Moreover, our various interests determine what inquiries we shall pursue, what concepts we will find useful, that is, they determine which truths there will be. But James is willing to draw radical consequences from this last idea, consequences that Peirce is not willing to draw, because of what he calls his "scholastic realism," his belief that ultimately only those concepts survive that correspond to real universals, which he called "Thirds." The element in James's thought that Peirce objected to is clearly expressed in "The Sentiment of Rationality." There James writes:

> . . . of two conceptions equally fit to satisfy the logical demand, that one which awakens the active impulses, or satisfies other aesthetic demands better than the other, will be accounted the more rational conception, and will deservedly prevail.
>
> There is nothing improbable in the supposition that an analysis of the world may yield a number of formulae, all consistent with the facts. In physical science different formulae may explain the phenomena equally well—the one-fluid and two-fluid theories of electricity, for example. Why may it not be so with the world? Why may there not be different points of view for surveying it? within each of which all data harmonize, and which the observer may therefore either choose between, or simply cumulate one upon the other? A Beethoven string quartet is truly, as someone said, a scraping of horses' tails upon cats' bowels, and may be exhaustively described in such terms; but the application of this description in no way precludes the simultaneous applicability of an entirely different description. Just so a thoroughgoing interpretation of the world in terms of mechanical sequence is compatible with its being interpreted teleologically, for the mechanism itself may be designed.
>
> If, then, there were several systems excogitated, equally satisfying to our purely logical needs, they would still have to be passed in review, and approved or rejected by our aesthetic and practical nature.[3]

This is the first statement (in the late nineteenth century!) by a "twentieth-century philosopher" of the idea that facts and values—or "interests"—are entangled, an idea that I will address later.

By the way, Peirce also rejected the fact/value dichotomy, but he did not reject the Kantian dichotomy between pure and impure interests,[4] and he insisted that the interest that drives pure scientific inquiry is utterly different from and purer than the interests that drive ordinary practical inquiry, while Dewey and James strongly disagree. But the disagreements—and they are very important—between Peirce and James should not obscure the fact that James, like Peirce, declares his allegiance to a notion of truth defined in terms of convergence, or "ultimate consensus."

2. MY EVALUATION OF THE PRAGMATIST THEORIES OF TRUTH AND MEANING

This essay is titled "Reflections on Pragmatism," and so it is appropriate for me to state what my own response to all of this is.

Both Peirce and James attached great importance to their (different) versions of the idea that "truth involves coerciveness, in the long run, over thought"—call this "the pragmatist theory of truth." One respect in which their versions are different, by the way, is that James held that the truth is what *will* become coercive over thought, meaning by that *human* thought, whereas Peirce eventually formulated (or rather reformulated)[5] his theory of truth in such a way that what is true is what *would* become coercive over thought, the belief on which all inquirers *would* be fated to converge, if inquiry were *indefinitely* continued, even by extraterrestrial species after the human race ceased to exist! Another respect is they had different accounts of the factors that cause beliefs to become "coercive over thought."

Although I think of myself as one who has learned a great deal from pragmatism, I don't think that the pragmatist theory of truth (either in Peirce's version or in James's) is correct. For one effect of the pragmatist theory of truth is to make the truth or falsity of any assertion about the past depend on what will happen in the future (or, in Peirce's case, on what "would" happen in the future if inquiry were sufficiently prolonged).

Consider any historical proposition whose truth-value is unknown and possibly unknowable (because all the records have been destroyed), say the proposition that "Boadicea was really called *Boudica.*" If James is right, this proposition is true just in case evidence will come to light in the future which will cause competent inquirers to conclude that this was Queen Boadicea's actual name; if Peirce is right, it is true just in case the world is such that competent inquirers *must* eventually find such evidence, even if it takes billions of years. I see no reason to believe either of these claims. I think that what makes a proposition about the past true is *what actually happened in the past*, not what *will* happen or what *must* happen in the future.[6]

In addition, I don't agree with James and Peirce that propositions are rules for conduct. And I also don't believe that a proposition's meaning can be exhausted by talking about what sensations it leads us to expect or what reactions it leads us to prepare (this is Peirce's "pragmatic maxim"). So, if I don't accept either the pragmatic maxim or the pragmatist theory of truth, why do I think the pragmatists are so important today?

The fact is that, although James was very keen on the pragmatist theory of truth, hardly any of his interesting metaphysical ideas actually *presuppose* it. This is something that Bertrand Russell, who detested the pragmatist theory of truth but was extremely impressed by James's theory of perception (which Russell regarded as a form of "neutral monism") fully understood.[7] And nothing of what I have praised and will praise in Dewey depends on the pragmatist theory of truth. In fact, in *Logic: The Theory of Inquiry* there is only one reference to that theory—in a footnote! And although I have said that I can't accept the pragmatic maxim, I can accept many of the particular applications of it that James and Dewey made.

What I have in mind is that the idea of asking of *philosophical positions*, of attempting to answer the great philosophical questions, what difference they have made and can make in practice, what difference they make to our *lives*, is a necessary first step toward bringing philosophy back in contact with human concerns, a first step to doing what Dewey asked us to do when he wrote that "philosophy recovers itself when it ceases to be a device for dealing with the problems of philosophers and becomes a method, cultivated by philosophers, for dealing with the problems of men."[8] Virtually every part of Dewey's philosophy exemplifies the determination to do just this. And in this connection, the part of Dewey's thought that is perhaps most relevant today, and is certainly still hotly debated, concerns his rejection of the still tremendously influential dichotomy between factual propositions and value judgments; and it is to that issue that I shall devote the rest of this essay.

3. DEWEY ON FACT AND VALUE

The rejection of the claim that there is an absolute dichotomy between assertions about facts and value judgments is the single most important idea of Deweyan pragmatism that I hope philosophers will come to accept in the future.

This dichotomy has by now become something familiar to lay people and not just a matter for discussion by philosophers and social scientists. Every one of you has heard someone ask, "Is that supposed to be a fact or a value judgment?" The presupposition of the question is that if it's a "value judgment," then it can't possibly be a "fact"; and, all too often, a further presupposition is that value judgments are "subjective."

This dichotomy was already widely accepted by analytic philosophers when I was a graduate student more than half a century ago. The logical empiricists, including my teacher Hans Reichenbach, claimed to have shown that ethical propositions only appear to be bona fide assertions; in reality, they lack truth-value, they said, and, indeed, they are outside the sphere of rational argument altogether. Important social scientists accepted the dichotomy as well; Lionel Robbins, one of the most influential economists of the 1930s, gave this view one of its most aggressive formulations:

> If we disagree about ends it is a case of thy blood or mine—or live or let live according to the importance of the difference, or the relative strength of our opponents. But if we disagree about means, then scientific analysis can often help us resolve our differences. If we disagree about the morality of the taking of interest (and we understand what we are talking about), then there is no room for argument.[9]

Yet this "self-evident" dichotomy is one that Dewey regards as baseless:

> Articles frequently appear that discuss the relation of fact and value. If the subject discussed under this caption were the relation of value-facts to other facts, there would not be the assumption of uniqueness just mentioned. But anyone reading articles devoted to discussion of this issue will note that it is an issue or

problem just because it is held that propositions about values are somehow of a unique sort, being inherently marked off from propositions about facts. . . . It is my conviction that nothing would better clarify the present unsatisfactory state of discussion of value than definite and explicit statement of the reasons [that this is supposed to be the case].[10]

Now that the fact/value dichotomy has become so widely accepted, it may appear naive of Dewey to claim that there can be facts about values. How can there be facts about what is and what is not valuable? What is more, Dewey suggests that such facts are just "space-time facts," that is, they do not depend on anything supernatural or "non-natural." (And he wrote this in 1944, long after G. E. Moore argued in his famous *Principia Ethica*, published in 1903, that if there are such facts, they must involve a "non-natural property"!)

But Dewey was not naive. He knew very well that his was a minority position. The first sentence of the essay from which I just quoted reads: "When I analyze the discouragement I have experienced lately in connection with discussion of value, I find that it proceeds from the feeling that little headway is being made in determining the questions or issues fundamentally involved rather than from the fact that the views I personally hold have not received general approval."[11] Let us see what Dewey meant by "the questions or issues fundamentally involved."

To do that, I want to look at certain well-known philosophical views that are diametrically opposed to Dewey's.

4. DEWEY'S NATURALIST OPPONENTS

One sort of opponent that Dewey recognizes but does not discuss in "Some Questions about Value" is the non-naturalist, the philosopher who holds that value propositions presuppose a non-natural or "transcendent" source of knowledge; in a footnote to that essay he writes that that view has been omitted "so what is said will not appeal to those who hold that view."[12] In a sense, the work of both Dewey and James is intended to show us that to assume that we need a transcendent justification for value propositions is only to make them seem occult, and they are anything but that—they are rooted in real, natural facts about human nature and about real human environments.[13] (Moreover, those who take the "transcendent" route in ethics have historically been opponents of fallibilism in ethics, and fallibilism, for pragmatists, is inseparable from democratic ethics.)

So this essay is addressed to naturalists in ethics. Dewey was well aware that among his fellow naturalists there were philosophers who regarded ethical utterances as "pseudopropositions."

In *The Unity of Science*, for example, after explaining that all nonscientific problems are "a confusion of . . . pseudoproblems,"[14] Rudolf Carnap wrote as follows:

> All statements belonging to Metaphysics, regulative Ethics, and (metaphysical) Epistemology . . . are in fact unverifiable and, therefore, unscientific. In the Viennese Circle, we are accustomed to describe such statements as nonsense. . . . This terminology is to be understood as implying a logical, not say a psychological, distinction; its use is intended to assert only that the statements in question do not possess a certain logical characteristic common to all proper scientific statements [i.e., verifiability—HP]; we do not intend to assert the impossibility of associating any conceptions or images with these logically invalid statements. Conceptions can be associated with any arbitrarily compounded series of words; and metaphysical statements are richly evocative of associations and feelings both in authors and readers.[15]

Dewey discusses this view (although he does not mention Carnap by name) in "Some Questions about Value." How then, *could* Dewey write (in the very same article) the words I quoted earlier, namely, "It is my conviction that nothing would better clarify the present unsatisfactory state of discussion of value than definite and explicit statement of the reasons why the case is supposed to be otherwise in respect to value." Didn't Carnap "state the reasons"?

Carnap did give a supposed reason. He said that value-propositions "are in fact unverifiable." This is certainly a reason that Dewey would have accepted, had Dewey agreed that it was the case. But the only reason Carnap had for saying that value propositions are unverifiable in 1934, the year that *The Unity of Science* was published, was the claim, accepted by the logical positivists and their "Vienna Circle" at that time, that the only verifiable propositions are observation reports such as "this chair is blue" (or, in an alternative version, "I have a blue sense-datum") and logical consequences of such propositions—a claim so extreme as to rule out all the propositions of theoretical physics, as Carnap later came to realize![16] From Dewey's perspective, this is no reason at all. (I will discuss subsequent, and more sophisticated, arguments offered by the logical positivists in the next section.)

Other defenders of the positivist view of ethical sentences simply claimed that it was the very "grammar" of ethical sentences to express emotions or "attitudes" (or, in Hans Reichenbach's version, to "command"), and not to state facts. But this is certainly not the surface grammar of such utterances: we do speak of some valuations as correct or true and others as incorrect or false, and we also discuss whether they are warranted or unwarranted. The emotivists' reply was that the surface grammar is "misleading"; but again Dewey would want to hear a reason for this claim that a nonreductive naturalist should accept, and he claimed (and I think that he was right) that no good reason had been offered. That one can be a naturalist in philosophy without being a reductionist is another idea of the classical pragmatists that certainly needs more advocates today!

Perhaps just because the attempt to show that the "logical" or linguistic properties of value sentences support emotivism has collapsed, philosophers who deny that value propositions can genuinely state knowable facts came to rely more and more on metaphysical arguments. Thus the late John Mackie argued in a book rather provocatively titled *Ethics: Inventing Right and Wrong* that although value sentences do indeed have the linguistic form of propositions, and are supposed to be capable of truth and falsity, warrant or lack of warrant, this is a metaphysical mistake.[17] According to Mackie's famous "error theory," all ethical talk rests on an error. The supposed error is the belief that there could be such properties as good and evil, right and wrong. Although Mackie published this claim thirteen years after Dewey's death, it is safe to assume that Dewey would demand a reason for this claim. And the only reason Mackie offered was that these ethical properties are too "queer" to exist![18]

In his brilliant study, *What We Owe to Each Other*, Thomas Scanlon discusses many of these questions concerning the normative and motivational force of ethical assertions and the complexity of the connections between valuing and desiring.[19] On Scanlon's "contractualist" theory, the moral motivation par excellence is the desire *to avoid an action if the action is such that any principle allowing it would be one that other people could reasonably reject.* And Scanlon responds to the question, "Why accept this account of moral motivation?"[20] by saying as follows:

> According to the version of contractualism that I am advancing here, our thinking about right and wrong is structured by . . . the aim of finding principles that others, insofar as they too have this aim, could not reasonably reject.

This gives us a direct reason to be concerned with other people's point of view: not because we might, for all we know, actually be them, or because we might occupy their positions in some other possible world,[21] but in order to find principles that they, as well as we, have reason to accept... there is on this view a strong continuity between the reasons that lead us to act in the way that the conclusions of moral thought require and the reasons that shape the process by which we arrive at those conclusions.[22]

I am not quoting Scanlon because I think that Dewey was a "contractualist" *avant la lettre*, but because Scanlon has well described how *one sort* of ethical claim can have motivating force in any community that shares one of the basic interests of morality. And the explanation he gives does not presuppose anything we ought to regard as "queer."

"But the motive Scanlon describes won't motivate anyone who is indifferent to what others believe and desire!" someone will object. True, but the claim that to count as genuine propositions, ethical utterances have to motivate even those who are indifferent to the interests and beliefs of others is yet another claim for which no good reason has been offered.[23] Ethical utterances do have various kinds of motivating force, and Scanlon has well illustrated how one kind of motivating force can be accounted for.

What Dewey would have disagreed with Scanlon about is (1) *the idea that there is a unique motive for ethics* and (2) that idea that all ethical judgments depend on "principles."[24] But even more than Scanlon, perhaps, Dewey would have emphasized that ethics depends on a concern—*concern* is too weak a word—an *identification* with the interests of others. Like Aristotle, Dewey believes that the reasons for being ethical are not apparent from a nonethical or pre-ethical standpoint; one must be educated into the ethical life, and this means that one's interests must be transformed. In that process, Dewey tells us, one does not simply acquire an interest in helping other people alongside of and independent of one's various interests in art, in work, in recreation, and so on; rather, all those interests are likewise transformed. In Dewey's account, the natural impulse of sympathy itself is transformed by being fused with our other impulses, and our other impulses and interests are transformed by being fused with sympathy. As he writes,

What is required is a blending, a fusing of the sympathetic tendencies with all the other impulses and habitual traits of the self. When interest in power is permeated with an affectionate impulse, it is protected from being a tendency to dominate and tyrannize; it becomes an interest in effectiveness of regard for common ends. When an interest in artistic or scientific objects is similarly fused, it loses the indifferent and coldly impersonal character [that] marks the specialist as such and becomes an interest in the adequate aesthetic and intellectual development of the conditions of a common life. Sympathy does not merely associate one of these tendencies with another; still less does it make one a means to the other's ends. It so intimately permeates them as to transform both into a new and moral interest.[25]

One thing all three of the "classical pragmatists" agreed on was that *we have to learn in the course of inquiry* what can and cannot count as a verification, and that there is no way of delimiting in advance what we can and cannot learn from inquiry and from the application of the results of inquiry. (The latter—the application of the results of inquiry—is, for Dewey, a part of inquiry, and, indeed, the most essential part.) For this reason, unlike Carnap, Dewey never appeals to a theory that purports to specify in advance what can and what cannot be "verifiable." And, unlike Mackie, Dewey is not a reductive materialist, and he does not pretend to have a principle that determines what is too "queer" to be a real property of things. What he did instead was develop a naturalistic picture of the ways in which intelligence can be applied to ethical problems, and especially to social problems. For Dewey, that there can be objective ethical truths follows from the fact that ethical problems are simply a subset of our practical problems, in the ancient sense of "practical"—problems of how to live—and it can be a *fact* that a certain course of action or a certain form of life solves, or better resolves, what Dewey called a problematic situation.[26]

5. AFTER DEWEY

In two recent books, I argued that the intellectual legs on which the fact/value dichotomy stood are now in ruins.[27] But to see that that is the case, one needs to bring together results that were certainly anticipated by Dewey and James but whose further working out required most of the second half of the twentieth century, and is, in fact, still continuing.

Specifically, one needs to bring together the observations (by different philosophers) of the way in which so-called factual and so-called evaluative predicates are mutually "entangled"—the way in which it is a fantasy to suppose that the predicates we use to give sensitive and relevant descriptions of human beings and human interactions can be "disentangled" into two "components," a "purely descriptive component" and an "evaluative component"—and the observation, first made long ago by Morton White, that Quine's demolition of the logical positivist dichotomy of theory and observational fact (Quine's "Duhemian" argument) also destroyed the logical positivist arguments for the fact/value dichotomy. It was the prestige of those arguments that had such a powerful influence on social scientists, such as the economist Lionel Robbins whom I mentioned earlier.

The logical positivist arguments in question depended on a *serious* effort, one continued over many years, to draw a clear line between factual propositions, theoretical postulates, mathematical-logical propositions (which they took to be "analytic"), and "pseudopropositions" (or "nonsense"), which latter included, according to Carnap, "all statements belonging to Metaphysics, regulative Ethics, and (metaphysical) Epistemology."[28] But how are we to determine just which terms are "nonsense"? "Observation terms" were supposed by the positivists to be *the* paradigmatic "meaningful" terms, but do we know that, for example, "stole" isn't an observation term, but "struck" is?

Commenting on this problem in 1956, Morton White dryly remarked that[29]

> [The positivists] now *propose* to *call* certain expressions meaningful to begin with and to call others meaningful if and only if they bear specified relations to those that were first called meaningful. In this way the criterion of meaning does not rise up from natural language, but is handed down in a legislative way. The theorist of meaning specifies a certain list of observable predicates or sentences which he *labels* as meaningful.[30]

Moreover, the positivist's assumption that the aim of science is prediction itself leads to a serious problem: to *predict* anything means (on the logical positivists' account) to *deduce observation sentences from a theory*. And to deduce anything from a set of empirical postulates we need not only those postulates *but also the axioms of mathematics and logic*. And, according to the logical positivists, these do not state "facts" at all. They are *analytic* (or "true by convention") and thus "empty of factual content." Thus the search for a satisfactory demarcation of the "factual" became the search for a satisfactory way of drawing "the analytic-synthetic distinction."

At this point (1950), however, Quine demolished the positivists' notion of the "analytic" to the satisfaction of most philosophers.[31] Quine suggested that the whole idea of classifying such statements as the statements of pure mathematics as either "factual" or "conventional" (which the logical positivists equated with "analytic") was hopeless. As he later put it:

> The lore of our fathers is a fabric of sentences. In our hands it develops and changes, through more or less arbitrary and deliberate revisions and additions of our own, more or less directly occasioned by the continuing stimulation of our sense organs. It is a pale gray lore, black with fact and white with convention. But I have found no substantial reasons for concluding that there are any quite black threads in it, or any white ones.[32]

But if we lack any clear notion of "fact," what happens to the fact/value dichotomy? As Vivian Walsh has written,

> To borrow and adapt Quine's vivid image, if a theory may be black with fact and white with convention, it might well (as far as logical empiricism could tell) be red with values. Since for them confirmation or falsification had to be a property of a theory *as a whole*, they had no way of unraveling this whole cloth.[33]

6. FACT/VALUE ENTANGLEMENT

Facts and values are entangled in at least two senses. First, factual judgments, even in physics, depend on and presuppose *epistemic* values. What the logical positivists were shutting their eyes to, as so many today who refer to values as purely "subjective" and to science as purely "objective" continue to shut their eyes is the fact that judgments of *coherence, simplicity* (which is itself a whole bundle of different values, not just one "parameter"), *beauty* (of a theory), *naturalness*, and so on, are presupposed by physical science. Yet *coherence* and *simplicity* and the like are *values*. Certainly, disagreements about the beauty or "inner perfection" (Einstein's term) of a theory are *value* disagreements.[34]

A second way in which values and facts are entangled might be described as "logical" or "grammatical." What is characteristic of "negative" descriptions like *cruel*, as well as of "positive" descriptions like *brave, temperate, just* (note that these are the terms that Socrates kept forcing his interlocutors to discuss again and again!) is that to use them with any discrimination one has to be able to understand an *evaluative point of view*. That is why someone who thinks that *brave* simply means "not afraid to risk life and limb" would not be able to understand the all-important distinction that Socrates kept drawing between mere *rashness* or *foolhardiness* and genuine *bravery*. It is also the reason that (as Iris Murdoch stressed in her important book *The Sovereignty of "Good" over Other Concepts*[35]) it is always possible to *improve one's understanding* of a concept like bravery or justice. If one did not at *any* point feel the *appeal* of the relevant ethical point of view, one wouldn't be able to acquire a thick ethical concept, and sophisticated use of it requires a continuing ability to identify (at least in imagination) with that point of view.

One may think of the logical positivists' fact/value dichotomy (and of the emotivist account of ethical language that goes with it) as the top of a three-legged stool. The three legs were (1) the postulation of theory-free "facts," leading to their dichotomy of observable fact and theory; (2) the denial that fact and evaluation are entangled; and (3) the claim that science proceeds by a syntactically describable method ("inductive logic"). The fact that even theoretical physics presupposes *epistemic values* means that if value judgments were really "cognitively meaningless," *all* science would rest on judgments that are (in positivist eyes), *nonsense*. That is why both Carnap and Reichenbach tried so hard to show that science proceeds by an *algorithm*, and the reason that Popper tried to show that science needs only deductive logic. Thus the failure of the third leg is also a failure of the second leg. But the second leg also broke because facts and values—ethical values—are entangled at the level of single predicates. And the first leg broke because the "two dogmas" on which it was based were refuted by Quine.

I wish to emphasize that the destruction of the fact/value dichotomy was a task that took many brilliant women and men and many years of the last century to accomplish (I say "accomplish" and not "complete" because philosophical tasks are never really completed). Those women and men are associated in the textbooks (with their unfortunate love of such classifications) with many different kinds of philosophy. Quine was a high analytic philosopher if there ever was one, and close to the logical positivist movement, even if he turned out to be its severest critic. Morton White was sympathetic both to Quine's brand of analytic philosophy *and* to Dewey's pragmatism. That there is no "algorithm" for doing science was stressed by Ernest Nagel, and also by the most celebrated "philosopher-scientist," Albert Einstein. The failure of the "disentangling maneuver" that was supposed to split up thick ethical predicates into a value-free "cognitive" component and a cognition-free "emotive" component was first seen by Philippa Foot[36] and Iris Murdoch, and then further discussed, more recently, by Ruth Anna Putnam, John McDowell, and myself.[37] Certainly the discussion has deepened and widened since Dewey's day. But James and Dewey were the pioneers.

3.

LOOKING AHEAD

What Are the Prospects for
Dewey's Philosophy in the Future?

Paul Kurtz

1.

The one-hundred-fiftieth anniversary of the birth of John Dewey is an auspicious occasion, for it celebrates the life and work of one of America's leading philosophers—if not *the* leading philosopher. If nothing else, his influence on public affairs beyond the academy qualifies him for that distinction. Surely, he was considered to be the most influential intellectual voice of liberalism for a good part of the twentieth century, as broadly construed.

I had the good fortune to have seen or met Dewey on a few memorable occasions. First, when I was on the program committee of the graduate students' philosophy club in 1948 at Columbia University, we invited Professor Dewey to speak. He appeared in Low Memorial Library to a packed house, where he received a huge ovation. He was recognized by his bushy white hair and moustache. He was rather dapper, dressed in a light grey suit. I recall how surprised he was at the turnout. In his usual soft-spoken voice, he said he thought that people had forgotten him. This talk was one of his last talks delivered to the students at Columbia and was later published in *Commentary*.[1] It dealt with the disparity between our scientific knowledge, forever changing, and the fact that our moral values are based on traditional habits, slow to change. After the talk I remember shaking his hand and how awed I was by his presence.

The next time that I saw Dewey was on October 20, 1949, at his ninetieth birthday party, held at the Grand Ballroom of the Hotel Commodore in New York City. Lest you think that I was granted a special privilege, I hasten to add that some fifteen hundred people were served a banquet in the ballroom, and as an impecunious student I overlooked the proceedings from a balcony. I had a great view of the birthday party below, which was a festive affair with addresses delivered by philosophers Ralph Barton Perry, Irwin Edman, and Sidney Hook. Other famous figures gave speeches, such as Supreme Court Justice Felix Frankfurter, Prime Minister Jawaharlal Nehru (who arrived late and was immediately ushered to the podium), labor leader Walter Reuther, and William Kilpatrick (head of Teacher's College, who heralded Dewey's contributions to progressive education); and there were messages from President Harry Truman and British Prime Minister Clement Attlee, among others.

Dewey was present with his second wife, Roberta Grant, and his children. He cut a birthday cake, which was served in his honor, and gave a brief talk encouraging those assembled not to despair about the vicissitudes of foreign affairs. The Soviet Union was then threatening Iran, and there was widespread fear of possible war with the West. In his remarks, Dewey said that he was always interested in political events. We should not become too pessimistic; for we need to take into account the long-range prospects of humankind, and Dewey remained optimistic about these. He informed the audience that he had been interested in many fields in his lifetime, such as psychology and education, but that he considered himself a philosopher first.

Dwight Eisenhower participated in the events of that week. He was then president of Columbia. Evidently, he was being groomed by Tom Watson, head of IBM, to run for the US presidency. I will never forget the brief statement by Eisenhower, the head of the European Allies in World War II. He got up and said (to paraphrase him from memory), "Professor Dewey, I congratulate you on your ninetieth birthday; you are the philosopher of freedom and I am the soldier of freedom!" Can you imagine any president since then uttering similar remarks! How far have we declined in public literacy! I should point out that there were some one hundred other celebrations of Dewey's birthday throughout America that week as testimony of the high regard in which he was held.

In retrospect, I think that a good deal of John Dewey's influence was attributable to his involvement in so many social and political causes and various professional organizations. He was a founding member and president of the American Philosophical Association and one of the founders of the New School for Social Research, the NAACP, the ACLU, and the American Association of University Professors. He was involved in so many liberal causes: the Committee to Defend Bertrand Russell, the Dewey Commission on Trotsky. He was honorary chairman of the Congress for Cultural Freedom and a signer of the *Humanist Manifesto* of 1933, and he wrote many articles for the *New Republic*. Unlike so many university professors who remain cloistered in the academy, Dewey was thoroughly *engagé*. Yet Dewey was a prolific author, and as his books were published, it was his philosophical outlook no doubt that established his reputation.

Another explanation for Dewey's acceptance by American intellectuals is that his philosophical outlook resonated with the practical streak in American life. Given the fact that nature is precarious and uncertain, Dewey's instrumentalism made sense, for there's a continuing need to solve problems in a frontier society. America had been an open and democratic society in which human initiative could modify the external world, realize human plans and projects, and fulfill our dreams of a better tomorrow. And there was a native pragmatic talent in American society, which was innovative and experimental, the only way to overcome obstacles and forge roads westward and to expand trade worldwide. The traditional ethnic, racial, and religious groups that came to these shores forced settlers to abandon the habits of the past and to resolve problems in new ways. Dewey expressed that attitude—it applied to statesmen and captains of industry and to the poor and dispossessed who were infused with ambition, seeking to succeed in the arts and sciences, commerce and the professions. It made sense to a rapidly expanding democratic, progressive, and well-educated public.

In my book, *American Thought before 1900*, I pointed out that it was difficult to find purely theoretical philosophical systems in the United States before the Civil War.[2] Jonathan Edwards reflected religious passions; Madison, Jefferson, and Hamilton were concerned with concrete political and social questions. John C. Calhoun defended the Southern outlook; and Abraham Lincoln defended American democracy. It was only when academic philosophy in the late nineteenth century developed in the universities that European metaphysical and epistemological theories were developed. And as we are all aware, pragmatism was introduced by Pierce, James, and Dewey to express the uniquely American philosophical view that ideas should be tested by their consequences in practice. John Dewey most succinctly outlined this approach already implicit in American institutions. So Deweyan thought was immediately found to be in harmony with the values of an achievement society. And this was adopted by conservative entrepreneurial businesspeople, as well as progressive working people and liberals.

On a personal note, I spent three years at Columbia preparing for my master's degree and doctorate, and reading everything that I could of John Dewey's work. I studied with Dewey's colleagues and students: Ernest Nagel, John Hermann Randall Jr., Herbert W. Schneider, Justus Buchler, Charles Frankel—and, earlier,

Sidney Hook at NYU. That period perhaps marked the high point of Dewey's influence. I spent several decades thereafter at various universities and colleges teaching courses on Dewey and American philosophy.[3] I witnessed how he came under heavy attack by conservatives after his death, conservatives such as Admiral Radford and Russell Kirk, who blamed him for virtually every ill in America, including the ideal of participatory democracy of the New Left. Meanwhile, interest in American philosophy per se declined, as importations from Europe—analytic philosophy, phenomenology, and existentialism—seemed to capture the attention of many younger philosophers and students.

Indeed, on October 20, 1959, the one-hundredth anniversary of Dewey's birth, there was a celebration at Columbia University. At that time, Randall complained that by then technical analytic philosophy and phenomenology, imported from Europe, were already eclipsing Dewey. Sidney Hook also delivered remarks at that time about Dewey's influence, and the centrality of "growth" in his philosophy.[4] Hook remarks that Dewey "was among the worst teachers of the world. He was completely devoid of the histrionic arts which a good teacher ... must summon up to awaken interest." Nevertheless, Hook affirmed that Dewey "was a great teacher for those students whose interests had already been aroused."[5] It was the power of John Dewey's ideas not only in philosophy but in the behavioral and social sciences, and their application to society, I submit, that had been the primary reason for his influence. As I have pointed out, John Dewey was overshadowed after his death, and philosophers seemed to have abandoned him as a more conservative mood developed and the Cold War took its toll.

All this changed three decades ago when Richard Rorty wrote about Dewey, and Hilary Putnam wrote on pragmatism, and—most important—the John Dewey Foundation (under Sidney Hook) and the Center for Dewey Studies (under Jo Ann Boydston) completed a critical edition of all of Dewey's writings, which was now available to a new generation of philosophers. This has led, as you are all aware, to a revival of interest in Dewey, with a growing literature about him; for Dewey not only talked about language but also engaged in *praxis*, and his constructive contributions to the problems of society were again appreciated, so that from the beginning of the twenty-first century many now recognize his important contributions. But here we are talking about his influence on philosophers, which is growing. Many of us now believe that we need to interpret Dewey for the broader public today (as in the past), and also point out his relevance to the rapidly changing planetary community—from India and China to Europe and Latin America—where science and technology are transforming the planet.

I should add parenthetically that the Center for Inquiry has focused on *inquiry*, which was central to the work of Dewey and Peirce. Our main task is to concentrate on the application of scientific methodology and outlook to the public arena, and to try to build centers devoted to humanistic ethical values: I call this a new *eupraxsophy*.

2.

Of special significance today is the fact that Charles Darwin had a profound influence on the pragmatists and especially Dewey. If we read "The Influence of Darwin on Philosophy," we see Dewey's account of the role of Darwin's theory of evolution in his thinking. This essay was published in the *Popular Science Monthly* (July 1909), one hundred years ago, when Dewey was only fifty years old.[6] Dewey opened his essay by observing that *The Origin of Species* marked an intellectual revolt in the development of the natural sciences. It undermined the presupposition that had dominated thinking that the universe was fixed and final, and that that which is absolutely permanent was considered superior to change and flux. The key issue, he says, was within science itself. This led to a new mode of thinking and a transformation of the nature of knowledge, morality, and politics.

The controversy with religion, according to Dewey, only intensified the intellectual challenges, but it did not precipitate it originally. What it did provoke was a new way of understanding nature. The classical Greek conception of the universe was exemplified by Plato's postulation of eternal essences and Aristotle's conception of fixed species. The conflict within science and philosophy was between a transcendental realm and the world of changing things.

For Dewey, Darwin's inquiries in the biosphere only continued the revolution in science that began with the advances of Copernicus, Kepler, and Galileo in physics, astronomy, and chemistry. For in posing questions and seeking explanations, scientists formulated hypotheses to explain observed data and test them experimentally. The rejection of first and final causes in the physical universe enabled the new science to proceed. Similarly for Darwin's principle of "natural selection," organic adaptations occur not because of any teleological design but because of variations that enabled organisms to survive or perish. There was no preordained plan, only chance and adaptation at work.

Since Dewey wrote his prophetic 1909 essay, evolutionary theory has expanded our understanding of the biosphere enormously; our conception of the human species has changed; new discoveries in the physical universe have also transformed our thinking exponentially; and this has far-reaching implications for the human prospect.

I think that these discoveries support the basic Deweyan philosophical approach. However, given the turbulent and random universe that we live in, these new findings may undermine the perhaps overly naive human confidence and optimism that prevailed in Dewey's time, so that today the challenge is so much greater than when Dewey wrote. Nonetheless, Dewey's use of the method of intelligence to solve the problems of humankind and the need for a new common faith for the planetary civilization that is emerging, I believe, will continue to make Dewey's philosophy relevant. This is all the more the case given the growth of fundamentalist religions in the late twentieth century to challenge modernism.

Evolutionary biology since Dewey's death has made remarkable progress. First, the fossil record has been expanded enormously. Of considerable significance is our awareness today of the great number of species that have become extinct. It is estimated that there are ten to thirty million species of which two million are known, and around a quarter of a million fossils have been uncovered. The total number of extinct species is unknown, though perhaps 99 percent of all species that have ever existed are now extinct. The incredible heterogeneity of life-forms beggars our imagination. They run in size from bacteria to whales and dinosaurs, from insects and ants to massive redwood tress. They include life-forms at the bottom of the oceans and in hot volcanic areas to fungi and algae existing in the ice of the polar caps. There is virtually an infinite variety of variations able to cling to life and survive in spite of seemingly impossible odds.

Life on our planet goes back an estimated 3.5 billion years ago. Most likely it began from a common ancestor, molecule, or cell that began to divide. From that primitive life-form evolved the immense number of branches in the form of species. Thus there is some genetic connection between all organisms on Earth, and the history of any species is a process of descent with modifications. Natural selection is the process by which evolution operates. The term *evolution* denotes *the change in the genetic stock of a species through time.* Darwin was unaware of the genetic theory that was later developed by Mendel, who studied the inheritance of traits in pea plants, which eventually became the science of genetics. An integrated theory of evolution was fashioned by the mid-twentieth century. This theory draws on a number of disciplines, including paleontology, ecology, anthropology, biology, molecular biology, and biochemistry.

The composite theory of evolution that developed a century after Darwin includes the following components: (1) a common ancestry, (2) a gradual process, (3) genetic mutations, (4) adaptations, (5) natural selection, and (6) speciation. Although there are general principles that apply to any species, the role of contingency and chance are important factors in what has occurred or will occur. In any case, the evidence for the general theory of evolution is today abundant, in spite of diehard creationists.

Second, the intriguing question that we face is *how* human evolution occurred. Charles Darwin proposed the theory that "man is descended from a hairy, tailed quadruped, probably arboreal in its habits," namely, the apes. Darwin thought that all species had a common ancestor. "The sole object of this work," he said in *The Descent of Man*, is to consider "whether man, like every other species, is descended from a prehistoric form."[7]

Darwin did not know about the great number of fossils of humans and apes that have been uncovered since his day, further corroborating his thesis. Based on this research, we may trace the origins of the human species to a common ancestor shared by both humans and apes. Today we have identified this as *Australopithecus*, which was intermediate between apes and humans and which existed somewhere between 5.3 million and 4.2 million years ago. All these beings became extinct 1.1 million years ago. There were several varieties of *Australopithecus*: *afarensis*, *africanus*, *robustus*, and *boises*. And, surprisingly, there were several hominid species, such as *Homo erectus*, *Homo habilis*, and *Homo sapiens*. *Homo habilis* existed between 1.5 million and 2.4 million years ago. It was named *habilis*, which means "handy man," because of the tools found with its remains. *Homo erectus* lived 1.8 million to 300,000 years ago. *Homo sapiens* (the "wise ones") have been identified as *the* human species. The discovery of Lucy in Ethiopia by the anthropaleontologist Donald Johansson in 1974 was an exciting find. She was an *Australiopithetus afarensis* female of between twenty and thirty years old, who walked upright and existed some 3.18 to 3.2 million years ago. Lucy is considered to be a transitional creature between apes and humans.[8] The same goes for the most recent discovery in Ethiopia of *Ardi* (short for *Ardipithecus*), which lived some 4.4 million years ago.

What is of special interest is that *Homo sapiens* are the only hominids that have managed to survive; all the other hominids have become extinct. It is unclear as to whether all the above are separate species. Fossils of *Homo erectus* have been discovered in Africa, Indonesia, and China. Jerry A. Coyne, the evolutionary scientist, observes that "about 60,000 years ago, every *Homo erectus* population suddenly vanished and was replaced by fossils of 'anatomically modern' *Homo sapiens.*"[9]

Similarly, *Homo neanderthalensis* "also disappeared." Coyne observes that when he was a student, evolutionary scientists believed that they evolved into *Homo sapiens*. But he says that this is now considered most likely incorrect, and "around 28,000 years ago, the Neanderthal fossils vanished." They were replaced by *Homo sapiens* who apparently supplanted every other hominid on Earth." "In other words," he opines, "*Homo sapiens* apparently elbowed out every other hominid on Earth."

When the theory of evolution was first proposed, many believed that humans were the "highest" species on the planet and that there was a progressive line of development until *man* emerged. Perhaps many pragmatists shared this confident faith in human powers. We now know that this romantic account is exaggerated and that *Homo sapiens* were in the end victorious due in no small measure to luck and pluck. It was a great battle to survive and there were no guarantees that *Homo sapiens* were bound to win out.

The current theory is that *Homo sapiens* originated in Africa approximately 50,000 to 60,000 years ago and then migrated to Europe, the Middle East, Asia, Australia, and Indonesia, eventually crossing the Bering Strait about 12,000 to 15,000 years ago (when it was frozen over) to North and South America. This would mean that *Homo sapiens* competed with the Neanderthals and *Homo erectus* for food, and perhaps even killed them off.[10] In the 1970s, a fairly radical hypothesis was thus proposed by paleontologists; namely, that *Homo erectus* and the Neanderthals "were actually two distinct species, not the ancestors of *Homo sapiens.*"[11]

The evolutionary scientist Carl Zimmer suggests that the key reason why *Homo sapiens* survived is that they possessed a larger brain, due to new mutations, which endowed them with the ability to fashion more sophisticated tools and to invent specialized technologies. They were able to fish, hunt, create clothing and jewelry, and etch drawings in caves. They were capable of symbolic representation and, in time, abstract thinking. *Homo sapiens* developed *language* to communicate with other humans and to transmit their technical and artistic skills to future generations. At some point, *culture* emerged, its successive advances retained in human memory and taught to the young, and began to characterize social groups. All this is intrinsic to Dewey's emphasis on the instrumental role of thinking in human behavior.

Also vital is the evolution of moral principles within social institutions. Human beings have survived in part because they depended on the extended family, which became the tribe. It is members of small groups or clans that learned that they needed to establish some rules of the game. There were moral principles, such as loyalty and attachment between parents and children, lovers and friends, brothers and sisters. And so moral rules emerged: I call them the "common moral decencies." This includes empathy and sympathy for members of the tribe and the willingness to defend them when threatened or when in dire need. Darwin himself notes that an "advancement in the standard of morality will certainly give an immense advantage to one tribe over another." He observed that a tribe that possesses in a high degree "the spirit of patriotism, fidelity, obedience, courage, and sympathy" and whose members were "ready to aid another, and to sacrifice themselves for the common good, would be victorious over most other tribes; and this would be by natural selection."[12]

Thus, morality in the last analysis emerged because of its functional value. Moral norms gradually evolved and became part of the cultural values that provided some cohesion within the social group. Eventually moral empathy was extended beyond the consanguineous tribe to the village, city, or state, and most recently to the whole of humankind. The term *coevolution* points to a powerful double factor in human evolution, which at a certain stage in human history becomes *gene-culture evolution*.

What is thus unique among all living creatures on the planet is the ability of *Homo sapiens* to create tools and instruments, to bend nature to human purposes, and to intervene in the world and change it. Robins build nests and beavers build dams, but that is virtually instinctive; humans create skyscrapers and spaceships to the Moon, and that is truly wondrous. They create new medicines to heal illnesses, new ways to produce food, and new vistas in which their imagination is able to soar. Here creative intelligence is able to function as a coping mechanism. Humans no longer need to depend on instinctive behavior in order to survive, for they can evaluate problematic situations in which they are involved; and they can consciously adapt to conditions or change them. They can modify their behavior and create new things to enjoy, new worlds—urban or rural environments—to live in, and new scientific, aesthetic, and philosophical creations to contemplate and appreciate. All other species are products of natural causes—genetic and environmental. Humans are able to understand the conditions under which they behave, and to transform nature to satisfy their wishes and desires. Cognition is thus the most effective tool of adaptation of *Homo sapiens*, and this allows for new cultural emergents to appear. No longer dependent on the slow process of natural selection to survive, humans can leap ahead and transform nature. Unfortunately, these new powers also enable the human species to wage wars of destruction. Creative human intelligence is the supreme instrument of human beneficence, but it can also be used for malicious purposes.

What seems apparent in reviewing the history and evolution of the human species on the planet is that it was fashioned by and responded to *contingent* events.[13] That *Homo sapiens* were able to succeed over competing species (*Homo habilis, Homo erectus, Homo neanderthalis*, and others unknown) in a turbulent planetary environment was due to ingenuity and chance. We are fortunate that we have come as far as we have and survived, indeed thrived. We have surpassed all other species on the planet. Like the dinosaurs of a previous period, we now dominate the planet. It is ours to possess and use. How things will work out in the end is indeterminate; that the human species will survive in the future is uncertain. Creative intelligence is the instrument of human greatness and achievement; but it may also be the source of extreme anxiety and fear, unless we can summon the courage to become what we want and preserve some integrity in spite of an awareness of our ultimate ontological fragility and finitude.

A quotation from George Santayana is especially appropriate here:

> . . . nature is contingent. An infinite canvas is spread before us on which any world might have been painted. The actuality of existent things is sharpened and the possibilities of things are enlarged. We cease to be surprised or distressed at finding existence unstable and transitory . . . but perhaps all existence is in flux even down to its first principles.[14]

3.

Questions emerge concerning the moral implications of coevolution to the future of our species; and these may become troubling as knowledge of how human evolution occurs becomes more widely known. This may become all the more apparent as the idea that there is a "perfect order" in the universe is finally shattered. We live in an orderly yet turbulent universe in which unexpected contingencies occur, and the only thing that we humans can rely upon is our own resolve to persevere and to do the best that we can.

If the human species is not simply a product of natural causal laws but of contingent events, what does this say about the historic convictions of humankind about the special place of the human species in the universe? Surely it undermines the confidence that an intelligent being designed an orderly universe and fine-tuned our planet so that the human species could emerge. Indeed, it is *not* that finely tuned; for accidental events have intervened and chance has invariably upset orderly development. Indeed, the unpredictable consequences of our choices are often not foreseen. Nor does any naive optimistic account of the human condition by naturalists and secularists suffice; for the role of haphazard events too often intrude to destroy "the best laid plans of mice and men."

If the human species follows the fate of virtually all other species on the planet and eventually becomes extinct, what does this portend about the human prospect? It is difficult to contemplate that there may *not* be any ultimate future for the human species on the planet Earth. We who have great confidence in science and reason and the belief that we *will* be able to save the planet in time may be overshadowed by the realization of how slender is the evidence for that faith. Indeed, in a highly technological civilization of the future, each generation may hold the destiny of humankind in its hands.

If we reflect on the fact that the human species goes back six hundred to a thousand centuries (60,000 to 100,000 years), we have little guarantee that we will endure even the next few centuries.[15] And this applies not only to our species, which may follow the course of other species and become extinct, along with other forms of life. One day Earth may become virtually uninhabitable. Destruction of the natural ecology, along with other unforeseen natural causes, may make it virtually unlivable, except for insects, worms, viruses, and bacteria— and they shall inherit the Earth!

The salient point is that we are uncertain about the human prospect ultimately, for what will be is dependant on unforeseeable contingencies and unpredictable threats to our future existence—if a meteor were to strike planet Earth, a viral infection were to wipe out significant portions of humanity, or an all-out nuclear war or some other catastrophic event were to ensue.

The role of indeterminate brute facticity intervening raises questions about the role of chance in history. One might well ask, what were the causal forces and contingent factors that shaped yesteryear; retrospective detective work is sometimes difficult to verify, but prognosticating what will happen tomorrow, next year, or centuries into the future is even more uncertain. Thus the contingent universe—fragile, precarious, doubtful—is a fact of nature, life, and culture. Seeing things in a realistic perspective is essential for wisdom; but this may also generate an ultimate hopelessness about the human prospect. One would hope not; for we can still live comfortably significant lives without worrying now about what will occur eventually in the remote future. It is similar to the statement that we all know today that each of us will die some day in the future. Meanwhile, live each moment fully. What will happen to future generations—including our own civilization—is an interesting speculative puzzle that we can do little about today. If our great-great-grandparents spent all their time fretting about how their great-great-grandchildren (still unborn) would fare, they would hardly have time to enjoy the multifarious possibilities of living their lives fully on their own. This is a realistic response to metaphysical angst about the unknown existential future of humankind.

Nevertheless, the moral quandary that the human species will increasingly face is the very survival of the species. This had been a central issue following World War II with the discovery of nuclear power and weapons of mass destruction, such as the atomic and hydrogen bombs.

There are other emerging problems of danger to our planet that lead to doubt about human survival. I am here referring to population growth, global warming, pollution, the depletion of natural resources. This raises the question, in what sense will John Dewey's philosophy be relevant to the future problems that humankind will undoubtedly encounter? I am not a prophet, and I do not have an answer to that question, but I point out that the methods he recommends in formulating the judgments of practice seem to me to be especially relevant to the rapidly changing world.

In the last century, competing naturalistic philosophies have emerged, sharing a common set of assumptions. They point out that the salvationist theologies of the past represent an escape into illusion about a mythic future, and these may lose their appeal. If god is dead, because he or she never existed, then supernatural mythic narratives of ultimate human salvation will not suffice because of a lack of evidence for any of the competing religious creeds.

Naturalists such as Dewey maintain that we need to draw upon science and reason to understand natural causes and cultural means, and we need to use this knowledge to directly intervene to ameliorate the human condition. The Deweyan option has been to develop science, education, and democracy to solve our problems, and we need to reconstruct our valuations in the light of this knowledge if we are to ameliorate the human condition. We need always to work within the context of existing praxis and culture. Our appraisals grow out of our valuations, which may be modified by inquiry.

Today we need a new naturalistic narrative in which our *planetary interdependence* is emphasized. We need to create a new, common faith, which Dewey suggested for earlier generations; but this needs to be truly *global* in dimension, one that emphasizes our planetary responsibilities and shared ethical principles and valuations. We need to create transnational institutions beyond the nation-state to cope with these problems.

We also need to develop a *new planetary ethics*—in which the inherent dignity and value of every person on the planet is recognized. We need to develop not simply a set of rational imperatives but also empathetic imperatives in which we cultivate a genuine feeling of affection for every person on the planet, an ethic that focuses on both reason and feeling for our planetary abode, and the human and other species that coexist on it: it must be a new planetary philosophy in which a set of shared ideal ends will motivate people to live and work together. Perhaps that may sound like a utopian scenario, but I submit that it is the most realistic option that we have. And it is entirely consonant with John Dewey's philosophical approach.

Part Two

INQUIRY AND KNOWLEDGE

4.

DEWEY AND THE
SUBJECT MATTER OF SCIENCE

Peter Godfrey-Smith

1. DEWEY AND REICHENBACH

In 1939, John Dewey was the first person to be the subject of a *Library of Living Philosophers* volume. The result includes meetings between Dewey and critics representing a range of philosophical schools and styles. There is a sometimes prickly exchange between Dewey and Bertrand Russell, and another with Hans Reichenbach. Reichenbach is sometimes classified as a logical positivist. This understates the originality of his views, though he was certainly an ally of the logical positivist movement. Reichenbach developed his own scientifically engaged form of empiricism.[1] He was sympathetic to Dewey and presents his essay "Dewey's Theory of Science" in the *Library of Living Philosophers* volume as one offering criticisms from a viewpoint that featured much agreement. So this is a useful exchange for thinking about how Dewey relates to other currents in scientifically oriented philosophy. I will start by looking at one of Reichenbach's criticisms, and Dewey's reply. I'll then use their exchange to navigate a path through several parts of Dewey's later philosophy, drawing primarily on *Experience and Nature* (1925) and *The Quest for Certainty* (1929). The main topic of this essay is the content of scientific theories, but for Dewey this question connects to many others.

Reichenbach claims in his essay that Dewey held a "nonrealistic" view of science. Reichenbach gives a series of quotes from Peirce, James, Dewey, and Mach. He takes all of them to express versions of the idea that scientific language that apparently refers to unobservable entities really just describe patterns in observables. Here is what he says about Dewey: "John Dewey calls the scientific object an 'instrumentality of multiplied controls and uses of the real things of everyday experience.'"[2] Reichenbach then says that the difference between pragmatism and positivism is that positivism treats the contents of the immediate world as "complex" and tries to reduce them further, to collections of sense data. Pragmatism rightly does not do this: "sense data are abstractions as much as are objects of physical science."[3] Reichenbach credits Dewey with this insight.

Reichenbach then patiently criticizes all such "nonrealistic" views. His main argument is that the inferences in science about unobservable objects are of the same kind as inferences used in everyday life to get us to conclusions about ordinary things that are hidden or misleadingly presented. Dewey seems opposed to the idea that the picture we get from science can correct and replace the common-sense picture of the contents of the world. But within everyday life, we engage in these corrections all the time, especially when we deal with mirages, illusions, and dreams. We find ourselves relegating various entities to a category of the illusory or unreal. Reichenbach thinks that science often does the same thing. When the correction science makes of a common-sense view is small, there is usually no need to talk about it *as* a correction and substitution, though strictly speaking this is what it is. We find this situation in the case of the comparison between the scientific picture of a wooden table and the common-sense picture. The common-sense view has it that the table is completely solid. Science sees it as made of atoms. Reichenbach sees this as a very minor, but genuine, correction.[4] Other corrections are more substantial. Reichenbach urges that we see our eyes and other senses as like speedometers, which successfully register states of environmental variables provided that conditions are appropriate. Visual illusions are cases where the speedometer is in inappropriate conditions or is not functioning properly.

Reichenbach was no doubt surprised when Dewey strenuously objected to his interpretation of him and insisted that he did not have a "nonrealistic interpretation of scientific concepts." Dewey suspected that the source of the misinterpretation was his (Dewey's) "identification of the scientific object with relations." He conjectures that Reichenbach must be one of the many philosophers who think that "relations have not the empirical reality possessed by things and qualities."[5] Why should *that* be diagnostic here, and give rise to the appearance of disagreement on what looks like a quite different topic?

2. RELATIONS AND QUALITIES

Dewey claimed that there had been a persistent downgrading of the reality of relations in much of the Western philosophical tradition. This he saw as a long-standing mistake. The claim that relations have often (rightly or wrongly) been accorded a second-class status seems generally fair. Two useful landmarks here are Aristotle and Locke. Aristotle saw the world as made up of substances and their properties (universals). A property inheres (in each case) in just a single substance; properties are all "monadic" rather than "polyadic." We can talk about situations in which things stand in a certain relation, but these cases must be analyzed in terms of how monadic properties inhere in substances.[6] Moving to the early modern period, in Locke we find a starker claim: relations have "no other reality, but what they have in the Minds of Men."[7] It has been common to see our talk of relations as not mapping directly to relational elements in the world itself but as having a more indirect application to a world in which real properties are always monadic. Our talk about intrinsic properties can represent intrinsic properties that things themselves have, but our talk of relations is not given this straightforward analysis.

Dewey opposed such views, and thought that their untenability had been made evident by the practice of modern science. Scientific theories provide our best examples of factual knowledge about the world, and science has learned that relations are what can most fruitfully be studied by organized inquiry, as Dewey explains in *Experience and Nature* (chapter 4). Science is concerned with patterns, correlations, and functional dependencies; it is concerned with what happens *here* when you prod things over *there*. Science has realized the importance and reality of relations in its practice, but philosophy is taking longer to catch up with the idea.

These points can be put in a still broader context. For Dewey, there are several things that the mainstream philosophical tradition has inherited from the ancient Greeks.[8] One is a view of knowledge as contemplation of being.[9] A couple of different aspects to this idea can be distinguished: the "being" that is contemplated is a matter of the forms or internal natures of things, and "contemplation" contrasts with intervention and transformation. A second and distinct inheritance is the idea that questions about knowledge have a special bearing on questions about what the universe contains; the objects that we *know* about are those that are "ultimately real."[10]

With the rise of modern science, contemplation was replaced by experimentation and intervention, and relations acquired a centrality to scientific knowledge. Once relations replace intrinsic properties as the subject matter of science, there is the possibility of asserting a metaphysical view that directly inverts the one that came down from the Greeks. A person might say that science has taught us that relations are what is real and intrinsic properties are mere constructs or illusions. One form of the "structuralist" tradition in philosophy of science supports views like this. I will look at that option below. But this is not Dewey's approach, and that is because of the second inherited error that he wants to correct, the idea that only things that we interact with cognitively or epistemically can be real. Dewey thought that insufficient philosophical attention had been paid to the nonepistemic or "noncognitive" side of our experience. What are presented as general theories of our interaction with the world are usually theories of our *cognitive* interaction with the world, theories of what and how we can know. These theories, in turn, are often used to make arguments about what the world contains. But those arguments are compromised because they are views based on only one part of our traffic with the world, the cognitive part. Philosophers suppose that if something is not the object of *knowledge* then it cannot figure in our experience *at all*.

Dewey argues, in contrast, that much of our experience of the world is not a matter of knowing about it, representing it, investigating it. There is also a great mass of noncognitive interaction with things: eating them, bumping into them, handling them, and habitually using them. Dewey sometimes describes this by saying that things can be *had* as well as *known*.[11] The term *having* is often awkward, and I am not sure how generally Dewey means to apply it—which interactions count as "havings"—but many of the ordinary perceptual encounters that go on constantly in our lives are in this category. Inquiry and knowledge comprise one facet of experience, which arises in particular circumstances. Cognitive engagement with the world arises when we encounter an obstruction or threat to our more habitual and unreflective activities. The cognitive side of life is embedded in a richer matrix of noncognitive engagement with the world. So if a person is going to make arguments about what the world contains based on premises about our interactions with it, based on premises concerning the nature of our experience, they should not restrict experience to its cognitive side.

For Dewey, in the noncognitive side of experience we encounter *qualities*. Qualities are contrasted with relations.[12] It is not clear how exactly Dewey intends to divide things up here. In current philosophy, a category that contrasts in a relevant way with relations is that of an *intrinsic property*. Roughly speaking, an intrinsic property of an object is one whose instantiation by that object does not logically depend on the existence and arrangement of any other objects. An *extrinsic* property is one that is not intrinsic.[13] Dewey's notion of a quality may be a somewhat a different category than this modern idea of an intrinsic property.[14] Qualities are also described in terms of their *immediacy*. In some places what "immediacy" seems to refer to is a kind of particularity or unrepeatability, which suggests the modern notion of a property-*instance* (or "trope"), as opposed to a universal.[15] Immediacy also sometimes looks more like a feature of our interaction with things, as opposed to a feature of the properties themselves, and Dewey also says that, strictly speaking, qualities exist in interactions between organisms and things external to them.[16] In that case, no qualities of objects would count as intrinsic in the contemporary sense. So it is an oversimplification to map Dewey's notion of a quality directly onto the modern idea of an intrinsic property, but Dewey does treat qualities as things that contrast with relations in how they attach to particular things, and also in their role within our lives. Most important, he says: "Genuine science is impossible as long as the object esteemed for its own intrinsic qualities is taken as the object of knowledge."[17]

This gives us Dewey's reorganization of the picture that came down to us from the Greeks. For Dewey, relations are known and qualities are "had." Neither is primary in a metaphysical sense, more real or more furniturelike. Neither is to be "explained away" in some manner that is not applicable to the other. They have different and complementary roles in our lives. The error of downgrading relations is rectified without making the error of installing relations in the position of metaphysical primacy once occupied by qualities.

With Dewey's picture laid out, a comparison can be made with another modern view that asserts that relations are the objects of knowledge. In philosophy of science, this view is now often known as "structural realism." It has links to an older "structuralist" tradition, going back through Bertrand Russell and Henri Poincaré, and also to some Kantian views.[18]

Structural realism was introduced in its contemporary form by John Worrall in response to epistemological arguments against scientific realism.[19] The "pessimistic meta-induction" holds that because the entities posited by most past scientific theories are now thought not to exist, the same fate is likely to befall the entities posited in our current theories.[20] Worrall argued that the history of science is less unfriendly to realism if we focus just on the "structural" claims that past theories have made. When theories are replaced, commitments made by the old theory about structural features of the world are often retained even though the entities posited by the old theory are abandoned. These "structural" features are networks of relations.

Some structural realists infer from these arguments that we can have confidence that our current scientific theories capture some structural features of the world with some degree of accuracy, but we should not hope for scientific knowledge of the nature of the entities that stand in these networks of relations. Ladyman calls this "epistemic" structural realism. It is also possible to claim, more strongly, that what we have learned from these facts about the development of science is that the world *consists* in pure structure; reality contains a network of relations with no individuals in the familiar sense standing in those relations. This is what Ladyman calls "ontic" structural realism.

Dewey, as we saw, holds that scientific theories describe relations. But Dewey differs from structural realism in both its epistemic and its ontic forms. The contrast with the ontic version is sharpest. From Dewey's point of view, the ontic version is an example of a view holding that if the cognitive side of our lives (exemplified by science) has no concern with some putative kind of entity, that is reason to think it does not exist at all. Dewey rejects this. The cognitive side of our lives is concerned with relations, and science is the most refined expression of that side of human life, but there is also the noncognitive side.

In recent discussions of ontic structural realism, some have argued that the view is incoherent; it makes no sense to say that the world could be constituted solely by a network of relations.[21] For a relation to be present, some particular entities related must also be present. Relations cannot be self-sufficient. Dewey asserted a version of this argument in 1925.[22] For Dewey, the incoherent version of structuralism comes about by combining the insight that scientific theories are concerned to represent relations with the mistaken tendency to think that a scientific inventory of the world is *the* inventory of the world.

The "epistemic" version of structural realism does not make an inference to any claim about the world's consisting entirely of relations. Epistemic structural realism is only a view about what we can know. This is closer to Dewey's view, but there are still some differences. Epistemic structural realism is usually a fallback from a simpler version of scientific realism, motivated by anxieties about our access to things other than relations. For Dewey, the fact that we do not know about the qualitative does not reflect the existence of some barrier or shortcoming, but instead is a functional matter.

> Things in their immediacy are unknown and unknowable, not because they are remote or behind some impenetrable veil of sensation of ideas, but because knowledge has no concern with them. For knowledge is a memorandum of conditions of their appearance, concerned, that is, with sequences, coexistences, relations.[23]

There is nothing about the qualitative that makes it inaccessible. Rather, these aspects of the world have a different role in our lives from what we investigate and know.

This brings us to a possible problem with Dewey's view, however. Dewey says that the qualitative is not remote because we have dealings with these features of the world, though they are not cognitive dealings. But these direct and noncognitive interactions would only seem to connect us with the qualitative features of what are sometimes called "middle-sized" objects (which Dewey calls objects of "primary experience"), rather than the intrinsic qualities of aspects of the world that are extremely small or that are otherwise removed from ordinary experience. What sort of relation do we then have with the intrinsic qualities of unobservable things? We can't know about them because they are qualitative rather than relational. And we can't apparently "have" them, because they are too far from ordinary experience. This makes it seem that there is one kind of natural feature that we really are cut off from. Dewey is opposed to philosophical views that assert gulfs and failures of contact, but it is hard to see how he avoids one here.

This problem connects back to the issues that concerned Reichenbach in his 1939 essay on Dewey. Here (with Reichenbach's ellipses removed) is the best of the quotations that Reichenbach uses to allege a "nonrealist" character to Dewey's thought:

> Put positively, the physical object, as scientifically defined, is not a duplicated real object, but is a statement, as numerically definite as is possible, of the relations between sets of changes the qualitative object sustains with changes in other things—ideally of all things with which interaction might under any circumstances take place.[24]

Reichenbach interprets this as claiming that what appears to be talk about hidden objects in physical science is really no more than talk about relations between observable things. Reichenbach has a point here: it is not enough to say that science is concerned with "relations" unless you say what sort of relations they are and what they are relating. The issue that Reichenbach wants to focus on in his discussion is whether apparent descriptions of unobservables in science are really just shorthand descriptions of patterns in the behavior of observable things. Once we look specifically at this question, it does sometimes appear that Dewey's view collapses to a more familiar empiricism, in which the role of scientific theories is to describe only relations between things we can observe. In his reply to Reichenbach, Dewey is determined to avoid such a view. When a scientific theory posits a "swarm of atoms" in explaining a physical structure of the kind we would ordinarily call a wooden table, Dewey does *not* want to deny that this invisible swarm really exists. He wants to deny only that it constitutes a "ghostly kind of table."[25] I am not sure if this reply to Reichenbach squares with everything Dewey says in *The Quest for Certainty*, but let's take him at his word: physics does try to describe swarms of invisible objects (atoms, and also "electrons, deuterons, etc.").[26] A swarm of this kind is a collection of things with qualities—things with intrinsic properties, at least. But then we face the problem raised above: what sort of contact can humans have with the intrinsic properties of objects that are far removed from ordinary experience? We don't seem to be able to know them *or* to "have" them.

3. KNOWING AND HAVING

At the end of the previous section, I began to turn from interpretation to criticism, and I will continue in that vein by looking more closely at the idea that scientific theories are concerned with relations. I will look at both Dewey's view and those of his structuralist relatives. I will give an argument against one kind of structuralism. The argument also has some bearing on Dewey's position, though difficulties of interpretation make its impact less clear. After that I will look again at our noncognitive interactions with the world.

Dewey and the structuralists hold that that science describes relations. They appear to be right that relations are central to much of what modern science describes. But is science *solely* concerned with relations? If so, what is ruled out?

In particular, is there a philosophical problem with the idea that science can reasonably attempt to describe the intrinsic properties of things?

Consider a table. What does science have to say about it? We can look for descriptions of how the table might interact with other things, but we can also look at its internal makeup. The table, we find, is made of wood. Wood is largely made up of cellulose and a chemical called lignin. Cellulose, in turn, is made entirely of carbon, oxygen, and hydrogen (as is lignin). A carbon atom is made up of protons, neutrons, and electrons. Those are all facts about the intrinsic makeup of wood.

There is certainly a role for structures and relations in this description of wood. Cellulose, for example, is not just an undifferentiated mix of carbon, oxygen, and hydrogen, but a combination of those elements in a certain arrangement. The arrangement is all that distinguishes cellulose from easily digested starch—their ingredients are the same. So when one looks inside cellulose, one finds a structure— a set of relations between parts. But when we do this we also gain knowledge of an intrinsic nature—knowledge of the intrinsic nature of cellulose.

Philosophers writing about knowledge frequently make use of a contrast between intrinsic properties on one side and extrinsic or relational properties on the other.[27] Knowing one of these is seen as a different matter from knowing the other. There is indeed a contrast of this kind between intrinsic and extrinsic properties *at* a given level in nature, but when we think *across* levels, things are different. Then the extrinsic properties of entities at level n may be part of the intrinsic nature of entities at level $n + 1$. When we learn about relations between carbon and oxygen within cellulose—for example, how they bond—we are learning something about cellulose's intrinsic nature. Looking across levels in a part-whole hierarchy, the relationship between intrinsic structure and external relations is "correlative" rather than being simply contrastive. When a whole has physical parts, the whole's intrinsic properties are due in part to the extrinsic or relational properties of those parts. They are also due in part to the intrinsic natures of the parts themselves, and the intrinsic properties of those parts can be handled the same way—as consequences of the inner natures and external relations of their own smaller parts.

Why might a picture like this be resisted? I will look at a couple of possibilities.

First, a person might say that the cellulose example is entirely compatible with the idea that science is exclusively concerned with relations. If someone discovers that wood contains cellulose, he or she is asserting a relation between those things—between wood and cellulose. Part-whole relations are, after all, relations. So where is the problem?

If someone says this, though, his or her view is entirely consistent with the idea that science describes the intrinsic natures of things. If "science is concerned with relations" in only *this* sense, then none of the distinctive theses of structural realism, or Dewey's view, are supported. All that is being said is that it is possible to express the content of scientific knowledge in a relation-asserting form. It then becomes unclear what the contrasts could be between this view and others. What is being ruled out? Even the idea that genuine knowledge is contemplation of essences would be compatible with this picture; we contemplate the relations between things and their essences.

Here is a second way of resisting the view sketched above. I said that wood contains cellulose, which contains carbon, which contains protons, and so on. But where will this bottom out? When we get to the fundamental constituents of reality, which have no parts, how can we hope to describe *their* intrinsic nature? (Perhaps there is no such fundamental level, but I will assume that there is for the purposes of discussion.) When we get to the fundamental level, all a theory can do is describe relations between entities at that level. Perhaps our theories can get no grip on the intrinsic natures of things at the fundamental level, and this undermines the claims we made about the higher levels.[28]

To this I would reply, even if we don't know *everything* about the intrinsic nature of cellulose (because its ultimate constituents remain intrinsically mysterious), we have still learned *something* about the intrinsic properties of cellulose when we learn that it contains three elements—carbon, oxygen, and hydrogen—arranged in a particular way. We have some knowledge of the intrinsic in this case, even if not total knowledge.

A third possible objection challenges the claim that it really is an intrinsic property of cellulose that it contains carbon. What this would mean is that a sample of cellulose would contain carbon no matter what the rest of the universe was like. Even if our table was the only thing in the universe, it would contain carbon. But physics may well speak against this picture. Perhaps if the rest of the universe were sufficiently different, it would not be possible for protons and electrons to exist at all. If *being a carbon atom* requires containing six protons, and protons do not exist in a one-table universe, then it is not an intrinsic property of the table that it contains carbon. Perhaps the state of the whole universe, or some large part of it, at time t is implicated in this table's containing carbon at time t.

In reply, perhaps it is true that the state of some large part of the universe is involved in the table containing carbon at time *t*. This is an issue within physics itself. Perhaps physics will determine that containing carbon is not intrinsic and will posit new intrinsic properties of objects like tables. Perhaps physics will instead become holistic in a way that implies that no proper parts of the universe have any intrinsic properties at all. Physics might come out that way and it might not. This conclusion could not be reached on the basis of general philosophical arguments about what can be known and how science works.

In this section so far I have sketched a view of how science is sometimes able to describe the intrinsic nature of things, and I have resisted structuralist arguments that it cannot do this. I have not tried to grapple with the special problems that arise in fundamental physics. My aim has been to show that in a large range of nonfundamental scientific work, the intrinsic is a straightforward target for scientific investigation, and the traditional contrast between knowledge of the intrinsic and the extrinsic can easily be misapplied. How much trouble do these points cause for Dewey? As I emphasized earlier, I am not sure how to interpret some parts of his treatment of the differing roles of relations and qualities. But Dewey was clearly attracted to a transformation of the Aristotelian view in which relations are downgraded and the intrinsic natures of things are the proper objects of inquiry. Dewey wanted us to "surrender the traditional notion that knowledge is possession of the inner nature of things."[29] Any view holding that science describes relations *rather than* the intrinsic and that understands as "science" fields other than fundamental physics has to confront the arguments given above. Whenever entities contain structured arrangements of parts (as molecules, organisms, and many other things do), there is no opposition between describing networks of relations and describing intrinsic natures.

Dewey's view has some other distinctive features. As noted earlier, when Dewey talks about qualities, sometimes he emphasizes a kind of particularity or unrepeatability. Then there is a different reason why science might be unconcerned with qualities: they are unrepeatable, and science searches for generality. But if so, showing that science is not concerned with qualities would not be enough to show that science was only concerned with relations. There would also be the question of the repeatable intrinsic features of things. Maybe science is concerned with relations *and* with the repeatable intrinsic features of things, such as *containing carbon*.

So far in this section I have looked at our cognitive engagement with relations and intrinsic properties. I have argued that science is not solely concerned with relations, in the sense in which relations are contrasted with intrinsic features. I now look at the flip side of this issue. Dewey thinks that relations are known while qualities are "had"—encountered in a nonepistemic way. I am not entirely sure whether he means to deny that relations can also be "had." That seems to be the flavor of the view in *Experience and Nature*: qualities are had but not known, relations are known but not had. But (unless I've missed it) I don't think the idea that relations are not had was asserted explicitly. Still, let's look at the version of Dewey's view that does assert such an inversion: the Greeks said that qualities are known and relations barely exist; the modern discovery is that only relations are known and qualities have their home in the noncognitive side of our experience. We looked at whether the intrinsic natures of things can be known. Can relations have the noncognitive role in experience that qualities have?

It is hard to assess this because these noncognitive encounters were not described in a very concise way. But clearly Dewey means to include our ordinary unreflective perceptual and active encounters with such features as colors, shapes, and solidity. And then I would argue that whatever a noncognitive encounter with a quality might be, the same sort of thing can exist in the case of relations. However we characterize our "immediate" practical encounters with colors and shapes, we have the same sort of encounters with arrangements and layouts—with the fact that this thing is next to this one, and this one is blocked by that one. Our noncognitive interactions with things in the world are encounters not just with the qualitative features of objects but also with the relations between them. In particular, we encounter things in their spatial and temporal arrangement. These relations between things are just as important to habitual behaviors, practical manipulation, and "enjoyments" as intrinsic qualities are, and are just as "immediately" experienced.

4. CONCLUSION

I have criticized some parts of Dewey's view of science in this paper, but this is also a collection of topics where I think Dewey shows much insight. Dewey is right that the development of science forces a break from the metaphysical downgrading of relations seen in much mainstream philosophy. Dewey is right that our cognitive or epistemic engagement with the world is embedded in a matrix of other kinds of engagement, and this fact is neglected in many philosophical treatments of experience. But, I have argued, Dewey's attempted redrawing of the scene is too stark. Too much of the shape of traditional philosophical views has been retained, resulting in an ungainly separation of roles.

In his treatment of science, Dewey is determined to avoid a view in which the scientific picture of the world and the picture found in "direct" experience are *rivals* of each other. The separation of roles Dewey reaches for (with science handling relations, and ordinary experience being the home of qualities) can indeed achieve this dissolving of rivalry: "The relations a thing sustains are hardly a competitor to the thing itself."[30] This maneuver works when the "things" exhibiting qualities and relations are things directly encountered in experience. Then scientific change—the replacement of one theory by another—would involve the discovery that we were wrong about some of these relations, or the discovery of further relations that had not been previously appreciated. The qualities experienced would remain the same, and there could be no rivalry between the scientific description and the ordinary experience; all the rivalry is between one scientific theory and another. But matters are different if science is partly about hidden and hypothesized entities far from ordinary experience—swarms of atoms, and so on—and is concerned with the intrinsic natures of those things as well as their relations. Then science gives us an alternative inventory of the things making up the world. Looking at this alternative inventory, we can ask whether it is a more detailed account of the same things we can recognize in ordinary experience or an account that shows something factually wrong with the picture we get in ordinary experience. This possibility is explored by Reichenbach in his essay on Dewey. For Reichenbach, the relation between a scientific and a common-sense picture of some part of the world may well feature conflict, rivalry, and replacement. It depends on what particular sciences determine. Rivalry might arise, and it might not. That is something to assess on a case-by-case basis. Here I side with Reichenbach. Dewey's account of science, for all its insights, comes too close to issuing a guarantee that rivalries of the kind that Reichenbach discusses are impossible— impossible, again, because the "relations a thing sustains are hardly a competitor to the thing itself." Dewey vigorously criticized other philosophies for trying to give guarantees of things that cannot be guaranteed. I think he ends up doing something like that here, and he also does so, I have argued, by drawing too much on the same metaphysical inheritance that he dissected and described so well. So on both these points, my criticism of Dewey is a Deweyan one.

5.

DEWEY AND DARWIN ON EVOLUTION AND NATURAL KINDS
A Pragmatist Perspective

Jay Schulkin

1. INTRODUCTION

Eighteen fifty-nine was a pivotal year that witnessed the birth of two of the greatest contributions to evolutionary science. The first of these was Darwin's revolutionary work, *On the Origins of Species*, and the other was the birth of John Dewey. Dewey was always biologically oriented without being a narrow biological determinist. Biological sensibility is pervasive in the orientation of the classical pragmatist, and particularly Dewey.

Two key factors seem omnipresent from a biological point of view: evolution and devolution. Evolution is manifest in great diversity of expression, ingenious modes of adaptation and extension—variation is key then in evolutionary expansion. But alongside evolutionary genius is the breakdown of function, devolution of expression, the converse of evolution.

The downward spiral leads to extinction, a key concept in evolutionary theorizing. Once one is grounded in biological categories, naturalism is a cornerstone of the perspective. The other pillar is realism; not naïve realism, where things simply are, but critical realism,[1] in which objects are not simply given, but are understood from a perspective. Critical realism requires a search for perspective and some sense of prediction, cephalic in origin, towards objects of various kinds. Dewey emphasized the first trend; Darwin emphasized both.

John Dewey's approach to the experimental method emphasized its link to Darwin and a philosophy of change, adaptation and retreat of certainty.[2] The cultivation of education is one of intelligence and problem solving, broadly understood and endemic across all areas of the human condition; authority is an achievement through experiment and self corrective inquiry, but never a certainty.

Dewey naturalized the philosophical quest to know and made it part of the empirical sciences, broadening the empirical sciences to take into account philosophical issues. Reflective inquiry pervades all inquiry; and our democratic ideals, our notion of progress, is in backing a philosophy of change, ushered in, in part, by the biological sciences. With the decline of necessity came a realistic sense of freedom of expression amidst the constraints of culture and our biology.[3]

I begin with a discussion about Darwin and Dewey and pragmatism, Dewey and naturalism, a discussion of evolution, and then move on to the basic cognitive adaptation and a sense of categories linked to objects and kinds. Finally, I address some ideas about evolution and cognitive coherence.

2. DARWIN'S IMPACT ON DEWEY

The impact of Darwin on philosophy was profound.[4] What appeared in his wake was a critical realism and naturalism[5] grounded in object knowledge and linked to organic habits, natural inference, and grounded reason. At times the reason was Aristotelian and oriented to object essences.[6] Dewey suggested that with regard to the mind and adaptation, questions are rooted in terms of change and function, context and resolution.

As Dewey put it, "Interest shifts from the wholesale essence back of special changes to the question of how special changes serve and defeat concrete purposes: shifts from an intelligence that shaped things once and for all to the particular intelligences which things are even now shaping; shifts from an ultimate goal of good to the direct increments of justice and happiness that intelligent administration of existent conditions may beget and that present carelessness of stupidity will destroy and forego."[7]

Pragmatists moved away, for the most part, from the defense of philosophical conundrums to an acknowledgement of the conundrums themselves and not necessarily their resolution. Problems about realism, good faith demands, and intellectual honesty require it. Doubts linger amidst the utter undesirability of our sense, an animal faith, a human faith. The backdrop is still naturalism; a modest, not overstated realism amidst this naturalism is still a requirement. Putnam[8] calls it "realism with a human face," or perhaps we could term it "naturalism with a human face"—and what other face could there be, since we are the frameworks of our own understanding, and the constructed edifice of that understanding is built on cephalic adaptive systems that evolved over millions of years.

For the classical philosophers in the field, pragmatism was grounded in naturalism and realism and was anchored in evolutionary perspective.[9] Evolution was a background whether narrowly or broadly understood. Amidst contradictions and an original sin (slavery), a sense of adventure amidst the plenty of nature seemed unbounded; natural piety was a normative goal and not the devolution of nature, a clearing of the wilderness, another dominant strain in the approach to the new land in North America, and less human purity and absolutism, but an experimentalism rooted in a naturalism and pragmatism, with a common sensibility about a virtual panorama of phenomena that impacts the human condition.

A common theme running through the transcendentalist through classical pragmatists is the discussion of nature; hard to avoid for nineteenth-century Americans, since most of their surroundings were rural, not urban. A natural piety could emanate quite readily in these circumstances; of course there was great variation in this natural piety and civic social justice.[10]

3. AN ORIENTATION TO INQUIRY

Myths of certainty or, as Dewey understood them, "quests for certainty," are replaced with frameworks that can be justified and inferences that seemed warranted. Dewey felt that often we live "in a world of hazards" and feel "compelled to seek security"; the perilous pervades amidst moments of reprieve. Amidst the ontologically pervasive, the natural desire is to seek comfort in uncertainty, a blanket cover against the endlessly perilous [precarious] sensibility that we find ourselves in; the forms of adaptation are as diverse as we are as a species.

With no Archimedean starting point, just good heuristics of problem solving embedded in cephalic capabilities, we move forward. Edifices of stone are replaced with more labile edifices, changing frameworks, workable, usable, reliable, and predictive, and anchored to self-correction, itself bound to inquiry and correction. The endless quest to escape the predicament, to quell the need for certainty, to eradicate the choices that we must make, is the omnipresent urge to forge and live in an edifice of comfort.

Dewey embraced this desire and coupled it with intelligent action and sustained humility. He may have exaggerated our conception of ameliorating the human existential condition of endless angst, as many of his critics griped,[11] but he sought an acknowledgement of our vulnerabilities amidst a steadfast conception of how ends blur into means of action, action replete with a thoroughgoing experimentalism and aimed towards controlled inquiry. He made no separation from other parts of our life; for him it is just that permutations are a dominant experience and they put the sense of control in perspective. It is no illusion; it is just never grandiose, and it need not be.

Dewey's philosophical sensibility is where ends merge into means, and where action is guided by ideas knotted to a thorough sense of the experimental and the empirical; the test of ideas is a normative goal in Dewey's experimentalism, tied to the reduction of the quest for certainty. As Dewey nicely expressed it: "the road from perceptible experience which is blind, obscure, fragmentary, meager in meaning, to objects of sense which are also objects which satisfy, reward, and feed intelligence, is through ideas that are experimental and operative."[12] Problem solving or intelligence is demythologized and naturalized in this intellectual landscape; the naturalizing of intelligence, problem solving anchored to human adaptation and human ideals of worth, is the normative goal of a thoroughly going naturalism, ripe for the human condition.

Dewey's naturalism is not anchored particularly to an overzealous reductionism, in which one explanation dominates at the expense of all else. Levels of explanation are one thing; a dominant way in which to understand our orientation to nature is another. Respect for nature, to kinds of objects, entails a respect for levels of explanation, from the molecular to the molar. This is a very modern perspective.[13]

Dewey's naturalism is also emboldened by his sense of the action of ideas and the continuity of philosophical perspective and science; the naturalism is embedded in his realism and the realism is bound to ideas in action, transforming and responsive to changing landscapes. It is a philosophical naturalism and realism embedded in developing predictable coherent forms of action.[14] Dewey's views covering the last forty years of his life are quite consistent with modern views of philosophical naturalism, less about essences to be discovered and more about coherent action.[15]

Naturalism is demythologized in terms of use and human duties, human interests and wondrous awe; gluttony and abuse are as readily available to our cephalic machinations as our control and inhibition, and considerations of future needs (despite the limitations). Clusters of properties hover around diverse forms of explanation[16] which embolden our inferences, tied to a real sense of the growth of knowledge[17] and a respect for our limitations[18] for which a community of inquirers[19] is the foundation, a foundation which is international in perspective.

4. EVOLUTION, CHANGE, AND ADAPTATION

Evolution is often popularly used as a synonym for glorified progression, but its key themes of variation and reproductive successes are biological variables rather than straightforward pathways. Evolution via natural selection is really about adaptation to niches, the opportunistic use of specific functions in more varied environments, and the development of novel functions for existing structures and molecules.[20]

Conceptions of geological and climate change already flew through the intellectual air that Darwin breathed. Charles Lyell's *The Principles of Geology* (1830–33) devotes several chapters to both concepts. As well as geographical and climate variation, species differences and even the idea of species extinction had become a core concept, as had the ideas of competition and survival, and resource availability and allocation.[21] All of these themes required a notion of kinds of objects, and a predilection for taxonomy. Authors of the twentieth century such as G. G. Simpson (*The Meaning of Evolution*, 1949) and T. C. Dobzhansky (*Mankind Evolving*, 1962) have acknowledged the continuing importance of these nineteenth-century foundations in the establishment of the modern evolutionary perspective by which we understand the rest of biology. Two factors especially, natural selection and variation in adaptation, remain key ingredients, and climate change and geographic/geologic shifts still shape our view of evolution.

At various points in our ecological history, there appear to have been bouts of rapid climate change that resulted in the extinction of species (e.g., 2.5 million years ago). There may have been another moment of rapid change within our own lineage that took place about 100,000 years ago,[22] possibly due to a greater preponderance of unstable environments. Evolution as a whole, and our evolution in particular, is replete with both change and stability. That possible climatic change at the 100,000-year mark may have facilitated dispersal of hominoids across the diverse regions we now inhabit, from the Arctic to the tropics, from deserts to rainforests.[23]

Geographic isolation also remains central to our understanding of variation, extinction, and speciation. As Darwin noticed and as we can still see clearly today, the same species separated by space and habitat in the Galapagos Islands produced two very different adaptations, a land-dwelling and an ocean-adapted animal, the iguana. Geography coupled with habitat selected for very different forms of adaptation.

Evolutionary theory also puts into context something about our original condition of knowing. The number of genes in the human genome turns out to be much smaller than was thought, and humans share 98 percent of our genetic code with the other great apes. Although no known precursor exists for syntactic competence in such primates, they are social animals and exhibit gestural responding, keeping track of the social milieu and other communicative elaborations, which are significant to evolutionary theory and to perhaps our own linguistic competence. In hominid evolution, abrupt changes seem to have taken place in the rapid expansion of symbolic expression.[24] Moreover, we have some evidence, including fossils, tools, and skeletons, that more than one modern form of the human species populated the earth at the same time, competing or perhaps cooperating for survival. Agriculture emerged in the range of 10,000 years ago, and written language approximately 5,000 years ago. This is quite recent when put in perspective.

The development of language, a symbolic representation of the world in which abstract sounds stand for objects, may have been the beginning of our desire to categorize. From hunter-gatherer to agrarian to industrial times, humans have tried to lend structure to what they see and to preserve it in some way. Dwelling together led to the sharing of workloads and efficient task completion, which afforded individuals more discretionary time. With this extra time, at some point, humans began creating visual representations of natural objects in the form of drawings and reliefs, some of the earliest of which have survived in the deep caves of southwestern Europe.

From this simple beginning of charcoal on a bare rock face, our ideas about nature have evolved with our culture and our ways of understanding.[25] Early humans originally understood nature through two primary categories: alive and lifeless. A classical and medieval cosmology based on the four elements eventually gave way to lifeless atomism, ethereal forms, and mechanical bodies. Now, lifelike properties infuse both animate and inanimate elements of the world, as we seem to be swinging back to animate nature.[26] Thus, our sense of nature evolves with our understanding, and has recently taken what is for many a gratifying turn towards an appreciation of wild places. The sensibility of the naturalist pervades the ways in which nature is depicted and can engender an appreciation for the diversity of species.[27]

In the nineteenth and early twentieth centuries, many theorists envisioned evolutionary progress as taking place gradually.[28] They theorized that as animals progressed at tasks, they became smarter and better adapted to their environments. Each stage in evolution was seen as linked to the past, building slowly and steadily from there. In the process, species transformed and new variants emerged. However, we are now fairly sure that evolution is not always slow and gradual, nor is it necessarily progressive. In fact, change might be radically discontinuous, indicating a radical break with preceding events, as seems to be the case with linguistic competence, as described above. Abrupt evolutionary change, like gradual change, may or may not be for the better. In this expanded view, great or small changes may occur over a relatively short period, provoking disequilibrium followed by periods of stasis, or a so-called punctuated equilibrium.[29]

Modern evolutionary theory provides a basic framework within which biological activity is viewed from a coherent perspective. That there are discontinuities within this framework may be due to our limited knowledge, or may be a reflection of the fact that the process of evolution is typified by breaks followed by periods of stasis. Not every feature of a biological entity is an adaptation, and adaptive arguments must be viewed with caution, as they often become circular. Evolutionary theorizing requires careful observation amid a core set of concepts (speciation, natural selection, etc.) that have determined the meaning of evolution. Evolutionary theory is rich in unresolved disputes, such as whether language evolved from gestures or from vocalization.[30]

From that first pointing finger or primate call, through cave paintings all the way to Darwin, we have come to utilize categories for understanding the changes of living things. Nature's purpose, while not intentional, is expressed in wondrous functional adaptations which in turn shape our perceptions of how the world is and what is in it.

5. REPRESENTATIONAL CAPACITIES

What emerged in our species was a highly linguistic, tool-using social animal, with an elaborate diversity of cognitive skills.[31] Early humans developed many forms of instrumental expression and tool use, and to go with these we engendered numerous cognitive adaptations, some broad and some specific. Cognitive expansion and fluidity, in which narrow adaptive abilities expand in use across diverse problematic contexts, has become a signal feature of the human mind. Evolution, for humans, could indeed be defined as the expansion into more and more novel cognitive performances through increased accessibility to core cognitive functions by our neural architecture. Key features of this cognitive fluidity are the integration of several orientations to coping with the world: social intelligence, technical abilities, diverse expression of natural knowledge, and, of course, language use.[32]

Language is a unique feature for our species, with its rich syntactical elegance and expansive capacities. Once syntactical language use emerged, our cognitive abilities seem to have increased in great measure, particularly our social discourse. The premium of our evolution is on our social contact and discourse, our communicative competence and praxis. This social contact and preadaptation, in turn, is vital for the formation of basic regulative events that traverse a wide range of rewards within the behavioral biology of our central nervous system.[33]

The cognitive capacity for representation probably started in our interest in edible objects: thinking about them, planning for and predicting their use. We don't tend to consider the roots of language and art as being planted in such humble beginnings, but the capacity to represent objects of diverse kinds is central to the evolution of the primate brain, and cognitive/behavioral capacities are, after all, primarily ways to engage the world, to compute probability and assess friendly or nonfriendly events.[34]

Our representations are also often social in nature. We are interested in others, and what they do. The representations we make are not simply pictures divorced from life, but active ways in which we engage the world. The outside world, the social world of others, is important to human flexibility, survival, and reproductive success. Representation often has the connotation of something divorced from the object, something that detaches, though, of course, some forms of representations are indeed that way. But representations of others, of those that we care about, do not divide us from others; rather, they guide the organization of cognition, and these cognitive or informational systems are inherent to the organization of action.[35] When we consider others, we want to comprehend their beliefs and desires, the way they are oriented, to what they are oriented, the tools they use, etc.

In terms of the mechanics of this representational urge, the traditional view of the brain sees the cortex as its only cognitive part. However, cognitive systems actually run across the brain. From cortex to brainstem, the central nervous system is knotted to rich information processing resources. Likewise, our social discourse, transactions, language, eating, and tool use are embedded in the social milieu and not divorced from it. Things like our motor capacity, our visual skills, and our social orientation evolved together.[36]

This dense, interdependent cognitive network we call humanity is really a fairly recent phenomenon. We—modern *Homo sapiens*—only emerged about 100,000 years ago. Agriculture, the move away from being a hunter-gatherer, developed in the range of 10,000 years ago. The domestication of dogs[37] and written language emerged something in the order of 5,000 years ago, so amazingly close in time to where we are and yet seemingly so distant from the complexities of contemporary life. But the common evolutionary feature through those years was cephalic accessibility, with a common demarcation theme between 30,000 and 60,000 years ago.

Pregnant within the brain are diverse rich information processing systems reflecting that expanding cognitive capability. Many regions of the cortex are tied to motor function. The motor regions are gravid with cortical functions. The wide range of tools we use in adapting to our environment reflects this evolution of cortical and subcortical systems in the brain. Tool construction and cognitive/motor systems are essential to the evolution of the brain. Tool use is an expression of an expanding cortical motor system in which cognitive systems are endemic to motor systems. For instance, regions of the brain are prepared to recognize differences between different kinds of objects and their uses, of which mechanical tools are an important subset, and frontal motor regions have been linked to the motor features of tool use.[38]

Tool use and its elaboration is a reflection of expanding motor capacity, rich with cognitive possibilities. Of course, we are not alone in tool use. Birds use sticks to build nests, chimpanzees and other primates use sticks to catch ants, or even kill prey on occasion. Significantly, the construction of tools by primates such as chimpanzees is often tied to a social context.[39]

In their tool using we can see the first glimmer of our ability to use objects, facilitating the expansion of our social milieu; for it is the expansion of cephalic function that underlies the tool use that serves physiological/behavioral regulation. An expanded motor system with diverse cognitive capacities no doubt is pivotal in our evolutionary ascent. It is not just that the evolution of the cortex or brain is knotted to social function; tool use and other diverse abilities are also knotted to the fact that we are social animals.

6. ANCHORED TO KINDS OF OBJECTS

Determining kinds of objects, their life history, and their development is the fundamental way in which we learn and know about the world. Aristotle describes plants in particular detail. While some of his observations are fanciful or even just plain wrong, they remain valuable for their reflection of what was seen through the classical world's conceptual lens. Thus, we are taxonomic animals from our earliest infancy; we categorize objects and we come prepared to discern events from that core orientation and perspective (e.g., the solidity of objects).[40]

Key categories about kinds of objects pervade the epistemological landscape. Cognitive predilection underlies action and inquiry. Categories of understanding converge at every step in our intellectual development, and symbolic and computational systems permeate all levels of human understanding. Generic categories of kinds, both naturally and culturally derived, are operative early on in ontogeny.[41]

An orientation to biological objects seems to be a core disposition in our cephalic organization. We readily accept this sort of categorization, and look for objects in our surroundings that fit into it. Environmental factors are essential to understanding our cognitive capabilities.[42] Our preparedness to note relationships and make categories is reflected in many forms of folk biological discourse (e.g., avoiding foul meat, searching for warmth and security, connecting with others in common bonds, and expressing ourselves symbolically), even though specific categories and ends may differ across cultures.

Diverse taxonomic characterization is the staple of cognitive coherence. But there is wide variation and diversity in our cognitive machinations and what we emphasize and what we do not. Some groups may even show a devolution of function about natural objects.[43] For instance, Atran's comparison of three- and four-year-old Mayan children and a group of Northwestern University students revealed that the toddlers could name more types of trees than the students.[44]

The landscape of human reason from a biological perspective, as Dewey understood it, is so knotted to objects and the discernment of their nature. Essences are thus not frozen in the depths of a cave, but core features are grouped together as constituting a kind of object, which allow one to function in the organization of action and the perception of an object.[45]

7. PRAGMATISM, OBJECTS, AND COGNITIVE COHERENCE

What constitutes an object is at the heart of what it is to know anything. We take it for granted, but the old adage "no framework, no knowing" permeates the epistemological landscape of coming to know and what is already known. The ongoing debate in Western philosophy between rationalism and empiricism is often couched as a radical separation between object and essence, but perhaps a better way to frame the dilemma is by degree rather than division. After all, the consideration of what something is, of whether it is a member of a category, requires having an idea and determining its consequences, at least to some degree, just as inducing a category from many instances requires having some idea of what the thing is.[46] The term "natural kinds" does not originate with Quine's famous essay, but the term gained a lot of mileage as a function of Quine's philosophy in some circles, and it captures an important concept, coupled with the empiricist philosopher's idea of an innate "quality space." In fact, the root of the concept of natural kinds is anchored to our biology, to our feel for natural objects, and to our ability to adapt to our surroundings. The human philosophical tradition of naturalism is very strong and, in one of its later manifestations, is a core feature of classical pragmatism.[47] A sense of objects as objects is rooted in our cognitive architecture, tied to our basic social and ecological adaptations.[48]

While the Scottish school of common sense was perhaps just too commonsensical to gain much renown as a philosophical school, the impact on Peirce is profound, Dewey just assumed an important prelude towards a sane view about kinds and a concerted rejoinder to the denial of objects and kinds in favor of a glorified inner mental space of contiguous associations (e.g., Hume). Moreover, Dewey, like Peirce, suggested before many others such as Wittgenstein or Quine that "we have not pure sensations, but only sensational elements of thought," and that "we have no power of intuition, but every cognition is determined logically by previous cognitions."[49] For Peirce, cognitive predilection underlies action and inquiry. What determines cognitive activity and behavior are expectations about an ongoing activity that is itself created from successful expectations.

Capturing something about kinds, of what constitutes nature, is what makes it intelligible, and this can be quite separate from simple use. In other words, knowing for Dewey is knotted to the natural history of the object in addition to our cultural evolution.[50] Behavioral adaptation figured importantly in Dewey's writings. He believed stability is sought amidst the endlessly precarious conditions in which one finds oneself, and categories are oriented towards adaptation, discovery, and engagement, not isolated internal representational space. "The natural and original bias of man is all toward the objective"[51]—toward the real world of adaptation and coherence.

What Dewey and later others understood was that cognitive architecture is inherent in the organization of action. Dewey's orientation is about cognitive-behavioral adaptation; there is no reification about concepts of objects. They are just assumed to be tied to knowledge as a kind of contact sport. Cognitive systems are action oriented and rooted in relationships to kinds of things, and kinds of actions towards things. Modern empiricism thus broke barriers between empirical and theoretical statements. The "empirical significance of the whole science" is understood as "pragmatic."[52] But it is a pragmatism knotted to building on what Goodman emphasized as "projectable predicates." How "entrenched" and reliable a term is reflects its encampment in a conceptual framework. In science, the issue is always empirical and testable, and the reliability of a term, say temperament, is over time, over use, over predication and explanation. The issue of induction is embodied in the conceptual frameworks of pragmatic use. Similarity, a notoriously and deceptively simple concept, is a defining property of belonging to a kind, a "family resemblance" of which some "standard of similarity is in some sense innate."[53] "Induction itself is essentially only more of the same: "animal expectations or habit formation."[54]

In pragmatism, theoretical sensibility is pervasive and underlies traditional distinctions between sensation and concepts (e.g., Rudolf Carnap, C. I. Lewis), best understood as "theory laden." The growth of science reflects the concept of expansion of our theoretical apparatus, our capacity to see new things. As Hanson put it, "the layman must learn (to be a) physicist before he can see what the physicist sees."[55] But perhaps the learning part is overstated, since evidence in cognitive science already holds quite a lot of expectations about objects. There is understanding, of course, but not necessarily a theory to put it in perspective. The child might know something about kinds of objects and their solidity, for instance, but what makes it up, explaining it, etc. is the stuff of science. In fact, while children might embody some notion of prelinguistic causation,[56] it is propositions, the stuff of linguistics, that tie causes to theories. Keeping track of objects is at the heart of our epistemological journey, and part of placating our fears is in our representing the objects in our world. As Hanson paraphrased Kant several hundred years later, "Nothing in sense datum space could be labeled cause or effect."[57] Hanson also said, "Interpretation . . . is operative in the very making of a system."[58] This is a view close to the later Wittgenstein and others such as Wilfrid Sellars, who held, like Kant, that "intuitions without concepts are blind."[59] In other words, seeing is always based on one's perspective,[60] and interpretation underlies all human social behavior and understanding. As a result, and echoing Peirce, abduction or retroduction is essential for hypothesis formation, and hence for category formation.

What Dewey described as "the precarious amidst the stable," the retention of a sense of an object's ontological permanence despite its movement and change through space and time, is thus both an appetitive and consummatory cognitive/behavioral adaptation. While we search for the essence of an object, we also derive satisfaction from capturing a family-like set of features. "Family resemblance" is for us a reliable way by which to predict the behavior of, and regulate our own behavior towards, the objects around us. The essence of an object, on the other hand, becomes "expressed in the grammar"; here the emphasis, as it was for many investigators, is on our linguistic competence at manipulating things and in our transactions with one another.[61]

We are, after all, preeminently linguistic animals and inherently social and historical. As Wittgenstein noted when discussing perception of a drawing that could be seen as either a duck or a rabbit, perspective matters; interpretation underlies perceptual coherence. Categories about kinds of objects must always satisfy the condition of conceptual coherence, usefulness, and prediction. Getting anchored is what matters—getting anchored to objects. What concerns us is utilizing the concept of, say, temperament in a way which picks out a set of properties that perhaps cluster together in a systematic way, a semantically meaningful way.

As Boyd notes, "Natural kinds is about how schemas of classification contribute to the formulation and identification of projectable hypotheses."[62] Boyd points to the projectable feature in our epistemological lexicon, citing Goodman. Reliable predictors of core features about kinds and objects are the epistemological backbone for cognitive coherent action. Predictive causal properties coinhabit the conceptual framework of events clustering together, and provide a context for what might be called "promiscuous realism" or perhaps "critical realism."[63] While John Stuart Mill introduced the term "natural kind" to our lexicon, the basic idea was already there and functioning. Pluralism, amidst realism, is emboldened by an expectation of classificatory systems, particular diverse forms of kind terms. Even categories like temperament have features that one can acknowledge and therefore keep anchored to a phenomenon without losing a sense of its category, and the cluster of properties that it is associated with. The move is away from a pernicious, overzealous rationalism, in which expectations about essentialism are discarded or toned down to real rational size, but anchored with a realistic view of nature. The term "natural kind" can be separated from traditional views about essentialism.[64]

Reminiscent of Dewey, John Dupré's discussion of kind-talk can be knotted to functional ends of explanatory discussion and desire, amidst diverse epistemologies and methodological functional tools with well-defined ends. In fact, as Dupré noted,[65] individuals have shied away from essentialist thinking in biological classification and/or tend to be minimal essentialists.[66] Quine emphasized a science that tied together naturalized epistemology, a subset of psychology, and eventually neuroscience, not his behaviorism and innate quality spaces but cognitive science and neural science.

The discussion, for us as pragmatists, is not about essences, but cognitive reliability, coherence, predictability, and adaptation. Category-based inductive processes have a firm modern basis in modern psychology. Category-based learning about objects is expressed very early on in ontogeny, and reflects cognitive adaptation (kinds of objects, animacy vs. inanimacy, facial responses). The core issue is the kind of categories: how general, how specific, and how culturally expressed. Temperament, to use one recurring example, is not a simple "investigative kind"; discussions of the emotions are more complex than leaves or trees, which are more simple exemplars of natural kinds and perhaps laden with normative judgments.[67] For our purposes, a cluster of properties knotted to biology and adaptation is enough to constitute a natural kind as long as the science can proceed in a meaningful manner.

Once one moves from essentialism to reliability in an inductive system, from philosophical essentialism to pragmatism, properties that cluster together work as a "natural kind." Thus psychological essentialism is a way to be rooted towards objects, the seen and unseen features of the kinds of objects in our world, an orientation easily noted in children. One can be a critical realist about kind-terms, as we are, anchoring a conception of temperament to biology and taxonomic cognitive tendencies, without reifying kind-terms into Platonic space, associated with rigid essentialism. Natural kind terms serve, indeed, as an important cognitive adaptation for grouping features of objects that may be inherently related to parts of biology. The fact that we are born to categorize is not the same as a form of rationalism. Realism about categories for kind-terms allows one to acknowledge psychological essentialism without an exaggerated expectation of absolute conformity to kind-concepts. We come prepared to group objects, one grouping of which is itself about the kind of objects. The kind of objects is about a piece of biology, and constitutes a kind of feature that pervades an object.

8. EXPERIMENTALISM AND AESTHETICS

Art, as Dewey so well understood, was part of the experience of inquiry; art as experience was not separate or for the parlor but endemic to inquiry: "aesthetic cannot be sharply marked off from the intellectual experience."[68] Aesthetic features are at the heart of the contours of basic research experience, the elegance of the design to the clinician's eye, history laden and dependent but building on the visual sensibility that defines our experiences and defines our species. Art as experience heightened the vital sense of worth in the context of human discovery; and it was something understood for ages, built into our biology, stretching back to cave paintings and our desire to represent our surroundings to make sense of our world. Dewey bridged the knowing process in which aesthetics was endemic to the events. The aesthetic experience focused on the form of the body, elegant, depicted in normal and pathological conditions: "Form was defined in terms of relations and aesthetic form in terms of completeness of relations within a chosen medium."[69]

Technological advances underlie Dewey's conception of the ascent of the epistemological engine, medical or otherwise; tools are embedded in his theories of seeing, knowing, orienting, perceiving. The tools for seeing the search for some control in understanding; the knowledge is endemically instrumental in use and can be aesthetic in scope, practical in use.[70] The point is that there is no separation in these cognitive functions tied to the organization of action and perception. The epistemological advances rested on the technological advances, so that medical or any other advances became a form of decision making. Artisan hands are endemic to a culture of discovery and discernment, to medical prognosis and medial advance, to patient healing or soothing. The practice of science long known rests on the tools of discovery, telescope, microscope; seeing through the lens of technology to advance to the sensory systems embedding, in interesting ways, of diverse understanding of objects. Art runs through the veins and pulse of science; the reconstruction of others, for instance, represents one small glimpse of the pervasive features of art in science.

In other words, art, as Dewey well understood, is endemic to human knowing; there should be no mythological sense of art, just the importance of enriching our experience as the human knower. Art unified in the expression is endemic to medicine, for art is part of the valuation of events; the impulse to know part of capturing the kind of illness, the expression of health, the development of a function.

9. CONCLUSION: EVOLUTION AND COGNITIVE COHERENCE

Cognitive adaptation lies in the doing of things for coherence of action in complex social environments, diverse ecological conditions, and social communicative functions. Objects for us are always in some sense social objects, and our preadaptive cephalic systems are expanded in use in social contexts. Core cognitive architecture is mostly about kinds of objects. To be sure, the linguistic competence of our species is itself an innate architecture with rich lexical hooks to semantic representations; language and the evolution of the neocortex, however, are also linked to social behavior, social contact, and social complexity. Regions of our central nervous system reach out to objects through our peripheral systems, through the construction of objects that allows us to expand our sensory systems. Inventions such as the microscope and telescope are such extensions of our seeing. Pervasive perceptual/cognitive capacities pervade the central nervous system. We reach out to the objects in space.[71]

A conception of biology and naturalism was tied to this sense of natural wonder embedded in the romantic sensibility. Natural philosophy for Dewey was rich with aesthetics and both appetitive and consummatory experiences; the exploration and discovery of nature was part of human self-reflection and development, was rich in organic self-regulation, sustenance, and rejuvenation, and was ripe with poetic beauty. A primal sensibility was pervasive in a continent brewing with possibilities and emboldened by a rich sense of nature, catalogued and noted by our species. Romanticism fueled an appreciation of the natural landscape, understood by Thoreau, mystically infused by Emerson, and demythologized by Dewey; technology was not an enemy but a tool for engagement. However, it can become the enemy when identified with knowing and the "scholar disappears."[72] Of course, amidst the elegance and respect was the slaughter of the bison, the degradation of nature; the devolution of our surroundings. On the one hand was a respect for the boundless resources and on the other a disregard for and a short-sighted view of nature. Human ingenuity is the wonder embodied in cephalic capacity; we invent, we change, we build, we can degrade the damage we do, the devolution we impose at least for now, and certainly in the past.

Dewey, and classical pragmatism in general, is anchored to objects, for which adaptation is primary. Looking at a particular object is noting a general feature; something quite general about a tomato, face, heart, etc. despite the variation; an orientation toward the generic properties of an object.

Dewey emphasized social cooperative sensibility to engage in cooperative inquiry towards a common end. It was a rather unique thing in philosophy, but then this was something quite different: a philosophy emboldened by what would emphasize community, purpose, and expansion of human experience, not isolated, but socially configured, responsible to one another and working as a joint enterprise. Cooperative behaviors were linked to a sense of human progress, grounded in a new sense of biology and human possibilities. Our evolutionary success is linked to social cooperative behaviors; "speculative biology and evolutionary theology" were fairly common.[73] Grounding intelligent action and functionalism in the behavioral sciences guided by worth, aims the normative goal of inquiry, rich in value and linked to diverse forms of appraisals linked to action and self-corrective inquiry. Dewey himself had always a broad array of critiques for human cultural evolutionary possibilities.[74]

A pragmatism embedded in a respect for nature is a formidable perspective, albeit difficult to realize.[75] This pragmatism includes a natural piety that reaches back to Emerson and can be found in Dewey. It includes an ethics of nature that can embolden a respect for nature and one another. It involves a recognition of the value of resources, where valuation is a highly embedded cognitive predilection.[76]

6.

RECLAIMING THE PRAGMATIST LEGACY
Evolution and Its Discontents

Arthur Efron

This paper, by a person who has no claim to being a scientist, is a kind of pep-talk on how pragmatists have been missing the boat when it comes to evolution, an exploration of how that has happened, and what issues are at stake. The paper started last year when I was looking through a new issue of *The Journal of Mind and Behavior.* It was a special double issue entitled "Evolutionary Biology and the Central Problems of Cognitive Science."[1] As is my habit when I receive my subscriber copy of *JMB*, I read the abstracts, sampled some of the argumentation, and checked through the list of references. I was hoping to find some reference to one of my old interests, Stephen C. Pepper. And, as always, I was looking for mention of John Dewey and other pragmatists. In one article, I did find what I was hoping for. It is the article by a philosopher named Robin L. Zebrowski of the University of Oregon.[2] But that was it: the other eight articles do not cite Dewey or James or Peirce. Zebrowski indeed cites William James, and names his article from a weird and whacky quotation taken from James. This James passage is one that is requoted from a book by Daniel Dennett. Dennett himself is quoted and cited all over the place in discussions of evolution, but is not a pragmatist, is he? Zebrowski also cites two books by George Lakoff and Mark Johnson. I believe they are pragmatists. Can we count Robert Brandom as a pragmatist? He is cited in another of the articles. Brandom has at least some connection with pragmatism.

So, in these nine articles, running to 216 pages of text, there is only one reference to Dewey. There are hardly any references to pragmatists. This does not seem right.

Zebrowski has a lot to say that is to the point of my paper. In his Abstract, the case is laid out: cognitive science is getting away from its "traditional thought." Frankly, I didn't even know it was old enough to *have* traditional thought. It is moving toward "evolutionary considerations." Here is the payoff quote: "This revision of cognitive science can trace its roots back to the American pragmatists, while still attending to even the most recent work in neuroscience and evolutionary psychology." In the article itself, we find this: "John Dewey set the stage for a successful cognitive science program when he wrote:

> . . . in laying hands upon the sacred ark of absolute permanency, in treating the forms that that had been regarded as types of fixity and perfection as originating and passing away, the 'Origin of Species' introduced a mode of thinking that in the end was bound to transform the logic of knowledge, and hence the treatment of morals, politics, and religion.[3]

That is from the opening of Dewey's book published in 1910, *The Influence of Darwin on Philosophy*. What an important book title that was! I don't think there was any earlier book title by any philosopher that sounded at all like this. Dewey had understood the high affinity between the idea of evolution and the philosophy of pragmatism. Pragmatists are perhaps the only major grouping in philosophy who (a) do not engage in a quest for certainty or "absolute permanency," who (b) do believe that change is unavoidable and can be a positive element in human life, who (c) do not privilege language over all the other things in life, who (d) welcome the findings of science but are not narrowly empirical in their outlook, who (e) have no use whatever for mind-body dualism, who (f) do not believe that violent revolution is a good way to solve social problems, and who (g) think that there is much bigger work for philosophy to do than to try to pin down permanently valid definitions of contested terms, or to construct foolproof logical propositions. In their theory of inquiry, they are unimpressed with the claim that a logical formulation is valid no matter what the societal context may be. Finally, in the life work of Dewey, pragmatism blended all its elements in a profound commitment to democracy as a way of life. There is nothing like this anywhere else.

1. QUALITIES OF DEWEY'S MIND

Rereading the title essay "The Influence of Darwinism on Philosophy," one hundred years after it was first given as a lecture at Columbia in 1909, leads to a renewed appreciation of the qualities of Dewey's mind. For one, he says nothing of his own disagreements with part of Darwin's theory. As Larry Hickman has pointed out, Dewey had already redefined Darwin's concepts of evolutionary "fittest," of the "struggle for existence" and of "natural selection."[4] But Dewey also had some basic differences with Darwin that I will have a look at near the end of this paper. Some of what he does say in 1909 is unexpected and, in one case, would be big news to all of us: the opposition to Darwinism that arose soon after the publication of *The Origin of Species* was not a conflict between "science on the one hand and theology on the other." The "issue lay primarily within science itself." So are we to think that organized religion was not a major opponent of the theory of evolution? Come on, Dewey, that is preposterous. Or is it? "Although the ideas that rose up like armed men against Darwin owed their intensity to religious association," Dewey declares, "their origin and meaning are to be sought in science and philosophy, not in religion."[5] When Dewey tells of the background of the scientific revolution that leads up to Darwin, would you expect him to be quoting Descartes on the progressive side? He quotes Descartes: "The nature of physical things is much more easily conceived when they are beheld coming gradually into existence, than when they are only considered as produced in a finished and perfect state."[6] You would expect him to cite Galileo, but might be surprised to hear this by Galileo: "It is my opinion that the earth is very noble and admirable by reason of so many and so different alterations and generations which are incessantly made therein."[7]

And although the essay is in honor of Darwin, you would hardly expect Dewey to bring out a basic contradiction in Darwin's mind and not even try to account for it. But Dewey has a point to make about this apparent discrepancy. Darwin asserts, in a volume titled *Life and Letters*, that it is "impossible to conceive this immense and wonderful universe including man with his capacity of looking far backwards and far into futurity as the result of blind chance or necessity."[8] Dewey goes on to say that Darwin's actual findings do not support any argument from design, or what we now refer to as Intelligent Design. Darwin, says Dewey[9] "holds that since variations are in useless as well as useful directions, and since the latter are sifted out simply by the stress of the conditions of struggle for existence, the design argument as applied to living beings is unjustifiable; and its lack of support there deprives it of scientific value as applied to nature in general."

Dewey's phrase, "living beings" comes from his major insight. The scientific revolution in astronomy was not capable of creating a new understanding of morality or logic. As for the development, prior to Darwin, of more and more precise knowledge of the structure of plant life, and of "the marvelous adaptation of organisms to their environment," those were changes that gave even more prestige to the argument from design. But Darwin, by showing that "living beings" are the results of natural selection, cut the ground from under that argument. Once "living beings" were accounted for in the way Darwin said, then the way was open "to transform the logic of knowledge, and hence the treatment of morals, politics, and religion."[10]

Toward the end of this essay, Dewey makes a qualifying admission. The claims he has been laying down here have been mighty bold, and they are going to be far from obvious. Philosophy, freed from the constricting ancient notion that "species" are fixed and final entities of existence, and equipped with understanding that "species" all have "origins," will now become "responsible." That is, "it will have to submit its hypotheses to test by the way in which the ideas it propounds work out in practice."[11] That is the archetypal pragmatist note for sure. But Dewey does not try to argue his readers into agreeing with this. His view in this essay is that huge changes in human thought do not occur by means of logical refutations of old ways of thinking. It is not a matter of falsifiability, as Popper was later to claim. "Old ideas give way slowly; for they are more than abstract logical forms and categories. They are habits, predispositions, deeply engrained attitudes of aversion and preference." We do not "solve" the old questions, "we get over them."[12] And as for himself, "in anticipating the direction of the transformations in philosophy to be wrought by the Darwinian genetic and experimental logic, I do not profess to speak for any save those who yield themselves consciously or unconsciously to this logic."[13]

2. ON THE TRAIL OF EVOLUTION THEORY

To return now to Colin Zebrowski's paper. Zebrowski's main point was that cognitive science had been born under the star of digital computation, but that nowadays most of the people working in it are moving to an embodied model of the cognitive mind.[14] The move to the body makes cognitive science a study of part of the evolution of the human mind. In that model, pragmatist approaches can flourish. The problem is that no one but Zebrowski seems to realize the roots that were once evident in the history of pragmatism.

Next I looked for one of the books cited by Zebrowski, a work entitled *Evolution and the Founders of Pragmatism* by Philip P. Wiener, published in 1949.[15] The first thing I noticed in this volume is that it has a Preface by John Dewey. Dewey had high praise for what Wiener had done: his book "completely annihilates the misstatements about the aim and tenor of the founders of the pragmatic movement that have flourished." I was expecting that this work would discuss Dewey as well as the connections with evolution forged by William James and Charles S. Peirce, but no, that's not exactly it. Wiener's book is about the group of early pragmatists in Cambridge, Massachusetts, who set about discussing and writing about evolution almost as soon as Charles Darwin's *The Origin of Species* had come out in 1859. By 1860 they were at it. James and Peirce do appear, but the most important name here was Chauncey Wright; he is also the one mentioned as delving into evolution by Louis Menand[16] in *The Metaphysical Club*. Wright was not the only one: there were also other early evolutionists among the pragmatists. Weiner has a chapter on the legal philosophy of Nicholas St. John Green, who, I must say, I had never heard of. There's a lot in this book about the evolutionary pragmatism of Oliver Wendell Holmes, Jr. My point here is that the pragmatists had an affinity with the basic concept of evolution which they realized at once. But does anyone today remember *Evolution and the Founders of Pragmatism?*

Because I am not a scientist, just an interested amateur and a pragmatist, I next went not to the university library but to Barnes and Noble, where I found *The Rough Guide to Evolution* by Mark Pallen.[17] It has a cover picture of a chimpanzee's face, facing me, and holding his chin as if deep in thought—or maybe the animal is just a little amused. Pallen's field is microbiology. Pallen has a forty-three-page chapter entitled "Philosophy and the Arts." It starts off with philosophy, and then quickly has to go on to the arts, because there apparently are not enough philosophers to talk about. But that start has two fine quotations, one from William James and one from John Dewey. The only other philosopher mentioned wrote much later than 1910: Karl Popper, who titled one of his books *Objective Knowledge: An Evolutionary Approach* (1972).[18] Popper drew analogies between the struggle for existence and the winnowing out of theories in science: through the process of falsification some theories gain increased fitness. But no matter how fit they may seem, they could always be displaced by future scientific discovery.

This is all well and good, but it is not very close to Darwin's concept of Natural Selection, let alone his theory of Sexual Selection. So, let's hear the two good quotations from James and Dewey. The James comes from his lecture of 1880, *Great Men and Their Environment*. According to Pallen, it starts with this statement: "A remarkable parallel . . . obtains between the fact of social evolution on the one hand, and the zoological evolution expounded by Mr. Darwin on the other."[19] And the Dewey, taken again from *The Influence of Darwin on Philosophy*, is: "Old questions are solved by disappearing, evaporating, while new questions . . . take their place. Doubtless the greatest dissolvent in contemporary thought of old questions, the greatest of new methods, new intentions, new problems, is the one effected by the scientific revolution that found its climax in *The Origin of Species*."[20]

After a while, I remembered that Henri Bergson had published his book *Creative Evolution* a few years before Dewey's essay, and I found that the theologian-philosopher Teilhard de Chardin had also had much to say about evolution. Bergson's version is invested with the premise that natural selection is not what accounts for evolution. Bergson also has the pragmatically incapacitating argument that human intelligence is not a prime value in evolution, except for a marginal part of intelligence that is still instinctive.[21] I could guess why Mark Pallen or other writers interested in the science of evolution today would not think of Bergson, even though his work is a serious response to Darwin. I have not read Teilhard, but I would guess his account of evolution was primarily theological.[22] (An instructive insight may be gained by first noticing that the Church did all it could to prevent Teilhard from publishing his book, and that in 2009, the head of the Vatican's Congregation for the Doctrine of the Faith has said that accepting the theory of evolution is no problem at all for the Church.)[23]

Before long I did make it to the library. I checked out several good books, but the one that gets the prize, in my inquiry, is *Philosophy and the Darwinian Legacy* by Suzanne Cunningham.[24] What Cunningham does is to carefully document and smartly criticize the denial, by two very famous and influential analytic philosophers, of the importance of the theory of evolution for philosophy. They succeeded in steering most of Anglo-American philosophy in just the opposite direction from where Dewey thought it was going. The two are G. E. Moore and Bertrand Russell.

Cunningham mentions the pragmatists as a group who did welcome evolutionary theory, but does not discuss their work. Cunningham's book ends with a masterful chapter entitled "Perception and Mind: A Darwinian Approach."[25] I think her reasoning there is pretty close to being pragmatist.

But to switch back to Barnes and Noble, a couple of other interesting things happened there. I had gone with the intention of buying a much-praised recent biography of Darwin, which I found all right on the shelf. But I never got it because two other books grabbed my attention. One was a huge hardbound volume by the late Stephen Jay Gould,[26] which I sat down with and began to read. I was thrusting myself into the full-fledged theory of evolution, explained with a wealth of empirical support, making use of the total technical vocabulary of the science, and maintaining a position which Gould unashamedly identifies as partisan. The book is 1,400 pages long, which is ample for making an argument. This raises the question of to what extent pragmatist thinkers should or could try to take sides in the intramural disputes of the theory of evolution. Gould is known as a partisan of the idea that the evolution of species sometime moves by relatively sudden jumps; he calls this "punctuated equilibrium." Change isn't always as gradual as Darwin supposed. But from what I could make out, that was only a part of Gould's partisanship. We would have to know a lot in order to intelligently contribute to the evolution battles. Can we avoid such controversies? That would be unlikely, but there might be certain ways to go about this, or to keep away.

3. TWO ISSUES IN THEORY

At this point it seems that at least one persistent controversy should be avoided. That is the old question of whether acquired characteristics can be passed along through genetic pathways to later descendants. Darwin himself had some belief in this, and other thinkers have supported the idea, one of them being the pragmatist James Mark Baldwin. Baldwin's theory, which dates back to 1905, has been given some support by no less an authority than Daniel Dennett.[27] But basically the idea is not proven, and for pragmatist purposes, it is not needed. Dewey was not one to suggest that if only we can build a good democracy, we could incorporate it in our genes and then pass it along to our heirs without further effort.

But wait! After showing this paper to my friend the sociologist Bill Harrell, I realized that I had just attacked a straw man. There actually is a whole field of evolutionary inquiry into inherited factors that does not make the same assumptions as Lamarck once did. To quote Harrell, "as behavior became a serious selective factor in evolutionary theory, some sense of teleology was bound to follow (merely random behavior was unlikely to be useful)." "Anytime developmental biology gets incorporated into an evolutionary scheme, the process of development in potentially changing circumstances begins to alter the selective pressures on the organism. It is not a matter simply of the potential built into the system at its beginning but how well it can adapt to an environment at different stages of a developmental cycle." A limited sense of intentionality comes into play, and has been explored by a number of researchers. "So, intentionality, understood as something other than an arbitrary cultural or psychological property, but as an aspect of species' being, raises issues for pragmatism which it needs to consider."[28]

The other book I found at Barnes and Noble is a hardback that is informative and comprehensive, and a good read too. I wound up buying it. It is by Jerry A. Coyne, and in its very title, there lies a problem for Deweyan thinking about inquiry. Coyne specializes in evolution and the origin of species. For twenty years he has been a member of the Department of Ecology and Evolution at the University of Chicago. He titles his book *Why Evolution is True*.[29] It is in the title that you can hear the problem. Coyne chooses to go against the protocol that would call evolution a theory. No, it is not just a theory, Coyne insists, it is true. It is obvious that one reason for his choosing such a title is the misperception by much of the lay public, that anything called a theory is just so much speculation. As just a theory, you can take it or leave it. But that protocol simply does not serve to describe evolution theory, and it provides a pseudo-weapon in the hands of those who want to deny the facts of evolution. Even Pope John Paul II said, in 1996, that evolution is "more than a hypothesis."[30]

I think Dewey, with his advice to make only those claims which have warranted assertability, would be against using the word "true" to describe the conclusions of the study of evolution. He avoids using the word "true" when he is discussing scientific findings. So, I think, would most pragmatists. But Jerry Coyne has good reason to disagree. Evolution theory is so strongly supported by the scientific findings that have accumulated by our day, that it is as good as true. Do we dare say so? Should we say so in our public statements and then add what qualifications are needed? There are many unresolved questions within the vast field of evolutionary inquiry. Coyne records several of them. They are not of the kind that would discredit the theory. The theory is true, and we can drop or at least not fix upon the term "theory": Evolution is True. Dewey, in the fourth paper in *The Influence of Darwin on Philosophy,* entitled "The Intellectualist Criterion of Truth," says that in science, an idea may become a *"proved* idea." But this does not make it "eternally true." If anyone were to make such a claim, she would just mean that the idea will be valid in *"prospective* modes of application which are anticipated." It will be "always at hand when needed," and that is "a good enough 'eternal' for reasonably minded persons."[31] In 1910, although Dewey was being careful about what Truth could reasonably be taken to mean, he is not quite as allergic to the term as he was later. When I checked a few pages in Darwin's own writings, I found he used Theory as a term for his larger generalizations, and was quite willing to say that many of his more restricted observations were "true."

Coyne's book turned out to be my favorite preparatory tool for constructing this paper. One of Coyne's surprising claims in *Why Evolution is True* is that the science of evolution can make, and has made, predictions that are valid. These confirm its propositions. The idea that no predictions are possible from a theory like evolution is quite mistaken. It does not predict the future—for that, as Yogi Berra said, is the one thing you should never try to predict—but it can make testable propositions of "what we should find in living or ancient species when we study them." Coyne lists six types of such predictions in his opening chapter. Besides those, evolution theory can make what Coyne calls "retrodictions," or findings that make sense only in the light of theory of evolution.[32]

Here, as an example, is the first of the predictions: "Since there are fossil remains of ancient life, we should be able to find some evidence for evolutionary change in the fossil record. The deepest (and oldest) layers of rock would contain the fossils of more primitive species, and some fossils should become more complex as the layers of rock become younger, with organisms resembling present-day species found in the most recent layers. And we should be able to see some species changing over time, forming lineages showing 'descent and modification' (adaptation)."[33] We can predict what type of fossils will be found in each rock layer, and we can be confident that the time-order will not be grossly violated. We should not find chimpanzee fossils in rocks dating from prior to the age of vertebrates. And we don't, no matter how many new digs have been undertaken, or will be undertaken.

Although Coyne rightly claims that we should be able to see evidence of *some* species changing over time, he does not cover up the fact that there are missing links. Many organisms never left us fossils, and it will never be possible to fill every gap in the record. Nonetheless, the accumulation of evidence we do have is overwhelmingly large. It is conclusive as to the fact of evolution, even though it cannot attest to every species change that has ever occurred.

4. PRAGMATIST WORK TO BE DONE

There is much more that I could summarize from Jerry Coyne's book. It is a very responsible and readable handing of the facts, and it is not chained to the goal of thoroughly refuting the believers in Intelligent Design. But let us go on to a further problem. What sort of aims might pragmatists have in view, when they reclaim their legacy and pay more attention to evolution and its theory?

I should think that the continuing interest of pragmatists in discussing evolution would be educational. Without education, without the ability to think critically, the chances for people to take a constructive part in creating democracy will be greatly reduced. This is plain old Dewey: Democracy and Education. But the job has not been done. James Campbell in *Understanding John Dewey* quotes a passage from the *Later Works* in which Dewey complains that "one half of the pupils in the last years of the high school think that the first chapters of the Hebrew Scriptures give a more accurate account of the origin and early history of man than does science."[34] As you know, the percentages are probably not much better today. The problem now is how to make the case in such a way that students attuned to the new electronic communication will want to understand it. In the public school systems, and even more so in the private religious schools, there often will be little support for effectively teaching the theory of evolution—especially if many of the high school science teachers themselves do not believe in it. (That has been shown.) But doing it online could be different: it could be a way for pragmatists to make an end-run around the lukewarm support for science that the schools now give. If you get out there online, you will be swimming around in a lot of junk theories, but you would still have a chance to make the educational case. I would be interested in hearing of any recent or new programs for teaching about evolution by using the channels provided by websites. Are there some out there now, some written with high school students in mind? The wishful result here is that one or two very popular pragmatist-evolution-teaching websites could do more educational work than thousands of classroom science presentations which either skip the topic or skimp it, or try to undermine it. Or maybe that chimpanzee face I mentioned earlier could be the start of a stealthy channel of pragmatist education on Facebook. The payoff for pragmatists in this educational effort would be the creation of a wider public who understand the affinity between pragmatism and evolution.

Another aim of pragmatists would be to provide critical intelligence to the findings reported by researchers, and to the arguments on evolution given by philosophers who are still afraid of where evolution is going to take them. I think the book *Darwinism and Philosophy*[35] might call for some critical resistance. It is edited by Vittorio Hösle and Christian Illies. There are seventeen well-argued essays here, doing some expert questioning of the assumptions underlying Darwinian biology. In one of them, by the philosopher David Depew, there is a treatment of the evolutionary thought of Dewey and James, which makes the disturbing charge that Dewey "ceased to follow developments in evolutionary biology after he had made up his mind in the 1890s how it worked." That might be true. But the reasons for it? Depew is not very convincing when he attributes this disinterest in evolution to Dewey's intellectual laziness, and he is hardly more persuasive in saying that at Columbia, Dewey was too occupied in defending himself against his Realist colleagues to maintain his interest in evolution. Under that pressure, Dewey "naturally took to arguing for his account of mental adaptation by increasingly philosophical and decreasingly Darwinian means."[36] That is just Depew's guess. A third reason, though, sounds more apt, although necessarily also speculative: when pragmatism became more interested in what physics could tell us—sometime around the middle of the twentieth century—it lost its interest in the science of evolution. That would make especially good sense when we remember the importance Dewey attributed to "living beings" as the effective link between philosophy and evolution. Still another reason, not mentioned by Depew, is that Dewey became discouraged over the misperceptions of the theory of evolution. In the concluding section of *Human Nature and Conduct* (1922), he has some bitter remarks: "The ethical import of the doctrine of evolution is enormous. But its import has been misconstrued because the doctrine has been appropriated by the very traditional notions which in truth it subverts. It has been thought that the doctrine of evolution means the complete subordination of present change to a future goal."[37] This is a perfectly awful attitude toward change, and is a travesty of what evolution really implies.

5. DARWIN WITHOUT NATURALISM?

Depew also has another serious charge to lay: Depew declares that with the coming of genetics, "pragmatic Darwinism as a whole became a degenerating research program."[38] This is a partisan conclusion, but it might also be good history. At least it records the fact that at some point, pragmatist involvement in evolution petered out.

Of the seventeen essays in *Darwin and Philosophy*, none of them is arguing for Darwinian naturalism. Now maybe naturalism, the topic of Thomas C. Dalton's fine book on Dewey, *Becoming John Dewey: Dilemmas of a Philosopher and Naturalist*,[39] is not a fully adequate philosophy. I wouldn't want to take a position on such a complex topic. But when I don't see a single argument for it in a volume of this kind, I become suspicious. I become even more suspicious when I see a whole section, containing six essays, devoted to the question "Is a Non-Naturalistic Interpretation of Darwinism Possible?"[40] Most of these philosophers and scientists want to limit the scope of the theory of evolution so that there is no threat to their religious or philosophical commitments. One, I noticed, is an atheist who says he is only interested, finally, in the problem of the origin of the universe. In the vocabulary of Stephen Pepper, this collection on *Darwinism and Philosophy* is only showing how a major theory like evolution can be fitted into any of the relatively adequate philosophical traditions, but that it takes a lot of pushing and shoving to make it compatible with Formism or Organicism or even with Mechanism. (Mechanism would have a tough time absorbing the theory of Sexual Selection). Only in "Contextualism," that is, pragmatism, is it a natural fit.[41] Depew does not think of that idea: for him there is simply a pluralism of possible "ontologies." I should think it would be good fun and good pragmatist work to subject this set of essays to critical judgment.

6. GENES SELFISH AND GENEROUS

The obstacle for pragmatists who want to comment on evolution today might be this: a lot of evidence has been gathered and interpreted in support of the idea that natural selection is a story of selfish survival. That idea is an oversimplification, since Darwin meant by the survival of the fittest, the cooperative as well as the competitive fittest. Today, one of the most famous books in the field of evolution is *The Selfish Gene* by Richard Dawkins.[42] The Selfish Gene metaphor gives new protective camouflage to the old idea of Social Darwinism that Dewey fought against.

In the logic of genetic evolution, David Depew writes, "any novel behavior had to be already licensed by a preexisting, even if only occasionally activated, gene complex."[43] Such is the consensus of scientists now, says Depew. This implies that Dewey's concern with human beings taking intelligent action based on their understanding of the problems encountered in social existence, is just a way of imagining novel solutions that are not supported by the evidence at the genetic level. Either that, or what we imagine we are doing to make society more democratic is only our illusion: it is our genes that make change possible.

Pragmatists will not want to deny the facts of selfishness as a factor in evolution, nor will they attempt to say that genetics is all bunk. Pragmatists, however, could undertake critical examinations of writings that rely too much on the selfish gene. I imagine pragmatist thinkers pointing out overstatements, and exposing the choice of methods that preclude finding anything but selfishness. Pragmatists could go further: they could encourage scientists to undertake studies of cooperation. If you do not even look, and if you don't expect to find evidence of survival enhanced by cooperative methods among animals or human animals, you probably won't. And if you do, you might also have trouble getting your findings published if there is a consensus in force among scientists against the cooperative hypotheses.

The larger pragmatist task would be to take on the consensus in evolutionary theory, if indeed it is such, which holds that the genes are the only things that finally matter. Reversing David Depew's reasoning, I might say that if the genes are the prior licensors of anything new, then how do we account for genuine novelty? That would be how the question might have been posed by Stephen Pepper.[44] What the reasoning from the all-ruling gene really shows is this: a condition for creating anything in this world must be that it is something doable within our genetic make-up. That is more of a truism than it is a worthy consensus. It does not mean that what is new is really not new, nor does it tell us that we might as well forget about what Dewey termed "The Construction of Good."[45]

Pragmatists might also encourage the gathering of evidence showing that natural selection does not preclude intelligent, localized adaptation within a given species. That is what Dewey seems to have been thinking about when he wrote "The Influence of Darwinism on Philosophy." When you read that essay you might get the uncomfortable feeling that the new thinking that accepts the transformation brought about by Darwin's discoveries will lead to nothing but the study of particular situations in specific conditions. Philosophers will no longer seek to construct generalizations that apply across the boundaries of many individual situations. But that would be making more than is warranted of the affinity between pragmatism and the theory of evolution. Evolution involves huge regularities within the different species that do exist. But there is at least some evidence to support what Dewey was looking for. I woke up to this idea when I read an account by the evolutionary scientist David Sloan Wilson, telling how he found two different bodily shapes of the same species of fish in the same lake. This finding required a computer analysis of the differences in order to ensure a statistically accurate comparison, not just an impression. Wilson and his young daughter were catching some bluegill sunfish in Michigan, not far from the Kellogg Biological Station. "We paddled our canoe into the middle of the lake and spent a pleasant hour catching bluegill sunfish. Then we paddled into a shallow weed-choked bay and caught some more that we kept separate from the first batch."[46] Back in his lab, Wilson and his research assistant measured them with calipers, and then "crunched them"—the measurements, that is, not the fish—"with a statistical method called discriminate function analysis, and behold! The fish that we had captured in the open water were shaped to cruise long distances and the ones captured in the vegetation were shaped to twist and turn through their spatially complex environment." Or so Wilson records, in his book *Evolution for Everyone: How Darwin's Theory Can Change the Way We Think About Our Lives*.[47] It's recent, published in 2007, and contains nary a single reference in its index to Dewey, James, Peirce, or pragmatism. Wilson does have some help, though, for pragmatists who agree that the educational job for evolution still needs to be done. He published an article in 2005 entitled "Evolution for Everyone: How to Increase Acceptance of, Interest in, and Knowledge About Evolution."[48]

7. THE EXPANDING FIELD OF EVOLUTION

This is the time for Deweyans and pragmatists of all kinds to get back into the discussion. By now, the "object of knowledge" that was Darwinism has shifted and expanded. It came to include huge amounts of fossil evidence; not much of that was available to Darwin. Then it took in the empirical evidence from basic genetics, which had not yet been discovered in 1859. Beginning in the 1960s, many evolutionary biologists adopted a new system of taxonomy, named cladistics, which improved upon the "living tree" model (or metaphor) that Darwin had used. Then molecular biology became part of the field. In a book entitled

Neural Darwinism,[49] Gerald Edelman told of similarities between the immune system and the nervous system. According to Mark Pallen, Edelman showed that "frequently used connections between nerve cells are selected from a pre-existing repertoire of cell-to-cell links in the brain, with developmental selection occurring before birth and experiential selection coming later in life."[50] Harrell again elaborates: "If the originating system is taken to be genes, the developmental process can be subjected to all sorts of epigenetic conditions which will not only effect the phenotypical expression of the genes, but can be transmitted from the organism to its offspring."[51] In the 1940s, scientists realized that the material substance of genetics was DNA. Evolution theory has now come to include the problems of understanding the meanings of DNA. In the new and proposed uses for knowledge of stem cells for medical purposes, and of information from genome studies that could encourage people to try to design their babies, there is an ocean of new ethical and social problems. The selective advantage of altruistic behavior has been documented in such works as *Unto Others: The Evolution and Psychology of Unselfish Behavior*.[52]

We need pragmatist contributions to these dialogues. One exceptional recent contribution (which I did not know of when I first wrote this paper) is *Living with Darwin: Evolution, Design, and the Future of Faith* by Philip Kitcher.[53] In 2009, the "object of knowledge" has expanded once again to include an evolutionary approach to the whole field of aesthetics. I now have read *The Art Instinct: Beauty, Pleasure, and Human Evolution* by Denis Dutton.[54] It received a long leading review where it was called "one of the most exciting and far-reaching philosophy books to reach the public in some time. As either an enjoyable reading experience or an instigator of further philosophical investigation . . . it could hardly be improved upon." Dutton cites such philosophers and aestheticians as Aristotle, Collingwood, Danto, Dennett, Derrida, Dickie, Fodor, Foucault, Goodman, Kant, Korsmeyer, Nussbaum, Searle, Sparshott, and Wittgenstein, but not a single pragmatist as far as I can determine.[55]

One person who seems to me to have begun to make way for a new pragmatist start on evolution theory is Thomas C. Dalton. But you have to notice where the passage occurs[56] within his erudite scientific discussion of Dewey's long struggle with and for naturalism. I have read Dalton's book only in spurts, because it is not absorbable in large doses. I was surprised to see recently that I had not marked up the pages where Dalton discusses Darwin and Dewey on evolution. How did I ever manage to skip those? Dalton finds that there was a problem with Darwin, a probable defect in his theory, that would create endless difficulty if it were linked with Dewey's philosophy. The difficulty has to do with Darwin's statement about the human mind in infants. In a word, he did not think there was one! Darwin, Dalton writes, "was a keen observer of human behavior. He noticed that pre-verbal infants appear to understand language, to correctly interpret facial and emotional gestures, and to express their own moods and needs. Nevertheless, he ruled out the possibility that this evidence suggested that infants possess minds."[57] Dalton locates the relevant text in Darwin's forgotten article entitled "The Biographical Sketch of an Infant."[58] Darwin held that the fears young children express—and here is the damaging quotation—such fears "are quite independent of experience." They are just a phylogenetic inheritance. Now that whole subject, of what is innate and what is created in experience, is too complicated to try to enter just here. But the phrasing "quite outside of experience" is the give-away. Dewey could never agree to that. Nor should he. I had not expected to be reminded of my own writing on the human infant, which I published a quarter of a century ago. But there it was, in my book, *The Sexual Body: An Interdisciplinary Perspective.*[59] I have a chapter that is loaded with empirical evidence that I had gathered, entitled "Reinventing the Asexual Infant: On the Recent 'Explosion' in Infant Research."[60] The evidence showed that the infant, even the neonate (under eight months old) is a sexual creature, but much of that evidence could just as well be used to support the attribution of mind or "self" or Deweyan "intelligence" to these very young people. In fact, that is what I say on the concluding page of my chapter.[61]

I will interrupt this narrative here, to bring you a special message from Darwin. Although Dewey was not a great theory-maker in the realm of sex, Darwin was. Dewey did recognize, in *Human Nature and Conduct*, that sex and sexual repression were major problems in civilized life. He wrote: "The intensity of the sexual instinct and its organic ramifications produce many of the cases that are so notable as to command the attention of physicians. And social taboos and the tradition of secrecy have put this impulse under greater strain than has been imposed on others."[62] The message from Darwin that I refer to was brought to my attention by Geoffrey Miller, in his book *The Mating Mind: How Sexual Choice Shaped the Evolution of Human Nature.*[63] Miller pointed out that Darwin gave serious attention to the facts of Sexual Selection, which was a far more original part of his theory than the famous Natural Selection. In Darwin's book, *The Descent of Man,*[64] he devoted only the lesser part of his text to the question of human descent, and gave the larger share, some 570 pages, to the topic of Sexual Selection. It is a selection process that works quite differently from Natural Selection: it involves choice. In about 70 of those pages, Darwin explored "sexual selection in human evolution."[65] But until recently, students of evolution virtually ignored this whole area of Darwin's research. (I think you can guess what the reasons were for such avoidance). Because philosophy is not without its connections to sexuality, this also must be counted now as part of Darwin's influence on philosophy.

The sort of evidence that I had gathered in 1985 complements Dewey's interest in research on the development of the mind of the infant, which he was convinced had an integral connection with the development of controlled motion in the human body. Almost unknown to Dewey specialists until Thomas Dalton's book, Dewey took persistent interest in the infant researches of the scientist Myrtle McGraw during the 1920s and 1930s. Dewey supported her work both with his encouraging words and by finding money to pay for her experiments. Dalton maintains that many of the assertions in Dewey's *Experience and Nature* as well as in *Art as Experience* come from his understanding of McGraw and of some other now-forgotten researchers on infancy.[66]

Evolution has equipped the infant, and even the neonate, with a great starting kit: with some of the qualities of mind that people need for their growth—growth, that is, in the larger Deweyan sense of the term. The genes, whether considered selfish or not so selfish, provide the ability to grow. But the growth takes place within the realm of experience. If Dewey was on the right trail, such early presence of mind in the infant will develop into maturity when motor qualities make for a creative interrelation of body-mind.

8. EMOTION IN DARWIN AND DEWEY

Whenever I reread Dalton's few pages on Dewey, Darwin, and evolution, I am more and more impressed. The theory of evolution Dewey adopted differed in another significant way from that of Darwin. There is a big difference in the theory of human emotion. This passage in Dalton taught me something. I had always assumed that Darwin's book, *The Expression of Emotion in Animals and Man*,[67] was basically valid. But Dalton, in a brilliant section entitled "The Development of Emotional Experience,"[68] shows that there was a real problem in that argument. Dewey disputed the notion that "human behavior is governed by emotional states that are widely shared among species." Dalton at this point is reviving a forgotten article by Dewey, "The Evolutionary Method as Applied to Morality." (1902)[69]

Dalton refers to Darwin's theory of *serviceable associated habits*.[70] I had not heard of it. This was supposed to tell us that habits seen in emotional behavior had originally developed to serve some primary need for survival, but then had changed into providing secondary purposes of expression. According to Dalton, Darwin "equivocated" about how exactly this change was supposed to have occurred. Darwin was up against "the messy problem of discontinuity among evolutionary processes." (Jerry Coyne, by the way, confronts that problem.) But the idea that emotions developed for one purpose and then were inherited by the organism to serve a related but other purpose is not well supported.

Dewey held that human emotions were too complex to say that certain easily recognized facial expressions in animals and humans give us the meaning of what is going on in the human being. Darwin, Dalton comments, was too uncomfortable with the inner workings of experience to take the complexity of emotions into account. That may be why he chose to focus on a few externally visible expressions. Dewey, though, did not think there were any purely affective states. Citing anatomical studies that had been recorded by Huxley, Dewey said in his 1902 article that "external similarity is no guarantee of identity of function." Dewey, Dalton writes, "found it difficult to see how the subtle differences between wariness, caution, concern, and fear could be distinguished simply by physical criteria alone."[71] Beyond that commonsensical objection, Dewey had a larger theory to refine, of the function of emotions. Here is how Thomas Dalton puts it. "Emotions, such as anger, grief, and sorrow, involved a sense of loss, violation, or incompleteness that is sometimes accompanied by feelings of divisiveness or precariousness. When these emotions are experienced, the perception of the world is altered and the capacity to complete or finish activities is diminished or partially suspended or inhibited. Consequently, during these episodes physical and mental effort is dedicated primarily to restoring the unity of perception and action and regaining an emotional balance."[72] When we hear such language, we know we are in true Dewey country. Darwin by his own thinking could not take us there. At the same time, Dewey's own theory is still subject to correction: is it valid, partly valid, or not at all valid? But assuming that Dewey is basically right in his theory of emotion, then the problem for pragmatists is to figure out how to explain this as a function, at least in part, of evolutionary processes. To say that human emotion has *no* relation to animal emotion is not a good answer, nor would Dewey have offered it, because it cuts off the possibility of finding any evolutionary continuity or commonality between animals and humans.

Darwin as the great liberating influence on philosophy is still important. With modern evolutionary theory, the impact is greater than ever. Dewey and other pragmatists realized early on their affinity with the theory of evolution. Dewey once was working on it. In *Cyclopedia of Education*, a five-volume work published between 1911 and 1913, he wrote the article "Evolution: The Philosophical Concepts."[73] He cross-referenced this to his articles in the same work on Adaptation, Adjustment, Conflict, Control, Environment, Function, and Stimulus-Response. But he couldn't do it all. Pragmatists today are missing something great if they do not reclaim their legacy in evolution and get to work on the many current issues and problems it touches.

7.

TWO TYPES OF PRAGMATISM
Dewey and Royce

Randall E. Auxier

1. PRAGMATISM IN THE POSTMODERN HOSPITAL

Pragmatism as a philosophical method provides a crucial way of addressing the relation of experience to existence, what might be called the "problem of immediate experience." Yet, William James seemed to be utterly defeated by this problem, if the hand-wringing of his interpreters (in addition to his own) is any measure. Dewey initially handled the issue with a postulate, the "postulate of immediate empiricism," later realizing that a postulate was not rich or concrete enough for his philosophy. Having thoroughly confused the relation of experience and existence in his 1925 *Experience and Nature*, which in spite of its popularity is one of Dewey's weakest books,[1] he rightly set out to address the problem of immediate experience in more promising ways. A series of essays in the early 1930s, "Qualitative Thought," "Time and Individuality," and "Experience and Existence," set Dewey on a much more defensible course. Drawing on this work, his two best books, *Art as Experience* and *Logic: The Theory of Inquiry*, handle the issue of immediate experience much more adeptly.

There is little need, at this time in the history of philosophy, to argue that pragmatism is a living option in philosophy. It is widely studied and discussed. After an hiatus of a quarter century, between the death of Dewey in 1952 and the publication of Richard Rorty's *Philosophy and the Mirror of Nature* in 1978, there has been a huge resurgence of interest in pragmatism.[2] But the gap in time had an effect, namely, that of altering and narrowing our common understanding of what counts as "pragmatism," so that while it is definitely alive in the present, it is on life support, and the electroencephalogram suggests to me that we would not be doing great damage to pull the plug, at least on what Rorty calls "pragmatism." What most people now understand by the term is something far narrower than even Dewey and James had in mind, let alone the other pragmatists of the first generation, such as Peirce and Royce. But I think pragmatism is not quite brain-dead. In what follows, I will address the narrowing of the life of pragmatism and do what I can to revive it (using Royce and some shock paddles), which means restoring to pragmatism a capacity to address immediate experience, reducing its nominalistic tendencies, and placing pragmatists in a position to do respectable descriptive metaphysics.

Royce not only regarded himself as a pragmatist (in a sense to be defined), in fact he *was* a pragmatist, and was so long before this approach to philosophy was called by that name. Yet all pragmatists have had a difficult time dealing with immediate experience, and Royce was no exception. This is the natural result of the limitations placed on pragmatic method in Peirce's early articles on the four incapacities, and his rejection of intuition and introspection as sources of philosophical evidence. And when philosophy supposes that we have no power of thinking without signs, mediation is introduced on a universal scale. In some ways, this is the Hegelian hangover of pragmatism, for Hegel was the archenemy of immediacy if ever there was one. The philosopher of mediation had good reason to deny the reality of immediate experience, since there is little hope of accurately calling it "rational," which is the only "real" for Hegel and his school. But pragmatists do not accept that the real is the rational; all of them allow that the real can be prerational, and that immediate experience occurs and is meaningful. To adopt a standpoint on philosophical thinking that sees *its* descriptions (rather than the experiences being described) as mediated, and to give philosophy no authority to claim ontological knowledge (this is the departure from Hegel) of what is altogether necessary in the being of the universe, is to find oneself in possession of mediated descriptions whose relation to immediate experience is less than clear. This is a significant problem, but for now it is sufficient to note that (initially at least) neither James nor Dewey had any clearer idea about how to handle the relation of *existence* (I use this term to denote both immediate and mediated experience, and whatever else may exist that is not currently experienced) and *experience* than did Royce. In fact, C. S. Peirce, among the pragmatists, probably has the best approach to immediate experience, in his phenomenology and theory of signs, but let us examine in a more general sense the legacy of pragmatism itself, and see where this leaves us relative to the problem of immediacy, and its relation to existence.

2. OUR FAITH IN THE WORK OF HISTORY

The term "pragmatism" encompasses a lot more historical territory than is often appreciated today in scholarly and philosophical circles. There is both an advantage and a danger in allowing the term to coalesce, as it has, around the meanings given to it by the thinkers whose ideas have stood the test of time; in this case, we speak mainly of James and Dewey, although Peirce has a very healthy following, and is even more influential in Europe and Latin America than in the United States.

The advantage of letting our present ideas about pragmatism suffice derives from our confidence that history sorts out for us the voices and ideas that are most worthy of our continued consideration. This confidence is often well placed. Those views do survive, most often, whose defenders have been the ablest, and in the case of "pragmatism," I do not dispute the judgment of history. Peirce, James, and Dewey represent three very different conceptions of philosophical pragmatism, all defensible today, all still very much a part of the ongoing development of philosophical thinking, and all showing different excellences towards which pragmatic thinking can tend. Each of these conceptions of pragmatism continues to enrich us, and the interplay among these views remains a source of new variations in our thinking. We could say, over the objections of some, perhaps, that the thought of Hilary Putnam and Owen Flanagan nicely embodies and extends the spirit of James, while Richard Rorty has built upon Dewey's achievements (in controversial but fruitful ways), and Susan Haack is an example of a thinker who builds upon Peirce's type of pragmatism.

As much as I admire all these contemporary philosophers, they are also the ones who put pragmatism in the hospital—which was better than letting it die in the gutter, frankly. But they are analytic philosophers, trained to believe that it is perfectly alright for a philosopher to lift whatever he or she likes and happens to agree with from any historical context, and use it for whatever purposes strike their present fancies, or more fairly, whatever seems most relevant to the problems with which they are occupied, however narrow those problems may be. I suppose that would not be such a bad thing except that nearly all analytic philosophers, from ignorance of history and the lack of an ethic of responsible scholarship (not to mention much pure laziness about reading closely and widely), end up reinventing the pragmatic wheel, and almost always either badly, or at least not as well as the wheels that were once in wider use. A mind is a terrible thing to waste; several generations of wasted analytic minds is a travesty. No one will read anything written by any analytic philosopher in a hundred years, but people will still read Dewey, James, Peirce, and yes, probably Royce. It is simply better philosophy than anything produced in the second half of the twentieth century.

The disadvantage of our blind faith in history comes in a small way from the possibility that genuinely valuable directions and meanings will come to be forgotten whenever history's judgment is imperfect, due to any of a thousand types of historical accidents of timing, trend, tides of popularity, and the like. But the greater source of disadvantage comes from our tendency toward an occluded view of the major trends themselves, in which we fail to understand fully the push and pull against which important ideas like "pragmatism" were formed. So, for example, we may (and often do) fail to understand fully Dewey's or James's own sense of "pragmatism" when we remain ignorant of the dialogue within which those views were formed. Thus, the interpreters and defenders of James who have not closely studied Royce, for example, remain blissfully ignorant of something they desperately need to understand. They will not grasp what motivates much of what James says about pragmatism, why he makes the moves he makes, unless they see the extent to which Royce's criticisms are pressing James's thinking, placing before him alternatives, and forcing him in some cases either to choose or to shift ground. James's journals clearly reveal the extent to which Royce's viewpoint challenged and pressed him.

This problem of failing to appreciate Royce is also acute among those who study Peirce. Royce was a figure very much at the center of the development of pragmatism, and although he criticized James's version of the idea, Royce regarded himself justly as a dedicated pragmatist. Long before this tendency in philosophy had the name "pragmatism," Royce was among the small handful of eminent philosophers working to develop it. For Royce, as for some of the others of that generation, such as Borden Parker Bowne, the arrival of the *label* "pragmatism" was not an event of any remarkable moment. Insofar as the label designated something worth considering, i.e., a practical turn in philosophy that recognizes the role of practical consequences in the further conduct of philosophical thinking, it was something they had embraced many years before.[3] The label itself was rather more like the advent of a new problem in philosophical nomenclature than the sudden birth of a new trend in thinking (the subtitle of James's 1907 *Pragmatism* indicates as much: "A New Name for Some Old Ways of Thinking").[4] And the problem with nomenclature became a serious distraction from the genuine issues at stake. The popularity of the label itself, early on, presented a temptation among philosophers to climb aboard the bandwagon without waiting to sort out the precise role of this tendency in philosophical thinking. In this case, the bandwagon itself certainly belonged to James, and Peirce rather quickly decided he did not want to ride, renaming his own approach "pragmaticism" as is well known. Dewey stayed aboard James's wagon a while longer, and when James died, Dewey seems to have taken the reins. In the first and second decades of the twentieth century, so much was written about pragmatism, both pro and con, that it became impossible to tell who was on whose wagon, and how many wagons there were, and who was driving any of them. A. O. Lovejoy's summary indictment of the movement in his "Thirteen Pragmatisms" nicely depicts the confusion.[5] It is also worth consulting John Elof Boodin's controversial article "What Pragmatism Is and Is Not" for the flavor of the debate.[6]

In the chaos, numerous important voices were lost to subsequent thinkers and scholars, including Royce's and two of his better students, William Ernest Hocking and John Elof Boodin.[7] Our understanding of pragmatism has been grievously diminished by this loss of memory, by the accidents of history, and by the fickleness of philosophical fashion. But my present aim is not to exhibit Royce's pragmatism in detail or to scold philosophers for being narrow, willful, and forgetful (at least, no further than I already have). My aim, rather, is to sketch in outline two different pragmatic temperaments and to recommend the restoration of the one now missing from contemporary pragmatism. I take very seriously and wholly agree with James' claim in "The Sentiment of Rationality" that a philosopher's temperament is simply crucial to grasping his or her thought, and to its formation. Frank Oppenheim, associating the pragmatism of Royce with that of Peirce in his magisterial study, *Reverence for the Relations of Life*, chooses the term "prophetic pragmatism" to describe something of the approach I will take in this essay.[8] I believe this is an appropriate label for the type of pragmatism I want to advocate, but my own efforts will be a bit more modest. I will attempt to fill out and supplement what Oppenheim has done. I believe pragmatism *should* be prophetic, and to this extent I find myself in sympathy also with the efforts of Cornel West, who has chosen the same moniker for his thought. But for my present purposes if I can succeed in staking out the importance to pragmatism of developing adequate ways of treating *ideals*, then I will be content. If the manner of handling ideals I will describe should also turn out to be "prophetic," so much the better. But a great part of pragmatism's difficulty with immediate experience is in knowing what to *do* with ideals, because ideals depend upon possibilities that pragmatists think are not immediately given.[9]

It may seem odd that the most abstract notions, such as ideals, would pose problems for pragmatists, when it is immediate experience, the most concrete mode of being, they struggle to describe and explain. But the two are connected. Pragmatism commits itself to dwelling in a human-sized world, leaving aside both the fundamental character of immediate experience, and the scope and necessity of abstract claims about the necessary characteristics of Being. Yet, even the mid-world has connections to existence, and it is in the concept of existence that the ideals and the immediacies are joined. Immediacy and ideal both point us toward not what is actually experienced, but toward what is *possible* for experience. Pragmatists want no part of transcendental arguments about possibility, but they cannot help employing both descriptions of immediate experience, mediated first by the descriptions themselves, and then by reflection upon those descriptions, and ideals, which unify the ends of practical action. In short, even a pragmatist needs ways of dealing philosophically with possibility, and possibility resides in existence, both the immediate and the ideal aspects of experience, and how these point toward the open universe of possibility.

3. ROYCE'S PRAGMATIC TEMPER

While Royce uses a fictional ontology and descriptive metaphysics to deal with the question of *existence*,[10] he employs pragmatism to address the issue of *experience*. For our purposes, pragmatism can be summarized as involving the following key ideas:

(1) a commitment to the primacy of *experience* as both the source and the final test of the value of philosophical reflection;

(2) that philosophical reflection is a kind of critical problem-solving activity that needs to take its impetus from genuine (as opposed to hyperbolic) doubt;

(3) that truth is understood in light of the way it addresses actual problems and genuine doubt in practice;

(4) that practice and practical consequences are the measure of the value of philosophy, not vice-versa.

We must add to this characterization the restrictions on philosophical thought found in the four incapacities and their consequences analyzed by Peirce, and also the critique of ontological necessity offered by Peirce and adopted by all pragmatists, including the recent schools. This is admittedly oversimplified, but it is enough to help us grasp Royce's pragmatic temper, and to grasp how it differs from the strains of pragmatic thinking currently dominant.

4. GENERALIZING EXPERIENCE: TWO TERRITORIES

Regarding the first of these characteristics of pragmatism, consider the following from Royce's 1895 address "The Conception of God" (before pragmatism was called by its present name):

> All that we know or can know ... must first be indicated to us through our experience. Without experience, without the element of brute fact thrust upon us in immediate feeling, there is no knowledge. . . . I absolutely accept this view. This is true and there is no escape from the fact. Apart from—that is, in divorce from—experience, there is no knowledge. And we come to know only what experience has first indicated to us. I willingly insist that philosophy and life must join hands in asserting this truth.[11]

The primacy of experience does not, for Royce, mean simply, as with Kant, that we cannot philosophize in the absence of experience *in general*. Royce insists rather that *particular* experience is the source of all knowing (perhaps readers will recognize in this one of the key principles of James's radical empiricism), and that what is known is never without its contextual dependence upon particular experience. There *is* no "experience in general," although we do experience generalities or general ideas, but only as the further clarification of practical, particular experiences that accumulate as the history of the individual truly grows. Royce means by "experience" approximately what Dewey and James mean by it, and all of them are in some way or another beholden to Peirce's articulation of the question. The primacy of immediate feeling and the elucidation or generalization of feeling into concept is the shared conviction of pragmatists, including Royce, although James alone among the pragmatists yields almost wholly to nominalism.[12] In other words, the idea that W. E. Hocking believed took him beyond Royce, the cognitive value of feeling, is in fact common to all pragmatists. Hocking did not recognize this idea as a pragmatic one.

Differences among the early pragmatists begin to appear when we consider both *how* feeling becomes concept, becomes generalized, and in the *extent* to which the resultant concepts can be trusted in terms of warranting our conclusions, especially our *philosophical* conclusions. In this domain, we can think of Royce as the most sanguine of the pragmatists, the one who places the greatest confidence in the scope of philosophical conclusions to provide us with a sort of warrant that justifies our claim to possess philosophical "knowledge," although Peirce is plenty optimistic, Dewey less so, and James might be thought of as allowing to philosophy the slightest degree of generalization of its conclusions.

The continuum of views here is reflective not only of the temperaments of each thinker, and perhaps also the degree of their commitment to radical empiricism (and Royce simply is not a radical empiricist, Peirce more so if not much, Dewey is thoroughly empirical but still allows for an occasional flirtation with idealistic conceptions of the "whole," while James is simply horrified by any such move), but also the extent of their respective commitments to the role and function of the a priori in addressing the practical life (which is the functional inverse of radical empiricism). The more a thinker tends to focus upon the peculiarities and accompanying complexities of a particular problem in relation to its own context, the less likely he is to give broad scope to any generalization of its solution to other contexts. Also the degree of genuine doubt, as the response to a problem, becomes a measure of the importance of the problem itself—the more pressing is the doubt, the greater the problem. And here is where differences in temperament begin to become differences in the estimation of the power and value of pragmatism and of philosophical knowledge in general. All pragmatists agree that the type of thinking called forth by practical problems is a substitute for direct action, and that when action is taken, reflective thinking has been completed. All pragmatists agree that where the action taken proves inadequate to solving the problem, we will withhold our affirmation that a "true" solution has been found. But regarding the relationship between *action* and *thinking* there is a world of *territory*—the place where psychology (or phenomenology) and philosophy meet (and where the problem of immediacy is posed). Alternatively, where the solution proposed by our thinking *succeeds*, there is another wide range of possibilities for its further generalization, and this is a second *territory*.

But these two territories, these types of pragmatism, fare differently in the hands of the dominant pragmatists. Where psychology (or phenomenology) and reflective philosophy meet, where the task is to explain in empirically responsible ways the process by which feeling or immediate experience becomes concept,

Dewey and James have held a great advantage in the judgment of history. Not only were both of them more accomplished psychologists than Peirce and Royce (which is not to say the latter two were unaccomplished),[13] but the growing tendency in the twentieth century to place greater confidence in this psychological aspect of knowing (precisely because it was more easily studied by scientific and other empirical methods than the second territory, i.e., how to generalize successful hypotheses, which relies on normative logic) has tended to elevate the Dewey/James type of pragmatism to the place of honor. The task has been to fill out this psychology with a descriptive phenomenology that will translate empirical claims into concepts that can be used by reflective philosophy, by attending carefully to the active contribution of consciousness to the immediate givenness of the object of experience. Indeed, their brand of pragmatism has effectively crowded out all other senses of the term "pragmatism." This result is not entirely to be despised, because after all, the process by which our concrete problems become our conceptual problems bears mightily upon our prospects both for understanding them and solving them.

But our historical emphasis upon this psychological territory, while it has yielded increasingly refined ideas about social epistemology and social psychology, has distracted us from the second territory, our norms regarding the generalization of philosophical results for practical purposes, and has occluded our sense of the full range of "philosophical" responsibility. For it is in this second territory, the effort to understand the relationship between a successful course of action and its proper generalization to other contexts, that issues of value, imagination, vision, and ideals resides. In this territory one needs a keen sense of logic, the capacity to create formalisms that permit proper generalization, that do not encourage illicit generalizations, and that can handle the functional role of universals (or exceptionless generalizations) as guides and limits to thinking. Peirce and Royce are very good at the creative formalization of thought, which for the purposes of pragmatism means the invention of restraints on inference that *prevent* the transformation of maxims drawn from particular experiences into bloodless abstractions. Such a logic adopts the norm of distinguishing logical possibility (in which necessity plays a crucial role) from temporal possibility wherein no abstract necessity is operative (whether in the form of causal laws or dogmatic metaphysical claims).

The Dewey/James pragmatism is notoriously weak in dealing with this side of the matter, while this is the very strength of the Royce/Peirce variety of pragmatism. Indeed, Dewey and James, not possessing the needed gifts for this kind of thinking, tended to be suspicious of any activity of this sort. Dewey was far better at creating formalisms than was James, but Dewey only achieved a fair competence with it after reading through Peirce's *Collected Papers*, between 1931 and 1934. He spent a lifetime failing to understand how and why Peirce was doing what he did (by his own admission), until the "light went on" around 1934, and Dewey was able thereafter to achieve some good results in logic, even if his results were quite modest compared to the logic of Royce and Peirce.

I am willing to call the Royce/Peirce temper (and talent) in this second territory "idealistic pragmatism," not only because Royce and Peirce each used the term "idealism" to describe what was being done, but also because I hope we are, in the present time, mature enough to be aware that the horror of idealism, warranted as it was by the excesses of that school in the nineteenth century, was an unfortunate over-reaction. It is difficult, if not impossible, to carry out any serious philosophy without at least *postulating* some conception of the Whole (that is, considering a *possible* Whole), for the purposes at hand.[14] Such a postulate does not entail the assertion that it as an ontological truth, only the pragmatic value of norms that apply to our thinking—the treatment of logic as a normative science. Thus, Royce and Peirce have significant commerce with the Whole, and even if they do call their systems versions of idealism, I think it is probably safe to set aside the term "idealism" and simply use the adjective "idealistic," to describe the philosophic temper of their versions of pragmatism. Let us pause over consideration of these idealistic versions of pragmatism to understand better how they operate.

5. IDEALISTIC AND RADICAL-EMPIRICAL PRAGMATISM

The difference between the radical-empirical pragmatism and the more idealistic pragmatism emerges most pointedly from cases in which the "problem" is primarily *intellectual* from the start, and the genuine doubt it inspires is *intellectual* doubt (and note that not all intellectual doubt is necessarily hyperbolic or Cartesian doubt; there are genuine intellectual problems). Here, Peirce and Royce will freely employ a priori thinking, especially the *reductio ad absurdum*, and without hesitation *carefully* generalize the results to other *intellectual* problems, especially philosophical problems. Success in addressing an intellectual problem gets the advantage of having used versatile intellectual tools (logic, mathematics, dialectic), and since these intellectual tools are *already* conceptual, their proper adaptation to other intellectual contexts is something that can be safeguarded by a thorough grasp of method and the proper employment and limitations upon logic. So long as one does not enter a hypothesis that works *formally* at cross purposes with some other generalization previously made, and so long as one discharges all hypotheses before hopping from one level of abstraction to another, the results of a good deductive argument one has employed in solving one intellectual problem can be employed in new intellectual contexts. Logic thus serves as a collection of *norms* for moving from a successful use of concepts, a successful inquiry, to different contexts.

Dewey and James are quite hesitant about the employment of logical tools across contexts, especially where universals (or exceptionless generalizations) are employed, not wanting to distinguish among generalizations in any way that requires final commitment between intellectual and practical problems. They do not accept the finality of a pure *reductio* (the sort that formulates propositions in universal terms, excluding the middle) as eliminating concepts from consideration in a given inquiry. This certainly protects them from making illicit moves in dealing with intellectual problems, but it also commits them to reinventing and rejustifying all their conceptual tools for the purposes of each new problem. Naturally they are willing to begin with generalizations carried over from previous inquiries, but these are ventured hypothetically and adapted to the particularities of the inquiry at hand. This means that even intellectual problems are treated in their particularity first, and their generality only later. In other words, the Dewey/James pragmatism is ponderous and unwieldy in dealing with very abstract problems, such as those one would associate with metaphysics *and its ideals*. And, the Dewey/James pragmatism also offers almost no hope for intellectual advance in such subjects as pure logic or in any domain of thinking that requires the development of new logical tools for handling other types of intellectual problems (beyond philosophy itself). Dewey professes this limitation on logic as a *virtue*, beginning with his 1903 *Studies in Logical Theory*, and continuing through his subsequent work in logic up until his 1931–34 epiphany with Peirce's *Collected Papers*. In 1903 Peirce assailed Dewey for this "genetic" principle in logic, which is utterly reductionist in the most narrow-minded sense—to reduce logic to the history of practical problems it has solved in the past, blocking the road of inquiry. Dewey was simply too slow-witted, logically speaking, even to grasp what he had done that set Peirce off on such a scolding tirade.[15]

So while Royce and Peirce were hard at work on the logic of relatives, Dewey and James remained fairly silent. This silence is not so great a problem until one enters the domain of pragmatic metaphysics, a domain in which even radical-empirical pragmatists need some footing in order to offer some account of the value and role of ideals and the Whole in setting out an ethics and a political philosophy. Here, Peirce and Royce have far better tools, and idealistic pragmatism has better metaphysics largely because it has better logic. With a solid metaphysics in place, something James never achieved at all,[16] and Dewey's work is partial and inferior (which is why Rorty cast it off, perhaps),[17] ethics and political philosophy become more manageable, less ad hoc, and more inspiring. That Dewey was good at ethics is undeniable, but how his virtue ethics exemplifies or connects to his muddled metaphysics will always remain unclear. Dewey's ethics does fold in nicely with his social epistemology, the first "territory" above, of which we may fairly proclaim him prince. But his metaphysics is a morass, amounting to not much more than lists of generic traits of existence with almost no analysis of how these generalizations are interrelated. Royce, by contrast, is, in my view, the best ethicist America has ever produced, and that is not surprising when one grasps how integrated his moral philosophy is with a clear, well-constrained hypothetical ontology and a developing modal logic of possibility. In short, Royce knows how to handle ideals and their relation to possibility.

So the principal pragmatists begin to diverge over the *relative* independence of intellectual problems from practical ones (none suggests a complete independence of course), and the fruit of this divergence is harvested in how to handle problems that require some significant degree of independence from present context (the problematic situation, concretely expressed), especially the role and existence of *ideals* in informing our present problems. This divergence results in differing conceptions of the scope of philosophy itself. We come here to our second point in my sketch above of the essentials of pragmatism, that philosophy is a kind of criticism that solves problems raised by genuine doubt. Royce is quite explicit about this point. For instance he says, "I am a student of philosophy. My principal business has always been criticism."[18]

But, while all the competitors seem to agree that philosophy is critical reflection, the view that it has some independence, its own problems and qualities of genuine doubt, was attacked by James and Dewey as "intellectualism." This is a true misunderstanding of Royce's position. In 1911, when Royce was called upon to make a response to Dewey's critique of absolute truth, he made the following remark:

I have earnestly asserted for many years that the so-called "pure intellect" is a myth. I believe, and so far quite in harmony with recent pragmatism, that all our human thinking is a part of our conduct, that the life of the intellect is always a constructive process, an activity, a fashioning of ideas, a committing of ourselves to assertions and denials, and adjustment of ourselves to our situation—in brief, I believe that our intellectual life is a part of the expression of our will. I decline then from the start to be classified with the so-called intellectualists. And now this position of mine is no recent concession of a half-repentant absolutist to the novel contentions of the popularly triumphant pragmatists. I expressed in print this general view about the relation of thought to activity more than twenty-five years ago. My own form of philosophical idealism has ever since been based upon it.[19]

This is illuminating with regard to what Royce means by "will," i.e., the term for conceiving of thought as a kind of conduct, commitment, and adjustment to the "situation," and it is worth noting that Dewey did not fully articulate his own conception of the "situation" as the bridge of experience and existence until nineteen years had elapsed from the time Royce said this. For now it is enough to be aware that restricting philosophy to reflective activity and granting to it a type of problematic situation that is intellectual in nature does not necessarily imply intellectualism. The issue turns upon the relation of will to thinking. Here Dewey takes the view that reflection is a break in the continuity of action, a pause for secondary activity upon the materials of primary experience. Royce is arguing for nothing more than this, although there may be room for disagreement about what instruments are appropriate to such reflective activity and their proper scope.

6. PHILOSOPHY AS CRITICAL REFLECTION (WITH A SMALL DIATRIBE)

While Peirce and Royce see *philosophy* as a fairly restricted kind of reflection upon certain kinds of problems that are *already* conceptual in character, Dewey and James want to include the *process* of conceptualizing the problem as one of the practical aspects of philosophy itself. Royce and Peirce will insist that the philosophical problem already comes in conceptual terms, and that philosophy can assist us in reconceptualizing it, and that this work is as much a priori as empirical, but Dewey and James are leery of this move. Effectively, Dewey and

James wonder whether *genuine* doubt can be inspired by a problem that is primarily (or even purely) intellectual. Is a primarily intellectual problem *really* a "problem"? Is it preventing us from acting? This depends upon whether thinking is a practical activity, since an intellectual problem can certainly inhibit the flow of our thinking. If thinking is an activity (and all pragmatists agree that it is, and is a part of conduct), then its inhibition by an intellectual problem can create genuine doubt. By 1938, Dewey was willing to say that a primarily intellectual problem can inspire genuine doubt, but James never came to the point of admitting it. How, after all, could one distinguish *hyperbolic* doubt from *genuine* doubt if one allows that "purely" intellectual problems do inspire genuine doubt? This seems like inviting Descartes (and all that is wrong with a priorism and dualism) back into one's philosophical tent.

But in some sense, Descartes is already *there*, in the tent, like an ill-behaved adolescent who must be disciplined. Dewey and James essentially put him in the "time-out" corner, which is ineffective with adolescents. It is not as if Dewey's *postulate* of immediate empiricism seriously confronts the mind-body problem (and one might as well call this the "time-space" problem, since that is what it became, or the existence/experience problem, or the problem of immediacy), especially when one has no logic adequate for explaining the *status* of a *postulate*. Dewey accomplishes nothing more with his postulate than Locke accomplished by saying that we only know our own ideas, yet there must be *something* beyond them, some *je ne sais quois*. Dewey's approach essentially says "let's just pretend the object of experience just *is* (i.e., exists as) the thing it seems to be," and he goes along his merry way for another three decades. The denotative method of *Experience and Nature* reworks this postulate into a simplistic theory of reference, but it remains no more than an ad hoc device for avoiding tough questions.[20] No wonder people dismissed pragmatism for so long, if that is all there is to pragmatism. Fortunately Dewey got better in the 1930s. And as damning as Dewey's sins are, they seem venal compared to those of James. Peirce complained about James's kidnapping of pragmatism very loudly, and with justice. Neither James nor Dewey is left with any serious, reflective tool for addressing the issue of immediate experience—just a handful of ungrounded postulates, or denotative references. And what is worse, each of them has, in his way, created a stumbling block to the development of solid phenomenology, by psychologizing or naturalizing (or both) the *concept* of experience.

But there are (at least) two ways to deal with this difficulty. One can peremptorily preclude as "intellectualism" all discussion of problems that does not answer to an empirical, practical problematic situation, as James and Dewey do, *or* one can restrict the role and authority of philosophical reflection itself to problems that have already received conceptual formulation, as Royce and Peirce do. These two ways of conceiving of the scope of philosophy are a further way of grasping the difference between our two "territories" described earlier. Unfortunately, each approach has a difficulty. The Dewey/James approach decapitates philosophy, forbidding it fully to use its powers of abstraction, for fear that it will put the head before the embodied heart and neglect or try to tyrannize the "problems of men," in Dewey's phrase, with "the abstractions of philosophers." Given the excesses of rationalistic philosophy in its history in the West, this is certainly a legitimate fear. Royce and Peirce, on the other hand, cut off philosophy at the knees, giving it scope and applicability only within the domain of human cognitive endeavors, and so they are obliged to introduce phenomenology and semiotics as, strictly speaking, *extra*-philosophical descriptive activities that enable us to give our problems an initial conceptualization. Then, and only then, can critical philosophical reflection deal with such problems according to its own proper methods.

In the end, however, the Peirce/Royce approach makes for better pragmatism. The reason is that phenomenology was, then, and remains the better horse to bet on than the gambit of depriving philosophy of functional universals, although it would have been difficult to know that at the time Peirce and Royce were restricting "philosophy" to reflective consideration of already conceptualized problems.[21] In Peirce's theory of signs and Royce's theory of interpretation, we find significant progress toward providing philosophical reflection with a concrete footing, a reflective description of the sources of its concepts. The "thirdness" of our being-in-the-world is interpretive existing, one phase of which creates concepts.[22] This, of course, is what phenomenology means for Peirce and Royce, and its interpretations are *required* for philosophy, although not properly speaking a *part* of philosophy. It turned out, as we know, that phenomenological description can be done in extremely productive ways, and (apparently) infinitely many conceptualizations of immediate experience can be accomplished through phenomenological description, by those with the talent for it, in ways that do not produce simplistic abstractions, and without giving in to rationalism, psychologism or an overstretched naturalism. Peirce and Royce had *some* talent in creating such descriptions, as did Dewey and James, but none of them had the talent of later phenomenologists, particularly Marcel (in the Roycean strain and temper),[23] the later Husserl (in the Jamesian temper)[24] and Merleau-Ponty (in the Deweyan temper).[25]

It may be argued, contrary to Peirce and Royce, that phenomenology *ought* to be classified as "philosophy" proper, although there is little question that Peirce and Royce denied to it that classification, but I do not think the issue is much more than a quibble. If phenomenology is not "philosophy" proper, it is certainly "philosophical." Many phenomenologists have claimed, on the contrary, that philosophy simply *is* phenomenology, but that is a hopelessly parochial view. Such phenomenologists spent a century pretending to be allergic to metaphysics and logic for fear that *all* metaphysics is *bad* metaphysics (again the heritage of rationalism's excesses), while they claim all pure logic is empty formalism. Phenomenologists heaved a collective sigh of relief when Husserl abandoned his approach in the *Logical Investigations* and moved on to *Ideas*; serious logic never returned to phenomenology, giving the phenomenologists an excuse not to learn it. But in recent decades it has become clear, I think, that these phenomenologists were mistaken. Phenomenologists have slowly begun the process of reclaiming metaphysics, and logic will soon follow. It always does. One cannot do philosophy without both metaphysics and its normative complement, logic.

While phenomenology has developed (whether it is a part of "philosophy" or not), and has restored the "legs" of philosophy as conceived by Peirce and Royce, enabling it to walk around (and providing it with a philosophical—as opposed to psychological or reductive naturalistic—path through the first territory), no complementary development has occurred in Deweyan/Jamesian pragmatism to restore to it the "head" it cut off, the capacity to do metaphysics and logic. This inability to deal with abstract thinking is most keenly problematic when Dewey and James (and their contemporary proponents, Rorty and Putnam) are obliged to confront *ideals*. Clearly Putnam does not want to concede that pragmatism must be nominalistic, and he wants to hold on to universals—even cultural universals, which are surely the most unpopular strain. But Putnam has not yet incorporated Royce and Peirce into his defense of universals. Until he does, he will be susceptible to Rortyan criticisms. It might be fair to say that neopragmatism is what happens to pragmatism when it refuses to deal with, formally and logically, the reality of ideals, or denies that ideals have any reality (and so embraces nominalism). Unfortunately, this refusal to become adept with ideals reduces pragmatism to an unending series of edifying dialogues, an exchange of opinions and efforts to communicate our private vocabularies, the effect of which on the world, and the academy, is *most* unpragmatic. Philosophy becomes an irrelevant chatter among eggheads. And that is what neopragmatism has become, except in the very few cases in which a contemporary pragmatist has broken the mold and dared to speak of ideals. Here, Cornel West comes to mind, as one who, in spite of what he sometimes says, is much more in the line and temper of Royce than of Dewey.[26] Perhaps this is why West is presently writing a book on Royce.[27]

While ideals are therefore treated as concrete concepts by Royce and Peirce, available for the work of philosophical reflection, they are bloodless abstractions in James's estimation, and at most promissory notes we borrow, using future action as collateral, in Dewey's view. One will not be able to keep a philosophy in play for very long without learning to work with ideals, and *that* requires a mastery of logic and metaphysics. In short, pragmatists in the James/Dewey temper will have to learn how to do *difficult* philosophy, something they have successfully avoided doing for about three generations, through disinclination, dullness of mind, and uninformed superstitions about the role of reason in philosophy. The inheritors of the James and Dewey temper, however, are such as to believe, quite dogmatically, that *all* metaphysics is *bad* metaphysics—and here we have nice examples among them of the methods of addressing doubt Peirce warned against, those of tenacity, authority, and the a priori method, which is what they have done in fixing their beliefs about the matter. Asked difficult and legitimate questions, followers of James and Dewey tend to repeat what their heroes said, as though that were an argument. Hence, the advocates of the Dewey/James style of pragmatism neither read nor understand Royce, nor Whitehead, nor anyone else who is difficult to understand, and they often dislike Peirce and do not understand him, even though they have developed a conscience about forcing themselves to read some of his simpler essays, once. Asking contemporary pragmatists to reconsider metaphysics is received as though one had asked them to go to church to get a little religion, an affront to any respectable intellectual these days, especially the followers of Dewey and James. Most of them would rather go to hell than try metaphysics. But most of them already have done some metaphysics, badly, and fail to grasp the situation, until they feel Rorty's pointy trident poking their collective behind. They do not want to inhabit nominalist hell, but they have no tools for invoking universals, or functional conceptions of the Whole, even as hypotheses.

Not all metaphysics has to be bad metaphysics; some approaches avoid the unholy trinity of logical, epistemological, and metaphysical necessity. Here I will content myself in noting that a dogma and prejudice *against* the usefulness of universals is unbecoming of a pragmatist, as is ignorance of historical context. James and Dewey certainly read Royce and did not sniff at him with superior dismissal. I do not see why a good pragmatist today who takes himself or herself to be developing the pragmatic line of thinking would imagine it is alright to dismiss what the progenitors of their movement thoroughly respected, even where they misunderstood or disagreed. If that is the attitude to be taken, pragmatists might as well become analytic philosophers, where it is widely regarded as praiseworthy to remain largely ignorant of the history of what one is studying. If philosophy is critical reflection, it would seem that being self-critical is required. That requirement reaches to a reconsideration of the prevailing attitudes about metaphysics and logic.

7. TRUTH IN PHILOSOPHY AND IN LIFE (WITH A FURTHER DIATRIBE)

So the question comes down, finally, to whether a pragmatist can afford to entertain ideals, and reason upon them in metaphysical and logical fashion, without ceasing thereby to be a pragmatist. Naturally, all pragmatists, no matter how nominalistic, retain *some* place for ideals in their philosophies (even Rorty professed ideal goals for public discourse), but there is great disagreement about how binding our reasoning upon ideals is, how determinate ideals are, how concrete. And thus we arrive at the third of my points in the initial sketch, namely, what makes a concept "true." Royce tends to follow Peirce in his estimation of what makes a concept "true," and it involves giving philosophy a broad authority to make judgments upon various *formulations* of ideals, and the formation of purposes, using a priori methods.[28] The justification for this view is that philosophy is a kind of social *practice*, and the ideas it endorses in one phase have practical consequences in later phases. There is such a thing as a *true* philosophical idea because a *true* one solves a *genuine* philosophical problem, and that is a very *practical* matter *for a philosopher*. Royce and Peirce do not think everyone should strive to be a philosopher, but for those who are philosophers, intellectual problems that have already received conceptual formulations do inspire genuine doubt—even if they may not inspire genuine doubt in persons who are *not* philosophers. Royce is forever saying that one need not accept *his* philosophy or *any* philosophy to appreciate and affirm the practical point he is making here or there, and when he says this sort of thing (in his lectures this type of remark occurs about every twenty pages), he is reaffirming his idea that philosophy is a fairly limited activity. This limitation of philosophy has come to be called the "deflationary" view, but I am confident that neither Peirce nor Royce would accept this label. They are not so much deflating the role of philosophy as recognizing that it is only one type of intellectual activity.

It is certainly important to the human community that *some* persons should be philosophers, and should contribute to our common life the benefits of that activity—conceptual clarity, tools for analysis and synthesis of concepts, teaching, and most importantly, the clear statement of *ideals* as possibilities for human living in the future. The pragmatic *truth* of philosophical ideas thus depends upon *how* those ideas resolve, for better or worse, *philosophical* problems. The result of a "true" philosophical idea is *philosophical* knowledge, the resolution of a philosophical doubt (which is the same thing). Philosophical knowledge can be contributed to the community in the form of clear and important words and actions (and asserting a proposition is an action) that demonstrate the reality of ideals as future possibilities for our common life, which is another word for "teaching" in the broadest sense. This is a kind of "possibilist" teleology, which is to say, it is *not* the ontological assertion of antecedently existing "fixed ends," but the recognition and excellent handling of the reality of ideals as future possibilities—without which we simply cannot plan our lives. Thus, Peirce and Royce are not only not averse to teleological philosophy (in this possibilist sense), they think it a strict requirement of doing *good* philosophy, a norm we really *must* adopt (and this is a moral not a logical "must"). Without it, speaking of ideals and possibilities becomes only a way of edifying our present selves, not planning for our future selves. It is not worth doing.

The Peirce and Royce type of pragmatism will go further, granting to philosophy an authority to determine, through argumentation, which ways of conceptualizing ideals are hopelessly unclear, contradictory, incoherent, irrational. Ideals that cannot be clearly explained, fitted within a system of ideals, related to one another in methodical ways, cannot be wholly dismissed, but must be reformulated until they become practicable contributors to an overall philosophical worldview, which is to say, these ideals are reworked until they are "true." In short, philosophy has authority over the ordering of ideals, assuming that reflection has been undertaken "scientifically," in the broad sense in which Peirce uses that term.

Dewey and James allow philosophy no such authority, even over its *own* problems, and will not embrace teleological language in any but the most provisional ways. Life, in their view, exercises judgment on philosophical truth, either by "growing" or failing to grow beyond generalizations that are no longer effective, or simply out-growing earlier statements of philosophical problems. In emphasizing such notions as "growth," Dewey is smuggling ideals into his valuational scheme, but do not ask him, or any Deweyan, to explain the philosophical meaning of such ideals. One simply receives an analogy or metaphor to biological flourishing, followed by the point that we *are* biological beings, as though that were an argument. It is as if Dewey's followers believe it is fine to hop back and forth from the biological to the moral domain of discourse without remainder and without an explanation. Since the philosophical question concerns "growth" as a *moral* ideal, one cannot answer it with a biological analogy, unless one is prepared either to reduce morality to biology, or to discuss also the formal *dis*analogies between moral growth and biological growth. But this analogy falls short no matter how well analyzed. Many people do a great deal of moral growing in the process of biological dying, for example, and we are hard pressed to characterize dying as biological growth or flourishing. This latter is a discussion most Deweyans are ill prepared to have, since they are often (not always) untalented or untrained in logic and logical relations, of which analogical reasoning is a subset.

Humans are certainly biological beings, and biological beings "grow." Humans are also moral beings, and seem to "grow" in some sense there. But the nutrition that fuels biological growth seems to be made of physical stuff, while the nutrition that "feeds" moral growth seems to involve the teaching and learning of ideals. It would make as much sense to learn how to understand and teach ideals as to learn how to cook, if one wishes to "grow."

8. CASHING IN (SEE ENDNOTES FOR OTHER DIATRIBES)

We are now ready for a brief consideration of the last of my four points about the essentials of pragmatism. What is the "cash value" of this difference between the

Dewey/James type and the Royce/Peirce type of pragmatism, for *life*. Whether today one ought to favor the radical-empirical pragmatism to the exclusion of the idealistic type in matters of *value* remains a bit unclear, but certainly we are aware, with this much time and distance from the initial discussions among these four pragmatists, that the inability of the radical-empirical pragmatism in its current popular manifestations to articulate a vision of ideals, one that inspires the moral admiration of philosophers and ordinary people, is one of the red marks on its side of the philosophical ledger of the twentieth century—and things are not looking any better for the twenty-first unless something changes.

The idealistic sort of pragmatism has not really had its "audit" at this point, for it has passed into trust without ever having its capital spent. Royce's nascent reemergence into philosophical prominence may provide that opportunity for pragmatic entrepreneurs who are willing to risk the investment, or perhaps it will remain in trust until another generation is heir to it. Much of what needs a new consideration, in my view, is contained in recent studies of Royce, including my own, but readers should be aware that there is far more in Royce than the current treatments contain. Royce is a pragmatist. And what can be said with a fair confidence is that the cash value of radical-empirical pragmatism is seriously occluded by its habit of ignoring the logical and metaphysical resources with which it might learn to handle ideals.

Part Three

CULTURE AND VALUES

8.

DEWEY'S UNFINISHED CULTURAL PROJECT

John Peter Anton

1.

Many decades ago, when I was a graduate student at Columbia University, I came across John Herman Randall's perceptive essay "Dewey's Interpretation of the History of Philosophy," where I read the following:

> ... in his thoroughgoing functionalism, his Aristotelian translation of all the problems of matter and form into a functional context—to say nothing of his basic social and ethical concepts—in countless vital matters he is nearer to the Stagerite than to any other philosopher.... It were not difficult to exhibit Dewey as an Aristotelian more Aristotelian than Aristotle himself.[1]

That was fine as far as it went and with all due respect to Dewey's own best student and heir. But what had puzzled me then and continues to this very day was the shifting of the meaning of philosophy, its nature and its functions in modern times and especially what it came to mean in Dewey's functional naturalism. I will not try to summarize what I have already written on Dewey's views on Aristotle in an article of mine.[2] The problem I want to discuss today is about Dewey's unfinished cultural project, which includes what happened to the good old philosophy of the Greeks, what transformations it underwent and how Dewey essayed to relate it to his conception of culture as *paideia*. The purpose of my paper is to throw some light on this unfinished cultural project and explain why it remains so. To begin with, the doctrinal element that makes the cultural project unfinished is Dewey's insistence on the instrumental role of reason that kept him so distant from Aristotle's principle of *noēsis noēseōs*, intelligence understanding itself. Dewey, as I hope to show, could not accept Aristotle's position of *nous* as being both a means and an end, in fact a supreme end. I will return to this difference. But I must first state why the unfinished problem of culture remains an open one for Dewey. Specifically, cultural change and with it the precarious elements of educational programs on which we depend for the formation of patterns of conduct remain fluid despite their successful though temporal efficacy. Therefore, pedagogy, while socially and individually indispensable, is destined to remain open, unfinished, if it is to respond to the constancy of social change.

I find it difficult to look into this problem without first raising the issue of Dewey's Aristotelianism, especially in view of his divergence from the classical meaning of philosophy. As a key to this issue I quote his view of what philosophy is, as stated in a 1933 article in the *Encyclopedia of the Social Sciences*:

> The conception of philosophy reached from a cultural point of view may be summed up by a definition of philosophy as a critique of basic and widely shared belief. For belief, as distinct from special scientific knowledge, always involves valuation, preferential attachment to special types of objects and courses of action.... Thus philosophies are generated and are particularly active in periods of marked social change.... The chief role of philosophy is to bring to consciousness, in an intellectualized form, or in the form of problems, the most important shocks and inherent troubles of complex and changing societies, since these have to do with conflicts of value.[3]

The issue I am raising is simple enough. How Aristotelian is this approach to the tasks of philosophy?

2.

One hundred and fifty years have passed since the day Dewey was born. In view of the multiple changes that have taken place in our lives we are entitled to ask how relevant is his philosophy today and whether it can affect the formation of cultural habits of individuals, given what has happened to the directions education has taken. The issue is "the pedagogy of *ēthos*."

Let me go back to certain passages from two of his works. He wrote in his 1946 "Introduction" to *The Problems of Men*:

> We have moved away from downright slavery and from feudal serfdom. But the conditions of present life still perpetuate a division between activities which are

relatively base and menial and those which are free and ideal. Some educators suppose they are rendering a service by insisting upon an inherent difference between studies they call liberal and others they call mechanical and utilitarian. Economic theories of great influence have developed out of and are used to justify the isolation of economic, commercial, and financial affairs from the political and moral. Philosophy relevant to present conditions has a hard task to perform in purging itself of doctrines which seem to justify this separation and which certainly obstruct the formation of measures and policies by means of which science and technology . . . would perform a more humane and liberal office than they now do.[4]

And in the last chapter of his 1931 *Philosophy and Civilization*, "Science and Society," he wrote:

It is not necessary for me to invade the territory of economics and politics. The essential fact is that if both democracy and capitalism are on trial, it is in reality our collective intelligence which is on trial. We have displayed enough intelligence in the physical field to create the new and powerful instrument of science and technology. We have not as yet had enough intelligence to use this instrument deliberately and systematically to control its social operations and consequences.[5]

One of the most serious trends in our time is the continuing professionalization of education as it aims primarily to supply our technocratic states with plenitude of labor skills and a mentality bent to carrying on profitable research. On the face of it, this prevailing trend seems to continue with noted indifference to democracy as political individualism and the quest for cooperative values in social life. As such it runs against the humanist tradition of the classical views of human nature. Such is the outcome of the prevailing view of *Homo technicus* and *economicus*, whereby the development of the human potential, our *entelecheia* as Aristotle would put it, takes a back seat to technical advancement and labor security. One of the ideological forces that granted this trend a notable priority was the use of social Darwinism to establish the hidden dominance of perennial change in social affairs.

From his early writings on logic and method in his 1903 *Studies in Logical Theory* to the 1920 *Reconstruction in Philosophy*, and then the 1931 essay "Philosophy and Civilization," Dewey has set the stage in his effort to formulate a final position of his understanding what philosophy should have been doing in modern times and needs to do in the future. In so doing he walked inside and outside the perimeter of the Aristotelian position. That is why I couldn't quite understand Randall's insistence on the "more than" praise of Dewey's creative extending of Aristotle. In the rest of my paper I will try to justify my reservations, but more than that use this background to explain what I mean by the unfinished cultural project.

Viewed in a different way, my paper is a brief comment on what Dewey meant by "philosophy" by taking into consideration his complaint in *Philosophy and Civilization* (1931) that American philosophy is but an empty and impotent striving, if by 'American' we mean something final, complete, and finished product. Dewey had already called for "a sincere outgrowth and expression of our civilization," one that "speaks the authentic idiom of an enduring and domi-nating corporate experience." Dewey has placed philosophy squarely within the framework of cultural change; nothing perennial about it except for "humble function" of the "coming to self-consciousness of our civilization."[6] Nevertheless, he concluded that such a philosophy is sincere philosophizing since "it confers upon scientific knowledge an incalculably important office" by philosophy itself.[7] Buried here is one aspect of the "unfinished cultural project." What is the other? We may ask. The emerging problem is that of education, what the Greeks, in their special sagacity called *paideia*. His numerous writings have shown clearly how Dewey, the educator, stressed the educational role of his prag-matism and instrumental experimentalism by placing special emphasis on the education of the individual, but an individual that was no longer conceived along the lines of the speculative products of the modern European culture "fixed in isolation and set up for himself."[8] Here again, Dewey, even if he does not acknowledge the model, is trying to recapture the Greek view of the education of the *politēs*, the social being of the modern individual.

3.

This issue brings me directly to Dewey's view of philosophy. His altering the meaning of the ancient conception of wisdom, *sophia*, calls for an explanation. Part of the issue is the parallel changing of the meaning of *philia tēs sophias*, *philosophia*, what they called the love of wisdom. The meaning has shifted to the activity of "philosophers" as skillful articulators of theoretical outlooks brought about through persistent reflection on determinate sets of logical and epistemological questions, mainly related to the problems of scientific truth. That the ancient *sophia* was relativized to stay in line with the steady rise of individualism is another issue, but what concerns my theme is the distribution of the initial classical task of philosophy to disciplines as they were gradually morphed into distinct pursuits as "philosophy of . . . ," leaving hardly any room for *philosophia* other what is done in introductory courses. When Dewey turned critical and castigated this trend, he also recommended reforming the pursuit of philosophy along the lines of his pragmatic naturalism; he went back to the Greeks and at one point considered a return to Plato's Socrates and the classical dialectic.[9] However, he stopped there for fear he might repeat the fatal error of the ancients: the spectator theory of knowledge. Be that as it may, Dewey rejected all the rationalist philosophies that claimed to be complete embodiments of wisdom. Philosophy for him became intelligence at work, a way of responding to cultural change through the scientific study of the social conditions that engender values and patterns of conduct as they initiate desirable changes in institutions and effect the inculcation of better and more efficient ways of solving persisting problems. In this regard, Dewey is not a "Greek philosopher" if by this we mean a spectator and theoretician of knowledge.

His view of philosophy assumes a special theory of human nature, quite different from that of Aristotle and yet quite close to it. On the one hand, he subscribed to a position that asserted human nature, excluding thus the absoluteness of change and asserting permanent features, however malleable, while on the other, he embraced cultural evolution or rather change primarily in the areas of conduct and social conditions. Again, he came close to the Greeks, especially Aristotle, but the similarities did not go very far. What Dewey had stubbornly excluded was the native property that determines human *entelecheia*. As a result he left out the possibility of permanent values, except for the ones he introduced through the back door, as a special type of consummate qualitative experiences. To support my point I need to refer to his 1938 essay "Does Human Nature Change?"

4.

Dewey's theory of human nature is too broad a subject to deal with in a brief paper. I will limit myself to few basic principles if only to show how close he managed to get to Aristotle's own.

Both share the view concerning certain changeless elements of human nature, but where Aristotle spoke of permanent *dynameis* Dewey talked about innate needs, by which he meant "the inherent demands that men make because of their constitution."[10] There is no *entelecheia* here, only needs such as food, drink, moving about, companionship, exhibiting energy, bringing one's powers to bear upon surrounding conditions, also "cooperation with and emulation of one's fellows for mutual aid and combat alike, the need for some sort of aesthetic appreciation and satisfaction, the need to lead and follow,"[11] to which he adds fear, pity, and sympathy. Then he moves to the required habits, "influenced by the physical environment and social custom."[12] What he means by *habits* is acquired ways of responding to special conditions, that is, acquired ways, not native elements. Human nature is such that while needs are permanent and native, social customs are not. Hence it is wrong to read back into nature cultural changes, reforms, improvements, or delusions.

The issue that emerges clearly here is that he says little about the sources of success and failure regarding the impact of habits, except that they remain contextual. Still, he insists that "civilization itself is the product of altered human nature."[13] The point is a difficult one to understand and may be hiding a contradiction. Of greater interest is his position on habits, which are not part of the original human nature, but they are morphed ways of responding to needs. After condemning the theory of human nature as unchangeable, he concludes:

> When our sciences of human nature and human relations are anything like as developed as are our sciences of physical nature, their chief concern will be with the problem of how human nature is effectively modified. The question will not be whether it is capable of change, but of how it is to be changed under given conditions. This problem is ultimately that of education in its widest sense."[14]

Hence the unsolved cultural problem emerges again. We have to wait until the sciences of human nature sufficiently mature to decide on the most appropriate educational program for the individuals to grow and attain their democratic way of life. What should we do in the meanwhile? What happened to the old dependence on political wisdom? Philosophy now, if that is what is at stake, can only engage as its main mission the pursuit of criticism of criticisms, recommending ameliorative habits without any prospect of formulating permanent values.

5.

In order to discuss the unfinished cultural project we can do no better than revisit Dewey's theory of human nature and ask why he insisted on leaving out any response or even trace of human *entelecheia*. This *lacuna*, if that is actually the case, helps us understand three issues, all left unresolved: (a) the unanswered question of permanent values, as both diachronic and transcultural; (b) the unavoidable relativism of the sociocultural contexts, which in turn assigns to philosophy a peculiarly limited mission restricted to the critical explication of the current patterns of institutions as they call for the adaptation of *paideia* to recommend such habits as they will enable the individuals to attain the highest possible level of immediate qualitative experiences; and (c) the open and unfinished cultural present, itself to be seen as changeable and malleable, but not as the carrier of absolute values, even at the highest level of qualitative immediacy as in art or religion.

The unfinished project thus turns out to demand the casting of the reforms for educational institutions mainly as programs capable of inculcating relevant habits for adjusting conduct as successfully as circumstances allow to the best of each individual's participation in community affairs. Since there is no best as highest and permanent values, especially in view of Dewey's cultural and social "Darwinism," now without Hegelian overtones, we are left with political fluidity and a constant demand for philosophical diagnosis of problems and discrepancies in the prevailing cultural *ēthos*. But what does the practice of philosophy amount to other than identifying problematic situations, generated in the activities of given cultures and recommending reconstructions and adjustments? To put it again in Dewey's way, philosophy becomes the never-ending functioning pursuit as critique of criticisms. The remainder of this outlook demands that the philosopher must know how to assess the cultural practices by accepting as his subject matter the set of institutional issues that call for critical investigation. But what stays out of range in this case is not the nature of human nature but the morphed habits that have acquired institutional acceptance as modal responses to needs, whether flexible or not.

6.

What is also missing in Dewey's account of cultural *ethos* at its best is what may be called the stating of a position regarding political *ethos* to correspond to what the Greeks called excellence, *aretē*. The term "virtue," of Latin origin, is hardly sufficient to cover the same ground. Furthermore, Dewey, on account of his cultural Darwinism, was led to adopt a contextual theory of virtue, or if one prefers, one of accommodating habits as culturally efficient to respond constructively to the social, economic, political, and other problems. There are, therefore, no permanent virtues, good for all cultures and all times. The permanence of *aretē*, whether in the singular or plural, has no place in the constantly changing cultural affairs in the diverse human communities, the insistence on its adherence notwithstanding; that is what Dewey called cultural ideology and dogma. This was one of the weaknesses Dewey found in the Greek way of life, namely, their insistence on having discovered and practiced, within certain limits, virtue (*aretē*) absolute, especially as regards the *aretē* of *phronēsis* and *theoria*, the practical and theoretical excellences.

Dewey's theory of human nature shows clearly why the plasticity of intelligence as a tool does not establish or even lead to the excellence of reason as a permanent and highest value on the same qualitative level as art and religion. For Aristotle, who assigned special significance to the permanent value of rational excellence as a supreme human attainment and with roots in the original structure of human nature, even the practical virtues are dependent upon the consummate development of human *noēsis*. It is a position founded on the principle of human *entelecheia*, as stated in the *De Anima*, where the initial endowment of the soul, the *noūs*, sets the foundations for the full theory of human nature. The statement "all human beings by nature desire to know," implies that knowing (*eidenai*) functions as a naturally urgent *dynamis* from the beginning of each human life. As a process it effects the constant coordination of desiring as the mover already implanted in the cognizing power. As such then this native potentiality has its own end, or rather *is* its own end as "first entelechy." As such, it serves the human being both as means, directing action and selecting from the available goods to satisfy our needs, as well as being its own end. Intelligence, as the power that distinguishes humanity from other living entities, emerges as the ultimate end of our natural *entelecheia*, regardless of social conditions or distinct cultural configurations. But not for Dewey; perhaps he suspected that this part of Aristotle might lead to a new type of Cartesian rationalism.

Still, both Aristotle and Dewey recognize the central place of political conduct in human life, although for Aristotle this type of conduct emerges as the highest form of group life. In fact it is indispensable for the completion of human fulfillment, *eudaimonia*, and this despite the crises due to frequent deviations from constitutional normalcy. It is the prospect of excellence, its attainment and continuous exercise that secures freedom and justice. Just the same, political normalcy and personal fulfillment cannot be had apart from the parallel development of intelligence as both means and end. Such then is the basis for social and political criticism in the case of Aristotle. That the "second philosophies," our special sciences, cooperate with first philosophy in refining the conduct of life, is a principle of inquiry Dewey adopted but with a different relevance to philosophy, as I have already stated.

If I were to restate the question about Dewey's Aristotelianism, to decipher Randall's dictum, I would have to emphasize, as I did, the difference between their corresponding versions of human nature. That both are naturalists, each in his special way, does not eliminate the basic difference that distinguishes their approaches to the role of philosophy. But to say that Dewey extended Aristotle's view as being more Aristotelian than Aristotle is not an accurate characterization of Dewey's approach to philosophy. Whatever else the difference may be, the residual problem that Dewey left unanswered remains: the unfinished project of culture, one that came with the acceptance of incessant change and the reformulation of the classical position regarding human nature. To be sure, by not including reason in the set of ultimate needs, Dewey saddled philosophy with a role limiting its scope to criticism of criticisms while at the same time eliminating the possibility of seeing reason as an ultimate end. If Dewey can be shown to be right, we have no choice but to conclude that pragmatic naturalism has advanced the case of philosophical thought beyond the point that the thinkers of Greece had achieved. It may be so, but it remains to be seen whether such indeed is the case. Another open problem? Yes.

9.

DEWEY AND THE MORAL RESOURCES OF HUMANISTIC NATURALISM

Nathan Bupp

> "The problem of restoring integration and co-operation between man's beliefs about the world in which he lives and his beliefs about values and purposes that should direct his conduct is the deepest problem of modern life. It is the problem of any philosophy that is not isolated from life."
>
> —John Dewey, 1929

1. A SECULAR NARRATIVE

Secular humanists are committed to a naturalistic view of the universe. Concomitant with this view is the realization that each of us gets only one chance to build a life of meaning and value—a grab at the brass ring on a perpetual carousel of time, as Joni Mitchell's haunting song "The Circle Game" suggests. For the humanist, a certain unflinching sobriety about the whole affair seems in order. There is within this sobriety a fervent commitment of the cultivation of the good life—the development of personal narratives that celebrate the natural world and lived experience—in the here and now. Key questions undergird these narratives: What is the character of the world? How ought we to live? What are the conditions of the good life? What limitations need we recognize? What flowerings and dispensations might we hope for? These are fundamentally human questions.

In short, what possible meaning(s) can we discover? What grounds do we have to suggest that meaning can be discovered at all? The marketplace of ideas is teeming with energy, as competing worldviews rush in, promising to provide the answer. On one side of the spectrum we find evangelicals and conservative intellectuals, many clustered around neoconservative think tanks and journals, who continue to beat the drum for that old time religion. They stubbornly maintain that only the sacred can assuage the need for meaning, purpose, and morality. They are haunted by the specter of a Godless naturalism unleashed on society, and pine instead for a theological narrative of supplication, salvation, and redemption, seemingly ignoring two millennia of secular philosophers, artists, and scientists who have addressed these same concerns, with much profit, quite independently of religion. On the other side, we have witnessed in the last few years the emergence of an assertive, uncompromising critique of religion, along with a new advocacy of unbelief. At the forefront of this movement is a diverse group of authors dubbed by pundits as "the new atheists."[1] There can be no doubt that together they have made an important contribution to the cultural conversation.[2] The problem is that *the rejection* of religion is not enough. Atheism in and of itself is merely a negative postulate. It may prevent us from being led down a primrose path, but it contributes nothing *on its own* to the illumination and possible resolution of contemporary human questions and concerns. To advance atheism without a concern for what comes next is to advance an impoverished, narrow perspective. One atheist philosopher who has clearly grasped the crux of the matter is Ronald Aronson, who stated:

> If the appeal of atheism relies on arguments or it casts itself as a messenger bearing cold hard truths, it will continue to fare poorly in today's world. For secularists, the most urgent need is for a coherent popular philosophy that answers vital questions about how to live one's life. . . . A new atheism must absorb the experience of the twentieth century and the issues of the twenty-first. It must answer questions about living without God, face issues concerning forces beyond our control as well as our own responsibility, find a satisfying way of thinking about what we may know and what we cannot know, affirm a secular basis for morality, point to ways of coming to terms with death, and explore what hope might mean today.[3]

John Dewey investigated similar (moral) terrain from within the framework of a comprehensive naturalism with manifest power, acumen, and penetration. It was an inquiry that spanned a lifetime, and his labors did not disappoint. The issues outlined by Aronson have taken on, I believe, a special urgency in our fragmented, technical, highly specialized contemporary culture. In this essay I wish to sketch a few variations on the task of self-definition—especially in relation to our confrontation of the problematic. By linking art, science, and experience (and relying on Dewey my touchstone) I will meditate on how this task might be approached through the construction of a genuinely secular, naturalistic narrative, along with the moral resources appropriate to this task in a secular age.[4]

Each of us has to confront the existential situation that *is* this world, with its admixture of positive potentialities and potential tragedies—a dialectic no phase of human life can escape. We are constantly constructing, revising, and amending our narratives—as individuals and as members of the human community. George Santayana believed self-definition to be "first and fundamental in morals."[5] Lionel Trilling's sensitive and carefully calibrated idea of "the sentiment of being" captures something essential about what this entails: "The sentiment of being is the sentiment of being strong. Which is not to say powerful . . . but rather, with such energy as contrives that the center shall hold, that the circumference of the self keep unbroken, that the person be an integer, impenetrable, perdurable, and autonomous in being if not in action."[6] Although the critical question as to how the human self abides in the world is extraordinarily complex, one solution to the problem is to look to experience itself as a fecund source of instruction. In fact, Dewey reminds us of something that virtually every serious student of human affairs comes to discover for herself, namely, that "common experience is capable of developing from within itself methods which will secure direction for itself and will create inherent standards of judgment and value."[7] Eschewing traditional, supernatural moorings, humanists look to the book of nature—not books of scripture, the "City of Man," not the "City of God"—in their attempts to understand the world and *construct* a life of meaning and value. The scene of this unfolding narrative is experience *in nature*. And protestations to the contrary notwithstanding, nature is the only game going.

In his classic collection of Dewey's writings,[8] John J. McDermott deploys the following process-oriented allegories:

experience as problematic
experience as pedagogical
experience as aesthetic

The important point to emphasis here is the transformative character of the process (with the emphasis on process), a *continuity* leading to a higher synthesis and perhaps the only moral imperative Dewey was willing to put his absolute stamp of approval on: growth.[9] Indeed for Dewey, the *summum bonum* is the individual's ability to come into genuine possession of all of his or her powers. This, however, is not a ready-made value; rather, it is an *achievement* that *takes time*. It is inextricably linked and dependant upon the moral posture we adopt towards the world—a byproduct, if you will, of the "qualities of mind and heart with which we greet and interpret situations."[10] Dewey's prescriptive ideal is the enlarged, expansive self: a resourceful human being deeply engaged in life, capable of drawing from a medley of intellectual and artful talents. It is just this process—coming into full possession of our powers—that I now turn.

2. THE NARRATIVE OF CONFLICT

Now, it may seem prosaic to point out the pervasive character of the problematic in our lives, yet it remains a central motif running through all of nature. A surprising and instructive parallel emerges when we consider Dewey's thought on this topic alongside that of religious thinker and psychiatrist M. Scott Peck—an individual who could not be farther apart from Dewey on a host of metaphysical issues.

Despite their differences, both Dewey and Peck place great emphasis on the tensive or *agonistic* phases of human life. Consider with me a few quotes. Dewey writes:

> Man finds himself living in an aleatory world; his existence involves, to put it badly, a gamble. The world is a scene of risk; it is uncertain, unstable. Its dangers are inconstant, nor to be counted on as to their times and seasons. Although persistent, they are sporadic, episodic. It is darkest just before the dawn; pride goes before the fall; the moment of greatest prosperity is the moment most charged with ill-omen, most opportune for the evil eye. Plague, famine, failure of crops, disease, death, defeat in battle, are always just around the corner, and so are abundance, strength, victory, festival and song. Luck is proverbially both good and bad in its distributions. The sacred and the accursed are potentialities of the same situation; and there is no category of things which has not embodied the sacred and accursed: persons, words, places, times, directions in space, stones, winds, animals, stars.[11]

M. Scott Peck writes:

> Life is a series of problems. Do we want to moan about them or solve them? . . .
> Problems are the cutting edge that distinguishes between success and failure.
> . . . Problems call forth our courage and wisdom; *indeed they create our courage
> and wisdom.*[12] (Emphasis mine)

Dewey again:

> Life itself consists of phases in which the organism falls out of step with the
> march of surrounding things and then recovers unison with it—either through
> effort or by some happy chance. And, in a growing life, the recovery is never
> mere return to a prior state, for it is enriched by the state of disparity and resis-
> tance through which it has passed. . . . Life grows when a temporary falling out
> is a transition to a more extensive balance of energies of the organism with
> those of the conditions under which it lives. . . . If life continues and if in the
> continuing it expands, there is an overcoming of factors of opposition and con-
> flict; there is a transformation of them into differentiated aspects of a higher
> powered and more significant life.[13]

And, finally, Peck once again:

> Wise people learn not to dread but actually to welcome problems . . . [because]
> it is in this whole process of meeting and solving problems that life has its
> meaning. . . . It is only because of problems that we grow mentally. . . . Problems
> do not go away; they must be worked through or else they remain, forever, a
> barrier to the growth and development of the spirit.[14]

Peck's use of the term "spirit" begs clarification. Peck articulates the familiar
theological perspective on difficulty: For him, problems are deliberately sent to
us by God to aid in our spiritual development. While Dewey, on the other hand,
saw the precarious and the problematic as endemic to all experience; a generic
trait *of nature*. Remove this minor quibble about the existence of God (tongue
planted firmly in cheek), and it becomes quite clear that they both see setbacks,
heartbreaks, disappointments, and just plain trouble as a necessity if the human
organism is to grow. A kind of *alchemical process* where the base metals of strife
and struggle gets artfully converted into the gold of moral growth. There is a
sense in which I, as a humanist, can hardly quarrel with Peck's notion of spiritual

growth; for he offers up an important qualification: In his introduction to *The Road Less Traveled* Peck writes, "I make no distinction between the mind and the spirit, and therefore no distinction between the process of achieving growth and achieving mental growth. They are one and the same."

Presaged by Dewey—and confirmed by second-generation cognitive science—is the fact that there is a rhythmic character to all of life. As Dewey pointed out, life consists of phases. Dewey saw this as a trajectory of harmony, loss, and reconstruction (stasis, conflict, resolution). Our lives, then, are punctuated by conflicts and problematic, indeterminate situations that demand resolution. *It is this continual rhythmic process—with a beginning, middle, and end that provides the background through which a narrative of growth can be weaved.* For Dewey, any attempt to avoid the vicissitudes of existence is, in the long run, harmful to the individual. "To a healthy man," he declares, "inaction is the greatest of woes." He urges instead an active and ongoing coping with difficult conditions; for to do so is to be in a learning situation: *experience is pedagogical.*

Fortunately for us mortals, resources abound. We have, in the words of Dewey, "working capital" from which to draw. This is the accrued wisdom of the past—certain standards that represent a deposit of common sense, and in many ways, they constitute the very bedrock on which civilization is built. These are the classical virtues and values. These are not absolute, and they need to be continually tested (and as is quite often the case, vindicated) by their consequences in practice. Still, they anchor inquiry, as they have emerged through long and edifying experience and represent a "storehouse of resources by which to move confidently forward."[15] Humanist philosopher Paul Kurtz has referred to these as the *common moral decencies* and the *ethical excellencies*, and they fortify us with a kind of *valuational base* we can draw upon—moral capital if you will, as we navigate the rapids that rise along the rivers of our lives.[16] Dewey struck just the right chord when he declared, "Imaginative recovery of the bygone is indispensable to successful invasion of the future, but its status is that of an instrument. To ignore its import is the sign of an undisciplined agent; but to isolate the past, dwelling upon it for its own sake and giving it the eulogistic name of knowledge, is to substitute the reminiscence of old-age for effective intelligence."[17]

3. THE IMAGINATIVE NARRATIVE

It is precisely in the notion of conduct, intelligently and artfully directed, that the confluence of science and art becomes pivotal. This is continuous with Dewey's notion of freedom. For Dewey, the human person is free to the extent that his or her conduct is intelligent and artful—essentially guided by the habits of mind of the scientist and artist. Such habits lead to the successful navigation of life's exigencies and their conversion into settled consummations. We are all moral artists operating in a precarious and ever-changing world. I have argued with my humanist colleagues (as others have) that what might be called a "third culture" is in order. We need to bridge the "two culture" divide between science and art and show that a genuine, absorbing, and ultimately satisfying humanism combines the best of both. In other words, we need to appeal to both the head as well as the heart.

A core humanist injunction is to extend the scientific ethos to all areas of human life. This was a central theme of Dewey's thought. The cornerstone of Dewey's analysis, however, was the recognition that scientist and artist are both engaged in similar activity. There is an aesthetic reordering of natural materials towards some desired end-in-view or "happy issue," as he called it. The painter, the mechanic, the poet, and the scientific investigator are all engaged in the reorganization and manipulation of natural materials: striving towards an end product that is unified and harmonious. Dewey says, "Thinking is preeminently an art: knowledge and propositions which are the products of thinking, are works of art, as much so as statuary and symphonies." Further he states, ". . . it can be seen that science is an art, that art is practice, and that the only distinction worth drawing is not between practice and theory, but between those modes of practice that are not intelligent, not inherently and immediately enjoyable, and those which are full of enjoyed meanings."[18] Dewey's thinking on the relationship of art to life requires some elaboration. The ideal he proffers is no mere aestheticism; the critical element, so operative in scientific thought, is never abandoned. Pure fancy has no place in the artful life. Conduct becomes artful when an aim or good *selected through a process of discrimination and reflective intelligence is deliberately pursued.* Conduct fails to become artful when it is driven by either blind routine at one extreme or blind impulse at the other.[19] So while stressing the continuities between art and science, in that both are forms of intelligent practice, Dewey illuminates the organic unity of thought, action, and value. This is exactly where science and art come together for the humanist.

The unfortunate reality, as Dewey saw it, is that the artistic and scientific approach are too often divorced from ordinary human aspiration by being confined to the laboratory or art gallery. Thomas Alexander writes, "Art reveals that experience is capable of being intelligently and creatively appropriated and transformed. Through art man is able to realize the potentiality for meaning and value to be directly embodied in the world. The moral taught by the arts is that when the self-conscious attitude of the artist toward his material has been extended to all experience, to the whole range of human life, then life itself is capable of becoming an art. When such an attitude prevails, the aesthetic dimension of experience will not be regarded as a special, limited, or effete kind of experience."

The function of creative intelligence is to aid our strivings toward an aesthetic ideal of existence, engaging our lives with the critical guided experimental intelligence of the scientist and the concentrated care, attention, and intensity of the artist. This includes, as Alexander points out, viewing the actual in light of the possible. The universe is not static, the future is not fixed—genuine possibilities for the realization of the settled and assured always remain open. This involves a deliberative and reflective kind of rationality, a dramatic rehearsal in the imagination of the possible courses of action available to us when faced with a problematic situation. Various forms of action are surveyed, including an imaginative appreciation of what consequences would be likely to follow if such actions were carried out. This is basically the ethos of science played out in imagination—the discovery of a problem, the suggestion of a hypothesis, the process of experimental inquiry, and finally a choice or plan of action is tentatively chosen (always open to revision) as a possible solution.

4. THE NARRATIVE OF UNDERSTANDING

Dewey made a powerful statement when he declared: "A culture which permits science to destroy traditional values but which distrusts its power to create new ones is a culture which is destroying itself." Unfortunately, the word *science* suffers from some rather cramped connotations, often limiting the public's perception of science to that of the image of the cold, calculating, emotionless scientist ensconced in lab coat and laboratory. Misunderstandings often follow, leading many to become confused, puzzled, and even frightened at the suggestion that science ought to guide and inform morals. And so the challenge faced by Dewey throughout his career as a public philosopher remains with us today, namely, the need to articulate a more living, full-bodied conception of science. A subtle shift in language can help achieve this. The notion of science becomes broadened and enlarged when we speak of the "scientific temper" or "scientific spirit," denoting a self-conscious attitude of mind or a constellation of cognitive dispositions extended to all of life. As Michael Eldridge has observed, Dewey wanted "to extend the intelligence found in science to the rest of our lives. It was a profound mistake to limit intelligent practice to only one part of our lives. The logic of the methods that had proven effective in dealing with the physical world could be adapted to deal with every part of our lives."[20] Dewey saw the "deepest problem of modern life" as one of "restoring integration and cooperation between man's beliefs about the world in which he lives and his beliefs about the values and purposes that should direct his conduct."[21] Paul Kurtz, influenced by Dewey, has stressed the term "critical intelligence" throughout his writings. Here we have a posture that can incorporate under its rubric common sense and practical wisdom. As Paul Kurtz has explained in his writings, critical intelligence refers to a capacity or disposition of mind, a method, attitude, or approach that can be used to understand, discern, and access relationships and cope with problems.

So paramount was this issue that Dewey felt the need to return to it, at age ninety, in one of his last talks, which was later published in *Commentary* magazine: "What has been accomplished in the development of *methods* of inquiry in physiological and physical science now cries out for extension into humane and moral subjects." Perhaps anticipating the kind of misunderstandings alluded to before, Dewey felt compelled to add a footnote which read, "The word 'methods' is italicized as a precaution against a possible misunderstanding which would be contrary to what is intended. What is needed is not the carrying over of procedures that have approved themselves in physical science, but *new* methods as adapted to *human* issues and problems, as methods already in scientific use have shown themselves to be in physical subject matter."[22]

It would carry us beyond the scope of this essay to articulate the vast, significant components of Dewey's rich theory of inquiry, science, and moral growth. Let it suffice for now to suggest that in Dewey, we find the elements we need to construct an elegant, passionate, and comprehensive response to the formidable and necessary task that is defining ourselves in relation to the vast wonder, mystery, and almost unfathomable deepness that is the cosmos. The key is to drink deeply from the well of experience—*reflectively*; to *have* as well as *know* experience. For nature is there, ready to, little by little, bit by bit, reveal her secrets, show us her ways, and chasten us with her wisdom. The concept I am hinting at here has been called *natural piety*. Yes, there is a form of piety open and available to the secular humanist. Santayana said: "(Natural) piety may be said to mean man's reverent attachment to the sources of his being and the steadying of his life by that attachment." For Dewey, natural piety represents "a just sense of nature as the whole of which we are parts, while it also recognizes that we are parts that are marked by intelligence and purpose, having the capacity to strive by their aid to bring conditions into greater consonance with what is humanly desirable. Such piety is *an inherent constituent of a just perspective in life*.[23] (Emphasis mine)

Towards the end of his magisterial autobiography *Persons and Places*, Santayana waxes eloquent about the balance and wisdom that come from long perspectives and broad foundations. It is perhaps only in the September of our years when we finally arrive at that place where, glancing back, we catch a sense of what we have really been engaged in all along. A project fulfilled and consummated by the creation of a complex, rich self. If we're lucky, a self differentiated, yet integrated; life *transformed into a liberal art.* Who is the protagonist in this story— is it the self, or is it nature? I must confess to waffling on this question. Yet I'm inclined to believe that they constitute an ever-shifting dialectic. The challenge is to always remain alert and sensitive to what can be called "the alternating scales of existence." On the human scale, initiative and intelligent action can make a real difference. When viewed from a broader, cosmic scale, we are reminded of the fragility of our achievements, the limitations of human power are revealed, and the recalcitrancy of a sometimes quite indifferent nature is brought in to sharp relief. To encounter the world, while simultaneously holding both perspectives firmly in mind—each one capable of compensating for something concealed by the other—is to survey the world from the standpoint of an enlarged vision. Above all, it is to achieve a certain intellectual dominion over our fate that is at once rich, balanced, and mature. Squaring our accounts with nature, and seeing all things in their proper station, we can then play out our Olympian *and* Promethean roles with scope, wisdom, and humility.

Dewey's melioristic approach seems especially attractive today. It provides at once an antidote to modern cynicism and pessimism and a sober, sound case for mature motivation and individual hope, for living in a precarious cosmos is possible only if we have some confidence in our ability to do so.[24] Our job is to learn how to dance with nature. John Dewey's seminal contribution was to show us how this might be done skillfully and meaningfully, employing the tools of critical and creative intelligence to enlarge and enrich present and future experience while rendering it more harmonious, stable, and secure.

ACKNOWLEDGMENTS

I must acknowledge the intellectual influence of a group of scholars, largely reflected in the ideas I present in this paper: James Gouinlock, John Lachs, John J. McDermott, and Tom Alexander. Their work has proven to be a constant source of inspiration and illumination. This paper is an expanded version of a talk originally delivered at the Center for Inquiry Summer Institute, August 2008.

10.

PHILOSOPHY AND THE CONDUCT OF LIFE
Dewey's New Paradigm

James Gouinlock

Metaphysics is commonly regarded as an esoteric discipline, but in John Dewey's hands it became directly pertinent to common life. I use *metaphysics* to refer to the systematic attempt to distinguish the most noteworthy characteristics of reality and to demonstrate the pertinence of such traits to human conduct and ideals. A metaphysics is developed in answer to the questions "What kind of world is it, really?" and "What manner of ideal goods does it offer, and what are its characteristic perils?"

Directly or indirectly, Dewey's philosophy was addressed entirely to "problems of men." He insisted that any philosophy that obscured such problems was not just an intellectual failure but was guilty of blocking pertinent inquiry into the conduct of life. Ultimately, such a philosophy impedes human effort and hence retards human growth and the realization of happiness. He observed, moreover, that the entire tradition of Western thought retains in its foundations the assumptions that guarantee just these futilities. Hence, Dewey examined the tradition body and soul, as it were, and supplanted it with one that was novel, comprehensive, and, I would argue, intellectually brilliant. We may say that his accomplishment was truly a new and powerful paradigm for addressing the generic problems of mortal existence.

The persistent ingredient in the metaphysics of the classic tradition is the assertion that being in itself constitutes an invariant standard of perfection for human conduct. Ultimate being, indeed, is the ordering principle of all lesser natures in an essentially static cosmos. Typically, these lesser natures are radically juxtaposed to the really real; they have a degraded reality, if you will, often called "becoming," "mere appearance," "the merely phenomenal," and others. Change cannot be predicated of true being; it belongs only to the realm of becoming. To be sure, the many different characterizations of true being have produced different standards of moral conduct and different alleged perfections. Platonic forms, Christian theology, and Kantian reason—to bring up three of the greatest examples—prescribe clearly different modes of conduct. Any incarnation of the tradition prescribes its own eternal and invariable norms, which must be observed throughout the great variations in the actual conditions of human existence.

The differences between the classic tradition and Dewey's naturalism are fateful for human self-understanding and the opportunities for a meaningful life. He was persuaded that the classical fixities were, more than anything else, needless constraints on human flourishing. He wished to liberate human conduct from such constraints and to show how we might thrive and prosper within the vicissitudes of the environment by learning how to function with nature's processes of change—with becoming, in traditional terminology. He contends that there is no changeless being or hierarchy of being and that the natural world is the only world there is. The varieties of existence open to our observation, investigation, and inference are all of a piece regarding their ontological standing. Of crucial importance, however, different existing entities have different potentialities—radically different, in most instances.

The liabilities of classic philosophies are much exacerbated in modern thought, where Descartes is the principal perpetrator. Descartes, as we know, produced the perfect and utterly opaque dualism of experience and nature. He assumed, first, that clear and distinct ideas are true, and second, that the object of purely rational cognition is the really real. Equipped with these assumptions, he concluded that nature is nothing but extension in motion (that is, matter) and mind nothing but a thinking thing. It is not extended and is fully independent of matter. (Never mind that Descartes himself fudged this distinction.) These really real natures can have no potentialities. They are fully actual as cognized. Nature, as Descartes presents it, can have no qualitative properties (it is just extension), and material processes produce no qualitative change. We ordinary mortals, on the other hand, doggedly believe that we live in a world swarming with qualities and marked by continual and persistent qualitative change. This is the world we try to live in and enjoy precisely by responding to such events, trying to adjust to them, evaluating and appreciating them, and even mastering them to some good end.

But nature, on Descartes' reckoning, is without potentialities. Still, he is not so audacious that he will deny the very existence of the qualitative. He simply transports the entire swarming mass of qualitative life inside of an impenetrable subjective prison, the mind, which can have no access to whatever sort of business might be going on outside of itself. Accordingly, for example, not one of us can ascertain whether other persons—or any other sort of creature, for that matter—even exist, never mind what sorts of behavior they engage in. Descartes' thinking makes practical life, including morality, unintelligible. It leads straight to Kant, whose categorical imperative is derived a priori and is applied a priori.

No philosophy, I believe, has left humankind so impotent. Dewey, in response, formulated his naturalistic metaphysics in deliberate contrast to the classic tradition, particularly Descartes. Dewey would develop a metaphysics that would provide us with a faithful understanding of the nature of things such that we might ally ourselves with it rather than be mystified and stymied by grossly mistaken assumptions.

It is the first task of Dewey's naturalistic metaphysics to establish the reality of qualities. They are not, in his argument, phantom beings or beings of dubious ontological standing. They are, like any other event, the outcome of specifiable and conjoint processes of nature. They are potentialities of natural events in discriminable interrelations. The fire is hot when it satisfies certain functions, including the infliction of peculiar feelings of pain on the epidermis. The heat is not an emergent property of the fire alone, nor is it nothing but a feeling on the skin. It is a consequence of many variables acting together, including the sense organs. When those conditions are satisfied, the fire is hot: It is the eventual function of this coalescence of processes that produces all these assignable qualitative results, including the searing pain. Withdraw the relevant conditions, and the functions we label as "heat" no longer exist. The point is that the properties of experience are properties of nature. Just as we learn how to produce and use heat, we may learn to contend with the entire variety of natural phenomena, including other creatures.

This is a massive and consequential change from the Cartesian worldview, and there is more. Dewey also discusses what he calls the "stable," by which he means effectual and discernible relations between natural events, occurring in ascertainable structures and sustained in existence by natural conditions for varying periods of time. The idea of the stable is Dewey's replacement for the belief that real forms in things can be assigned only to the highest levels of being. Accordingly, though nature is a flux, it clearly produces patterns and regularities, but they will undergo change when something novel is introduced into the process. Mind, for example, is not an original and changeless essence; neither is human nature fixed and unchanging, and neither are the things that we call goods, duties, and so on.

A further contradiction to the classic tradition is Dewey's notion of the precarious, by which he refers to those events in experience that are disruptive, destructive, resistant, intrusive, and the like. The precarious is not a subjective existence; it is a public event that is genuinely problematic—like muggings, wars, floods, famines, natural disasters of all kinds, and good fortune as well. These are not "mere appearance," not an inferior realm of being discontinuous with true being—that is, mere becoming, as the classic tradition would have it. They have full membership in natural existence.

We are constantly besieged by the precarious. It is essential to recognize that it is not an anomalous occurrence but belongs to a matrix of identifiable natural processes. If we become cognizant of the continuities organic to the precarious, we might contrive some remedy for its intrusions and even harness its powers. In the terms of Dewey's metaphysics, we might engage the situation by means of discovering the continuities of the precarious and stable, followed by vigorous activity to reconstruct the situation. The classic tradition, Dewey charged, taught arts of acceptance, while his metaphysics teaches arts of control.

When we deliberately attempt to convert the precarious into a stable and welcome outcome, we have initiated what Dewey calls a "history." A history is any process of qualitative change. Nature is abundant with them: beginnings, variations, additions, subtractions, incorporations combined into (sometimes) integrated processes with identifiable outcomes. When an acorn bonds with earth, water, nutrients, sunlight, seasons, and much else, it becomes an oak, and it participates in further functions, such as being host to insects, birds, and animals. A collaboration of many conditions is required, and any of these is subject to change and will change, most notably in human activity. Such delightful confluences and such basic media of conduct must remain metaphysically unreal to Descartes.

Histories are most noteworthy for Dewey when their outcome is deliberately foreseen and a plan of action is conceived and undertaken to achieve it. This outcome Dewey denominates an end, thereby identifying a still further trait that had been denied to nature in modern philosophy. In Dewey's typical usage, goods are a subset of ends, but whether he speaks of ends or goods, they do not enjoy the status of absolutes. Indeed, the provisional idea of the outcome directs our inquiry, but this idea is itself modified in light of inquiry, which will disclose all kinds of resources and pitfalls in a proposed endeavor and prompt us to revise the choice of a particular end in view. The inauguration of such histories is a response to a problematic situation, the likes of which occur in every human endeavor; the history is successful if the problematic conditions are brought to a consummatory end. In many—perhaps most—situations, the problem is a shared predicament, and the inquiry, deliberation, and conduct are undertaken by individuals in concert. This, in germ, is what Dewey means by social intelligence.

Scientific inquiry—or some prototype of it—is essential to this process. We are undertaking to effect a reordering of natural phenomena so that they might become accomplices in our striving and achievement. Clearly, some manner of disciplined inquiry is required to know how nature's processes are interrelated: actual and potential relations of dependence must be ascertained. This is especially true when social engineers propose sweeping changes in prevailing institutions. At the same time, nature imposes its own sort of discipline on us. Nature's potentialities are not invariably beneficial, obviously. If our deliberations are in error (or are fatuous, for that matter) nature's ways will disappoint and perhaps punish us. We are chastened, and perhaps we will know better next time.

Inseparable from Dewey's analyses is his characterization of the nature of science, and, as we know, he had much to say about that. I will spare us a summary of his accounts of experimental method. I need remark only that inquiry is initiated within the contingencies of experience, with its troubles and opportunities; and to contend with them effectively we advance an experimental hypothesis. The hypothesis proposes that the introduction of specified changes in the situation will eliminate the trouble and bring about the desired changes. We undertake the conduct directed by the hypothesis, and inquiry terminates when the conduct succeeds as predicted or fails. If students are bored, for example, we hypothesize that the introduction of a more interactive mode of instruction would arouse them, and we try it out.

Experimental inquiry is not that of the passive spectator. It requires active engagement with nature, and what inquiry discloses is not static essence but the determination of how variations in a given process are correlated with variations in another. We might introduce our own variations. Dewey contrasts this understanding with the prevailing stance of the classic tradition. He repudiates the notion that scientific knowledge is a direct grasp (by reason?) of natures beyond the confines of Cartesian subjective mind. Once more, Dewey's philosophy sets aside the arcane speculations of the tradition and substitutes an analysis of inquiry that exhibits its potentialities to empower experience. (In Dewey's customary usage, the terms *science* and *intelligence* are all but conflated. Intelligence, if anything, has more generic connotations, so science might be denoted as "intelligent inquiry.")

I have been offering a sketch of Dewey's comprehensive critique of the classic tradition in philosophy. Organic to his critique is a generic theory of the nature of nature that discloses the availability of potent instruments of thought and conduct that hitherto have not been available to us. This integral activity of man and nature is Dewey's new paradigm of conduct. It is in fateful contrast to that of the classic tradition. Recall that according to the latter, the end of conduct exists antecedently to any problematic situation, independently in fact of human aspiration and inquiry. Traditionally conceived moral inquiry, indeed, is more in the nature of a fool's errand: it is innocent to the development of the experimental method that would enlighten and vitalize our conduct. Our nature as agents, moreover, (according to the variant offerings of the tradition) is also regarded as essentially given, and the ends appropriate to it are likewise preestablished in the wholly ordered cosmos. The proper function of females, for example, is given in their inherent and eternal nature. According to such thinking, as Dewey exposes it, there is a disjunction, a discontinuity, between the alleged antecedent good and the good that would arise from one's analysis of the variables in a given situation. This discontinuity he commonly names "the dualism of ends and means."

Inasmuch as the absolutes of the classic tradition are fictions, their supposed guidance is in truth some sort of prejudice and very likely, in Dewey's view, an imposition on vital human potentialities. His opposition to all this is encapsulated in his expression "the construction of good." The ends or goods that we seek are not already given as from the brow of Zeus but are put together from natural resources, where we must assess the peculiarities of our situation, take account of our own abilities and aspirations, consult our accumulated wisdom and the experience of others, and likewise acquaint ourselves with the real possibilities and variations of the conditions at hand. Thus, with overt exertion and art, we would construct our good. Dewey was confident that we then would do much better for ourselves, individually and collectively, than by adhering to the nostrums of tradition.

The construction of the good is the quintessence of Dewey's new paradigm. As we have seen, this mode of conduct is literally inconceivable within the assumptions of the classic tradition. It becomes intelligible only with a radical reconstruction of the obfuscations of classical metaphysics. Dewey's philosophy becomes, if you like, the champion of experience rather than its apologist, and it is one of the masterworks of philosophy. His philosophy is neither a mere assortment of insights nor a series of essentially unrelated analyses. It accomplishes, rather, the great philosophic task of articulating a full, comprehensive, and integrated vision of the nature of things—or, as we might also put it, of the full nature of the human condition. Its characterization is replete with an arsenal of human powers forged in concert with nature. The entire opus is coined with thoroughly humanistic intent. It is truly an epochal achievement.

Having made such an assessment, I might seem the inconstant student if I also suggest that I find significant gaps and weaknesses in his thought. Nietzsche says something to the effect that one does a disservice to his teacher if he remains always and only a pupil, and that is a view to which Dewey fully subscribed. So I proceed in good conscience.

Three points are pertinent here. First, Dewey could give the impression that he had an exaggerated view of the noxious effects of the classic tradition, and he evidently turned his back on many of its riches. In historical fact, many a culture has demonstrated an ability to change its institutions and practices in response to major threats to its survival or to newfound opportunities for prosperity and thriving, let their absolutes be what they may. Then, curiously, their previously fixed ends undergo change to be conformable to the new reality. The point here is that putative moral absolutes do not always prove immovable when cultural adaptation becomes imperative or patently helpful. Moral criticism, then, might be directed as much to cultural practice as to the reigning moral dogmas. Dewey in fact was rather gifted in this sort of analysis.

These comments are not a denial that the infliction of cruel and oppressive moral requirements is common, and a critique of the worldview that justifies or even sanctifies these requirements is necessary. It would be especially effective when conjoined with cultural criticism. It is likewise of great consequence in any case to investigate and discriminate the resources of conduct that are potential in the nature of things.

Second, Dewey was so impatient with the classic tradition that he was evidently resistant to searching it for profound insights and its store of wisdom. On this, Dewey might have learned from Santayana, who was exceptionally talented at discerning the wisdom embedded in the human record. Ancient sages, for example, might be remarkably perceptive about the passions, evils, ideals, and forms of moral nobility revealed in their history, and these perceptions were recorded in religion, myth, poetry, literature, philosophies, and written histories. There is matchless wisdom in Plato's dialogues, regardless of the literal truth of the theory of forms. Even discounting his theory of final causes, Aristotle's Ethics and Politics are alive with vital wisdom that could thrive in any age, if one had the wit to appropriate it.

Dewey was evidently too eager to keep on with other matters, but this is a surprising bent in a man who was first, last, and always a moralist. Such a person typically welcomes wisdom from any source. Love of wisdom, after all, is not the last stage before moral dogmatism. It might even ward off dogmatism.

Dewey provides a great and matchless service in his critique of the classic tradition, and his inclusive and penetrating accounting of the nature of things is truly a philosophy of liberation and empowerment. Even so, it is disappointing that he withdraws from any serious attempt to discern and articulate a sampling of the great fulfillments of the human condition. Such renderings are not merely edifying in an offhand way; they are lessons in life, and they provide powerful inspiration. Moral growth and dedication are quickened by the appreciation of exemplary persons and ideal loves.

Apparently, Dewey was temperamentally unsuited to this sort of thing. But this and other such ventures are vital to one of his major themes: the practical realization of the new paradigm of conduct requires the emergence of a moral agent that is almost without precedent in human history.

This leads us to my third and final criticism: Dewey conceives of an "ideal" moral agent who would, however, be ineffectual in the real world. Dewey, so to speak, put almost all his chips on the strategy of inculcating social intelligence and its associated virtues: those familiar with the norms of experimental thinking, and who are habituated to it, will save the world. Educators will be the chief instruments of this awakening by teaching and implementing experimental inquiry in all phases of schoolroom life. One who would be fully scientific must be a fallibilist, welcoming of new ideas, willing to accept or reject ideas on the basis of intersubjectively warranted testing, sensitive to the interests of others, and sufficiently adaptable to fundamentally revise one's life practices and allegiances, if need be, so far as social intelligence requires. I have never met such an agent, and I don't have much hope that I will.

The sources of irrationality, for example, are evidently deeper, more complex, and much more persistent than Dewey supposed. It is commonplace to witness individuals who have attained high distinction in scientific pursuits and are at the same time fanatically resistant to any sort of argument that challenges their religious, moral, or political views. Many generous and decent people remain impervious to any challenge to their basic loyalties. We are familiar with individuals who feign kindness and tolerance while being deceitful, manipulative, controlling, insensitive, and ruthless for power. Especially in conflicts where the stakes are high, such people will be heavily represented, and many of them will attain positions of authority and dominate the rest of us. We can say about as much for each of the seven deadly sins—about how deep seated and virulent they are.

In short, I am skeptical that the intelligent agent in Dewey's sense is much of a possibility, and insofar as there are few who are capable of it, they would be well advised not to practice it openly to avoid being devoured by the others. For better or worse, moral argument typically carries large doses of prejudice, hatred, resentment, compromise, intransigence, threat, authority, submission, and bruised feelings; it commonly has little effect on the antecedent moral convictions of the respective participants.

Insofar as moral discourse might be truly efficacious, it requires resources in the individual to which Dewey gives scant attention: classical virtues such as courage and justice, for example, temperance, a sense of duty, and practical wisdom. These are not so much acquired in formal teaching as they result from initiation into traditions and customs that are sustained by virtuous conduct. This sort of learning, to be sure, tends to be conservative and hence suspect to Dewey. But perhaps he was not sufficiently appreciative of how much virtue and justice in our tradition we are heir to and how worthy of preservation they are.

There are further issues, to be sure, about the nature and acquisition of desirable traits in would-be moral beings. I believe Dewey falls short on such themes, so I do not share his enthusiasm for social intelligence. I do share his enthusiasm for intelligence and intellectual candor. One can have the highest regard, as I do, for his revolution in philosophy without subscribing to every part of it.

11.

DEWEY'S FAITH

Ruth Anna Putnam

Once he had abandoned both the faith of his childhood and absolute idealism, Dewey rejected all forms of supernaturalism, a position he maintained for the rest of his life. Dewey was a naturalist in two senses. He held that no appeal to nonnatural or supernatural entities, beings, or powers could legitimately play a role in dealing with philosophical problems. That, of course, was and is the position of the overwhelming majority of post–World War I philosophers at least in Europe and the English-speaking world. Philosophers did not and do not feel obliged to defend that position; it was and is taken for granted.

Dewey was a naturalist also in a second, more profound, and thus more controversial sense. He held that a belief in a supernatural being had pernicious effects on one's ability to deal with social or personal problems. On the one hand such beliefs, especially as part of a historical religion, give rise to theological problems that cause brilliant minds to spend their time trying to solve these problems instead of dealing with the practical problems of their times. Thus, in particular, they reflected and disputed about "The Problem of Evil" instead of seeking ways to deal with the particular evils they actually faced. On the other hand, it seemed to Dewey that if one believed that the deity is both omniscient and all powerful and intervenes in the world's affairs, one would either, from a sense of total helplessness, become despondent, or else become indolent from believing that a good deity would take care of all problems.[1]

Of course, not all religions are deterministic, not all conceptions of a deity are of an omniscient, omnipotent Being who acts in the world, but Dewey thinks particularly of Christian, and specifically of Calvinist conceptions. These are deterministic and, as he points out near the end of *A Common Faith*, committed to a separation of the damned and the saved. Dewey is moved to exclaim, "I cannot understand how any realization of the democratic ideal as a vital moral and spiritual ideal in human affairs is possible without surrender of the conception of the basic division to which supernatural Christianity is committed." And then he adds, a point to which we shall return later, "Whether or no we are, save in some metaphorical sense, all brothers, we are at least all in the same boat traversing the same turbulent ocean. The potential religious significance of this fact is infinite."[2]

The final remark comes as a surprise. What does a naturalist mean by "religious" or why should he care about religious significance? Indeed, why would Dewey at age seventy-five produce a book that some characterize as his philosophy of religion? I believe that Dewey would have preferred to speak of his philosophy of religious experience; for he values religious experience while opposing religions.

1.

What then is the difference between a religion, any religion, and an aspect of experience that Dewey called religious? For my purposes here, let us follow Dewey in defining a religion, say, Christianity, Islam, animism, etc, as an instantiation of the Oxford Dictionary definition of "religion" quoted by Dewey, namely, "Recognition on the part of man of some unseen higher power as having control of his destiny and as being entitled to obedience, reverence and service."[3] A religion in this sense is an institution that involves, among other things, a creed, that is, a body of beliefs that are accepted on the basis of some authority, ultimately on the basis of revelation. This is a crude characterization, but for our purposes it will suffice. A religion also involves rites and ceremonies. I believe that these are of considerable importance in the life of a faith community, but they are not the targets of Dewey's critique.

The multiplicity of conceptions of the higher powers, of what counts as obedience and worship, and of the motivation for these is cited by Dewey as a reason, among others, to reject all of these conceptions. But the fact that some sort of religious conception is found in almost all human societies suggests, though Dewey does not say so explicitly, that experiences appropriately called "religious" are found in virtually all communities. He believes, moreover, that this aspect of experience is enormously valuable and would be even more valuable as well as more widely, indeed universally, accessible, if it were freed from all connection to the traditional religions and to belief in the supernatural.

What then is the great value of the religious aspect or function in experience? Before he responds to this question, Dewey is concerned to distinguish his view from that of philosophers or theologians who appeal to the fact that individuals have religious experiences, that is, experiences *they* describe as awareness of the presence of God, as evidence of the existence of a supernatural deity. One cannot help but think of William James's *Varieties of Religious Experience*.[4] But Dewey does not mention James, and, indeed, James does not claim that the numerous religious experiences he discusses prove the existence of a deity as conceived by Protestant Christians or, indeed, by adherents of any other religion. James is not a Christian, but he is also not a naturalist. Religious experiences are, he holds, evidence for the existence of the divine, that is, some superhuman consciousness, but not for what he calls "over-beliefs" concerning its nature. But I digress.

Dewey offers an example of the kind of reasoning he rejects. An unnamed author asserts, "I resolved to stop drawing upon myself so continuously and begin drawing upon God." He then describes a daily routine of meditation and concludes, "That was thirty years go. Since then I have had literally not one hour of darkness or despair."[5] Dewey agrees that the episode "illustrates a religious aspect of experience" but insists that it is the man's Christian upbringing that causes him to interpret his experience in terms of a personal God whose existence is then said to be proved by the experience. All that is proved by the experience, objects Dewey, is the existence of a complex of (natural) conditions that have brought about a reorientation followed by an inner peace. Strictly speaking, then, it would seem to be this complex of natural conditions to which the word "God" refers when the man says that he began to draw upon God, although, of course, that is not what the man means. As we shall see later, neither is it what the word "God" means for Dewey.

Let us return to Dewey's characterization of religious experience. He writes, "The actual religious quality in the experience described is the *effect* produced, the better adjustment in life and its conditions, not the manner and cause of its production.[6] It is, of course, this effect that Dewey finds so valuable. To put it succinctly, Dewey holds that if an experience leads to a dramatic and lasting positive readjustment in one's attitude to life, one has had a religious experience, and such an adjustment is immensely valuable. Dewey speaks here from his own experience. As mentioned by Rockefeller, as a young man reading Wordsworth, Dewey had what he later called a "mystic experience." Rockefeller describes it as "blissful" and that "his worries and fears seemed to fall away and he was filled with a sense of deep trust and oneness with the universe."[7] Dewey said to Eastman, as quoted by Rockefeller, "Everything that's here is here and you can just lie back on it. . . . I've never had any doubts since then—nor any beliefs. To me faith means not worrying. . . . I claim that I've got religion and that I got it that night in Oil City."[8] However, Dewey misrepresents his own views; as we shall see soon, faith means more than not worrying. Dewey called the experience a "mystic experience" because it was purely emotional and to some degree ineffable.

It is now obvious why Dewey held that religious experiences are more common than we think. They are more common because when persons who have not internalized the beliefs and concepts of a particular religion or are not committed to belief in a supernatural being have such a transformative experience, and they do have them, they do not label the experience religious. Instead they may say, "I found the meaning of my life," or, as Dewey himself said, "I ceased to worry." This leaves me to wonder why Dewey insists on the word "religious."

2.

Let us return to the characteristic mark of a religious experience in Dewey's sense, the fact that it is followed by inner peace, by the ability to survive even tragedy without sinking into depression. What happens in the experience? One comes to see the things one values most forming a unified whole, one ceases to feel oneself torn this way and that by this or that ideal. Or, again, one sees the world as in some sense ordered rather than torn apart by the conflicting aims of different nations, classes, or religions. Although this "seeing" is an act of the imagination, it is not, Dewey points out, fanciful. On the contrary, the unifying and unified ideal has real effects in real life, and prompts choices and actions that will transform an unsatisfactory, that is, a nonideal situation into one that is more satisfactory, closer to a realization of the ideal.

One's ideals control one's conduct, and in so far as they are moral ideals, one can be said to have moral faith. However, warns Dewey, "What has been said does not imply that all moral faith in ideal ends is by that fact religious in quality. The religious is 'morality touched by emotion' only when the ends of moral conviction arouse emotions that are not only intense but are actuated and supported by ends that are so inclusive tat they unify the self."[9] Immediately thereafter, Dewey explains, "The religious attitude signifies something that is bound through imagination to a *general* attitude. This comprehensive attitude, moreover, is much broader than anything indicated by 'moral' in its usual sense, The quality of attitude is displayed in art, science, and good citizenship."[10] Dewey has moved, I believe, beyond a naturalistic reading of so-called religious experiences to a naturalistic characterization of the religious life or the religious individual. In ordinary English a religious is a monk or nun, a person whose life is directed by a very specific and comprehensive ideal in all, even in its most minute aspects. Generally, Dewey says, if your conduct is guided in every aspect of your life by a unified moral ideal, then your attitude toward that ideal, the emotional tone that permeates your life, is like that of a monk or nun toward God; it is thus appropriate to call it a religious faith.

There are, I think, two ways of reading Dewey's account of the meaning, or at any rate *his* meaning, of the word "religious." He may be saying that some scientists, some artists, some good citizens are so single-mindedly devoted to their research, their artistic endeavors, their social/political activities that one can say—in fact, we do say—science, or composing, or fighting for the rights of the mentally limited is their religion, or that they do what they do religiously. But surely this is too trivial; Dewey offers more than an analysis of a secondary use of the word "religious." Moreover I would want to question whether mere single-mindedness is a good thing; morally repulsive ideals can be and have been pursued single-mindedly. Yet clearly, "religious" is for Dewey a term of commendation.

3.

It seems more plausible to read Dewey as follows. It is impossible, he believes, for an intellectually honest educated person in the twentieth or twenty-first century to accept any of the historic religions literally. Fundamentalist creeds contradict science outright; liberal versions of these religions, abandoning piecemeal particular items in their historic creeds as these conflict with scientific discoveries, find themselves on a slippery slope that can only lead to total rejection of the creed. But that does not mean that what is valuable in a religion, namely, that it gives meaning and unity to life, must be given up.

This raises the following question. When you remove from any of the historic religions all the factual claims, anything that might conflict with what science in the broad sense discloses, what is left? In the best case, what is left is moral guidance. Here one expects an account of what might be left. Thus others say such things as Buddhism teaches compassion, Christianity teaches humility, etc. Dewey is oddly parochial on this point, claiming that the historic religions other than Christianity and Judaism fail to provide moral guidance because they fail to ascribe moral qualities to the deity. This strikes me as doubly misguided. On the one hand, other faiths ascribe moral qualities to the deity or to the founder of the faith. On the other hand, imitatio dei is not the only way in which theistic religions provide moral guidance. Moreover, Dewey objects to Judaism and Christianity precisely because, so he claims, they ascribe religious value to certain moral qualities *because* they are embodied in the deity. In contrast, Dewey holds that certain moral qualities have religious value *because* they are all-encompassing. Once again Dewey has emphasized the difference between a religion and the religious quality of experience but not, so it seems to me, elaborated his conception of religious value.

Dewey makes his point again, but ultimately confusingly, in terms of the meaning of the word "God." For Christians—let us confine ourselves to them because basically the many forms of Christianity, particularly of Protestantism, are what Dewey has in mind—for Christians the word "God" refers to "a Being having prior and therefore nonideal existence."[11] For Dewey the word stands for "the unity of all ideal ends arousing us to desire and action." Or "the ideal ends that at a given time and place one acknowledges as having authority over one's volitions and emotions, the values to which one is supremely devoted, as far as these ends, through imagination, take on unity."[12] God, so understood, is not a Being and has no independent existence. According to Dewey, "Here as afar as I can see is the ultimate issue as to the difference between a religion and the religious as a function of experience."[13]

4.

What then are the ideal ends whose authority over us Dewey takes to be so obvious that he need not argue for them? Here and there Dewey offers lists, such as, "justice, affection, and that intellectual correspondence of our ideas with realities that we call truth,"[14] or "justice, knowledge, beauty."[15] But such lists are always incomplete, at once too abstract and too specific. What we really need to know is where our ideals come from, since a Deweyan God cannot be understood as a preexisting source. The answer is that we begin with goods actually enjoyed, "the goods of human association, arts, and knowledge. The idealizing imagination seizes upon the most precious things found in the climacteric moments of experience and projects them. We need no external criterion and guarantee for their goodness. They are had, they exist as good, and out of them we frame our ideal ends."[16]

We begin with experience, with experiences that are experienced as good. But while we need no external criterion of the goodness of these consummatory experiences, we may learn that the price we pay to have or to prolong some of these experiences is too high. We can only begin with experiences as experienced, but we need not persist in our initial valuation of them; indeed, we must be prepared to reevaluate them. We know that Dewey insists on this modification when he writes in a different context, that is, in the context of a theory of valuation. Here, in *A Common Faith*, he is content to give a rough outline of his view. In any case, however good some consummatory experiences may be, our situation as a whole is not satisfactory, not ideal. So, we use our imagination to develop visions of a better world, an ideal world, but one that is related to the present world. Dewey speaks of a rearrangement of existing conditions. We do not fashion our ideals de novo. As is the case with knowledge, so it is with valuation. We stand on the shoulders of past generations, we modify in light of new experiences, we pass on an improved vision. So, at least Dewey, the inveterate optimist, would have said.

5.

In his reply to his critics in the volume devoted to him in the Library of Living Philosophers, Dewey tells us that he wrote *A Common Faith* in order to make "explicit the religious values implicit in the spirit of science as undogmatic reverence for truth in whatever form it presents itself, and the religious values implicit in our common life, especially in the moral significance of democracy as a way of living together."[17] Why does Dewey speak of religious values, and why is it important to make them explicit?

Let us proceed in a Deweyan spirit. What was the problematic or unsatisfactory situation that prompted Dewey's reflections on religion? *A Common Faith* begins, "Never before in history has mankind been so much of two minds." There are those who, with Dewey, hold that the scientific method broadly conceived, also called the method of intelligence, is the only method leading to true belief because it is ever open to self-correction. On the other side there are those who recognize revelation, as transmitted in sacred scriptures, to be an alternative source of truth. No one holds that revelation is the only source of truth, but when revelation conflicts with what science claims to disclose, these people hold that science must give way.

In fact, the situation was and continues to be more complicated. Liberal members of faith communities tend to give up specific propositions of their creeds when these conflict with science, but they hold on to a basic belief in a supernatural deity. Thus not only is humanity as a whole divided, but many individuals are divided within themselves. Moreover, Dewey pointed out, religions (again he thinks particularly of various variants of Christianity) tend to support moral and political values that are remnants retained from earlier ages. Opposition to birth control or to same-sex marriage may serve as contemporary examples. Once again liberal members of these faith communities experience an inner conflict: their conscience is shocked by some of the alleged moral judgments of the supernatural deity.

Here one is tempted to wonder why these liberal religionists, as Dewey calls them, do not go all the way and give up the belief in the supernatural? Why don't they recognize that the stories told in their scriptures are myths to be interpreted as metaphors? Why don't they frankly admit that the morality ascribed to the deity is outdated? Let us approach a response to this question obliquely.

In *The Quest for Certainty* Dewey reminds us, "There are, again, moments of intense emotional appreciation when, through a happy conjunction of the state of the self and of the surrounding world, the beauty and harmony of existence is disclosed in experiences which are the immediate consummation of all for which we long." Of such experiences Dewey says that they set "the measure of our ideas of possibilities that are to be realized by intelligent endeavor," that is, by "actions that are directed by thought, such as are manifested in the works of fine art and in all human relations perfected by loving care."[18]

I quote this for two reasons. On the one hand to remind you once more of the crucial role played by consummatory experiences in Dewey's own world view. On the other hand because a few paragraphs later Dewey, having once again objected to the intellectual content of religions that comes into conflict with science, characterizes, "[t]he religious attitude as a sense of the possibilities of existence and as devotion to the cause of these possibilities."[19]

Science together with imagination discloses the possibilities of existence; the religious attitude is devotion to the cause of realizing certain of these possibilities. Why then should there be a conflict between science and religion? In the last chapter of *The Quest for Certainty*, Dewey gives an answer that is more interesting, more thorough then reference to particular propositions of some religious creed that contradict relevant propositions of science. Rather what the liberal religionist will not give up is the philosophical dogma that "the reality and power of whatever is excellent and worthy of supreme devotion depends upon proof of its antecedent existence, so that the ideal of perfection loses its claim on us unless it can be demonstrated to exist in the sense in which the sun and stars exist."[20]

This is Dewey's answer to my question a few paragraphs ago, why don't liberal Christians, liberal Jews, liberal religionists in general give up the belief in a divine Being, in Higher Powers, in short, in something supernatural? The answer, Dewey claims, is that these liberals believe, wrongly according to Dewey, that they themselves would cease to love justice and mercy if they did not walk humbly with their God, to use the words of the prophet Micah.

As the Oxford Dictionary definition makes clear, religious belief is belief in "higher powers." I am not convinced that such a belief involves a belief in the antecedent existence of our highest ideals "as the sun and stars exist." William James pointed out that an egg is a possible chicken, it is not a chicken already existing in some other realm. Out of an actual egg an actual chicken may emerge if certain further conditions obtain. Our highest ideals *may* be realized if we devote ourselves to their realization; their realization becomes more likely if others join our efforts, and, a religious person may add, their realization becomes even more likely if God (the Higher Powers) cooperates with us. William James developed such a conception of God in the last chapter of *Pragmatism*, writing, "Monotheism itself, so far as it was religious and not a scheme of class-room instruction for the metaphysicians, has always viewed God as but one helper, *primus inter pares*, in the midst of all the shapers of the great world's fate."[21] No doubt, Dewey spoke from experience of some Christians he had known when he thought that belief in a supernatural deity might encourage inaction. However, we can likewise speak from experience of the devotion with which members of traditional faith communities have devoted their efforts to realize possibilities dear to Dewey's heart. I am thinking of men like Dr. Martin Luther King, women like Mother Teresa, or the activities of South- and Central-American liberation theologians. Nothing follows from these examples. I am, however, inclined to think that the supernaturalism Dewey opposed so passionately was a belief in an omniscient and omnipotent God. In contrast, the deity in which we not only have a right to believe but are better off believing, according to William James, is, as already mentioned, in some sense finite. I see no reason why "liberal religionists" need to give up belief in such a God.

I have digressed. Dewey claims that there would be no conflict between science and religion if the metaphysical assumption that our highest ideals must exist antecedently were given up. This means, he writes, not only "that a religious attitude would surrender once for all commitment to beliefs about matters of fact whether physical, social or metaphysical. . . . Nor would it substitute in their place fixed belief about values, save the one value of discovering the possibilities of the actual and striving to realize them.[22]

Dewey's last comment strikes me as more revealing of his deeper concerns than the attacks on supernaturalism as source of factual, though false, beliefs. Note, by the way, that an understanding of values as evolving as we try to realize them is compatible with a Jamesean finite deity as well as with a Deweyan metaphorical God.

What then were Dewey's positive views? Dewey begins his essay "What I Believe" by distinguishing two senses of the word "faith." In the older sense it refers to a body of propositions believed on the words of an authority, ultimately on the basis of revelation. It is a belief that such and such is the case. In the newer sense faith is a commitment to act. "Faith in the newer sense," Dewey holds, "signifies that experience is the sole ultimate authority."[23] Of course, Dewey's faith in experience comes as no surprise. Is this not just to say again that science broadly conceived is the only intellectual authority? No. In the context of referring to a willingness to act, to say that experience is the only authority is to reject the authority of revelation, or more generally of the religions, as source of our ultimate values. Because moral codes or conceptions of the good based on revelation or sacred literature are backward looking, they insist on behavior suitable for an age when humans confronted nature helplessly. Such codes may require behavior that has become positively harmful; more often, they are silent on the questions that new technologies and new social and economic conditions bring to the fore.

To say that experience is the ultimate authority is to say that we are free to adjust to new circumstances, that we are able to develop new conceptions of an attainable better future. Such new conceptions will then motivate us to aid in bringing that future about. For Dewey, the revolution in methods of gaining knowledge, that is, the triumph of the scientific method, is far more important than any particular knowledge we have gained in the sciences from anthropology to zoology. The natural sciences have taught us that everything existing undergoes change. But, Dewey notes with chagrin, most people (he thinks particularly of Christians in the United States) think that in religion, morals, politics, and economics everything is fixed: Christianity is the final religion, capitalism is the final economic system (though it may need some minor adjustments), and the institution of marriage and the family will endure in its present, i.e., twentieth-century shape. Seventy-five years later we have barely begun to challenge that litany. But a philosophy of experience, Dewey believes, will accept the reality of change even in social, moral, and religious matters and will attempt to direct these changes. "It is not called upon to cherish utopian notions about the imminence of such intelligent direction of social changes. But it is committed to faith in the possibility of its slow effectuation in the degree in which men realize the full import of the revolution that has already been effected in physical and technical regions."[24]

Another popular error Dewey opposes is the idea that there must be one purpose to everything that happens, one grand meaning. People seek such meaning in the historic religions, or failing to find such meaning, they sink into despair. Dewey, the eternal optimist, says that there are many meanings, interconnected. And then he wrote, "Search for a single, inclusive good is doomed to failure. Such happiness as life is capable of comes from the full participation of all our powers in the endeavor to wrest from each changing situation of experience its own full and unique meaning. Faith in the varied possibilities of diversified experience is attended with the joy of constant discovery and of constant growing. Such a joy is possible even in the midst of trouble and defeat, whenever life-experiences are treated as potential disclosures of meanings and values that are to be used as means to a fuller and more significant future experience."[25] What Dewey here described is, I take it, what he meant by the religious quality of some experiences.

6.

In conclusion, I want to return to one declaration of Dewey's and to one question I asked. The statement is this: "Whether or no we are, save in some metaphorical sense, all brothers, we are at least all in the same boat traversing the same turbulent ocean. The potential religious significance of this fact is infinite."[26] Since the religious is, for Dewey, what is of ultimate and inclusive moral significance, I conclude that Dewey's faith, his faith in the sense of what motivates him to act, is faith in democracy as a way of life, both social and individual. On the occasion of his eightieth birthday, now seventy years ago, Dewey characterized democracy in this sense as follows. "[D]emocracy is a *personal* way of individual life; . . . it signifies the possession and continual use of certain attitudes, forming personal character and determining desire and purpose in all the relations of life."[27] (This is not the place to elaborate Dewey's all-encompassing notion of democracy; indeed, it is not a task to be undertaken in one essay.)[28] Dewey himself wrote about his conception of democracy over and over again. Generally we think of democracy as meaning, ideally, that every adult human being contributes equally to the construction of the good, where we mean, of course, every living human being. But Dewey concludes *A Common Faith* by reminding us, "The things in civilization that we most prize are not of ourselves. They exist by grace of the doings and sufferings of the continuous human community in which we are a link. Ours is the responsibility of conserving, transmitting, rectifying and expanding the heritage of values we have received that those who come after us may receive it more solid and secure, more widely accessible and more generously shared than we received it. Here are all the elements of a religious faith that shall not be confined to sect, class or race. Such a faith has always been implicitly the common faith of mankind. It remains to make it explicit and militant."[29]

12.

JOHN DEWEY'S SPIRITUAL VALUES

Larry A. Hickman

As we celebrate the 150th anniversary of the birth of John Dewey, it would perhaps be good to recall that he was a deeply spiritual person, both personally and professionally. As we know, however, Dewey's spirituality was not defined by organized religion. It was instead a part of his commitment to a philosophically informed version of naturalism. He was an ardent opponent of supernaturalism, but he thought that both militant theism and militant atheism constituted dogmatic positions. Given the sometimes egregious insinuations of supernaturalist religious commitments into the social and political life of this country (and it is probably best that I do not start on a list of examples, since there would be no time left for the remainder of my presentation), I believe that his message is as relevant to our own time and place as it was to his.

In a 1935 letter to his friend Max Otto, for example, he wrote: "I feel the gods are pretty dead, tho I suppose I ought to know that however, to be somewhat more philosophical in the matter, if atheism means simply not being a theist, then of course I'm an atheist. But the popular if not the etymological significance of the word is much wider. It has come to signify it seems to me a denial of all ideal values as having the right to control material ones. And in that sense I'm not an atheist and don't want to be labeled one."[1]

In this statement, which is both clear and succinct, Dewey captures the ambiguities of the term "atheist" and its cognates in popular and philosophical parlance. If he is provided none but a choice of belief in God or no belief in God, then because he rejects supernaturalism he must acquiesce to the term "atheist."

Many years later, in his introduction to the ninth volume of Dewey's *Collected Works*, Milton R. Konvitz wrote that "[Dewey] attacks 'aggressive atheism' and 'militant atheism'; but what of an atheism that is not aggressive, not militant? Well,

Dewey does not say, and one does not venture to say for him. But the fact remains that while he condemns supernaturalism, he finds a place for God—not much of a place, but still there it is; he condemns militant or aggressive atheism, but does not say he condemns atheism when it is not militant or aggressive."[2]

It is true enough that Dewey made himself clear in *A Common Faith* about what he regarded as those extreme positions. He thought that militant atheism and militant supernaturalism alike suffer from their preoccupation with human beings in their isolation. He thought, moreover, that the militant atheism of his time also suffered from lack of piety: "its attitude," he wrote, "is often that of man living in an indifferent and hostile world and issuing blasts of defiance."[3]

But his letter to Max Otto, written in 1935 after the publication of *A Common Faith*, appears to resolve the issue that Konvitz raised about "nonmilitant" atheism. If the only alternatives are theism and atheism, then Dewey is an atheist of the nonmilitant variety.

But there is a second sense of "atheist" in this passage, and it is one with which Dewey refuses to identify. He had written in *A Common Faith* that "a religious attitude . . . needs the sense of a connection of man, in the way of both dependence and support, with the enveloping world that the imagination feels is a universe. Use of the words 'God' or 'divine' to convey the union of actual with ideal may protect man from a sense of isolation and from consequent despair or defiance."[4] What, then, are we to make of the fact that Dewey, the self-described (nonmilitant) atheist, nevertheless seems to write approvingly of use of the terms "God" and "divine"?

Once again, Max Otto can help us sort this out. In his 1940 book *The Human Enterprise: An Attempt to Relate Philosophy to Daily Life*,[5] Otto built on his correspondence with Dewey. He distinguished between a "cosmic" atheism, which he rejected, and a "moral" atheism, which "denies the reality of ideals, purposes, and values as genuine elements of human experience and hence of 'reality.'"[6] Employing Otto's terms, we may say that Dewey is thus a *cosmic* atheist, but not a *moral* atheist. As such, he confirms "the reality of ideals, purposes, and values as genuine elements of human experience and hence of 'reality.'"

Terminology is still somewhat problematic, however, because the antonym of "moral atheism" in Dewey's vocabulary is not "moral theism," but "moral idealism."[7] It is true that Dewey acquiesced to the term "God," but it was in a sense that hardly fits the standard definitions of theism. His use of the term is in fact similar to that of University of Chicago theologian Shailer Matthews, who had written in 1931 that: "God is our conception, born of social experience, of the personality-evolving and personally responsive elements of our cosmic environment with which we are organically related."[8] One of my former graduate students, who called my attention to Matthews's work, glossed his definition as follows: "It is our adjustment with those elements in our environment which produces personality and a life of meaning."[9] I submit that the record of Dewey's published work and correspondence indicates that he would have found in this statement very little with which to quarrel.

If the opposite of moral atheism is not moral theism but moral idealism, there are also scores of passages in which Dewey identifies moral idealism with spirituality. But he also warns us that the term "spiritual" has suffered considerable abuse. It should be used with care to denote an attitude toward culture that rejects crude forms of materialism. "The facts named by 'culture'" he writes, "also include the whole body of beliefs, attitudes, dispositions which are scientific and 'moral' and which as a matter of cultural fact decide the specific uses to which the 'material' constituents of culture are put and which accordingly deserve, philosophically speaking, the name 'ideal' (even the name 'spiritual,' if intelligibly used)."[10] I ask that you note that Dewey has selected the adverb "intelligibly" here, where his even most diligent readers might have expected to find the word "intelligently." His point, I take it, was to suggest that even if the term "spiritual" is used *intelligently* (as he intends to do), it may not be *intelligible*, and this because of its long history of abuse.

But how, more precisely, does Dewey characterize that abuse? Simply put, there has been an unwarranted separation of the material from the spiritual in ways that hinder the realization of spiritual or ideal values in the material world. This has occurred in a number of ways.

For one thing, there have been some traditions, especially those heavily dependent on institutionalized religious dogmas, that have attempted to monopolize spiritual capital. This, he says, "may in the end be more harmful than monopoly of material capital."[11] Dewey was not opposed to treating the spiritual as "capital." In an early (1891) essay that bears the title "The Scholastic and the Speculator," Dewey in fact encouraged what we today might call a "venture capitalism of ideas." He discouraged the conservative, scholastic type of spirituality that "has always been gathering in wealth from the wreckage of time and hugging the salvage to itself to set out its full meaning." He preferred the radical, speculative type of spirituality that throws "its fund out again into the stress of life; it must venture its savings against the pressure of facts."[12]

Second, the spiritual factor of our American tradition has been occluded and displaced by entrenched economic inequalities. "Instead of the development of individualities which [our tradition] prophetically set forth, there is a perversion of the whole ideal of individualism to conform to the practices of a pecuniary culture. It has become the source of inequalities and oppressions."[13] On this point Dewey was anticipating the distinction made later by C. B. Macpherson between "possessive" and "developmental" types of individualism,[14] and applying it in the sphere of spiritual life. This is of course a point that he also developed at length in *Individualism Old and New* and *Liberalism and Social Action*.

Third, the long tradition of philosophy bears a considerable share of the responsibility for this debilitating split in experience. "It is equally important," he writes, "that we realize that ["spiritual" activities] are truncated and tend toward abnormality in the degree that they do not eventuate in employing and directing physical instrumentalities to effect material changes. Otherwise that which is called spiritual is in effect but indulgence in idle phantasy."[15] Elsewhere Dewey castigated much of the history of philosophy for its intellectualist tendencies, which is to say, the centuries-long love affair of philosophers with empty abstractions and their avoidance of the "checks and cues" that constitute evidence that inquiry is involved in the domain of concrete, existential affairs.

It seems clear that we are not yet free of this type of vicious intellectualism, vicious because vacuous, although it now tends to express itself in terms of an intellectualism of out-of-control tropes rather than out-of-control essences. Here, for example, is a recent statement by a highly regarded French philosopher of religion, a former Director of Philosophy at the Sorbonne who at present holds a distinguished appointment at the University of Chicago: "To classify a man is to downsize him as a human being, because he could not be classified any other way than according to an order and measure (models and parameters) that come to him from elsewhere, which is to say from the workings of my rationality."[16] Further, and even more remarkably, this philosopher writes, "Knowing man thus requires referring him to God the incomprehensible and thus by derivation to grounding incomprehensibility in the incomprehensible. . . ."[17]

I ask you to note that in place of this dialectic of concepts that circles around to bite its own tail, this exercise in intellectualism that glories in talk of "grounding incomprehensibility in the incomprehensible," Dewey prescribes a moral idealism that is rooted in a natural world—including its social components—that has become increasingly comprehensible.

But of course it is only fair that we hold Dewey the Pragmatist to his own requirement that we spell out the conceivable practical consequences of our ideas. We must therefore ask what, more precisely, he means by moral idealism?

Here is a sample passage from his 1908 *Ethics*: "[W]hen the values of material acquisition and achievement become familiar they will lose the contrast value they now possess; and human endeavor will concern itself mainly with the problem of rendering its conquests in power and efficiency tributary to the life of intelligence and art and of social communication. Such a moral idealism will rest upon a more secure and extensive natural foundation than that of the past, and will be more equitable in application and saner in content than that with which aristocracies have made us familiar."[18]

It is thus fair to say that Dewey was deeply spiritual. But it is also important to note that his spirituality was not vacuous: it grew out of a philosophically informed and refined version of naturalism that is worlds away from the type of valueless or soulless materialism that has quite often been associated with atheism and agnosticism, even if for the most part unfairly, especially by agents of various religious institutions. Dewey's spirituality grew out of a naturalism that denies any ontological split between what is material and what is spiritual, or ideal. He demands that "spiritual functions shall be integrated with the ultimate conditions and means of all achievement, namely the physical, and thereby accomplish something beyond themselves." And he drives his demand home with a pointed remark about American society:

> Until this integration is effected in the only place where it can be carried out, in action itself, we shall continue to live in a society in which a soulless and heartless materialism is compensated for by soulful but futile and unnatural idealism and spiritualism. For materialism is not a theory, but a condition of action; that in which material and mechanical means are severed from the consequences which give them meaning and value. And spiritualistic idealism is not a theory but a state of action; that in which ends are privately enjoyed in isolation from means of execution and consequent public betterment.[19]

This theme—the rejection of soulless materialism and unnatural spiritualism alike, and promotion of a variety of naturalism in which the material and the spiritual are understood not as inhabiting separate spheres, but rather as two aspects or functions of situations as they have been judged to require attention and amelioration—this is a theme that he would develop in his essay "Antinaturalism in Extremis," published in 1944 as the lead essay of *Naturalism and the Human Spirit*. For Dewey, "matter" is treated as a conceptual tool that complex organisms utilize to deal with perceived problems. And "spirit" is treated as a conceptual tool that complex organisms utilize to deal with perceived problems. Neither matter nor spirit have ontological priority within our experience: both are tools that are abstracted from the constraints and facilities of our experience, and that function in a variety of ways.

I ask you to recall the words of the title of the book I just mentioned: it is not *Naturalism* or *the Human Spirit*, but *Naturalism* and *the Human Spirit*. Taking pains to distance himself from mindless materialism, Dewey devotes most of that essay, as he says, "to the contrast which exists between charges brought against naturalism (on the ground of its identification with materialism) and the facts of the case."[20]

Two further features of his essay are worth noting. First, Dewey's naturalism as it is characterized here is not complex: it involves little more than a rejection of supernaturalism and respect for the conclusions of the natural sciences. (Elsewhere, of course, Dewey commits himself to other varieties of naturalism that have been termed "ethical" and "methodological.") Second, he firmly rejects the old Greek and medieval split between matter as something base and "the spiritual" as superior. Dewey is thus combating attempts by antinaturalists to monopolize the term, to identify all of spiritualism with the futile and unnatural variety. He is, in short, attempting to reconstruct the terms.

Despite the clear reference to "spirit" in the book's title, however, some of its readers apparently did not get the point. In his reply to the naturalists, W. H. Sheldon distinguished between two types of materialism: one, the view that matter is mindless, solid stuff; the other the view that consciousness is "at the beck and call of the physical."[21] He charged Dewey and the other Columbia naturalists with the second type of materialism. Since the naturalists have identified themselves with conclusions of the natural sciences, and since the natural sciences are concerned with physical or material verifiability in the spatio-temporal realm, then naturalists must be materialists. They therefore deny knowledge of the mental or spiritual. Q.E.D.

In Sheldon's view, naturalism "leads to or implies that in the last analysis all processes in the known universe, mental, spiritual, vital, or what not, are wholly at the beck and call of the processes we have agreed to call physical, and therefore the only reliable way of control over nature—and over other men—is secured by knowledge of spatio-temporal distributions. That is the only materialism that counts, that has bearing on human life and the prospects of man's future."[22]

In their response, "Are Naturalists Materialists?" Dewey and his colleagues Sidney Hook and Ernest Nagel responded by scoffing at the idea that any serious reader could have understood them as claiming that the spiritual is at the "beck and call" of the physical. Of course naturalists can account for "qualities and behaviors called mental and spiritual.... But these qualities and behaviors of organized wholes are not additional things which are substantially distinct from the properties and behaviors of spatio-temporal objects in their organized unity."[23]

This, by the way, was hardly a new position for Dewey. In 1901 he had offered a course at the University of Chicago on "The Evolution of Morality" that addressed this very subject. (We are fortunate that his students hired a stenographer to record his lectures and distribute them to the members of the class. These lectures have been edited at the Center for Dewey Studies and will, along with others, be available later this year.)

So Dewey's position regarding matter and spirit was hardly new when *Naturalism and the Human Spirit* was published in 1944. Already forty-three years earlier Dewey's students had heard him speak of the "development of the sense of the mental self, of the spiritual self, that is, of the self as somehow or other distinguished from physical things, and operating on a higher plane than do physical things, and subjecting the latter [physical things] to a subordination and regulation for purposes that concern the self. This is not a metaphysical consciousness;" he continues, "this means simply circumstances tend to set it off as a mental reality and that setting of it apart and giving it a set of distinctive characteristics has been influential in ethical development." Here Dewey is addressing the spiritual in a sense other than its identification with moral ideals. He is discussing a spiritual self, the development of a mental reality by means of which moral idealism becomes possible. So much for Sheldon's charge that the Columbia naturalists construed the spiritual as being "at the beck and call" of the physical.

In other words, Dewey's naturalism can account for spiritual values because the construction, reconstruction, and maintenance of spiritual values is a part of the natural function of human beings, including the maintenance of a self. The projection of ends-in-view, of ideals, of aspirations, of plans of action, is as natural to human beings as walking or chewing. To understand the spiritual aspects of human life it is necessary once and for all to put aside the dualism of mind and body, of matter and spirit, and to embrace the fact that mind—the spiritual in its natural and honorific sense—has evolved through eons of human and non-human history as the effect of countless adjustments to changing conditions. Increased complexity; enlarged spheres of imagination and projection; what Dewey terms "dramatic rehearsal"; and the tools that human beings use in the techno-sciences and that can only be termed ideal or conceptual: all of these have arisen out of the actual practices of embodied human beings in a world of pushes and pulls, of facilities and constraints—of what C. S. Peirce called "secondness."

In all this I am suggesting that Dewey's understanding of spiritual values is as relevant and important today as it was during his own time. It is especially important in the context of what appear to be the endless cultural wars—the polemical pyrotechnics that have come to contaminate the battleground struggles between religious fundamentalists and their opponents who have been called "the new atheists."

Since this phenomenon is pertinent to my topic, I would like to address the issue more fully. In a recent review[24] of Ronald Aronson's book *Living without God*,[25] *New York Times* writer Peter Steinfels wonders whether Professor Aronson might best be termed "a new new atheist." He points out that Aronson has called "for a coherent popular philosophy that answers vital questions about how to live one's life." The new atheism, quoting Aronson, "must answer questions about living without God, face issues concerning forces beyond our control as well as our own responsibility, find a satisfying way of thinking about what we may know and what we cannot know, affirm a secular basis for morality, point to ways of coming to terms with death and explore what hope might mean today."

Why have I inserted Aronson's list here, into the context of a discussion of Dewey's contributions to our understanding of spiritual values? Because if we were to add to the list the requirement that the new new atheism must also articulate the parameters of a sound humanistic pedagogy, then I submit that we would have a list of issues around which some of Dewey's major contributions to the public discourse of the first half of the twentieth century were advanced. In the context of the public debates of our own time we would probably have to place Dewey among these "new new atheists."

It is certainly well known to readers of Dewey's writings that in a series of major publications that include *A Common Faith*, *The Quest for Certainty*, *Ethics*, and *Human Nature and Conduct*, Dewey sought to deal with precisely those issues in ways that exhibited his own developing sense of spiritual value. In my view, his work is especially pertinent regarding the last item on the list: what hope might mean today. Unlike many European philosophers, then as now, Dewey's antifoundationalism did not lead down the path to nihilism; he instead put antifoundationalism to work in the service of enriching the meanings of human life.

Even those who are sympathetic to my suggestion regarding Dewey's contributions to the issues referred to in Aronson's list, however, might nevertheless agree with those of his critics who object that Dewey never dealt adequately with the penultimate item, namely, "ways of coming to terms with death." Reinhold Niebuhr, for example claimed that Dewey's naturalism attempted to evade "death, as the final evidence of the ambiguity of the human situation," by the "promise of social immortality." Dewey's position, he wrote in 1949, "is perilously similar to Hitler's dictum: 'It is not necessary that any of us should live. It is only necessary that Germany should live.'"[26] (Neibuhr's comment comparing Dewey to Hitler put him in the company of Mortimer Adler, by the way, who had done something similar a decade earlier, in 1939, when he claimed that Dewey posed more of a threat to democracy than Hitler. Adler then called for the "liquidation" of professors of Dewey's ilk.)[27]

It is true that despite having lost two young children to the ravages of disease—Morris at age two and a half to diphtheria, and Gordon, at age eight to typhoid—and having suffered the loss of his wife Alice in 1927, just seven days short of their forty-first wedding anniversary, Dewey had very little to say in print about "coming to terms with death." In my view, this is because Dewey thought of death as a part of life, and because he had as little concern for his own death as Socrates had had for his. In *Human Nature and Conduct* he put the matter quite clearly. "There is a conceit fostered by perversion of religion which assimilates the universe to our personal desires; but there is also a conceit of carrying the load of the universe from which religion liberates us. Within the flickering inconsequential acts of separate selves dwells a sense of the whole which claims and dignifies them. In its presence we put off mortality and live in the universal. The life of the community in which we live and have our being is the fit symbol of this relationship. The acts in which we express our perception of the ties which bind us to others are its only rites and ceremonies."[28] This is a statement with which many Buddhists would be quite comfortable.

At this point I want to pass beyond the discussion of the ways in which Dewey's spiritual values were grounded in his naturalism. I cannot hope in any event to treat the issue of naturalism in the detailed and insightful way that Phillip Kitcher has done, for example, in his essay "The Naturalists Return" published in 1992 and in his publications since that time. I want instead to turn, very briefly, to some of the ways that Dewey's spiritual values manifested themselves very concretely on behalf of an enriched democratic society, and then to conclude with a statement about the role of Dewey's "secular humanism" vis-à-vis his spiritual values.

For Dewey, a moral ideal without concrete action is little more than an empty abstraction. And one of the moral ideals that Dewey held most dear was freedom of speech. Given Dewey's times and places, this was hardly an abstract ideal for him. We today can imagine only with great difficulty the conditions that obtained in the American academy during the period of World War I, from 1914 to 1918. As Jim Campbell notes in his remarkably fine-grained history of the early years of the American Philosophical Association, *A Thoughtful Profession*, "the American system of higher education became fully involved with the war when it was virtually nationalized in 1918."[29] He quotes Charles Franklin Thwing, who reports that "the colleges became, like the railroads, essentially government institutions. All [male] students who entered the American colleges in the autumn of 1918, either as freshmen or as upperclassmen, being eighteen years of age and of physical fitness, became by their entrance, soldiers of the United States. . . . An essential military camp was established on every campus."[30]

Dewey's Columbia University colleague James M. Cattell, who had been a major influence in bringing him to Columbia after his resignation from the University of Chicago in 1904, was fired by the university's Board of Trustees in 1917. Among his other offenses was that he had lobbied for a bill that would have protected the rights of conscientious objectors. Two other Columbia professors were dismissed for alleged unpatriotic antiwar activities.[31]

Dewey responded to the political repression and abridgement of civil rights that seemed ubiquitous during World War I, and which included the terminations and resignations of some of his close colleagues at Columbia, by working with Jane Addams, Roger Baldwin, Clarence Darrow, Felix Frankfurter, Norman Thomas, and others to establish the American Civil Liberties Union in 1920. He was also a founder and first president of the American Association of University Professors, a founder of the NAACP, a member of the League for Industrial Democracy, and chair of the commission of inquiry into the charges brought against Leon Trotsky. This is of course only a partial list of Dewey's participation in organizations dedicated to the public good. His correspondence reveals the enormous amount of time he spent, time taken from his busy schedule of teaching, writing, and publication, in order to help secure those values that he termed spiritual and that he thought central to the enrichment of democratic life.

Finally, there is the more specific question of how we are to understand Dewey's spiritual values in the context of his role as signatory to the humanist manifesto. That is a question that I attempted to address in a brief contribution to *Free Inquiry* in 2005. Dewey's spiritual values, I suggested, embrace "an expansive humanism that provides platforms for working with religious humanists. Some strands of Buddhism, Unitarianism, and even liberal Christianity, for example, share with secularists a common commitment to humanism as Dewey defined it in his essay "What Humanism Means to Me": [viz] 'an expansion . . . of human life, an expansion in which nature and the science of nature are made the willing servants of human good.'"

As we celebrate the 150th anniversary of Dewey's birth, I ask you to recall that Dewey's "humanism thus provides tools for fostering broad-based coalitions . . . founded on the idea that the tests of belief—whether secular or religious—lie not in origins but consequences. Within such arrangements, secular humanists can and should work with religious humanists to isolate and undercut forms of both soulless materialism and unnatural spirituality, where those practices are preventing rather than promoting the growth of individuals and communities."[32] These ideas, I believe, are among the most important of Dewey's spiritual values.

Part Four

LIVED EXPERIENCE

13.

REREADING DEWEY'S
ART AS EXPERIENCE

Joseph Margolis

1.

I t's remarkably difficult to specify the decisive key to the great thicket of John Dewey's *Art as Experience* (1934). Everyone who reads the book is surprised by its force and running confidence. And yet, almost no one can state in a plain way (no one has) just what its promised contribution comes to. Certainly, in our time, Dewey is largely ignored as an aesthetician or philosopher of art: efforts to give him his due tend to blather about what Dewey calls "a consummatory experience" and veer off with a knowing look about the Darwinian cast of his naturalism—about the ultimate source of aesthetic experience in animal sensibility. And yet, read obliquely, these are indeed the right clues to feature, if—that is, only if, as I would insist—they are rightly subordinated to what Dewey was aware, what he regularly signaled he was aware, remained the essential unsolved philosophical problem posed by the fine arts, which, viewed more globally, he realized was also the abiding puzzle of the human condition itself.

The point is: the very title of Dewey's book, which, rightly perceived, signals its being the mate of *Experience and Nature* (1925, 1929), perhaps then its offspring and successor, collects his most sustained effort to apply his naturalism, his metaphysics, to the densest space of encultured life, without ever resolving the general question of the relationship between physical nature (biology, most particularly) and human history and culture.

Dewey was aware that the answer required the fresh invention of a conceptual vision that would bring his Hegelian and Darwinian themes to bear in a spare and closely focused way on the analysis of a work of art (on *its* metaphysics, to speak plainly) and, correspondingly, the analysis of human beings viewed in terms of what accounts for their being uniquely able to produce art and to respond as they do to art's notable presence in every society. Dewey, I daresay, was unable to answer his question commandingly, though his answer was perched on the very edge of discovery. I take his question to be effectively the same as the question Plato, more understandably, was unable to answer in Socrates' elenctic conversations about virtue, for Plato lacked (if I may say so) both Hegel's understanding of the historicity of culture and Darwin's sense that the fully formed species, *Homo sapiens*, must have developed very slowly from hominid and prehominid forms that (themselves) could never, in their own right, have broached either Plato's or Dewey's question.

That is, I surmise that Dewey was aware that his own habit of biologizing the genesis of specifically human sensibility and intelligence (his constant emphasis on the continuing presence of our animal powers in whatever humans manage to accomplish culturally) must still be insufficient for answering the original question. Hence I charge that Dewey never succeeded in answering his deepest question, in *Art as Experience*, and, furthermore, that the whole of Western philosophy has still to advance a satisfactory answer. The conceptual resources needed were never sufficiently understood until well into the nineteenth century: they have hardly been mastered to this day.

If so, then perhaps the best part of Dewey's contribution rests with its bringing us to the very edge of a deeply needed philosophical transformation that Dewey himself was unable to capture perspicuously. I take this to explain, at least in part, Dewey's perseveration on the theme of "experience"—in particular, the theme of "a consummatory experience"—which strikes us now as a rather poor blunderbuss of an idea, a vestige of older Idealist strains perhaps, that accomplished little more than hold in place whatever Dewey believed would need to be properly explained if ever we were to succeed in our analysis of the arts. The same is true of Plato's Socrates, who could never dismiss the Parmenidean fixities he saw no useful way of applying to what we would now regard as the materials of cultural history.[1] Parmenidean invariance and Idealist "experience" have little in common except their being habituated barriers to grasping the "next" phase of philosophical invention. "Experience," in Dewey's idiom, is hardly essential to the pragmatist gains Dewey envisages.

Plato's Socrates was unable to disentangle the novel regularities of the cultural world from Parmenidean fixities in a way that would permit him to abandon invariance in favor of the flux of history in solving the problem of defining the virtues; and Dewey was unable to characterize the distinctive features of artworks (*a fortiori*, the defining features of human culture itself) except by way of a strong disjunction between the seeming material nature of the "products of art" (a view he shared with Santayana) and his innovative notion of "a consummatory experience," a psychologized apotheosis (possibly due to his Darwinized reading of Santayana's theme of experienced pleasure—but in any case the key to his own distinctive formulation of the aesthetic). I intend no estimate or comparison of the importance of either undertaking. But if Plato failed in the elenctic dialogues, then to suggest that Dewey failed in *Art as Experience* need not be read as a disaster.

Hegel's extravagant guess at the public presence of the conserving regularities of cultural history and change, we may conjecture, made it possible, for the first time, to discard any supposed need to insist on conceptual invariances of any kind: Socrates lacked any such luxury. And the dawning significance of Darwin's discovery, perhaps more neo-Darwinian than Darwinian, has now begun to signify the artifactual (hybrid) nature of the human self itself—in effect, the embodied mate of culturally informed artworks, themselves inseparably embodied in and reflexively emergent with respect to mere physical or biological media or materiae.[2] (You may already glimpse here the thread of a promising answer to Dewey's question.) If I am right about this way of reading Dewey, then, perhaps, Dewey's *Art as Experience* prompts us to admit that we, too, have yet to grasp the true continuity and difference between biology and culture.

In short, my conjecture is that *Art and Experience*, more than any other of Dewey's books, provides a compelling brief for a grand solution to a puzzle Dewey was not prepared to claim he could supply; but, anticipating its solution, he dutifully assembled all the driving evidence he could muster to persuade his most attentive readers to address the mystery that remained.

I mean that, short of a century ago, Dewey confronted us with a paradox that should have eked out a satisfactory answer by now, a paradox he was aware Santayana had already effectively drawn attention to, some forty years earlier, in *The Sense of Beauty* (1896). It's worth remarking that, in the original edition of his history of aesthetics, Monroe Beardsley explicitly mentions (though much too briefly) the close connection between the nerve of Dewey's *Art as Experience* and the central paradox of Santayana's *Sense of Beauty*: "The experience of art, Santayana begins [Beardsley remarks], is a pleasure, a positive and intrinsic value. This pleasure, like other sensations, can be transformed by the mind into 'the quality of a thing.'"[3] Beardsley then cites Santayana's sensible intuition but plainly uncompelling argument: "If we say that other men should see the beauties we see, it is because we think these beauties *are in the object*, like its color, proportion or size," a remark that obviously has more in common with Hume than with Kant.[4] Beardsley adds to this a bit of Santayana's treatment of his own paradox: "This projective transference, says Santayana, 'is radically absurd and contradictory', since beauty is a 'value', which can exist only in perception."[5] Just so. That's to say: Santayana saw the importance of resolving the paradox but never answered the call.

I suggest that Dewey accepted Santayana's challenge as his own: contrived to replace Santayana's Humean-like emphasis on the pleasure/beauty paradox with his own catch-all of a consummatory experience, which, in some distantly Hegelian spirit, colored by the Darwinian cast of his own book, joins indissolubly the subjective and objective aspects of an aesthetic episode. Dewey may have secured a gain of sorts thereby, but he risked too much on the innovation: he left the deeper issue completely unresolved, subject to an unwanted dualism. Beardsley notes Santayana's later emendation: that is, that beauty is not "subjective" (or "objective") but "neutral"[6]—which is hardly an improvement on what it replaces. Beardsley leaves the matter there.

Still, Beardsley scores significantly in drawing out of Dewey's *Experience and Nature* (published well before *Art as Experience*) the following oddly tepid foray into the distinction between biology and culture—which Beardsley reads (correctly) as signifying Dewey's belief that he and Santayana were committed to naturalism in much the same way in speaking of the arts, whatever their deeper differences might be:

> There are [Dewey says] substantially but two alternatives. Either art is a continuation, by means of intelligent selection and arrangement of natural tendencies of events; or art is a peculiar addition to nature springing from something dwelling exclusively in the breast of man, whatever name be given the latter. In the former case, delightfully enhanced perception or esthetic appreciation is of the same nature as enjoyment of any object that is consummatory. . . . That, in this process, new meanings develop, and that they afford uniquely new traits and modes of enjoyment is but what happens everywhere in emergent growth.[7]

Beardsley does not see the decisive failing of Dewey's remark: he himself, of course, betrays a similar disinclination to distinguish sharply between biology and culture. Culture, I should say, is always a *sui generis*, metaphysically signifi-cant transformation of biological competences (made possible by the feat of mas-tering a first language and the functional emergence of what we call the self), however *that* transformation effects a cognate form of physical materiae.[8]

If there is anything that counts as the signal difference between the Kantian and Hegelian philosophies, apart from construing Kant's transcendental ques-tions as *a posteriori* posits within the open-ended span of historied inquiry, it's Hegel's grand effort to isolate the *sui generis* metaphysics of cultural life itself.[9] What could Dewey have meant by the phrasing, "something dwelling exclusively within the breast of man, whatever name be given to the latter"? He means the hybrid transformations (the histories) of cultural life that count as the fullest expressions of human freedom. He means, more pointedly, the repudiation of what, reading what he's written, has come to be called "museum art," which severs (he claims) the connection between art and "the common life," construes art as an elitist concern, and reads museums—Dewey actually says, "most European museums"—as "memorials of the rise of nationalism and imperialism."[10] He has a point, but he goes too far: what must be redeemed cannot be rescued by invoking consummatory experience. It requires attention to the distinctive struc-ture of what we are prepared to call a work of art—a painting for instance.

Art is nothing if not culturally formed, informed, grasped by creatures sim-ilarly formed. Dewey is perfectly clear about all of this in the full argument of his book; but at the critical point at which the distinction is positively needed he turns away, resists whatever might otherwise seem to introduce a discontinuity involving our animal origins, or a dualism between an elitist conception of art and the commonalities of human life so dear to his own vision,[11] or the admis-sion of the compositional unities of art that might threaten to reintroduce the excesses of Idealism. It may even help to explain Dewey's extremely dampened acknowledgment of his own Hegelian proclivities. (There's no mention, for instance, of G. E. Moore's attack on "organic unities" of Hegel's sort, in *Art as Experience*, which notoriously appeared some ten or so years before Dewey's own book appeared. To be honest, I sense a loss of philosophical nerve on Dewey's part.)

I take this to be a piece of the inherent weakness of Dewey's dialectic of "experience" and "*an* experience" ("a consummatory experience"). The better maneuver (if I may call it that) lies on the very surface of his argument, but Dewey is not prepared to seize it.

Dewey's phrasing is hardly an accident. For when he turns to address the arts, he begins this way:

> It has been repeatedly intimated that there is a difference between the art product (statue, painting or whatever), and the *work* of art. The first is physical and potential; the latter is active and experienced.... In the previous chapter, I emphasized the dependence of this final work upon the existence of rhythms in nature; as I pointed out, they are the conditions of form in experience and hence of expression. But esthetic experience, the work of art in its actuality, is *perception*. Only as these rhythms, even if embodied in an outer object that is itself a product of art, become a rhythm in experience itself are they esthetic.[12]

Here, Dewey clearly avoids admitting the primacy of the cultural: he means to capture whatever it might signify, by admitting the "art product" (a mere physical object) and the "work of art" (now transformed into a creaturely experience). But that can't possibly be enough. I don't mean to say that Dewey actually ignores the cultural complexity of art. But when he speaks of culture directly (which is remarkably rare in *Art as Experience*), he says no more than this:

> As the developing growth of an individual from embryo to maturity is the result of interaction of organism with surroundings, so culture is the product not of efforts of men put forth in a void or just upon themselves, but of prolonged and cumulative interaction with environment. The depth of the responses stirred by works of art shows *their* continuity with the operations of this enduring experience. The works and the responses they evoke are continuous with the very processes of living as these are carried to unexpected happy fulfillment.[13]

Culture is admitted only when it is, or can be, easily absorbed within the biology of animal life.

I glimpse in all this Dewey's paraphrase of Santayana's materialism (and paradox) and the stubborn adherence to the biologized idiom of "experience" and "an experience." I doubt it can be enough for a philosophy of art, though it has a distinctive Darwinian ring—and relevance. It's certainly not the case that Dewey fails to consider what are usually regarded as the aesthetic features of particular works of art.[14] But when he actually focuses on "esthetic experience," he's clearly more interested in how our engagement with the arts enhances life itself:

> To grasp the sources of esthetic experience [he says] it is . . . necessary to have recourse to animal life below the human scale. . . . It is mere ignorance that leads . . . to the supposition that connection of art and esthetic perception with experience signifies a lowering of their significance and dignity. Experience in the degree in which it *is* experience is heightened vitality. . . . Because experience is the fulfillment of an organism in its struggles and achievements in a world of things, it is art in germ. Even in its rudimentary forms, it contains the promise of that delightful perception which is esthetic experience.[15]

If the point of all this is clear—as it surely is—then Dewey resolves Santayana's worry by tethering our interest in the arts to the enhancement of the pleasure of life itself. That's not enough for our understanding of the arts, but it's well on its way to a reformulation of Dewey's *ethics*.

I have no objection to Dewey's theme: it's a genuinely lovely sentiment—and hardly false for that reason. Dewey's argument is impeccable in its own terms:

[*a*] Form is a character of every experience that is *an* experience.

[*b*] Art in its specific sense enacts more deliberately and fully the conditions that effect that unity.

[*c*] [Form therefore] marks the matter of an experience that is carried to consummation [that is, "*to its own integral fulfillment*"].[16]

I see little room for improvement here: the argument's the nerve of Dewey's entire doctrine. But it vaporizes the conceptual connection between the metaphysics of a work of art and the consummatory moment that putatively transforms the "material thing" into "an experience" (agreeing, thus far at least, with Santayana); Dewey then adroitly moves the entire discussion onto the more strategic (already prepared) plane of discourse meant to engage the formulation of the good life.[17] Dewey means that there must be a proper fit between our engagement with the "thing" itself and our "experiencing" it: the consummation, he assumes, is pertinent all right; but how *that* part of the analysis proceeds vis-à-vis the normal questions of the philosophy of art is hardly Dewey's primary concern. *Art as Experience* is really an essay in moral philosophy, now sometimes fashionably termed "aestheticization"—opportunistically advanced as a reading of Wittgenstein's dictum, "ethics and aesthetics are one" as yielding the supposedly pragmatist proposal that "the aesthetic [is rightly] the preferred model and criterion for the good life."[18]

2.

Beardsley sees "nearly all" of Dewey's themes (in *Art as Experience*) as having "been made explicit [already] in *Experience and Nature*": for instance, the "basic category of 'experience' as the interaction between organism and environment— not the subjective pole only, but the whole transaction—man's 'doing and under-going' as [Dewey] says in *Art as Experience*"; also, what Dewey calls "histories" (in *Experience and Nature*), "the prototypes of '*an* experience' in the later book ... of a 'sort' [like other, more standard experiences, that nevertheless] afford 'consummations.'"[19] But Beardsley nowhere challenges Dewey's deeper code, which obscures the full import of his (that is, Dewey's) verdict, namely, that the "art product" (as in painting) must be no more than a mere physical object—a dictum that must be false, if artworks are able to be expressive or representational or semiotically significant; *and*, second, that the "work of art" has no constitutive physical properties at all (in the sense of the art product) since it is "transformed" into "an experience" involving the "product"—which formulation must then also be false or paradoxical, being the inverse of Santayana's claim).[20] Dewey's "dualism" is perfectly plain here.

I confess I find Dewey's argument an embarrassing extravagance, almost a dereliction of duty. I salute Dewey's biological exuberance but hardly its philosophical exhaust. I'm certain an analogous argument could be mounted so as to link the would-be "consummatory" experience of intellectual satisfaction and the pursuit of science—without ever providing a proper sense of what to understand by the enterprise of science! There's the worry. Read in the light of pragmatism's extraordinary revival at the end of the twentieth century, it would be a mistake not to offer any clue at all to the correction needed.

I have my own conviction in this matter, which I take to be congenial to pragmatism's newest prospects and the known demands of the philosophy of art. But I have no wish to recommend my view as a replacement for Dewey's account. There's no possibility of that: *Art as Experience* rounds out Dewey's vision in a remarkably apt way that, very probably, only Dewey could have shaped. It leads wherever it leads, in fulfilling the expectations of *Experience and Nature*. Nevertheless, succeeding there, it fails to meet the needs of the philosophy of art in whatever spirit now collects contributions from the most diverse sources. I'm afraid Dewey's solution could bring pragmatist aesthetics to a screeching halt if ever it became our paradigm. Perhaps it matches Santayana's paradox; but it nowhere attempts to answer either puzzle. It couldn't possibly succeed by turning away from the analysis of the "art product" to the analysis of "consummatory experience."

Let me suggest, therefore, a minimal thread of philosophical reflection that pragmatism might well consider pursuing, that would (I would say) be entirely congenial to Dewey's (and to the rest of classic pragmatism's) avoidance of reductionism and dualism—and florid Idealisms—as well as to Dewey's attraction to historicity and Darwinian themes. It would need to be bolder and more explicit, metaphysically, on the matter of cultural emergence and the *sui generis* distinctions of the cultural world itself; also, more hospitable to the possibility, within the space of cultural emergence, that the human self (whose analysis has plainly baffled the entire history of Western philosophy) may prove (I think it will) to be a historied, functional, emergent artifact of cultural processes centered preeminently in the mastery of a home language and what such mastery makes possible among the diverse primate (infant) offspring of *Homo sapiens*, whose own parental generations have already been transformed into societies of apt selves.

My own view is that these adjustments are needed *now*, not merely to save pragmatist aesthetics from Dewey's near-stalemate, but to bring any comprehensive, current philosophy of art into reasonable accord with the most salient themes of Hegelian and Darwinian theory looming over the entire space of Western thought. I would say Dewey fails to bring the Hegelian themes to bear on the analysis of the structure of a work of art—*a fortiori*, on the analysis of the interpretation of artworks.

The argument would have to be grounded in the contrast between two very different sorts of evolutionary process that are themselves complexly intertwined in the career of what we count as the human: one, neo-Darwinian evolutionary biology, which includes the biochemistry of genetic forces; the other, the artifactual evolution (and effects of such evolution, incarnate in biological processes) of true language and what language makes determinately possible in the way of further, culturally significant, *sui generis* (artifactual) transforms of what otherwise belong entirely to physical and biological nature. The theme is absent from the reflections of the classic pragmatists—but I would say, it's more congenial there than in a large part of Western philosophies of art.

The transformation of hominid primates (human infants!) into apt selves is, of course, the single most important, most extraordinary feat achieved through the confluence of biological and cultural evolution (species-wide) and of developmental biology and enculturation (individually, ontogentically so to say). My thought is that the whole of Western philosophy has, in speaking of the formation of persons or selves, fatally restricted itself to the presumed paideutic (read: Aristotelian) details of what I call "internal *Bildung*"—if we agree to follow recent suggestions (notably triggered by John McDowell), however deprived of Darwinian inspiration or (frankly) any grasp of the inherent limitations of a merely Darwinian account of selves.

To be pertinent at all, internal *Bildung* must, I dare claim, be indissolubly linked to the larger processes of what I name "external *Bildung*"—meaning, by that, the gradual evolution of certain prehominid primates leading to the original advent of *Homo sapiens* and Neanderthal and, thence, to the very different cultural evolution of prelinguistic communicative skills reliably transmitted by socially acquired (but biologically embodied) means, from prehominid species, culminating in the invention of true language.[21] The deep lesson that results from bringing the neo-Darwinian discovery of the late formation of language and artifactual selves into accord with the Hegelian reading of *Bildung* lies with the historied contingencies of the self's career and the contructivist nature of our theories (the self's theories) of the natural and cultural world.

The key to pragmatism's best prospects (I would say, the whole of philosophy's prospects) rests with acknowledging and elaborating the implications of the artifactual nature of the self, which give an entirely new meaning to the themes of historicity (regarding languaged thought) and cultural creation (involving the arts and political life at least).[22] I take the artifactual nature of the self and of works of art to be so closely matched, metaphysically, that we are pretty well obliged to concede (*a*) that artworks can be produced ("uttered," as I prefer to say) only by artifactually constituted selves; (*b*) that whatever is uttered in the way of exercising human agency entails a *sui generis* form of causality that cannot be specified in accord with any merely "relational" models of causality standard among the physical sciences (the Humean sense, for instance, or any cognate sense) that treat cause and effect as mutually independent: "utterance," as in deliberately raising one's arm or in executing a pas de deux or in speaking, is logically too "close" a linkage to fit the Humean model, though external causal regularities can always be recovered within the molar bounds of artifactual agency (the action of Michelangelo's tools, for instance, on shaping the marble of the *David*, or, indeed, the "external" influence of Cézanne on the Cubists); and (*c*) the unique features of agency, cast in terms of the transformation of physical and biological factors into determinably and discernibly encultured elements (as in uttering expressive, representational, symbolic, semiotically significant "things"), account for the effective transformation of material things into cultural artifacts.

This very small but essential philosophical adjustment, missing in Dewey (and Santayana), completely obviates the need for Dewey's and Santayana's paradoxes. There may be many ways in which the adjustment may be effected: that now proves to be an entirely subsidiary matter. But what's decisive here is that every such maneuver rests on a principled distinction between biology and culture. The idea is all but ignored in the entire history that runs from Aristotle to our own day—notably, in Dewey, where it shouldn't have been missed, unless you favor the lax sense in which Aristotle's biology might be able to be read as permitting a systematic distinction between biology and culture—to include the disjunction between biological and cultural evolution.

Apart from the Darwinian and neo-Darwinian opposition to admitting any *telos* in evolution and epigenetic development *and* apart from the perceived need to distinguish carefully between the logical behavior of physical and cultural concepts, the artifactuality thesis challenges in the most fundamental way the very idea of natural norms (of truth as well as of the value of agental commitment). All questions of cognition and rational freedom must go completely constructivist wherever we link internal and external *Bildung*: which (I would argue) *is* the constructivist upshot of Hegel's entire critique of Kant,[23] once we reach the pragmatists' incorporation of Darwin's themes.

I think this means that Dewey was distracted for some reason in insisting on the aesthetic primacy of consummatory experiences, which risks leading us into a needless cul-de-sac. (Remember Santayana.) Because, on the best argument, Dewey seems to have failed to notice that the resolution of his own and Santayana's paradoxes, viewed in accord with neo-Darwinian discoveries, would have allowed him to explicate the ampler, more daring resources of his own Hegelian inspiration—in effect, to unify his theories of art, morality, history, and the metaphysics of the self and culture in a manner powerful enough to have won out over the extremely hesitant, recent efforts of analytic philosophy to recover Hegel by another route.[24]

Dewey's *Art as Experience* is (I think we must conclude) a poor but vigorously advanced detour into a most implausible solution of his own version of Santayana's paradox. In fact, I can't see how he would ever have favored such a move if he had actually freed his philosophy from the remnants of the post-Kantian Idealism he worked so hard to discard. Surely, he remained entangled in the thought (as is sometimes also true of William James, who favors an empiricist analogue of Idealist or Kantian representationalism) that "experience" retains some animal assurance of a realist connection to the world. But that this would have vindicated (in aesthetic contexts) the consummatory role of Dewey's claim (about having "an experience") or that it could have counted as a solution of the paradox Dewey shares with Santayana is more than difficult to make convincing. These last questions, of course, are merely expressions of textual scruple: what is defensible regarding what is "given" in the consummatory way—applied to different works of art—still counts against the reading.

14.

JOHN DEWEY AND THE
ONTOLOGY OF ART

Russell Pryba

1. INTRODUCTION

Arecent exhibition at the Hauser and Wirth Gallery in New York featured the performance artist William Pope L.'s "reinvention" of Allan Kaprow's installation piece *Yard*. In 1961 Kaprow, one of the founders of the Happening, filled the courtyard of the Martha Jackson Gallery with tires and objects wrapped in black tarpaper.[1] He instructed visitors to "rearrange the tires." Pope L.'s "reinvention" entitled *Yard (To Harrow)* consisted of over 1,200 tires and stacks of presumably filled body bags illuminated by hanging red lights and accompanied by the sounds of a narrative read by an Obama impersonator. In addition to the differences in presentation, materials, and social context of the two installations, the opening of Pope L.'s recontextualization of *Yard* was attended by the usual institutional trappings of the art world: velvet ropes, security guards, and long lines.

If one subscribed to the Institutional theory of art[2] (a view that Dewey would reject as the contemporary heir of the museum conception of art) then the velvet ropes and security guards would indicate that Pope L.'s *Yard (To Harrow)* is a candidate for aesthetic appreciation fully endorsed by the art world. Given the institutional status of *Yard (To Harrow)* there is no question, the Institutional theorist would argue, that it is an artwork. This difference alone is enough to alter the meaning of Pope L.'s and Kaprow's versions of *Yard*. In 1961, *Yard* was a daring foray into the avant-garde, a precursor of performance art, and a glaring reminder that all art is, and always has been, participatory, an interaction between a human being and an environment. In 2009, Pope L.'s *Yard (To Harrow)* cannot be said to evoke the same challenges to the categories of art as

Yard initially did in 1961. Rather, it is a reminder that even un-art, as Kaprow came to call his work, can be taken in by the artworld and be given a certain status by an institutional fiat. In the intervening years the very meaning of climbing on, and interacting with, tires has subtly shifted from being a challenge to the very categories of art and to the distinction between art and the meaning of everyday life to a reminder of the power of the art world to appropriate challenges to its own authority.

In addition to the differing perspectives on the relationship between artworks and the institutions of art that *Yard* and *Yard (To Harrow)* provide, focusing on the historical distance between the two works can illustrate how the two works have very different meanings. For example, Pope L.'s *Yard (To Harrow)* possesses political meanings that are by necessity absent in *Yard*. By adding an Obamaesque voiceover narration, and replacing the tarpaper with body bags, *Yard (To Harrow)* raises questions about the juxtaposition of the politics of hope with the ongoing involvement of the United States in two armed conflicts. In the context in which *Yard (To Harrow)* is presented, used tires and body bags can both be understood as omnipresent, yet too often overlooked, externalities of the American automotive way of life. Read in such a way *Yard (To Harrow)* makes visceral the costs of maintaining the luxuries of modern American life by literally showing how these costs pile up. What is significantly different about the audience's experiences of the two *Yards* is more than the perspective they present on matters of local importance to the art world. Rather, both works, taken together, point to the important role that social context plays in transmitting and framing the meaning of a work of art. That *Yard* is a Happening makes it clear that the work is an experience rather than an object. This format makes it easier to abstract the transactional aspect of art from the experience of the work itself in a way that is often harder to glean in a more "ontologically stable" work such as a painting or sculpture. Thus, *Yard (To Harrow)* stands in relation to its own time and place as well as commenting directly on its relationship to Kaprow's *Yard*. By standing in this relationship, *Yard (To Harrow)* cannot be said to embody the same sort of daring challenge to art itself as did *Yard*. Yet, the seeming inability of *Yard (To Harrow)* to exist otherwise than as a reference to *Yard* is augmented by the complexity of new meanings that it provides by illustrating the role of the context of the experience of a work of art to the work itself.

Both Kaprow's work and Dewey's aesthetic theory present the same challenge to aesthetics, what might be called "the disappearance of the art object." The term "art," for both Dewey and Kaprow, does not signify an object at all but rather an activity—an experience that is marked by a pervasive qualitative wholeness that sets it apart from the stream of ordinary experience as *an experience*, as aesthetic. Art for Dewey is a triadic relation comprised by artist-art product-audience. Further, the triadic relation as a whole is located in a cultural context that partially determines the way that a work of art will be experienced. What is culturally determined in this sense is the range of possible salient meanings that a work can have within a given context. Whereas a participant (Kaprow dubbed them "happeners") in Kaprow's 1961 *Yard* might have been concerned with challenging the conventions of artistic presentation amenable to the confines of the art world (or with simply having a new and possibly weird experience) a participant in Pope L.'s *Yard (To Harrow)* might be concerned with the relationship between the two *Yards* or with simply being seen at an anticipated art world event. What is in evidence in comparing the possible experiences available to the participant in each instance as it pertains to Dewey's aesthetic theory is that when one node of the triadic relation which constitutes a work of art changes not only does the work of art change but new vistas of meaning are opened up as well.

That Kaprow's un-art should serve so readily as an example of Dewey's aesthetics is not surprising given the documented influence that *Art as Experience* had upon Kaprow as a young graduate student at Columbia in the early 1950s. In the introduction to Kaprow's collection of essays, *Essays on the Blurring of Art and Life*, the curator and art historian Jeff Kelley draws attention to the notes that Kaprow left in the margins in his copy of *Art as Experience*. These notes include "art not separate from experience" and "environment is a process of interaction."[3] Those familiar with Dewey's *Art as Experience* recognize these ideas from Chapter One, "The Live Creature." Dewey's diagnosis that the arts in the Western world had been set apart from the vital processes of human life as it is lived is significant for understanding the influence that the exposure to Dewey's theory had on Kaprow's artistic development. The effect of the severance of art from life had, as Kelley puts it, "been to idealize 'esthetic' experience by assigning it to certain classes of culturally sanctioned objects and events. These, in turn, were sequestered from the currents of communal life according to the boundaries of taste, professional expertise, and the conventions of presentation and display. ... Even the capacity to *have* an esthetic experience had been estheticized, becoming the purview of experts.... Art per se became the exclusive site of esthetic experience."[4] Kaprow's importance then, for Kelley, is that he worked to "shift that site from the specialized zones of art toward the particular places and occasions of everyday life."[5] That is, he worked to put Dewey's theory into practice. The art world's absorption of the initial challenges that *Yard* raised as to the appropriate materials and presentation of a work of art has the consequence of making aesthetic experience more passive, both mentally and bodily. It serves to counteract the exact point that Dewey and Kaprow emphasize regarding aesthetic experience. As Kelley puts it, it serves to aestheticize aesthetic experience by severing it from the broader context of everyday experience from which aesthetic experience emerges. Since *Yard (To Harrow)* is comfortably situated within the channels of the contemporary art world, it is robbed of the ability to effectively raise the question of the relationship between art and life in the same way as *Yard* did when it was first presented.

There is a particular passage in *Art as Experience* which may help to discern Dewey's influence on Kaprow, whose later un-art activities included having people carry cinder blocks up flights of stairs, washing a friend's kitchen floor with nothing but a Q-tip and saliva and even brushing his teeth. In this particular passage Dewey illustrates the distinction between an emotional expression that is aesthetic and the mere discharge of an emotional impulse by way of the example of an irritated person setting out to clean a room:

> Irritation may be let go like an arrow directed at a target and produce some change in the outer world. But having an outer effect is something very different from ordered use of objective conditions in order to give objective fulfillment to the emotion. The latter alone is expression and the emotion that attaches itself to, or is interpenetrated by, the resulting object is esthetic. If the person puts his room to rights as a matter of routine he is anesthetic. But if his original emotion of impatient irritation has been ordered and tranquillized by what he has done, the orderly room reflects back to him the change that has taken place in himself. He feels not that he has accomplished a needed chore but has done something emotionally fulfilling. His emotion as thus "objectified" is esthetic.[6]

In addition to illustrating the potential suggestive influence that *Art as Experience* had on Kaprow's later un-art activities, the above quotation also illustrates Dewey's awareness of an important feature of the metaphysics of art: embodiment. The difference, for Dewey, between the mere discharge of an emotion and an expression (the difference between the anesthetic and the aesthetic) is that in an expression the emotion becomes "objectified"—that is, it is embodied in an object or event. In this case the orderly room embodies the emotional irritation that itself becomes ordered through the process of putting the room in order. Thus, for an emotion to be aesthetic, it has to embodied in an object in such a way for the object to reflect the process of change that has taken place in the agent themselves. This is an important point to stress because it provides a way of understanding the relationship between Dewey's claim that art is an activity and the resulting objects that are produced through that activity. It is not simply that an activity has to be consummatory for it to be aesthetic, but further that the result of the activity is that aesthetic qualities may become embodied in an object or event. We need not take Dewey literally in this passage and restrict that which can be embodied in an object to emotions. Rather, it can be taken to indicate a general metaphysical point about artworks, that they are, as Arthur Danto has put it, *embodied meanings*.

In what follows I elaborate on the role of embodiment in Dewey's aesthetic theory and indicate the way in which it provides a point of convergence with Joseph Margolis's cultural ontology. Before addressing this point, I shall address some preliminary concerns regarding speaking of Dewey and the ontology of art and present the background of Dewey's metaphysics in such a way as to assuage any initial misgivings.

2. THE PLACE OF METAPHYSICS IN DEWEY'S PHILOSOPHY

Given Dewey's and Kaprow's joint emphasis on reconnecting art and the everyday by way of drawing attention to art as experience, it may appear as though there is little, if any, room for the ontology of art in Dewey's aesthetics. This is particularly so if the ontology of art is understood as investigating the peculiar being of artworks qua objects and the aesthetic properties that those objects possess independent of any aesthetic experience of them. On this interpretation of the role of the ontology of art, Dewey's aesthetic theory might be understood as providing reasons why one should abandon the ontology of art altogether! Given this construal of the purpose of an ontology of art, there would be little point in attempting to indicate how it might be fruitfully incorporated within Dewey's larger critique of metaphysical dualisms. This might be termed the "Rortian option" for understanding the place of the ontology of art, and metaphysics more generally, in Dewey's philosophy.[7] To insist that Dewey's aesthetic theory can be reconciled with the ontology of art understood in this narrow way is to misread Dewey and to fail to grasp the significance of the reconstruction of the philosophical tradition that he attempted. It is to fall back onto the claim that one can fruitfully investigate the properties of artworks outside of the transactional situation that constitutes the core of Dewey's naturalistic approach to philosophy and art.

However, one need not adopt Rorty's interpretation of Dewey's metaphysics or view investigations into the ontology of art as excluded by Dewey's aesthetic theory. Rather, Dewey can be seen as offering a positive metaphysical theory that isolates the "generic traits" of experience by way of his emphasis on the interactions that take places between the organism and its environment, both physical and cultural, which are always encountered by way of "the situation." Richard Bernstein has stated this reading of Dewey as follows:

> Dewey argues that the claim that qualities are either exclusively mental or physical, subjective or objective, is based on a mistake. Qualities as experienced belong to a situation or context. A situation cuts across the dualism of subject and object, mental or physical. More precisely, these distinctions are instituted within an inclusive context or situation. Mental and physical, subject and object are not independent realms; they are functional distinctions instituted within situations for specific purposes.... Questions, then, of the type "Are qualities merely mental or physical?" are misleading. Any specific quality may be classified as either or both, depending on the specific situation and the purposes of the classification.[8]

Thus, following Bernstein, questions like "Are aesthetic properties located in the art object or are they merely subjective?" would be indicative of an ontology of art that Dewey would reject. Yet, it would remain permissible to inquire into the ontological status of artworks, what they are about and how they embody that meaning, in terms of a functional distinction that serves to make the overall situation in which aesthetic experience occurs better understood. To speak of Dewey and the ontology of art is not to read into Dewey a bifurcation of the experience of art into the separate realms of subject and object. Rather, it is to select qualities that artworks possess as "objective" in order to more fully understand the role that artworks play as one node in the triadic relation that, for Dewey, constitutes a work of art. It is the claim of this paper that without an understanding of the contribution that artworks qua artworks make to aesthetic experience, it will not be possible to understand Dewey's aesthetic theory as a whole. That artworks are experienced as *having* aesthetic qualities within the context of the situation as a whole should not be reduced to the claim that those properties are located exclusively in the art object. However, given that artworks consistently comprise one aspect of the situation where an aesthetic experience is likely to occur (although this clearly not a necessary condition for aesthetic experience for Dewey), it is reasonable to investigate the relationship of artworks qua objects to the situation as a whole. This is not to claim that artworks are the special and exclusive site of aesthetic experience. It also does not deny that other objects of experience may in fact lead to aesthetic experience. It is simply to recognize that artworks, more than any other cultural product, are experienced as *having* aesthetic qualities. So long as this fact of experience is not reified into a form of realism that places those properties exclusively in the art object rather than in the situation, it is not inconsistent to speak of the place of the ontology of art in Dewey's aesthetic theory.

There is a second reason that it is permissible and perhaps helpful to provide an ontology of art that is consistent with Dewey's larger metaphysical commitments. It is well known that while working on the unfinished reintroduction to *Experience and Nature*, Dewey lamented his optimism regarding the possibility of reconstructing the meaning of "experience" in such a way to make his theories properly understood. If he were to rewrite *Experience and Nature*, Dewey says, "I would abandon the term 'experience' because of my growing realization that the historical obstacles which prevented understanding of my use of 'experience' are, for all practical purposes, insurmountable. I would substitute the term 'culture' because with its meanings as now firmly established it can fully and freely carry my philosophy of experience."[9] However, the reason for preferring the term "culture" to "experience" is not justified solely in terms of the difficulty of altering the historical connotations of the term "experience." Insofar as Dewey stressed the continuities between the religious, aesthetic, political, economic, moral, etc. rather than the compartmentalization of each into their own distinct spheres, the term "experience" was inadequate for illustrating the "reciprocal interconnections" between them. Further, the accustomed meanings associated with the term "experience" in philosophy seemed to all to readily support the idea that the aesthetic, religious, political, economic, moral, etc. were in fact distinct spheres of experience rather than phases of one overarching "experience" that could be fruitfully understood through descriptive metaphysics. Dewey continues, "instead of separating, isolating and insulating the many aspects of a common life, 'culture' holds them together in their human and humanistic unity—a service which 'experience' has ceased to render. What 'experience' now fails to do and 'culture' can successfully do for philosophy is of utmost importance if philosophy is to be comprehensive without becoming stagnant."[10] That contemporary philosophy has become the purview of a few specialists working in heavily compartmentalized areas of inquiry is a testament to the stagnation that Dewey feared would result from the neglect of the philosophy of culture.

At the very end of his career Dewey moved away from a "philosophy of experience" to a "philosophy of culture" because only a philosophy of culture could bind together the features of a "common life" in a "humanistic unity." Since part of that unity is comprised, but not exhausted by, the material aspects of culture, a metaphysics of culture would be required in order to identify the generic traits of the various areas of human endeavor that had frequently been treated as isolated from one another by the history of philosophy. The choice between a comprehensive philosophy and philosophical stagnation rests upon providing a philosophical account of culture that incorporates both the ideal and material aspects of human life. This, in turn, would require an ontology of culture which is both thoroughly naturalistic and nonreductive. Seen in this way elucidating an ontology of art that is consistent with Dewey's naturalism is a propaedeutic for providing a more general metaphysics of culture which could accommodate the kind of comprehensive vision for philosophy that Dewey saw as necessary toward the end of his life.

Finally, any tension that may exist in speaking of the ontology of art within Dewey's philosophy of art is mitigated when the ontology of art is understood nonreductively. That is, the ontology of art does not necessarily focus exclusively on the material constituents of the work of art as might be feared by those who are apprehensive about accommodating ontological investigations within Dewey's philosophical project. On the contrary, some contemporary formulations of the ontology of art, such as Joseph Margolis's, reinforces Dewey's rejection of dualism and reductionism. What is revealed by looking at artworks qua objects is that they are a special kind of entity, cultural entities, which possess, in virtue of their location in the existential matrix of a particular culture, properties which are irreducible to the material objects from which they emerge. These emergent properties, labeled as "Intentional properties" by Margolis, are what mark off culture as *sui generis*. Further, since culture is itself fully historicized, recognizing the status of artworks as "cultural emergents" explains the metaphysical possibility that artworks change meaning over time. Construed this way, the ontology of art is not the investigation of the timeless nature of artworks enshrined in metaphysics but rather a description of the continually unfolding process or *history* that every artwork is. The ontology of art, following Margolis, is one part of a larger metaphysics of culture that enables us to focus and isolate, in reflection, the peculiar metaphysical status of art and other cultural entities. This in turn can illuminate how culture operates within, while simultaneously penetrating, our experience. Further, it is only through a metaphysics of culture that it can be most fully understood how "culture" denotes the overall context in which all experience, aesthetic or otherwise, occurs. Seen in this manner, the ontology of art is not anathema to Dewey's philosophy of culture but rather it is a necessary piece of understanding what culture is, by what means it is transmitted, and how culture itself is the context or situation in which all "experience" ultimately takes place.

3. DEWEY'S AESTHETIC THEORY

According to Dewey the term "art" does not denote "things" but rather an activity. The "aesthetic" is not a set of properties that are best instantiated by a certain class of objects called "artworks" but is rather the quality of activity or experience that is consummatory and marked by unity rather than being disruptive or inchoate. This is the difference between experience and *an experience*. For Dewey *an experience* has "its own individualizing quality"[11] that sets it apart from the undifferentiated stream of experience. Art then is a quality of activity—specifically the quality of being aesthetic or consummatory. Yet, Dewey does not remain silent regarding the material constituents of works of art, or what he calls the *product of art*. In fact, in making the art product/art work distinction, Dewey is an important antecedent to Joseph Margolis's more recent distinction between the physically embodying medium of a work of art and the culturally emergent entity that the artwork *is* (where "is" here is not the "is" of identity but rather the "is" of embodiment). Although Margolis does not follow Dewey in claiming that the term *artwork* denotes an intrinsic quality of activity or experience, as we shall see Margolis's ontology of art is compatible with Dewey's analysis of the art product and how it serves as a material base from which artworks emerge. Even if one were to ultimately reject Dewey's view that art is experience, or his expression theory, Dewey can still be understood as suggesting a nonreductive ontology of art. Reading Dewey in this way not only illustrates why Dewey is an important historical antecedent of more fully developed antireductionist ontologies of art like Margolis's but also can serve as the framework for developing a cultural realism that can avoid the persistently lurking charge that Dewey's aesthetics is idealistic.

In Dewey's analysis, an art product (a painting, sculpture, building, poem, etc.) is only potentially an artwork. It achieves actual artwork status when it is taken up as part of an individual's experience in such a manner as to be aesthetic—as *an experience*. Thus, the physical embodying medium of an artwork is "self-identical throughout the ages. But as an artwork it is recreated every time it is esthetically experienced."[12] The trouble arises when one considers what Dewey means when he claims that an artwork is *recreated* every time it is aesthetically experienced. One way to read this claim is that an artwork is not completed until it is taken up as part of an individual's experience, a reading that is supported by Dewey's analysis of the triadic relation between artist–art product–audience that constitutes the work of art. Therefore a functionally infinite amount of artworks can emerge from the product of art because of the different relationships in which it stands to different people at different times in different contexts. Another, more problematic way of taking this claim is that each individual (re)creates a *different* work of art when they experience it aesthetically. It is undoubtedly true that different people bring different funded meanings to their individual experiences of a work of art. Art means different things to different people, and this is greatly impacted by the background knowledge that a person brings to his or her experience of a work of art. But I think that we should resist the idea that the artwork *goes out of existence* when it is not being experienced aesthetically and that different people create different works when they experience them aesthetically.

This difficulty in part results from the limitations of English terms to adequately express what Dewey intended theoretically. However, the difficulty in speaking about art as experience is that the artwork seemingly exists prior to being experienced as *an* experience and yet is also a consequence of that experience having taken place. Nor is this tendency of speech confined to Dewey. Commenting on the significance of *an* experience having occurred, Philip W. Jackson claimed:

> What is special about such occurrences is not simply that their parts hang together to form a whole. Nor is it simply that we find them to be momentarily satisfying. What adds to their importance are the enduring changes that they produce. They leave in their wake a changed world. The contents of the world have been increased by one more painting or poem or piece of music and, more importantly, both the experiencer, whether artist or art appreciator, and the object experienced have changed. The experiencer changes by undergoing a transformation of the self, gaining a broadened perspective, a shift in attitude, an increase in knowledge, or any of a host of other enduring alterations of a psychological nature. The object of experience changes through the acquisition of new meanings. These meanings, once disclosed are potentially communicable to everyone. They thereby augment the fund of interpretive possibilities available to all who subsequently come upon the same object or event.[13]

Jackson nicely indicates the tension in Dewey's thought that I wish to emphasize. If *an* experience truly produces one more painting or poem or piece of music, then there is no hope of anyone ever subsequently experiencing the *same* painting, poem, or piece of music. It is important not to conflate the acquisition of new *meanings* with the creation of new *artworks*. This is more than a simple failure of language to express the complexity of Dewey's thought. Rather, it indicates the place in which an ontology of art is required to augment Dewey's theory of art as experience in order to explain how it is possible that artworks acquire new meaning(s) over time without simultaneously confusing the individuation conditions for that work. It is not controversial to claim that an interpretation completes a work of art and thereby different interpretations may, in some sense, constitute different works. However, it is far more ontologically economical to explain how, in virtue of their ontological status as cultural entities, artworks can bear multiple and divergent interpretations rather than multiplying entities every time an artwork is experienced anew. One need not give up on the ability of art to change the world or the transformative power that art possesses to improve the self. However, these abilities have to be reinforced by being able to give an account of what an artwork *is* that permits it to be experienced and understood in a variety of, often divergent, ways. There can be no doubt that if, for example, one were to read some illuminating piece of art criticism before experiencing a specific work of art, then that piece of art criticism would become part of the situation in which the artwork is encountered. However, what has been produced is not necessarily a new painting but rather a painting-under-an-interpretation.

Most encounters with art do not produce new interpretative possibilities that can be said to challenge the received meanings of the work. A truly novel interpretative possibility, one that alters the situation through which a work of art is encountered, does in fact change the way in which one experiences a work of art. However, there must first be an understanding of how artworks can in fact bear meanings (through embodying them) before it will be possible to have anything theoretically fruitful to say about acquisition of *new* meanings. In other words, it is the ontological status of artworks as culturally emergent entities, with determinable, rather than fully determinate natures (as physical objects are thought to have), which grounds interpretive practices. Previous interpretative possibilities and meanings are embodied in a work of art prior to any particular individual experience of that work, whether that experience ends up being aesthetic or not. This is so because these meanings are a part of the culturally salient features that a work of art possesses, built up over time, and which become part of the context in which that work is subsequently encountered. If we were completely ignorant of what artworks *are* it is hard to see how we could ever experience them aesthetically. Since artworks are culturally emergent entities, their metaphysical nature comprises a part of every situation in which a particular work is experienced. In order to explain the possibility of having an aesthetic experience of a work of art, it must already be seen as something that is a potential bearer of culturally significant meaning but also that that meaning is open to (re)interpretation. Explaining how artworks embodied their meanings is a task for the ontology of art. Therefore, in the absence of an adequate ontology of art, Dewey's emphasis on the triadic nature of the experience of art cannot be completely described. Part of the situation or context of an aesthetic experience is an account of culture that explains how cultural entities are meaningful.

4. TOWARD A DEWEYAN ONTOLOGY OF ART

Since the art product/work of art distinction is central in Dewey's aesthetics and is the textual support for connecting Dewey's own aesthetic theory with Margolis's nonreductive ontology of art and cultural realism, it is prudent to more carefully observe the way that Dewey draws the distinction. In the following passage Dewey draws attention to the claim that artworks do not have fixed natures:

> The *product* of art—temple, painting, statue, poem—is not the *work* of art. The work takes place when a human being cooperates with the product so that the outcome is an experience that is enjoyed because of its liberating and ordered properties. If "art" denoted objects, if it were genuinely a noun, art-objects could be marked off into genera and these subdivided into species. This sort of division was applied to animals as long as they were believed to be things fixed in themselves. But the system of classification had to change when they were discovered to be differentiated in a stream of vital activity. Classifications became genetic, designating as accurately as may be the special place of particular forms of continuity of life on earth. If art is an intrinsic quality of activity, we cannot divide and subdivide it. We can only follow the differentiation of the activity into different modes as it impinges on different materials and employs different media.[14]

The first thing to note about this passage is that Dewey refers to products of art as paintings, sculptures, buildings, and poems. I do not think that this is Dewey merely being less than careful with his language. Paintings, sculptures, buildings, and poems are cultural artifacts that only have meaning in the context of the collective life of a community. As cultural entities they possess properties (namely, cultural or Intentional properties) which the physical objects of which they are comprised cannot possibly possess. Secondly, for Dewey, the claim that artworks cannot be subdivided is a consequence of their not being "things fixed in themselves." Therefore, the various art forms—painting, sculpture, poetry, and architecture—do not represent a classificatory scheme for different sets of objects but rather are different modes into which the activity of art can flow. An interesting consequence of this view is that, for Dewey, the questions that inevitably arise regarding the art status of new media that were not traditionally categorized as art, such as film, would not arise. It should be no surprise that art, understood as an activity or an event in the way that Dewey understands it, should find new outlets for creativity in materials and media that are equally capable of leading to the kind of consummatory experience that is paradigmatic of the aesthetic. The prejudice of confining art to the fine arts as defined by Hegel has no place in Dewey's aesthetic theory, as we would expect it would not. That we have grown accustomed to relegating art and the aesthetic to the paradigmatic forms of the fine arts is, in Dewey's view, a consequence of understanding the work of art as an object.

However, an ontology of art that recognizes the historicity of cultural entities, and thereby recognizes that they do not have fixed natures, would likewise permit the kind of genetic analysis of artworks that Dewey presumably thought could only be accounted for by speaking of art in terms of a quality of activity. This would allow for one to comfortably speak of art as an activity while also questioning the nature of artworks as cultural entities because neither alternative would exhaust the description of what art is on its own accord. Rather, they both represent features of the situation that may be highlighted, in reflection, in an attempt to better understand the situation in its totality. Further, both views (that art is an activity and that art is a cultural emergent) entail the historicity of artworks as a result of their being irrevocably embedded in the ongoing stream of communal human life. Margolis and Dewey defended complementary views insofar as both deny that artworks have fixed natures. According to Margolis since an artwork is an "utterance" of culturally enriched human selves, artworks have "histories" rather than "natures."[15] To claim that artworks are "things fixed in themselves" would be to deny the historicity of human life. Margolis's use of the term "utterance," which explicitly invokes the idea of communication, rests comfortably alongside Dewey's emphasis on the communication that takes place between an artist and an audience through the medium of an artwork. Artworks, and cultural entities generally, would not be possible if there were no culturally bound entities like human selves who could convey meaning(s) through an embodying medium to other culturally fluent selves. Therefore, the ontology of cultural entities, for Margolis, relies on the ontology of human selves. Since selves, for Margolis, are metaphysical "hybrids" of biology and culture, artworks as utterances of these selves are likewise metaphysically peculiar entities that are partially comprised of, but not exhausted by, a physical object in the same way in which human beings are partially comprised of but not reducible to a body.[16] That the meaning of artworks is in some sense dependant upon those that hear what the artwork "utters" is not cause to give up the notion that it can be fruitful to understand artworks as objects, albeit objects with less than fully determinate natures, in certain situations. Rather it is cause for developing a theory of the ontology of art that recognizes and explains how meaning is embodied and conveyed through art objects.

A summary of Margolis's view regarding the ontology of art would be helpful in elucidating this point. The following is a tally of the central claims of Margolis's ontology of art.

1. Physical nature and culture are distinguished primarily in terms of what lacks, and what possess Intentionality.
2. Intentionality is a term of art that meant to mark off a family of *sui generis* properties confined to the cultural world—these include expressive, representational, stylistic, rhetorical, symbolic, semiotic, linguistic, traditional, institutional, and genre-bound properties.
3. The cultural cannot be reduced to the physical because of possession of Intentional properties that the physical world necessarily lacks.
4. Yet, cultural entities are embodied in natural or physical entities and their properties are correspondingly incarnate in natural or physical properties.
5. Cultural entities emerge from physical entities.
6. Intentional properties are inherently interpretable, determinable but not determinate in the way we suppose physical properties to be.
7. Cultural entities have historied natures, or are histories, because Intentional properties, which form their natures, are themselves historicized and alterable as a result of the ongoing practice of reinterpretation, under the condition of historically changing experience.[17]

Margolis's ontology of art can treat artworks as objects without falling back on the claim that they have fixed natures by positing a *constructive or cultural realism* that recognizes the reality of culture, and thereby of artworks, in virtue of their possession of Intentional properties. This view explains the relationship between culture and nature in a nonreductive way, thereby, in the spirit of Dewey, avoiding the dualism of culture and nature. The advantage of Margolis's over Dewey's view is that the individual experience no longer bears the responsibility for accounting for the existence of a work of art. Rather, culture itself, which provides for the very possibility of the existence of human selves, experience, and artworks in the first place, can account for the distinction between a cultural entity and the physical thing in which it is embedded. This analysis avoids the implication that any individual aesthetic experience literally (re)creates or completes the work of art and thereby avoids the implication of idealism that has plagued Dewey's aesthetics from the onset. Margolis recognizes the significance of

Dewey's denial of the ontic/epistemic distinction and constructs his ontology of culture using this Deweyan insight as a guiding principle. Thus, Margolis is capable of capturing many Deweyan themes regarding both pragmatic metaphysics and aesthetics while simultaneously providing a theory of the peculiar kind of entities that artworks are.

Now to return to the point regarding Dewey's use of words painting, sculpture, poem to refer to the product of art. In Margolis's idiom this would amount to a category mistake. If it is permissible to treat the product of art as roughly equivalent to the physically embodying medium of a work of art, then the product of art is not a painting at all but rather paint on canvas. But is there any evidence to support this reading of Dewey? Does Dewey recognize and endorse the embodiment claim that is central to Margolis's formulation? Dewey does seem to recognize the importance of the material object as a condition of the very possibility of aesthetic experience:

> A work of fine art, a statue, building, drama, poem, novel, when done, is as much a part of the objective world as is a locomotive or a dynamo. And, as much as the latter its existence is causally conditioned by the coordination of materials and energies of the external world. I do not mean that this is the whole of the work of art; even the product of industrial art was made to serve a purpose and is actually, instead of potentially, a locomotive as it operates in conditions where it produces consequences beyond its bare physical being; as, namely, it transports human beings and goods. But I do mean that there can be no esthetic experience apart from the *object*, and that for an object to be the content of esthetic appreciation it must satisfy those *objective* conditions without which cumulation, conservation, reenforcement, transition into something more complete, are impossible. The general conditions of esthetic form . . . are objective in the sense of belonging to the world of physical materials and energies: while the later do not suffice for an esthetic experience, they are a *sine qua non* (an essential condition) of its existence.[18]

It is clear that Dewey recognizes that the aesthetic partially relies on the physical world but that this is not the whole of the work of art. The world of physical materials and energies is an essential part of the aesthetic but is not a sufficient condition for the aesthetic. This claim directly corresponds to the relationship of the cultural and the physical in Margolis's view. For Dewey, as we have seen, a work of art is done when it is taken up into an individual's experience and experienced aesthetically. Yet, Dewey's use of the phrase "work of art" here indicates the tension. If the work of art is only done when it has been aesthetically experienced it seems odd that it could be transformed into something more complete. This could easily be explained away by indicating that Dewey failed to observe the difference between his technical usage of the term "work of art" and its common meaning. But this is exactly the point! This slippage indicates that aesthetic experience is of artworks but does not complete or create them. Even Dewey seems here to be unable to shake the pervasive tendency to understand artworks as objects, albeit objects that are distinct from the physical world in which they are embodied. Just as the locomotive is only actually a locomotive when it produces consequences beyond its bare physical being, a work of art is only actually, not merely potentially, a work of art when it does the same. Yet, it appears on Dewey's view that the function of the work of art is to produce aesthetic experience. This runs contrary to the thread in Dewey's thought which rightly emphasizes the potential of anything to be experienced aesthetically. It also subsumes art under the tyranny of the aesthetic. It is not difficult to imagine an artist who sets out to create a work of art that functions in ways other than producing aesthetic experience.

5. CONCLUSION

I have not been arguing that we should completely abandon the important analysis of aesthetic experience that Dewey provides in *Art as Experience*. Rather, I have suggested that we should modify our understanding of aesthetic experience to be the experience of an artwork, whose existence is already secure in virtue of the cultural environment in which it is indissolubly embedded and in which aesthetic experience takes place. Aesthetic experience can still be understood as an interaction between an organism and its environment with the addendum that this environment is one in which artworks already exist, sustained by the very thing that sustains the existence of human selves, their location in a culture. Aesthetic experience does not complete or (re)create an artwork. The environment with which the live creature interacts *is* culture and as a part of that environment, artworks already possess significant consequences for human beings that extend far beyond their physical being. In aesthetic experience we may recognize and take up that meaning in our own individual experience but we need not worry that in the absence of aesthetic experience artworks and other cultural entities will collapse back into the physical world from which they emerge.

15.

NARRATIVE NATURALISM

Judy Walker

I n our time, John Dewey might be called a "religious humanist," although if he were able, he might object. I am a secular humanist. Dewey's philosophy informs many of my most significant interactions, but I do not explore in them, as Dewey did, what it means to be religious. Naturalistic philosophy and the sciences support the assertion that religious experience is meaningful in quality, not that meaningful experience is religious in quality. We can achieve a full sense of direction and personal identity through a creative, narrative method of working within natural experience with no sense of the supernatural. My method is drawn from a multidisciplinary study with philosophical naturalism at its core. I hope that my thesis will be put to use, then tested for its efficacy.

For some, meaning in life is not a pressing concern, but it is for me and for many others everywhere. There are those who respond with much goodwill toward religion but also those who think that they have been very damaged by it. In the cultural debate, this is the great divide. We must engage in thoughtful conversation and form coalitions for common ends. Can we do so while preserving distinctions that make a difference? In the public square, in studies and in the polls, semantic confusion is rampant, and implicit interpretations often frame the issues. Connotations count.

Following Dewey, philosophical naturalists are able to describe and defend quite effectively our ability to lead the fullest possible lives. As a species, we seek meaning in many contexts; with the assistance of the sciences, philosophical naturalism is more than capable of providing it. Science is more than just one language among many for describing the world and how it works. No other ways of knowing should exclude or contradict without good evidence the best that science has to offer. Fortunately, there is much common ground among the sciences, the humanities, and the arts, although in the past it has often been lost in translation. The success of science, naturalism, and an ethical, inclusive humanism depends in no small part upon our willingness to use terminology that could help to dissolve the sort of problem that should not need to exist.

Richard Rorty thought that "a talent for speaking differently, rather than for arguing well, is the chief instrument of cultural change."[1] There is a place for argument but also one for changing the subject's parameters when they no longer suit our purposes. Rorty follows Dewey in thinking that some large and complex issues can pragmatically be evaded; they disappear when they no longer seem relevant or necessary.

Just as there is no one "Absolute" with a capital A, there is no one "Meaning" with a capital M. We value the multiple perspectives in our philosophy. Still, we may think about the biggest questions that do converge, especially when we are suffering. Looking forward, do we have hope? Looking back, can we say that we have reached our personal and professional goals? Did we deal well with inevitable conflict and loss? Did we attempt to help others and to further good in the world? Will we tell the stories of our lives to ourselves and others with understanding and, in largest measure, with joyful satisfaction? Will it matter that we ever lived? Philosophy, as the love of wisdom, is all about meaning. Meaning is amenable to study and is ours to create, not to "find" in the sense that there is an ultimate answer for all.

In *The Poetics*, Aristotle famously said: "A whole is that which has a beginning, a middle, and an end.... [T]he plot... will thus resemble a living organism in all its unity, and produce the pleasure proper to it."[2] I see this as Dewey's problem-solving cycle of sentient life, one that forms a mode of conduct that can produce an intensely felt quality of exhilaration, achievement, and fulfillment. This primary narrative of meaning is both scientific and aesthetic, without reduction or exclusion. When Dewey urged that scientific, philosophical naturalism should be seen as a stance that can address a wide variety of natural, social, and practical problems, he successfully articulated an inclusive match between the methods of science and the emotional, inspirational advantages of aesthetics. Experience that he often called "religious" is included in this synthesis.

Although Dewey talked more about art than about narrative, he never ignored the temporal, dramatic nature of reality, because he saw art as an activity, a process of perceiving the environment and of making decisions about it. He thought of the ordering of experience as an aesthetic project overall. He felt the rhythmic pattern of critical inquiry itself, making a five-point analysis of observation that is easily reducible to three aspects less difficult to remember: situation, study, and solution—the equilibrium of habits, the disruption of harmony, and the attainment of growth.[3]

Dewey's action-oriented, aesthetic philosophy has stood the evidentiary test of time. Meaning for Dewey has a productive, positive, and unabashedly affective quality. He knew the importance of managing both emotion and thought, even though the neuroscience to support his view had not yet been articulated. And he emphasized the development of good habits of mind to achieve chosen results. Dewey prefigured the findings of cognitive scientists with his willingness to talk about imagination in his explorations of the mind. He directly addressed the art of creating meaning in a way that stressed its transformational quality without relying upon a transcendent realm which exists apart from the natural world. Dewey knew that the exercise of choice in problem solving has a deeply passionate component that should never be ignored, as emotion is necessarily put to the service of reason.

Robert Solomon said, "It is because we are moved, because we feel, that life has a meaning."[4] This reflects emotion's etymological sense of movement, of being moved, of motivation. Philosophical naturalism is already completely prepared to incorporate what science has shown, and now we can use the scientifically supported value of passion to our advantage. Our advocacy of science and philosophical analysis no longer will seem so cold to so many people; it will no longer seem that something important is missing, something that can be offered only by religion and religious practices in a cultural bargain that sacrifices knowledge on the altar of feeling. Ignoring emotion at their peril, many proponents of philosophical naturalism have tacitly ceded too much of its wide-ranging territory to religion. We must renew instead our understanding of Dewey's primary emphasis on the felt qualities of life. Emotionally satisfying, meaningful experience is a crucial component of what humans need, but we don't have to be religiously inclined to get it.

The neuroscientist Antonio Damasio has shown that reason and emotion are inseparable.[5] Reason *includes* emotion, an important point that those who contrast reason to religion should consider. Damasio confirms that emotions are crucial to the decision-making process. We can educate our emotions but not suppress them entirely, nor should we. This is not to say that in all situations we should act upon our emotions without any critical thought. We all know that such an approach can be a recipe for disaster. But we should learn to use our emotions wisely, because they provide us with important information about how we are doing as we make our way in the world. We can readily catch ourselves in the act of knowing and feeling as we explore our environment through time. Damasio says that "you know you exist because the narrative exhibits you as protagonist in the act of knowing."[6] In other words, you are the movie-in-the-brain, emerging within the movie.[7] With your physiologically embodied, emotionally laden reason, you create, moment by sequenced moment, your autobiographical self.

Our passions are informed—and transformed—in the entirely naturalistic process of inquiry. This has been Dewey's position all along.

The expansion of reason's connotations in this way will enable an entirely naturalistic humanism to address much more directly the alleviation of emotional suffering. No one wishes to be enmeshed in a deeply troublesome situation. But there is meaning to be made in the process of resolving it. Psychological studies show that a victim can become a protagonist by incorporating trauma into a new, more stable narrative, emphasizing what of benefit has been learned from the experience.[8] The trauma is not ignored or excised; it is contextualized, so that it no longer operates as the central, defining theme. Damasio asserts that suffering puts us on notice that our decision-making strategies should change.[9] After trauma, the felt quality of the experience can become one of accomplishment through the development of a new sense of self. Dewey, too, saw that problematic situations are opportunities for growth. This call to action is central to his philosophy, with an imaginative, creative, and aesthetic orientation permeating his entire analysis.

It is time to broaden our aesthetic sensibilities again, as Dewey did. Dewey often mentioned imagination in his work. He said that "the connection between imagination and the harmonizing of the self is closer than is usually thought. The idea of a whole, whether of the whole personal being or of the world, is an imaginative, not a literal, idea."[10] He also defined an imaginative experience as "what happens when varied materials of sense quality, emotion, and meaning come together in a union that marks a new birth in the world."[11] Imagination, like emotion, no longer exists as a concept implicitly opposed to reason. All ideas are imaginative, which is fine—as long as there is thoughtful inquiry to back them up. Susan Haack says that "imaginative speculation is essential, but imaginative hypotheses have to stand up to evidence."[12] Ruth Anna Putnam concurs: "To say that one has developed one's philosophical position in response to the moral impulse, or in response to any other passionate concern, is not to say that one does not have or has not given intellectually compelling reasons for that position."[13] We should take an informed and ethical approach to our imaginative activity.

Imagination is closely connected to creativity. Damasio stresses that progress has been made toward building "a two-way bridge . . . between neurobiology and the humanities, thus providing the way for a better understanding of human conflict and for a more comprehensive account of creativity."[14] Creativity is our imaginative, aesthetic identity in action. Problem solving is creative. That's good, because we have to do it all the time.

As I delved into research primarily in philosophy, but also in psychology, cognitive science, and literary theory (including new subdisciplines often called "cognitive narratology" and "evolutionary literary studies," which reach out sincerely to the sciences), I started to see a pattern, a rhythm, a familiar method of ordering experience throughout. It was the basic movement of narrative:

> beginning—middle—end
> stability—crisis—resolution
> observation—testing—conclusion
> situation—study—solution
> understanding—doing—making
> being—doing—becoming
> epistemology—ethics—aesthetics
> truth—goodness—beauty

We can use story cycles like these deliberately to our advantage to acquire knowledge, act ethically, and create meaning in our lives.

Narratives enable our ability to transmit the felt qualities of our experience to others and even to ourselves. They bring both order and emotional resonance to any significant situation. Narratives are inherently aesthetic, indicating that critical analysis is also an art. Our ends-in-view, goals, highest aspirations, and ideals deeply inform the plots of our lives. The scientific, narrative trajectory of problem solving (and, better yet, of problem *finding*) can easily include the positive connotations of productivity, inventiveness, and constructive, ameliorative development. Critical inquiry is therefore generative, effective, imaginative, and creative. This is a fully organic understanding.

I found that scholars in many areas have explored the significant role of narrative in the creation of meaning. From philosophy, for instance, Mark Johnson calls the journey to narrative wholeness in experience the "source—path—goal" schema,[15] adding cognitive science and linguistics to Dewey's assertion that an organism's inquiry about its world involves the rhythm of an initial state, the encountering of a problem or conflict, and its resolution, resulting in the felt quality of fulfillment, growth, or transformation. Johnson also follows Dewey by stating that "our imaginative rationality is the chief means we have for dealing critically, creatively, and sensitively with the novel situations that arise for us each day."[16] And as Thomas Alexander says, "To preserve the narrative, dramatic structure of existence, for Dewey, is to preserve the dimensions of the possible and the actual; these are . . . dimensions of nature."[17] Narrative in this case is not merely descriptive; both implicit and explicit stories reflect an inherent structure of the mind. We often consider a variety of alternatives and possible future outcomes before we act. Dewey called this a "dramatic rehearsal." At the end of each such story, we have a point of view from which we imaginatively perceive the situation's outcome as a whole. Owen Flanagan supports the vital role of narrative, as well: "Many thinkers have converged on the insight that a narrative conception of self is the 'essential genre' of self-representation. . . . We narratively represent our selves in part in order to answer certain questions of identity."[18] He agrees with Daniel Dennett, who metaphorically calls the self "the center of narrative gravity" to explain the idea that we are all, in effect, the narrative agents and novelists of our lives.[19]

From other fields, anthropologist Pascal Boyer, like Antonio Damasio, says that the narrative drive "is embedded in our mental representation of whatever happens around us."[20] Similarly, evolutionary psychologists John Tooby and Leda Cosmides say that "stories are told in a way that mimics the format in which experienced events are mentally represented and stored in memory, in order to make them acceptable to the machinery the mind uses to extract meaning from experience."[21] Cognitive narratologist Manfred Jahn notes that "the cognitive sciences themselves have begun to recognise the 'storied' nature of perception, sense-making, memory, and identity formation."[22] Social psychologists Kristin Sommer and Roy Baumeister state that "the evidence suggests that the process of organizing and describing life events in narrative form facilitates the development of meaning."[23] And cognitive psychologist Steven Pinker indicates that "the basic script of an agonist tending, an antagonist acting, and the agonist reacting . . . underlies the meaning of the causal constructions in most, perhaps all, of the world's languages."[24]

The *agon*, a Greek term for "conflict" or "contest," can be used to represent the second stage of the narrative cycle of beginning, middle, and end or of stability, crisis, and resolution. Johnson also highlights the agon around which the narrative turns, leading to resolution in a structure that "provides the most comprehensive synthetic unity that we can achieve."[25] Seen in this way, a struggle, or even great suffering, can become a challenge, a problem to solve, with the realistic possibility of personal growth. Tragedy is no longer the final, felt outcome of an extremely problematic situation. Its victim can regain autonomy by turning the meaning of the past into future ameliorative action. Narrative transforms suffering.

I've developed a mnemonic device which helps me to be mindful of my greatest challenges and most important goals. I call it the *triagon*, a term I coined to symbolize my deliberate use of narratives when I need them. It reflects a framework for the many ways to state the cognitive, situational sequence of stability, crisis, and resolution. With another nod to the Greeks, I see it as an *organon*, a tool or instrument for acquiring knowledge. Aristotle mentioned the three modes of the human *ergon*, or work: knowing, acting, and producing—the *theoria*, *praxis*, and *poiesis* of daily life.[26] The *triagon* reflects my secular humanism as a naturalistic worldview with its principal philosophical components of epistemology, ethics, and aesthetics supported by the scientific method of situation, study, and solution. I see the *triagon*'s movement through a situation's big or little wholes which have a narrative's beginnings, middles, and ends.

Dewey continually comes to mind. Larry Hickman has commented on the similarity between Dewey's triadic template and C. S. Peirce's conception of categories.[27] Kim Díaz calls it Dewey's rhythm of "inception, development, and fulfillment."[28] Observations like these from our philosophical tradition bring to the *triagon* key reminders of the emotional, aesthetic, imaginative felt quality of the process of thought, turmoil, and transformation; situation, suffering, and growth; mind, motivation, and meaning. This method, this narrative, is the being, doing, and becoming of knowledge, ethics, and identity. It is the nature of inquiry itself.

The *triagon* moves from stability, through conflict, toward an integrated improvement through time. Irving Singer said that the number three establishes "a sense of reconciliation."[29] The *triagon*, with its inclusion of the agonistic in experience, helps me to put into proper sequence all that I have tried to think and learn. Although I know I am no blank slate, I am able to analyze my circumstances more effectively by seeing them as manageable, consciously narrated stages that help me to focus on the ameliorative, transformative, felt quality of my life.

The *triagon* is also a way to tell the story of a naturalistic, humanistic life as a creative work of art. As I read Nietzsche's evocations of "life as art," I wondered what such an analogy could mean for the practice of philosophical naturalism today. Alexander Nehamas explains that "Nietzsche . . . looks at the world in general as if it were a sort of artwork; in particular, he looks at it as if it were a literary text."[30] For individuals, life as art, narrative, or literature can be seen as the real representation of a bildungsroman, a story of the coming of age of those of any age, depicting the journey of a protagonist in the shaping and maturing of his or her personality. Charlotte Bronte's *Jane Eyre*, Somerset Maugham's *Of Human Bondage*, James Joyce's *A Portrait of the Artist as a Young Man*, Thomas Mann's *The Magic Mountain*, and Virginia Woolf's *To the Lighthouse* are great examples of the genre.

The transformation of daily decision making into an autobiography is an aesthetic experience. But some narratives are better than others. We must develop our plots with ethical as well as creative intention. When I view my life as an artistic whole to which I aspire, I think of it as more understandable, inventive, and emotionally integrated. When I consciously try to produce results of value to myself and others, my life becomes more meaningful. Using the *triagon*, I think of hindsight, foresight, and insight, each with ethical responsibilities attached. Nietzsche's "joyful wisdom" is within our reach as a worthy part of any satisfying form of self-creation.

Nevertheless, I know that it is unrealistic to expect that I will feel calm, centered, and enthusiastic at every moment. I realize now that I need to recognize the point at which I am in the grip of the middle part of a problematic narrative. I try not to shove my acknowledgment of emotion aside in an ill-conceived attempt to find some immediate relief. As I consider my suffering without rushing the process, I become more confident that I will feel in time the peaceful, hopeful satisfaction of a job well done, in spite of the tragedies in my past, the continuing difficulties I must face, and the acknowledgment that I will die. For me, calling my experience "religious" has not been necessary; it is aesthetic in every most exalted sense. As Dewey said in *Art as Experience*, "The moment of passage from disturbance into harmony is that of intensest life."[31]

I call that movement, that narrative, that culminating and transformative experience *sublime*. The sublime should be seen as an adjective more than a noun, though to say so is heresy against its philosophical and literary history. It has no actual existence, either in an order above our daily experience or below a religious domain in any essential way. Instead, we may use it, or other words like it, to explain what "religious" experience actually is. As the artist Agnes Martin has stated so well for all of us, "The artist tries to live in a way that will make greater awareness of the sublimity of reality possible."[32] I see in the sublime the connotations of a process derived from the implications of its etymology: it defines a threshold, an adventure. The sublime can be used to describe the ameliorative, transformative resolution of a triagonic, narrative encounter with conflict. We may use it to remember that fear, sorrow, or pain can be contextualized in a middle stage of a naturalistic narrative, not suffered as a tragic inevitability. We will not remain at the brink of an abyss; we will move instead toward a greater understanding.

There is risk in this adventure and also great reward. There is a feeling of ascendancy at this threshold, without the confusion caused by any supernatural implications. As Paul Kurtz would say, there is no need for a "transcendental temptation." When any final burden of personal misfortune is lifted in a narrative, transformative sequence, it feels like freedom. I think of the sublime as what Dewey meant by the imaginative, felt quality of wholeness as a metaphor for meaning. It exemplifies the feelings of exhilaration and joy that we can achieve at the end of a successful situation. This elevated outcome is made more powerful by science, not less. Profound joy can be produced by cultivated, natural habits of thought; the feeling is the same. Joy is joy.

"Religious" experience is meaningful in quality; meaningful experience is not "religious" in quality. Meaningful experience is fully ours to make, and its story is ours to tell.

Part Five

PRAGMATISM AND POLITICS

16.

JOHN DEWEY AND THE EARLY NAACP

Developing a Progressive Discourse on Racial Injustice, 1909–1921

Susan D. Carle

That Dewey was involved in founding the NAACP is well known, but the extent of Dewey's continuing commitment to the NAACP's racial justice agenda is commonly underestimated. In the NAACP's first decade, the period on which I focus here, Dewey served on the NAACP's Committee to Aid Federal Education, and wrote frequently about race as an aspect of social diversity in both the United States and other countries. Dewey's story of gradually developing racial consciousness presaged progressive white Americans' gradual awakening to the evils of racial injustice. By the late 1910s, Dewey's writings are replete with references to the value of diversity of all types—specifically including race—in promoting the richness and vibrancy of American social and political life. These ideas were central to his vision of American public education as preparation for citizens' participation in democracy.

Although Dewey is often criticized for not saying enough about race,[1] I will argue that these critiques look for Dewey's contribution in the wrong place. Dewey's blend of activism and writing about the benefits of racial pluralism paved the way for the development of a discourse about what we today call multiculturalism, as well as opening the eyes of moderate white progressives to the evils of racial injustice. Dewey thus deserves recognition for his work as a race theorist, not so much for developing ideas that pushed forward the vanguard—Dewey quite wisely left that task to others better situated to do it—but for heralding a moderate progressive discourse about racial injustice that could move the nation's political center in a more racially sensitive direction.

The basic facts concerning Dewey's involvement in the founding of the NAACP are well known: In 1909, Dewey lent his name to a call for a conference, spearheaded by progressives William English Walling, Oswald Garrison Villard, and others, that led to the NAACP's founding, thus establishing the first national biracial organization dedicated to improving race relations and the position of African American citizens in the United States.[2] The immediate impetus for this call for a conference was a 1908 race riot in Springfield, Illinois, the birthplace of Abraham Lincoln, but the factors underlying the NAACP's founding were far more long standing. The conference built on decades of work by race activists, most but not all of them African Americans, including such leading social reform luminaries as W. E. B. Du Bois, Ida B. Wells, and AME minister Reverdy S. Ransom, as well as John Dewey's good friends from his Chicago years at Hull House Jane Addams and Florence Kelly, and a host of other progressive American intellectuals and activists.

On paper, Dewey's role in the founding of the NAACP was significant but not profound. The mere fact that Dewey lent his name to the call for the 1909 conference was an important and meaningful act, as conference convener Villard well understood. Courting the support of wealthy Columbia University English Professor Joel E. Spingarn, Villard wrote in the fall of 1910, "we shall shortly take the liberty of laying before you the work of our NAACP in which Prof. Dewey is so much interested."[3] Joel Spingarn, along with his brother, lawyer Arthur Spingarn, would come to play vital roles in the NAACP's management and leadership throughout its first several decades. Villard's persuasive tactics in dropping Dewey's name clearly had their desired effect.

A second way in which Dewey lent his support to the fledgling NAACP was by delivering a short speech at the 1909 Conference. Dewey's speech, memorialized in the records of the conference, was helpful and supportive. At first glance, its theme—namely, that science did not support popular notions of African racial inferiority—might be considered a bit simplistic, especially when compared to the many ambitious orations by other participants who expounded on their moderate socialist or progressive political visions and outlined grand strategic and organizational plans. On deeper scrutiny, however, as I will argue shortly, Dewey's speech deserves to be better appreciated for his characteristic way of zeroing in, with plain language, on the crux of the issue at hand. But before sketching the intertwined development of Dewey's thought on race and his contribution to the development of a progressive American discourse on the evils of racial injustice, I must first make the Deweyan move of situating Dewey's interest in the NAACP in its social context.

1. DEWEY'S BACKGROUND

Dewey was born in 1859 in the far northern community of Burlington, Vermont. In the year after his birth, the total population of Burlington numbered 7,700, of which only 46 were African Americans. By the time Dewey left Burlington after college in 1882, its population had grown to 11,300, but the number of African Americans remained small, at 116, a little more than one percent of the population.[4]

Thanks to the work of Harvey Amani Whitfield and others, we know a bit about Burlington's African American population in this time period. In 1880, three-quarters of the 116 African American men and women residing in Burlington worked as laborers or servants. One African American woman worked in the professions; all others were domestic servants or did not work outside the home. Among African American men, one-third worked in skilled occupations, including as carpenters, printers, shoemakers, or barbers.[5] There appear to have been no African American churches or other distinct social institutions, and by the 1880s African Americans had begun to move away from Burlington as occupational opportunities for them continued to decline, a trend true throughout small-town New England.[6]

There is nothing in Dewey's personal history that suggests that he developed particular sensitivity to race issues, in either a positive or negative direction, in his early years; he may instead have been much like the whites Du Bois describes in the New England community of Great Barrington, Massachusetts, where Du Bois was raised in a very similar time period (between 1869 and 1885), in which the color line was drawn painfully on social issues but was not particularly salient in matters of general community life and education.[7]

Nor does it seem that race relations were salient in Dewey's mind when he began his academic career. Dewey's move to the University of Chicago in 1894 inalterably changed him, however, by nurturing his interest in social reform activism. Dewey developed a close friendship with Jane Addams and began an intense association with her settlement community, Hull House, where he was a frequent, sometimes almost daily, visitor. When Dewey moved to Chicago in the summer of 1894, his wife, Alice, and their older children departed for a long European tour, leaving Dewey and his youngest child alone in their new city. Dewey's almost daily correspondence with his much-missed family gives us special access to his developing political views during this period.[8]

The timing of Dewey's move to Chicago threw him into the midst of late nineteenth-century urban labor and social strife. Dewey arrived just as the American Railroad Union's (ARU) Pullman strike, led by president Eugene Debs, was getting underway. The strike quickly extended through sympathy actions to Chicago's stockyards and many other work sites. Marked by great violence and property destruction, the Pullman strike stands at the intersection of labor relations and civil rights history as a one of a number of major labor conflicts that resulted in brutal striker violence against African American workers.

The Pullman strike reflected a site of social contradiction: the ARU's members asked Chicago's laborers to support them in their efforts to gain better wages and living conditions in Pullman company towns, but they ignored the facts that African Americans were barred from jobs and housing with the Pullman Company, and that the ARU excluded them from membership. In a cynical, race-baiting tactic common among industrialists of the period, Pullman hired African American strike breakers during the ARU strike, and in industries hit with sympathy strike actions, such as Chicago's meat-packing plants, African American workers tended to decline requests that they walk off their jobs in support of the all-white ARU.[9] Quite irrationally under the circumstances, the ARU expected a different response. The resulting situation prompted much indiscriminate race-based violence and inflamed labor-related race tensions that would continue in Chicago for decades.[10]

The racial dimensions of the Pullman strike received much news coverage at the time,[11] but the progressive white activists centered at Hull House seemed oblivious to it. In their eyes, the strikers were unmitigated heros. Thus, in his letters to Alice, Dewey describes his developing attitudes as follows:

> [T]he strike is lost, & 'Labor' is rather depressed. But if I am a prophet, it really won. The business made a tremendous impression . . . the exhibition of what the unions might accomplish, if organized and working together, has . . . given the public mind an object lesson that it won't soon forget. I think the few thousand freight cars burned up a pretty cheap price to pay—it was the stimulus necessary to direct attention [and] get the social organism thinking.[12]

Even given the benefit of hindsight, I think it fair to direct some criticism at Dewey, Addams, and other white progressive activists for their seeming obliviousness to the white-on-black violence of the Pullman and related strikes in Chicago. African American activists in Chicago during the same period, such as

Reverdy Ransom, who would later join Dewey and Addams at the founding convention of the NAACP, had a very different view of the racial dimensions of Chicago's labor strife.[13] But before becoming *too* critical about this split of perceptions between African American and white activists, it is important to put late nineteenth-century understandings of the concept of race in historical context. At that time the term "race" meant something quite different than that term connoted later in the twentieth century. To late nineteenth-century thinkers race signaled, not a binary opposition between black and white, or between persons of color and so-called Caucasians, but instead a division of the world's people into a number of distinct groups along axes that represent an amalgam of characteristics we today distinguish, including national origin, language, culture, and ethnicity. As no less an authority than W. E. B. Du Bois put it in 1897, a race "is a vast family of human beings, generally of common blood and language, always of common history, traditions and impulses, who are both voluntarily and involuntarily striving together for the accomplishment of certain more or less vividly conceived ideals of life."[14] Du Bois thus wrote of the world's eight races, attributing distinctive strengths of character and disposition to each:

> The English nation stood for constitutional liberty and commercial freedom; the German nation for science and philosophy; the Romance nations stood for literature and art; and [each of] the other race groups [is] striving, each in its own way, to develop for civilization its particular message, its particular ideal. . . .[15]

Dewey's writing in the period prior to 1900 used the term "race" in a manner similar to Du Bois's conception. In his frequent writing on education, for example, Dewey proposed that "every religion has its source in the social and intellectual life of a community or race";[16] and "education proceeds by the participation of the individual in the social consciousness of the race."[17] Similarly, Dewey stated, "[e]ducation being a social process, the school is simply that form of community life in which all those agencies are concentrated that will be most effective in bringing the child to share in the inherited resources of the race."[18]

Dewey frequently used the term "race" in connection with his ambivalent musings about a then-popular educational approach known as "cultural epoch" theory. This theory posited that the stages of a child's intellectual development corresponded with the stages of "racial development": just as "the race" went through stages in the development of civilization, from nomadic to agricultural life styles, and then to interest in reading and writing, so too was children's intellectual development believed to proceed in this sequence. Dewey expressed reservations about this theory,[19] and this growing skepticism about "physiological philosophy" helped pave the way for further development of his understanding of race as a social construct.[20]

By the turn of the twentieth century, Dewey had made his turn towards social psychology, laying the groundwork for the connections his later work would draw between developmental psychology, pedagogy, and his theory of participatory democracy. Thus, in the period between 1900 and 1910, many of Dewey's writings continued to use the concept of race with connotations spanning national origin, ethnicity, culture, and social group, but did so in reference to the need to preserve the pluralistic make-up of American society. Drawing on his observations of and lessons learned from Hull House and projecting them as a model for public school education generally, Dewey wrote about "[t]he power of the public schools to assimilate different races to our own institutions, through education given to the younger generation."[21] But Dewey also warned against what observers in "both New York and Chicago" had noted—namely, that "in some respects the children are too rapidly ... de-nationalized," losing "the positive and conservative value of their own native traditions."[22] In later work Dewey would draw further on this model of public schools as ideally both fostering political commonality and preserving social differences in teaching a new generation the citizenship skills necessary for participatory democracy.

The Deweys left Chicago for New York City in 1905. There Dewey remained interested in the settlement house movement, which had an equally or even more vibrant and complex presence in that city, though his involvement was nowhere near as intense as it had been in Chicago. But the Deweys were on friendly terms with many New York City settlement house leaders such as Lillian Wald,[23] and it was from some of these leaders, both African American and white, through a complicated series of alliances and institutional developments beyond the scope of this paper, that the NAACP was born.

In New York City, Dewey focused much of his energy on his relations with fellow Columbia University faculty. Many of Dewey's biographers have written about the importance of Dewey's relationship with Franz Boas, who was pioneering new ideas in anthropology that rejected old stereotypes about the naturalness of race and superiority of the Anglo-Saxons. Dewey also developed close relationships with the faculty at the Columbia Law School, then a hotbed of new thinking about the relationships between law, social science, and politics. Dewey helped shape the thinking of the young Karl Llewellyn, who along with Dewey would go on to be a long-term supporter of the NAACP.[24] This new generation of legal scholars saw law as a potential tool for shaping a more just society, ideas critical to the motivation of the founders and early leaders of the NAACP.[25]

2. DEWEY'S CONTRIBUTIONS TO THE NAACP DURING ITS FORMATIVE FIRST DECADE

In light of Dewey's many connections to progressive activists and intellectuals in New York City, it would be far more surprising if Dewey had *not* been involved in the founding of the NAACP than that he was. Dewey expressed his support for the initiative to form the organization in a number of ways. Along with about sixty others, including his old Chicago settlement house friends Jane Addams, Florence Kelley, and Mary McDowell, and his New York acquaintances Lillian Wald and Columbia University economist Edwin Seligman, Dewey lent his name to the Call issued in early 1909 to announce plans for a large organizing meeting.[26] He further lent his name to the smaller, somewhat more select "Committee of Forty" of the National Negro Committee, which purportedly reflected persons who had attended organizing meetings for the conference.[27]

The organizing plan for founding the organization sought to bring together the wealth, social influence, and power of elite white progressive reformers with the expertise of African American activists who had been working for many decades on racial justice issues. This combination had some benefits but also some drawbacks. In the benefits column, the early NAACP was able to survive its tenuous infancy, unlike several primarily African American national civil rights organizations with similar agendas that had come and gone in the past, including the Afro American League, the Afro American Council, and the Niagara Movement.[28] In the negatives column, some of the white founders of the NAACP who insisted on exercising control over the organization's affairs exhibited attitudes on race that can only be described as "insensitive," at best. The number of white social activists who believed in complete racial equality was very small and by no means included all members of the NAACP's inner circle. Of those persons, white social worker Mary White Ovington was probably the most deeply committed to racial justice, as shown by her years of work in establishing and living in New York City settlement houses for African Americans and her several decades of devotion to fundraising and management tasks for the NAACP. Others, such as Villard and Walling, did not even believe in unrestricted interracial social mixing.[29] Even Addams was known to express views concerning the social inferiority of African Americans.[30] In this context, I believe Dewey's speech at the 1909 founding conference is best read as a gentle effort to address this central problem of deeply imbedded white attitudes of racial superiority.

The records of the 1909 National Negro Conference evince the enormous energy and optimism of the moment. A broad cross-section of prominent academics and activists delivered a total of two dozen speeches. Most of the participants, including Du Bois, Ransom, Walling, and Ovington, were committed to the mild democratic socialism popular among progressives of the period. Most of the talk at the conference was of bringing about a new political and social order in which white and black workers would recognize their common interests, unite in a progressive, nondiscriminatory labor movement, and work for a more economically and socially just society in which the forces of capitalism would be constrained and equal political rights for all would be achieved.[31]

The conference organizers carefully sequenced the order of the formal speeches. The first set of speeches focused on "science" and appeared to reflect the organizers' strategy of beginning with a focus on evidence that persons of African decent were not biologically inferior. Columbia University anthropology professor and physician Livingston Farrand, an associate of Franz Boas, gave the first substantive speech summarizing this scientific evidence and offering the rather convoluted conclusion that "it is absolutely unjustifiable to assert that there is trustworthy evidence for the view that marked differences of mental capacity between different races exist; that if they exist they are certainly of a much slighter extent than would appear from hasty observation;" but that "on the other hand it is equally unjustifiable to assert that no differences exist."[32]

The second speech, delivered by Burt Wilder, a professor of neurology and vertebrate zoology at Cornell University, was well intended but quite bizarre by contemporary standards. Following pages of quotes from scientists who argued for the theory of innate biological differences between the races, and including photos and charts comparing the brain sizes and weights of African Americans and orangutans, baboons, and white murders, Wilder concluded that "the average brain-weight of Obscure American Negroes is a little . . . less than that of obscure American whites," and with "Negroes more frequently than with whites does there occur prefrontal deficiencies," but "many Negro brains weigh more than the white average and many white brains weigh less that the Negro average" and "some white brains present [deficiencies] of the prefrontal lobe and some Negro brains do not."[33]

Progressive Columbia economist Edwin R. A. Seligman followed with shorter and more tactful remarks, although they too fell short of an insistence of absolute equality across the races. Emphasizing "the necessity of distinguishing between the individual and the group and the danger of making unduly broad generalizations," Seligman suggested that "there is nothing more tragic in the whole of human experience than the lot of that American Negro, cultivated, refined gentleman, who at the same time is thrown into the cauldron and fused with a mass of his unhappy and more unfortunate brethren."[34] Nevertheless, Seligman added, "we can expect to see the elevation of the great mass come about only very, very slowly."[35]

Next came John Dewey. Beginning his even shorter speech with an apology for taking the audience's time, Dewey explained he only appeared because "it gave me the opportunity to express my sympathy with the purpose of this gathering."[36] In contrast to the other speakers, Dewey plainly asserted that science showed that "there is no inferior race" and therefore that "the members of a race called that should have the same opportunities of social environment and personality as those of a more favored race."[37] Emphasizing the importance of equality in opportunities in education, Dewey argued that, "from a strictly scientific standpoint" and "leaving out all sentimental and moral considerations," it should be seen as the "responsibility of society as a whole today to see to it that the environment is provided which will utilize all of the individual capital that is being run into it." Dewey further proposed that "a society that does not furnish the environment and education and opportunity of all kinds which will bring out and make effective the superior ability wherever it is born is not merely doing an injustice to that particular race and those particular individuals but is doing an injustice to itself by depriving itself of that social capital."[38]

The modesty of Dewey's speech does not mean that it was not significant. His point was that the key institutions of American society could not be excused from their responsibility to provide equal opportunities to citizens regardless of race. In focusing on the basic fact of equality, Dewey put his finger on the nub of the issue: until white Americans truly rid themselves of race prejudice, as manifested in a host of key institutions including education, racial injustice was destined to continue.

In his later writing on race, Dewey had a great deal more to say about the relationship between race prejudice and the conditions for just economic and social orderings, as I discuss below. But even in this first lecture on race issues, Dewey hit on the core of the question presented to white Americans—i.e., equality in all key social and political institutions—in a manner in which his fellow "scientist" speakers were not yet capable of articulating.

Dewey's speech focused on education, and his involvement with the early NAACP after the founding convention likewise focused on this central preoccupation. Indeed, a matter unappreciated in Dewey scholarship to date is his continued involvement with the NAACP in its early years after the moment of its founding. A review of NAACP records reveals that Dewey remained involved in the NAACP through much of the 1910s. In a list of the NAACP's leadership prepared in December 1910, Dewey's name appears as a member of the General Committee, with friends including Kelley, Seligman, Wald, Clarence Darrow, and others. By this point Addams and others had taken on larger roles as Executive Committee members, and by the next year Dewey's name no longer appears on lists of General Committee members. Dewey does, however, continue with a more selective participation, by agreeing to serve on the organization's Committee to Aid Federal Education.[39] This committee reported to the NAACP Board of Directors and focused its efforts on passage of federal legislation to help fund local education, especially in the areas of literacy and vocational training. Dewey actively championed this effort, agreeing to attend meetings with federal officials and giving at least one speech in 1916 about the importance of improving African American education in the South as well as new immigrant education in the North.[40]

By the middle of the decade, the NAACP Committee to Aid Federal Education appeared to have collapsed due to squabbling among board members that had nothing to do with Dewey.[41] At this point, Dewey's attention turned primarily to the European conflict, but he continued to think specifically about race in this context, noting in a 1915 speech, for example, his concerns about how "the mystic identification of Race, Culture and the State" was connected through social movements with "Germany's political ambitions."[42] Here and elsewhere Dewey began to link the myth of race with the kind of nationalism he abhorred.[43] Dewey's observations as to the pernicious use of that mythology in the European context helped drive home for Dewey the perniciousness of race groupings in the United States as well. At the same time, Dewey—always a nationalist even though a gentle one, as Alan Ryan has noted[44]—began to develop his theory of the special virtues of American society based on the particular strengths of American pluralism. Dewey did so by linking his wartime preoccupations with his central interests in public schools and pedagogy.

3. DEWEY'S WRITING ABOUT RACE AND AMERICAN EXCEPTIONALISM

By 1916, in *Democracy and Education*, Dewey was explicitly bringing together his thoughts about public education and pedagogy with his growing concern about the evils of racism in both Europe and the United States. In that work Dewey expounded at length on his views about the connections between public school education, political socialization, and the development of the conditions necessary for the flourishing of democracy. The concept of diversity had emerged as central to Dewey's theory as he again drew indirectly on his observations of Hull House in writing:

> In the olden times, the diversity of groups was largely a geographical matter. There were many societies, but each, within its own territory, was comparatively homogeneous. But with the development of commerce, transportation, intercommunication, and emigration, countries like the United States are composed of a combination of different groups with different traditional customs. It is this situation which has, perhaps more than any other one cause, forced the demand for an educational institution which shall provide something like a homogeneous and balanced environment for the young. Only in this way can the centrifugal forces set up by juxtaposition of different groups within one and the same political unit be counteracted. The intermingling in the school of youth of different races, differing religions, and unlike customs creates for all a new and broader environment.[45]

In other words, diversity on race and other grounds both provides part of the rationale for the institution of the public school—i.e., to perform a socializing function in providing unity in difference—but also provides material for strengthening and enriching education and political socialization by teaching the skills of flexibility and adaptation across ever-changing and multicultural social environments.

The interwar period found Dewey's focus less preoccupied, for a time at least, with developments overseas. But Dewey continued to write about the evils of racism, including America's domestically grown variety, devoting an essay to the topic in 1921.[46] In this lengthy essay entitled "Race Prejudice and Friction," Dewey first returned to the central matter of race prejudice on which he had focused in his 1909 speech for the NAACP, but this time made many more passes over the topic. Dewey's core explanation of prejudice started with irrational psychological reaction: "Some force cuts short our thinking and makes us jump to a conclusion." Prejudice thus "is something which comes before judgment and prevents it or cuts it short," the result of "biases originally springing from instincts and habits which are deep in our natures," or an "instinctive aversion of mankind to what is new and unusual, to whatever is different from what we are used to." Drawing examples from across a range of history and geography, Dewey initially turned to the history of China, where Dewey first delivered this essay as a speech. Dewey noted the "anti-foreign waves which have swept over China at different times," as well as "the attitude of the earlier immigrants to the United States towards later comers."[47]

But Dewey did not treat all forms of prejudice against outsiders as equivalent, nor did he dodge the particular intransigence of race prejudice against persons of African descent in the United States. Turning to that question, Dewey suggested that physiologic factors, including facial features and color, could "serve as a nucleus about which many other things cluster" so that they "afford a physical basis upon which feelings otherwise effervescent come to rest until they share in the permanence of the physical trait."[48] But this somewhat dithering musing about the causes of prejudice against persons of African descent was not what gave this essay its punch; instead, Dewey argued, moving from the fuddling to the provocative, that individuals' race prejudice was not the real problem at all.

Dewey proposed that the real problems of racial injustice rested at the levels of the political and economic. These were the forces, Dewey argued, that changed "race prejudice into racial discrimination." It was not prejudice but its manipulation in the interests of political domination, as in the examples of slavery in the United States and the British domination of India, that "create the belief in superiority on one side and inferiority on the other." The dominant political group develops "arrogance and contempt" for those it dominates, along with "an uneasy subconscious feeling that perhaps the subject people is not really so inferior as its political status indicates," producing a still more "noisy and aggressive" expression of superiority. Here Dewey observed parallels with "prejudice against women as a class" and the political subordination of women.[49]

Dewey's conclusions offer insights still relevant to this day. To Dewey "[w]hat is called race prejudice is not then the cause of friction. It is rather a product and sign of friction which is generated by [other] deep seated causes," including politics, economics, and international relations. Race, Dewey proposed, became "a sign, symbol, which bears much the same relation to the actual forces which cause friction that a national flag bears to the emotions and activities which it symbolizes, condensing them into visible and tangible form."[50] Thus, Dewey proposed, "[u]niversal disarmament would be a more powerful factor in soothing race prejudice than any amount of enlightenment of cultivated persons can be," and "only by profound economic readjustments can racial friction be done away with."[51]

How insightful these words are today, in a much changed context but one still charged with interconnections between geopolitical conflicts, global economic inequality, and hatred based on race, religion, and national origin. Dewey's contribution in this essay reflects his characteristic manner of putting his finger directly on the issue at hand—namely, the *structural* aspects of racial subordination. Thus Dewey's work on race not only heralds our contemporary preoccupation with diversity or multiculturalism, but in this essay, in particular, is able to discern the link between racial oppression and the maintenance of an unjust geopolitical order.

5. CONCLUSION

Although the scope of my project ends with the first decade of the NAACP's existence, it bears noting that Dewey's commitment to the NAACP continued into later decades. In 1932 Dewey spoke at the NAACP Annual Meeting[52] and he lectured before African American teachers in Baltimore, whom, Dewey reported to his friend Albert Barnes, "impressed me as a fine lot of people."[53] Dewey continued to correspond with Barnes about their shared interest in African art, signed an NAACP public letter in the 1942 Odell Waller race and criminal justice matter,[54] gave a very generous financial contribution to the

NAACP of $1,000 (in 1950s dollars),[55] and received a justifiably laudatory telegram from its leader on the occasion of his nintieth birthday.[56]

On Dewey's death in 1952, NAACP National Secretary Walter White wrote to Dewey's second wife expressing the organization's condolences and noting its memory of Dewey's participation at its founding as well as the fact that he was "unremittingly and uncompromisingly a supporter of the fight for full citizenship rights for the American Negro."[57] True words, plainly spoken, but more could have been added to note that the story of Dewey's involvement with the early NAACP reflects the intertwined development of Dewey's thinking about race, the work of the NAACP, and the development during the early twentieth century of a progressive American discourse about both the positive virtues of racial diversity and the political evils of structural racial subordination.

ACKNOWLEDGMENTS

I owe special thanks to John Shook and Larry Hickman for inviting me to take part in this project; Loren Goldman and Michael Elderidge for generously allowing me to mine their encyclopedic knowledge of the literature on Dewey; and all the conference participants at the John Dewey's 150th Birthday Celebration for exciting presentations, stimulating conversation, and helpful feedback. Dewey would have been enormously pleased to find himself in such company.

17.

PUBLIC REASON VS. DEMOCRATIC INTELLIGENCE

Rawls *and* Dewey

Judith M. Green

Concerning how to deliberate democratically about important matters of public life, many contemporary liberal political philosophers may tend to think that they can draw insights from either John Rawls or John Dewey, but not both. Their theoretical styles are very different, and their proponents tend to give papers at different conferences and to publish in different journals. Rawls frames his advice about democratic deliberation in terms of "public reason," with detailed attention to questions about constitutions, basic institutions, and how to achieve fair interpretation and operation of these in contemporary societies indelibly marked with what he calls "reasonable pluralism." Dewey frames his advice in terms of developing and employing "democratic intelligence" in problem-focused inquiry about matters of community concern. Even their differing uses of that last concept—community—are thought by some, including Robert Talisse, to require a choice between their rival research platforms, which Talisse argues should be a choice against Dewey's theoretical framework and in favor of a contemporary Peircean reframing of Rawls's approach. My purpose here is to show that Talisse has been too quick to bury Dewey, and that we should instead continue to value and to learn from him. However, this does not require rejecting Rawls's final contributions to ideal theory, but rather critically combining them with Dewey's best experience-based insights and those of other pragmatists, classical and contemporary, in order to develop more general, ideal-guided, yet context-sensitive political theories that offer illuminating, transformatively effective guidance to actual, nonideal democratic deliberation in our real-world conditions of the twenty-first century.

Such a combination is not as absurd as Talisse would have us believe. Rawls's account of public reason in his final works, especially *Political Liberalism* (1993,

1996), *The Law of Peoples* (1999), and "The Idea of Public Reason Revisited" (1999), focuses on creating and sustaining a constitutional democratic society regulated by legitimate laws that are adopted through public deliberative processes that include those whose conduct its norms effectively govern, not only in their public dealings with one another, but throughout their comprehensive doctrines. Thus, in the ideal liberal society he imagines, in order to clarify what is at stake today in experienced democracies like the United States, "reasonable" citizens are committed to constitutional democracy *all the way down*, not just as a strategy or *modus vivendi* they have adopted because they have reluctantly concluded that they cannot succeed in persuading those who hold differing "reasonable comprehensive doctrines" (religious or secular), or in imposing their views on them. Contrary to Talisse's comparative account in several recent essays, Rawls's account of public reason frames *a way of life* for diverse but reasonable Rawlsian constitutional democrats, as does democratic intelligence for Deweyan pragmatist democrats. Moreover, both Rawls and Dewey are wary of including nondemocrats in deliberative processes; both draw on history and recent events in framing their accounts of the democratic ideal; and both suggest that important changes in American society are required if it is to fulfill that ideal.

Nonetheless, the ways of life and democratic commitments of Rawlsian constitutional democrats and Deweyan deep democrats may differ on at least five other matters:

(1) concerning the completeness, consistency, and stability of the fully integrated webs of life-guiding beliefs and personal commitments Rawls calls the "comprehensive doctrines" of "reasonable" people, which Deweyans would challenge concerning their frequency of occurrence and their desirability, acknowledging more gappiness and tension among elements of the worldviews of thoughtful, open-minded people in pluralistic, democratic societies, and favoring more flexibility in their deployment and growth;

(2) concerning Rawls's pre-1996 rules against public critiques of the comprehensive views of other reasonable democrats and against bringing the contents and language of one's own larger vision of life into public deliberative contests, rules which Rawls grounded in the epistemological claim that it is impossible for people who hold different views to persuade or even to understand one another—both the rules and the epistemological claim being unacceptable to Deweyans;

(3) concerning backward-looking vs. forward-looking and ideal vs. actual

theoretical orientations that lead to differences concerning what is to be done in nonideal societies, what if anything can be said about the formation and transformation of comprehensive doctrines or worldviews, and how liberal democrats should approach deliberations with holders of antidemocratic views;

(4) concerning the focal kinds issues and occasions that call for democratic deliberation, and the kinds of actors who do and should participate in these;

(5) concerning the nature and role of communities, and why these matter.

In spite of these important differences, I believe Rawlsian constitutional democrats and Deweyan deep democrats have important things to teach one another, and that Talisse exaggerates the gap between these two paradigms by misreading both of them.

In my view, Rawls's account of *public reason*, as a key aspect of his final version of ideal political theory, has three important lessons to teach contemporary Deweyan pragmatists.

Rawls wisely distinguishes what he calls "reasonable" people, their political views, and their larger comprehensive views, from "unreasonable" people and their views, focusing his account on what is owed by reasonable people to other reasonable people, while making no claim that one must seek to make reasonable proposals understandable and acceptable to unreasonable people.

Among the reasonable, he included those who hold religious comprehensive doctrines as well as those who hold alternatively structured background views that may include controversial ideas about philosophy, science, economics, ethnicity, or other matters, *if and only if* these views pass two tests: (1) they regard others as free and equal persons entitled to human rights; and (2) in political matters, they are committed to reciprocity in giving reasons that can be understood and accepted by reasonable others who share their commitment to a liberal constitutional society, but not share their comprehensive doctrine.

In his final work, Rawls argued that doing ideal theory has value because it clarifies some key points, while recognizing that it must take lessons from history and can never be regarded as final; in fact, he continued to revise his ideal political model of "justice as fairness," including his account of public reason, always thanking his critics for helping him to see where his earlier claims needed to be modified.

At the same time, I believe that Dewey's account of *democratic intelligence*, especially when complemented with helpful insights from Jane Addams, George Herbert Mead, Alain Locke, and contemporary pragmatists working in their stream of ideas, has three important lessons to teach Rawlsian constitutionalist liberals:

Dewey and the classical pragmatists focus collaborative inquiry or deliberation on understanding and transforming *specific problems* effectively, focusing on ends-in-view relative to the pursuit of the always-vague democratic ideal, and typically involving *a combination of actions* in what Rawls calls "the public sphere" with those in what Rawls calls "the background culture."

Dewey and the classical pragmatists learn from and value the history of philosophy, but they focus on *the diverse experiences of problem-focused struggle of ordinary men and women* (historical and contemporary) in framing issues for transformative philosophical inquiry, clarifying and amplifying the *actual, multiple meanings of concepts* instead of offering stipulative definitions, and progressively building up *an ideal-directed general theory* as a resource or tool for guiding contextually differing courses of future experience.

Dewey and the classical pragmatists treat the *boundaries among various cognitive and value domains*—the political, the scientific, the moral, the religious, the aesthetic—as *fluid and open-textured*, distinguishing one from another only to sharpen the focus of a particular inquiry, while recognizing that individuals and societies *continuously and mutually exchange meanings and values across domains* in dynamic ways that are conscious or unconscious, voluntary or conflictual, progressive or retrogressive relative to shared ideals.

Concerns about the possibilities of combining such important insights from Rawls and Dewey that Talisse has raised are based on a series of misunderstandings:

Taking Rawls's *stipulative definition* that "community" means a homogeneous association as an authoritative account of the term's *ordinary philosophical meanings* as well as the *empirical qualities of actual communities*;

Failing to notice Rawls and Dewey's *agreement* that *the basic needs of all* must be met by a liberal or even a decent society as a *precondition* on other personal rights, as well as the acceptability of basic institutions and political procedures;

Accepting Rawls's dualism or strict barrier between the public sphere and the background culture, whereas Rawls himself had given up this idea by 1996, when he reframed *Political Liberalism* in his introduction to the paperback edition;

Extending Rawls's liberal reciprocity norm to require making public policy proposals understandable and acceptable to those who hold unreasonable views, including fundamentalists and absolutists of all kinds;

Taking Dewey's "democracy as a way of life" to entail homogeneity in views and values among all the members of a community, in combination with assuming that shared experience means uniformity; and

Claiming that Dewey believed that the sciences are to settle all public matters—or at least, that the methods of "hard" sciences like physics and chemistry are to be rigidly followed in all other domains of collaborative inquiry—even though Dewey actually proposed that we reconstruct how we understand "the scientific method" and apply it outside the sciences only in domain-appropriate ways.

I have time today to address only two of Talisse's misreadings, which are valuable in so far as they stimulate us to consider what contemporary democratic theorists who are drawn to Rawls's work as a touchstone and those who are drawn to Dewey's may be able to learn from one another. The two topics I propose to address here are Rawls's use of the concept of "reasonableness," and Rawls's and Dewey's differing uses of the concept of "community."

"The essentials" of public reason Rawls cities in the introductory passage to "The Ideal of Public Reason Revisited" (1999) are acceptance of "a constitutional democratic regime and its companion idea of legitimate law,"[1] noting that the institutional forms such regimes may take are varied. Thus, Rawls's conception of *public reason* operates as *a normative sorting criterion* for separating those comprehensive doctrines that are compatible with liberal constitutional democratic societies and legitimate law from those that are not compatible. Citizens who hold one of what he calls a "family" of "reasonable comprehensive doctrines" agree in employing public reason in their public or *exoteric* relations with those fellow citizens who also hold comprehensive doctrines that pass this test. Although they may employ additional, different norms of reasoning in their nonpublic, *esoteric* interactions with those who share their particular comprehensive doctrine, they never reason even privately in ways that reject or undermine constitutional democracy and legitimate law, nor do they silently tolerate others doing so. Rawls's "ideal normative conception of democratic government" focuses on the conduct of its reasonable citizens and the principles they follow.[2] It is not a purely formal or institution-focused conception of democracy, Rawls insists, but one that states norms of *reasonable* democratic citizens' *conduct* and of the *reasoning* this conduct involves. How *unreasonable* citizens and their comprehensive doctrines are to be treated is determined by the principles of justice in an ideal constitutional democratic society, which he discusses in a later section (7.2) of "The Idea of Public Reason Revisited." Thus, Talisse's recent claims that

Rawls's conception of public reason requires that the democratic public actor somehow succeed in persuading antiliberal, antiegalitarian religious fundamentalists concerning the reasonableness of public policies that would require coercive application, and that liberal democrats who truly respect their fellow citizens' comprehensive doctrines should be prepared to send their children to religious fundamentalists' schools, reflect grossly mistaken readings. Rawls's own account of "public reason" has the *opposite* implications, applying primarily to interactions among those who share it, not to interactions with those who reject its essentials, and furthermore requiring reasonable citizens to *criticize and attempt to undermine acceptance* of the views of unreasonable citizens if these constitute threats to a democracy's continued existence, or at least to the scope of its actualization of the ideal.

Three years earlier, in Section 5 of his new Introduction to the 1996 paperback edition of *Political Liberalism*, Rawls closed some of the previous distance between Dewey's ideal of democratic intelligence and his own ideal of public reason, reframing a "wide" version of public reason that operates in *both* the background culture and the political culture. As in "The Idea of Public Reason Revisited," the scope of his discussion is limited to reasonable persons who hold one or another of an open-ended, changing "family" of reasonable liberal comprehensive views (complete or partial) within a constitutional liberal democracy that is both largely just and inherited by its current participants at least several generations after its founding, so that "reasonable pluralism" is an experienced fact of life for them within a liberal background culture that has shaped their own views. Unlike Wittgenstein's "family resemblances," which are overlapping patterns of similarity without any universally shared set of necessary and sufficient core elements, Rawls's "family" of reasonable people and their comprehensive doctrines may differ in countless ways, but they share a set of four necessary and sufficient conditions he specifies in the Introduction to the paperback edition of *PL*: (1) they view all of their fellow citizens as free and equal persons; (2) they are committed to reciprocity in the practice of giving reasons for their proposals, claims, and public values that are framed in ways that they sincerely believe diverse reasonable others will be able to understand and accept; (3) they are committed to liberal constitutional essentials; and (4) they accept the fact that a plurality of differing comprehensive doctrines can and do satisfy the criteria for reasonableness, though not all comprehensive doctrines meet these tests.

Whereas in the 1993 hardcover edition of *Political Liberalism*, Rawls had argued that the content and language even of reasonable liberal comprehensive doctrines must be kept sharply separate from public political discourse, he explicitly withdrew this requirement in the 1996 revised paperback introduction: "I now believe, and hereby I revise VI:8, that such [reasonable comprehensive] doctrines may be introduced in public reason at any time, provided that in due course public reasons, given by a reasonable political conception, are presented sufficient to support whatever the comprehensive doctrines are introduced to support. I refer to this as the proviso and it specifies what I now call the wide view of public reason."[3] In further rethinking his 1993 discussion of the examples of the Abolitionists and Martin Luther King Jr. as invoking religious language to support and persuade others of the antiracist, proinclusive transformations in American political institutions, public policies, and cultural habits they believed our liberal constitution and our democratic ideal require, Rawls acknowledged that they *could have given reasons* that fellow citizens who held differing yet reasonable comprehensive doctrines could have accepted as reasonable, and thus, were in no way transgressive of the norm of public reason in framing their own reasons as they actually did. This means that Rawls had given up a dualism in favor of a duality, to use Dewey's language, in order to focus attention on *a public communicative context, purpose, and function* that includes *a greater degree of reasonable pluralism* than do many other communicative contexts, purposes, and functions in various institutional and interpersonal arenas in the "background culture," such as church services, university classes, scientific research projects, business exchanges, benevolent association meetings, and family gatherings. Rawls acknowledged that experiencing such "wide" public reasoning processes may lead and has led reasonable people to change their political views over time. Given the freer flow Rawls was prepared to affirm between public reasoning concerning political views and the language and contents of nonpublic comprehensive doctrines, the experience of reasonable diversity in the political domain must be expected to influence comprehensive views to change over time, as he acknowledged they generally tend to do. This is all that would be needed to open up a Rawlsian discussion of the legitimacy and respectfulness of efforts to "deepen the democracy" of reasonable people's background beliefs, feelings, nonpublic institutions, and habits of daily living, as Dewey, Addams, Mead, Locke, and contemporary pragmatists in their stream have proposed.

Rawls himself acknowledged that there are various ways of arriving at his broad conclusions about what democratic public reason includes and hot commitment to its requirements can be achieved: "The content of public reason is not fixed, any more than it is defined by any one reasonable political conception."[4] Interestingly enough, Rawls was more inclusive in his suggestive listing of broad kinds of comprehensive views than are many contemporary Deweyans— he includes some framings of religious views as reasonable, though he sometimes assumes more orthodoxy among those who hold these views than he should, e.g., among American Catholics like me. Yet Rawls's inclusiveness is not as broad as Robert Talisse reports when he confuses Rawls's "fact of reasonable pluralism" with the fact of an even wider range of "unreasonable" views that fail to meet Rawls's four criteria. Fundamentalisms of all kinds are almost by definition "unreasonable" in Rawls's view, as they are dangerous to democracy in Dewey's view and disruptive to cosmopolitan deliberation in Locke's view.

The two-fold issue of how to understand what a *community* is and what its role should be in contemporary liberal political theory is a crucial one for theory and transformative practice—an issue that divides communitarians as well as Deweyan pragmatists from libertarians and strict Rawlsian constitutionalist liberals. Their differences about "community" affect not only the differing political ideals they advocate, but also the ways in which they interrelate on-going historical experience with ideal goals, their theoretical starting points, and the underlying ontologies that indicate what these should be. Broadly, for communitarians and Deweyan pragmatists, *communities* are experienced historical realities to the same extent that *individuals* are; the two are always experienced together, as intertwined in their functioning and in their mutual definitions relative to one another, and as exemplifying both commonalities and differences in their identifying characteristics, which follow the pattern Wittgenstein called "family resemblances." Communities so understood typically are *conflict ridden* because of their diversity, unsettled or inconsistent comprehensive views, and changing members, ideas, and contexts; such conflicts can destroy them or can help them to progressively reorganize and grow. *Societies* as communitarian and Deweyan pragmatist thinkers understand them are made up of practically overlapping, often conflict-ridden, sometimes intentionally interlinked national, international, and transnational communities that in the twenty-first century, span the globe—through telecommunications that allow work groups to be located thousands of miles apart; through personal travel as well as commerce in goods that may be partially created in various places; and through the emergence of global problems for all that require coordination of differing local solutions or adjustments to take account of differences in local experiences.

In contrast, although libertarians and Rawlsian constitutionalist liberals disagree about many things, the *social contract* tradition they share leads many to treat both *communities* and *societies* as artificial, and only *individuals* as real in an originary sense. In Rawls's later philosophy, in which he focuses on the political aspects of his theory of "justice as fairness," his ideal liberal society differs from actual ones in that no one can enter it from outside or leave it except by death. His purpose in imagining such an ideal liberal society, including its political dimensions as these would be shaped by rational and reasonable people, given "the fact of reasonable pluralism," is to clarify how it is reasonable to think about our goals and responsibilities to one another in our "largely democratic" society, the kind of constitution we should and actually do have, how our basic institutions should operate, and how we should deal with people who live in four other kinds of actual societies (nonliberal but decent societies, outlaw states, conditionally deprived societies, and benevolent absolutisms). Rawls's ideal society differs from libertarian ones in two important ways: first, liberty is always conditioned by certain kinds of requirements of equality; and second, shared social obligation to meet the basic needs of all takes priority over any other understanding of our individual rights and duties to one another. For both libertarians and the later Rawls, however, communities are artificial, homogeneous, and focused on meeting a differing set of needs and goals than those that are proper to the political domain. Rawls's limiting definition of "community" is purely stipulative, serving the purpose of contrasting more homogeneous modes of association in what he calls "the background culture" with "the fact of reasonable pluralism" that public reason must take account of in the political sphere of his ideal model of a constitutional liberal society.

So at one level, these two broad groupings of contemporary liberal political theorists are simply talking past each other on the issue of community, based on different uses of the term. On other levels, however, their differing uses of the term reflect and produce differing ontologies, differing uses of ideal theory, and differing problem-solving focuses. These important issues need our attention—more attention than I can give them today.

When the seriousness of the concerns Talisse has raised has been reduced, if not eliminated, the value of critically combining potentially complementary insights from Rawls, Dewey, Addams, Locke, and Mead becomes discussable. As a resource for guiding fruitful inquiry, more attention is required from contemporary pragmatists to the general ideal-guided characteristics of democratic deliberative inquirers, constitutions, basic institutions, procedures, and background cultures that have emerged and are now emerging in differing world contexts. Rawlsian liberals must continue to develop Rawls's final insights about the dynamic quality of individuals' political views over time and due to their deliberative transactions with diverse reasonable others within largely democratic societies, about desirable processes of osmosis between their political views and their comprehensive views that may lead to progressive developments in both domains, and about the acceptability of employing tropes and concepts from religious and other aspects of reasonable comprehensive views in explaining and advancing particular political proposals and wider reframings of issues. At the same time, both Rawlsian constitutional liberals and Deweyan pragmatist liberals must give more attention to nonideal deliberations within societies that have liberal democratic constitutions, within societies that have some other kind of political structure, and between societies that have differing kinds of political structures.

On this occasion of celebrating John Dewey's 150th birthday, please let me conclude by drawing on complementary insights from Rawls, Dewey, Addams, Locke, and Mead, as well as from my own experiences in urban planning and electoral politics, to offer a few preliminary guidelines for democracy-minded participants in public political deliberations that include both reasonable and unreasonable citizens within societies that have liberal constitutions, but are still far from fully actualizing the democratic ideal. First, try to size up the views of your fellow deliberators: Are they reasonable in Rawls's sense? What kind of comprehensive view (complete or partial) do they hold? Then try to size up their level of open-mindedness: Are their views rigid? Are they absolutists of one kind or another? Do they value the kind of give-and-take based on information and reasoning that leads everyone to change views somewhat, or do they seek only to defeat or convert others? Then try to size up the level of their interest in mutuality: Do they seek a mutually beneficial solution, or do they seek to dominate, to carry only a bare majority, to use their role in the deliberation to influence powerful others, or perhaps even to use up others' time and energy unproductively so that they will drop out of the deliberative process, and the important decisions will be made on some other basis?

If your fellow deliberators seem unreasonable, a red flag should go up in your mind about the likelihood that investment of your time and energy in deliberation will be productive; if you decide to deliberate with them in spite of their unreasonableness, you will probably have to translate your political proposals into nonliberal terms that make sense to them in light of their background views, recognizing that support for democratic practices as a *modus vivendi* in Rawls's narrow, nonideal sense may be as much as you can expect from them, and that their deeper values and loyalties may actually be incompatible with your own. If your fellow deliberators do not seem both open minded and interested in mutuality, you should seriously consider whether the opportunity costs of deliberating with them will be too high, so that your time and energies may be better employed in some other way: sending in someone else you both respect to deliberate with them, trying to sideline them from the deliberative process by encouraging them to contribute their efforts in some other way, building up alternative deliberative forums, educating others, marching, lobbying, blogging, writing books, making films, making music, and creating other kinds of cross-difference interchanges that share and challenge participants' deeply held values and habits of thought and expression.

In these ways we can advance the actualization of what Rawls calls "attainable utopias" and Dewey calls the ideal possibilities within the best moments of experience we have already had, even in the conflict-ridden, non-ideal would in which we now live in the twenty-first century.

18.

DEWEY'S ETHICAL-POLITICAL PHILOSOPHY AS A PRESENT RESOURCE

Gregory Fernando Pappas

> **Better it is for philosophy to err in active participation in the living struggles and issues of its own age and times, than to maintain an immune monastic impeccability.**
> —John Dewey, "Does Reality Possess Practical Character?"

The relevance or vitality of Dewey's Ethical-Political philosophy is a function of its use as a present resource. Dewey made two important contributions that I wish to highlight because they bear directly on today's problems. First, in Dewey's philosophy, we find tools of diagnosis and understanding of how ideological oppositions may have contributed to our present economic-political crisis. Secondly, there is in Dewey a positive proposal in regard to what sort of politician is needed if we are ever to transcend how opposing ideologies have dominated politics. I will also address recent criticisms of "Pragmatism" in politics, i.e., those that worry that President Obama is a Pragmatist or exemplifies the practices recommended by Pragmatism.[1]

1. IDEOLOGICAL OPPOSITIONS IN SOCIOPOLITICAL DISCOURSE

For Dewey, ideological oppositions in sociopolitical matters have had a long history. The oppositions are based on untenable dualism that, in practice, has led to a dogmatic and narrow-minded approach to problems. Ideological oppositions are an obstacle to the sort of intelligent and context-sensitive deliberation/communication that Dewey thought was needed in a democracy. He thought that, throughout history, one of the most common ideological oppositions has been between forms of individualism versus collectivism. The opposition between these types of political theories is of consequence because they each prescribe a particular form of inquiry about social problems.

Political theories that center on individual natural rights and the notion of negative freedom are suspicious of all collective action because such collective action tends towards regimentation, mechanical and mass uniformity, censorship, and suppression. Collectivism, for its part, considers organized action as the source of all that is good and civil in nature. Both views assume an untenable dualism between the individual and the social but, more importantly, they share the same dogmatic approach to problems. For the individualist, social organization (government) is at best a necessary evil, and it tends to be oppressive. Therefore, social problems are analyzed in terms of how individual initiative, freedom, incentives, and independence have been suppressed by some collective action or organization. The collectivist, on the other hand, tends to analyze problems in terms of the disintegration and instability created by a rampant individualism that has undermined social order or communal bonds. Depending on who represents the status quo in this debate, one accuses the other of the present problems, but neither one cares to examine situations on their own merits. Hence, Dewey referred to them as dangerous opposing doctrines that seem to exempt us from the responsibility and the hard work of ameliorating social problems in light of their contextual uniqueness. "The person who holds the doctrine of 'individualism' or 'collectivism' has his program determined for him in advance."[2]

The existence of these opposed schools of thought would be inconsequential if it were only a historical artifact. Unfortunately, the Libertarians and Communitarians hold sway in our society, and continue to apply their peculiar way of analyzing to try to solve our *current* problems. This is not the place to go in depth about this ongoing debate, but I trust that what has been said already is sufficient to make anyone suspicious of any efforts to interpret Dewey as belonging to either camp. Instead, Dewey was simply a "contextualist" who, however much he cherished community, avoided prejudicing the communal over the individual good.

It seems plausible to believe that recently (since the second half of the twentieth century), parts of the world have been living under the assumption of a related but more significant opposition. Here is some recent commentary on this matter:

The irony of the post–Cold War period is that the fall of Communism was followed by the rise of another utopian ideology, which created the laissez-faire financial system that has now disintegrated. In America, a type of market fundamentalism became the guiding philosophy.[3]

For the better part of half a century after World War II, democratic capitalism built its modern framework against the backdrop of its death match with totalitarian Communism. In the two decades since the fall of the Berlin Wall, the American model of capitalism, largely unchallenged by ideological alternatives and increasingly dominant around the world, drifted toward what conservatives viewed as a more pure form of economic liberty and what liberals came to view as misguided free-market fundamentalism.... But now, as the United States and other nations look for lessons in the wreckage from the excesses of that period, political leaders are confronting uncertainty about what economic structures and values should define capitalism's next chapter.[4]

One common assessment of our current situation (implicit in the quotes above) is that going too far in the direction of capitalism has caused our present global crisis. As Dewey feared, the argument between socialists and capitalists has been used to describe our situation, and that argument dominates our current political discourse which forms an excuse for precluding constructive action. Most political analysis and commentary today assume that, in the map of possible political positions, there is a left and there is a right—each one defined according to opposing policies and values. These labels are applied to countries, political leaders, and Supreme Court justices. One obvious objection to this way of approaching problems is that reality is very different, or that we are relying on "a map" that oversimplifies the actual political landscape. Perhaps, but I will set this issue aside and instead consider how Dewey's philosophy can be useful in addressing this last common assessment of our recent problems in terms of ideological oppositions.

Dewey warned us about the dangers of historical shifts between opposing ideologies, and provided a philosophical framework to move beyond those ideologies. Dewey was concerned with how oppositions tend to invade our thinking and lead people somehow to believe that they must choose between them. This myopic way of thinking is what leads to extremism, and to entire societies moving in a pendulum between one extreme to another. For some reason, humans fall prey to fixing a one-sided extremism with a craving for the opposite extreme. This is often called a "backlash," but Dewey thought of it in terms of a nonreflective pattern of compensation. We tend to fall easily into this pattern because within the experience of one kind of excess, its contrary seems desirable. The desired excess might represent the direction towards which we should aim, but we must not confuse direction with final aim. Extremism is appealing because it is easily noticed and it seems to represent a position of strength. But Dewey argued otherwise. It is when we live within an extreme that we are the most vulnerable, because we are more likely to compensate by shifting to the opposite extreme. Extremism is also appealing because it offers simple answers to complex problems, and the quest for simple answers is part of the quest for certainty.

In his capacity as a philosopher, Dewey sought to undermine the philosophical views that propounded dualisms and thereby sanctioned the idea that we are stuck between extreme options. He said, "[t]he modern world has suffered because in so many matters philosophy has offered only an arbitrary choice between hard and fast opposites."[5] Philosophy, as criticism, is needed to unearth these prejudices and to suggest better ways to live. This is what Dewey tried to do when he proposed his democratic contextualism.

2. DEWEY'S DEMOCRATIC CONTEXTUALISM

Dewey had an approach to the important questions that are the basis of ideological debates among politicians such as: What is role of government and markets in the ideal society? Should we have more taxes? More regulation? More public investment? Where and how much is too much? Should we rely on the market to fix the problem of health care? How do we make these decisions? Dewey's personal stand on these and other questions was often misunderstood. He was in fact subject to criticism from both sides of the political spectrum. People at contrary extremes perceived Dewey's position as a disguised threat to their desired extreme. At the very least, it was hard to figure out what Dewey advocated. Was he on the left or was he on the right? The same thing is happening now with Obama (more on this later).

Dewey's politico-philosophical stand is, however, clear once one makes a genuine effort to read what he wrote. Dewey stood for the values and virtues of democracy as an ideal. For Dewey, every question regarding what should be socialized or otherwise left to market forces must be considered on its own merits. On this point, Dewey could not have been clearer:

We have to consider the probable consequences of any proposed measure with reference to the situation, as it exists at some definite time and place in which it is to apply. There cannot be any universal rule laid down, for example, regarding the respective scope of private and public action.[6]

Even if Dewey—in his time—may have favored a more socialized economy to remedy particular problems, it would be a mistake to call him or his philosophy "socialist" or left. His heart was with democracy *as a way of life*, and his approach to means and problem solving is a radical, nonpartisan *contextualism*.

Contextualism is a view about good judgment and decision making. Dewey's contextualism can be expressed in a negative or in a positive way. His contextualism refutes the notion that judgments which do not follow rules are necessarily arbitrary. Dewey is against the notion in philosophy that one can or should set up criteria or rules in advance to determine good judgment in a situation. Context matters in a profound way in all areas of life where judgment is needed. Whether a feature of an action counts as a reason to do it (or not) is dependent on the context. Whether a stroke of green in a painting contributes to the beauty of a painting depends on what other colors and lines are present. The green that helps with the beauty of one panting may be what ruins another painting.

In today's political climate, it is not easy to be a contextualist about the appropriate means to democraticize our experience (Dewey's normative stance). Consider the implications. A contextualist may require that we resolve one problem by market means and another through government intervention, or even that we treat the same problem differently at different times. Such an approach by a politician today would probably be perceived as a sign of indecision, a character flaw, or what has been called "flip-flopping." For many, political integrity is personified by standing fast to one's ideological (preconceived) way of dealing with a problem, no matter what. Granted, a genuine contextualist politician may at times be difficult to distinguish from an opportunist politician, insofar as both seem flexible. For Dewey, however, there is a profound difference between these characters in both their methods and the result. Now, all of this strikes me as particularly relevant today since people are trying to figure out where Obama stands on many issues and, as with Dewey, he has been criticized on all fronts.

Neither the left nor the right can make sense of Obama's economic philosophy or lack of one. Is he center-left, right-center, or is he just another politician capable of reaching across the ideological spectrum for convenient reasons, but without a moral backbone? Could it be that Obama is instead a contextualist, and hence a Deweyean Pragmatist? The label "Pragmatism" has been used to describe Obama's view. "Mr. Obama is stepping into the debate characteristically intent on avoiding polarizing labels, and his advisers describe his philosophy in terms of pragmatism rather than ideology."[7]

Ever since the publication of Chris Hayes's article entitled "The Pragmatist" in the December 29, 2008 issue of *The Nation*, there has been much discussion, especially in Internet blogs, about the extent to which Barack Obama's thought and action can be located in the tradition of American Pragmatism. Hayes and Mitchell Aboufalia have even made us aware of the indirect historical and bio-graphical similarities between Obama and John Dewey.[8] Others have considered these speculations a "stretch," or find them unhelpful in the attempt to decipher where Obama stands in relation to his contemporaries. In my view, it is too early to offer a judgment about Obama's pragmatism. I am only interested in the debate insofar as it is revelatory of how many conceive Pragmatism today, and how the debate presents an opportunity to address some objections that have been raised about it. More importantly, my goal is to introduce Dewey's Prag-matism as alternative approach to deliberation and problem solving in the polit-ical arena, and contrast it with recent attempts to articulate what "Pragmatism" entails in politics.

3. THE VARIETIES OF PRAGMATISM IN CONTEMPORARY POLITICS

Pragmatism is appealing today because it points to a new style of politics that transcends the partisan and ideological divisions that have marred the history of political deliberation. However, there are different senses of 'Pragmatism' that are used today when referring to politicians. To be a 'pragmatist' sometimes means simply to be "expedient" and "efficacious" in resolving problems and pur-suing one's interests. At first blush, there seems nothing inherently bad about this; in fact, we wish many of our leaders had this quality. The problem is that, in politics, "expedience" is an excuse to achieve self-serving aims (power, fame, re-election) or to acquiesce to the status quo that benefits the interests of the few.

Hence, a "pragmatist" in politics could well refer to the politician who is just a practical opportunist and is usually contrasted with the politician that bases his decisions upon theory, ideas, or some fundamental principles and values. Richard Posner has, however, given a positive spin to this type of pragmatism. He characterizes his "everyday pragmatism" as "the mindset denoted by the popular usage of the word 'pragmatic,' meaning practical and business-like, 'no-nonsense,' disdainful of abstract theory and intellectual pretension, contemptuous of moralizers and utopian dreamers."[9] For Posner, there is nothing inherently problematic about the "self-serving" aspect of a "pragmatist" politician. This is only problematic for those who hold unreasonable ideals (utopias) about politics and democracy. Posner thinks we need to be neo-Schumpeterian "realist" about what to expect from democracy. Democracy is merely a procedure, "a kind of market,"[10] a "competitive power struggle among members of a political elite . . . for the electoral support of the masses."[11] It should be clear that Posner is using "pragmatism" in a way that, while common, is far from "Pragmatism" as a philosophy that includes John Dewey.

In his *Nation* article, Chris Hayes is aware of the ambiguity of the use of the term "pragmatism" in politics and is hopeful that Obama will be a "pragmatist" in the more philosophical and Deweyan sense. He writes:

> Pragmatism in common usage may mean simply a practical approach to problems and affairs. But it's also the name of the uniquely American school of philosophy. . . . This tradition is a worthy inheritance for any president, particularly in times as manifestly uncertain as these. And if there's a silver thread woven into the pragmatist mantle Obama claims, it has its origins in this school of thought. Obama could do worse than to look to John Dewey, another one-time resident of Hyde Park and the founder of the University of Chicago Laboratory Schools, which Obama's daughters attend[ed].

There are, however, others that are not so optimistic about Obama, precisely because they are worried that he may be a Pragmatist in the philosophical sense. They have raised criticisms of Pragmatism as a philosophy because they feel it falls short of what is needed today in the political arena. While many of these critics are seeking a postideological way to do politics, they find Pragmatism as an alternative to be shallow, empty, without a moral backbone, and ultimately a view that sanctions politics as usual. For instance, a recent editorial in the *Christian Science Monitor* asserts a critic's concern about relying on Obama's or anyone else's Pragmatism as a guide to lead a nation. "Policy devoid of clear ethical theory creates a nation without principle, and a nation without principle is a nation on stilts." "An analysis of what pragmatism really means explains why Mr. Obama's plan has not (and cannot) work. It also reveals the emptiness of pragmatism as national principle."[12] Hayes voices a similar concern when he says, "Obama may have told Steve Kroft that he's solely interested in 'what works,' but what constitutes 'working' is not self-evident and, indeed, is impossible to detach from some worldview and set of principles."[13]

The concern behind the remarks critical of Obama is clear: unless Pragmatism in the philosophical sense can convince us that it has enough substance beyond repeating the vague assertions that it is committed to "what works" instead of ideology, it is hard to see a significant difference between it and Pragmatism in the narrow expedient sense. Obama may be a Pragmatist in the philosophical sense, but that makes him susceptible to the same problem of a Pragmatist as a self-serving opportunist—not enough of a moral backbone to avoid relativism and to change the pessimistic or cynical view that many have about politicians.

I am sympathetic to these recent critics of Pragmatism. Part of the problem is that, although pragmatism is often mentioned as the alternative to ideological politics, outside of the academic world there has been very little effort to articulate what Pragmatism means. I have already suggested the importance of "contextualism," but more is needed to answer the critics. It is not enough to reply, as many scholars in Pragmatism have, that Pragmatism in politics is more than mere political expediency because Deweyean Pragmatism is committed to deliberation, experimentation, fallibilism, and social intelligence. None of these broad prescriptions address moral values, and in fact seem perfectly compatible with a politician that has these commitments and traits but lacks the sort of moral character needed in an ideal democracy.

The recent "normative modesty" of Robert Talisse and Cheryl Misak[14] in restricting the understanding of Pragmatism in politics to an epistemology is also insufficient. Their argument does not address the concerns of the objectors who are searching for more *moral* substance. These recent epistemologists of Pragmatism seem to put great faith in the inculcation of proper epistemic habits (e.g., concern for truth, reasoning well, etc.) but are these habits sufficient to ensure we have democratic political leaders? A politician may be a fallibilist and abide by epistemic principles. He/she may base policy decisions on reasons, arguments, listening to others, and evidence. Yet this seems compatible with someone driven by money and power instead of care for the people that he or she represents. Nor does being epistemically responsible guarantee moral integrity. Seemingly most people who are cynical about politics think of politicians as "moral" failures and not just epistemic failures. We wish to hold politicians morally responsible and not just epistemically responsible.

Granted, to have excellent epistemic habits avoids ideologues, wishful thinking, and dogmatism, but doesn't the Pragmatist politician need some sort of moral commitment in order to avoid becoming the opportunist, self-serving politician that "flip-flops" on positions and is willing to compromise on the basis of mere expediency? I think this is the intuition behind those who want to defend Obama by ascribing onto him some ideology, at least vaguely conceived as some conceptual framework or set of principles to stand on. Otherwise, Obama would remain susceptible to becoming just another "Pragmatist" politician in the narrow, opportunistic sense. Here is how Hayes puts it: "while ideology can lead decision-makers to ignore facts, it is also what sets the limiting conditions for any pragmatic calculation of interests . . . Principle is often pragmatism's guardian."[15]

Dewey's Pragmatism is, however, not susceptible to the objection of lacking a moral backbone because moral values, virtues, and commitments are integral to his conception of the ideal politician. How is this consistent with the well-known notion that a Pragmatist is committed to "what works"?

4. THE PRAGMATIST'S COMMITMENT TO "WHAT WORKS": THE IDEAL CONTEXTUALIST POLITICIAN

The vague commitment to "what works," often cited as key to being a Pragmatist politician, has not helped with the moral reputation of Pragmatism. For many, this vague commitment appears as either spineless, as an empty assertion, or as leading to an unwanted relativism. Let us examine some of the most common reasons for these impressions and concerns, and how Dewey's Pragmatism would answer those critics.

For some critics, to state "what works" does not answer the important questions. For them, "what works" raises the questions: "For whom?" "For what?" "What works" is always relative to some ends that people may disagree on.

People may derive different judgments about "what works" because they have disagreement about ultimate ends-values. Consequently, we must first determine the desired ends.[16]

Dewey scholars reply to the "ends" objection by noting the objector's impoverished understanding of Pragmatism. For Dewey, the means and ends distinction is functional. Dewey argues that ends can be subjected to evaluation by its means and other contextual factors. This is an unsatisfying reply to the objectors because it does not address their implicit need for an ultimate standard of evaluation of *both* means and ends. The objector finds "what works" empty because he/she cannot conceive how "what works" in a particular case can be determined without presupposing some general standard or criterion of "what works." But the objector is asking for precisely that which Dewey denies and cannot provide given his contextualism: in matters of evaluation and judgment, there is no ultimate single criterion for a right judgment across all situations. For Dewey, "what works" is not what meets a standard but "what fits or resolves *this* present problematic situation." Dewey's approach can be called a type of "relativism" but it is a relativism to each situation as the ultimate context that grounds our judgments. "What works" has to remain a general, empty, and vague assertion because "what works" is different in each situation. Saying more tends to defeat the purpose of the expression.

The ideal Pragmatist politician is sensitive to context. Sensitivity to context means, among other things, that one does not impose a single end or a universal criterion across problematic situations. A politician that tries to deal with contentious issues by always seeking answers that reach consensus or bipartisan support is not a Pragmatist in Dewey's ideal sense. Sure, sometimes the problematic situation is such that preventing legislative gridlock trumps everything else, but we rely on the judgment of the ideal politician to figure out what the situation calls for, and other goals, ends, obligations, and values are to be given consideration in that deliberation. One implication of the notion of the ideal contextualist politician is that he/she is more unpredictable than those who are ideologues or those who adhere to one single end or criteria. One may argue that politicians should be predictable, but it is not obvious why predictability is so desirable.

For other objectors, the problem with Pragmatism in politics is not that it lacks a criterion of "what works," but that the presupposed criterion is narrow and leaves out moral values and principles. In the political arena for example, it is assumed that the politician that is committed to "what works" believes that deliberation, decisions, or judgments should be based solely on some type of scientific or cost-benefit calculation. Bronsther says:

> For James, things are "true"—and thus we ought to accept them and act upon them—insofar as they "work" for people, making their lives more satisfactory. Through philosophical [P]ragmatism, the ethical questions of politics became scientific questions. A lawmaker was to assess a policy's impact on the real world."[17]

Why is the opposition to dogma and ideology and the Pragmatist's corresponding emphasis on inquiry so often understood as implying scientism or consequentialism?[18] Granted, to inquire about policies "that work" may require science and deliberating about possible consequences. It does not follow, however, that consequences (of any particular kind) or science determines the ultimate criteria of judging "what works" in a particular situation.

Bronsther and others are suspicious of the Pragmatist's rhetoric in appealing to "what works." They see the appeal as naïve, and the rhetoric to be a way ignoring or avoiding moral values, moral discussion, moral ideals, and moral disagreement:

> He [Obama] presumes that policies forged by reason, evidence, and "unbiased" expertise—those policies that "work"—will garner the support of all reasonable members of Congress and thus bridge partisan divides. He bases his belief in the possibility of national and political consensus on this faulty argument. Consensus has not emerged in Washington because disagreement exists.... What "works" for liberals doesn't work for conservatives.... The deeper partisan disagreements are ethical and philosophical.[19]

The assumption in Bronsther's criticism of Pragmatism seems to be that "what works" requires deliberation about value-neutral facts or that "what works" entails the primacy of an impartial or value-free standpoint in deciding policy. First, this interpretation assumes a dualism between facts and values, something that any good philosophical Pragmatist would deny. Moreover, the Pragmatist does not assume a priori (prior to a situation) and naïvely that there is more agreement about facts than there is about values. Ideologues often cling to ideals, theories, and values in such a way as to ignore facts. A Pragmatist emphasizes facts, concrete circumstances, present situational needs and possibilities, but she does not ignore the important function of ideals, theories, and values in deliberation and good judgment. Let's make this clear.

Pragmatists are utterly opposed to decisions and judgments guided by ideology, as implied by the contextualism already explained. We must be careful, however, not to conclude that Pragmatists therefore hold the contrary view: that one must remain neutral or empty in regard to principles, ideas, ideals, concepts, and values or to any of the content that is associated with "ideology." For the Pragmatist, there may be here a false dichotomy. We are not caught up with an either/or situation, e.g., either there are politicians whose decisions are ideologically driven or they are purely focused on "what works" in a situation (in some value-neutral way). The truth of the matter is that even the most ideological person or politician has some degree of situational flexibility, and even the person most willing to compromise and be flexible is usually committed to something. Finding the proper balance between openness and commitment is in fact part of what is ideal, according to Dewey.[20] If having an "ideology" merely means the inclusion of principles, ideals, and values in political deliberation, then Pragmatists (at least Dewey) had one: it is called "democracy." I suspect, however, that most people would find this last sense of "ideology" too broad to be useful, especially in politics where "ideology" is used to describe the "ideologue," someone who is contrary to Pragmatism.

Dewey does not think that his contextualism, and the openness and flexibility that it requires of us, to be incompatible with wholehearted commitment to ideals, principles, and values. The latter are, in fact, part of the contextual resources (tools) in a situation that are needed to determine relevance. Sometimes these tools provide useful standpoints that can help in deliberation, but they do not specify the specific course of action. In some cases, principles may be what keeps good political leaders "anchored," and prevents them from going down the "slippery slope" in their flexibility and compromise. Hence, a general demand for some principles or values to guide a politician's deliberation seems reasonable. What is not reasonable, for Dewey, is the expectation that these principles and values need to operate in deliberation as criteria or standards that determine judgment. "What works" does not mean not guided by principles. Instead, it means that what is a justified or proper course of action cannot be determined in advance of the problematic situation that calls for judgment. In facing social problems, one should try to do "what works" and not what some absolute principle or antecedent criteria tells him/her. The Pragmatist is very flexible. She is even willing to "test" principles in light of present problems. Yet she does not enter the situation empty handed or "neutral" among values, nor should she try to do so.

Far from an empty or value-free assertion, "what works" in Dewey's version of Pragmatism presupposes a "thick" or substantive normative standpoint. "What works" means that which ameliorates or resolves the particular problematic situation calling for our judgment. However, Dewey has a substantial prescription about how this resolution should be accomplished. According to Dewey, we must try to come to judgment by being sensitive and open to the present and unique problematic context, while also being guided by democratic values and principles. This is a different prescription from doing what is most expedient (as in the "Pragmatist opportunist") or what safeguards the validity or subsistence of an ideology. It is also a different prescription than to pursue truth or any of the epistemic goals of the recent epistemic Pragmatists.

Dewey's contextualism is part of a normative ethical philosophy, with substantial recommendations about character, dialogue, and community, that is found in his ethical philosophy. In a democracy, reasonable judgments require characters that transact with others who are equipped with certain habits, such as sensitivity and openness to context. Dewey also mentions virtues regarding our treatment of others, such as trust, tolerance, and empathy. This is not the place to examine all the character traits of the ideal "Pragmatist" politician that is needed for Dewey's ideal of democracy *as a way of life*. I must, however, say something about empathy since it refutes the notion that Dewey's Pragmatism prescribes an impartial, value-free standpoint in the political arena. Furthermore, Dewey's view on empathy could be considered as another reason in favor of the view that Obama is a Deweyan Pragmatist.

5. EMPATHY AS A DEMOCRATIC VIRTUE

From the standpoint of Dewey's philosophy, impartiality has been overrated in the history of ethical and political theory. "Impartiality" can be a virtue but only in some contexts—and there is no such thing as absolute impartiality. Selectivity and partiality are at bottom unavoidable traits of any inquiry. Dewey says:

> It is not concern which is objectionable even when it takes the form of bias. It is certain kinds of bias that are obnoxious. *Bias for impartiality is as much a bias as is partisan prejudice, though it is a radically different quality of bias.* To be

> "objective" in thinking is to have certain sort of selective interest operative. One can only see from certain standpoint but this fact does not make all standpoints of equal value. . . .[21]

Strict objectivity or impartiality is a myth. Pragmatists are suspicious of the separation of inquiry and facts from value. Inquiry starts with, and cannot totally divest itself from, values and the normative to achieve a neutral "objectivity" from a "god's-eye view." For the classical Pragmatists, values are unavoidable. Where there are always partialities, the only reasonable question is: which partiality is best? There are better and worse "biases" relative to their capacity to disclose the scope and depth of the situation:

> A standpoint which is nowhere in particular is an absurdity. But one may have an affection for a standpoint which gives a *rich and ordered landscape* rather than for one from which things are seen confusedly and meagerly.[22]

Which "habits of desire and imagination"[23] one brings to a situation will determine one's selectivity, and hence the scope and depth of the present situation that is being immediately appreciated (had) and reflectively examined. There are habits that provide the agent a rich, broad landscape upon which to deliberate and to act, and there are others that in comparison are constraining, one sided, and narrow. Dewey prescribed "the fostering of those habits and impulses which lead to a broad, just, sympathetic survey of situations."[24] Empathy and openness are two valuable "undergoing" habits in this regard.

For Dewey, whether our experience is wide or narrow depends also on the extent and depth of what he called sympathy, but today is known as empathy. To exchange places—emotionally and imaginatively—with another is the only way to widen our intellectual horizon in situations and to determine effectively what ought to be done. As Dewey said, this is the most "generous thought." On the other hand, "a person of narrow sympathy is of necessity a person of confined outlook upon the scene of human good."[25]

The rationalist tradition in moral and political theory has assumed that the avoidance of a distorting partiality in deliberation, and the guarantee for considerate and just treatment of others, requires the adoption of the universal and objective standpoint provided by reason. Dewey cannot make sense of an impartial and universal standpoint. However, Dewey holds that the closest we could get to a similarly broad intellectual standpoint—that might be useful for deliberation—is with the aid of sympathy. "Sympathy . . . furnishes the most reliable and efficacious intellectual standpoint. It supplies the tool, par excellence, for analyzing and resolving complex cases . . . for an effective, broad, and objective survey of desires, projects, resolves, and deeds."[26] The concern implied by a genuine sense of justice cannot be accounted for by the intellectual capacities associated with the impartiality of reason, it requires sympathy. "A person entirely lacking in sympathetic responses might have a keen calculating intellect, but he would have no *spontaneous sense* of the claims of others."[27] Failure to treat others (beyond one's social group) as equals is not a deficiency in the ability to perform a reasoning process from a formal principle of justice, nor is it a result of failing to grasp intellectually and abstractly the respect in which all people are equal. Justice ceases to be a virtue if it is not fused with sympathy. It is through sympathy that one can appreciate what justice demands because it makes possible for us to understand what each person needs in a vivid and more reliable fashion. Hence, Dewey claimed:

> [T]o put ourselves in the place of another, to see things from the standpoint of his aims and values . . . is the surest way to appreciate what justice demands in concrete cases.[28]

Let us return to the topic of Pragmatism and the notion of an ideal politician. For Dewey, there is nothing problematic about a politician being partial or biased with regard to moral values and ideals. Dewey would admit that not all biases are the same. A bias towards the values of democracy in our political leaders is important to avoid such practices as imposition and oppression. For Dewey, avoiding narrow partiality, and therefore respect for pluralism and inclusivity of understanding, requires what Obama has recently called "empathy" in his stated criteria for Supreme Court justice. On the campaign trail, Obama said that he would want his Supreme Court nominees to have "empathy." Notice in his remarks to Planned Parenthood (July 17, 2007) how Obama seems to be contrasting the impartiality of an umpire with empathy:

> You know, Justice Roberts said he saw himself just as an umpire. But the issues that come before the court are not sport. They're life and death. And we need somebody who's got the heart to recognize—the empathy to recognize what it's like to be a young, teenaged mom; the empathy to understand what it's like to be poor or African American or gay or disabled or old. And that's the criteria by which I'm going to be selecting my judges.

Critics of Obama's criteria consider his view a threat to the "objectivity" and "impartiality" needed to be a good judge. Empathy seems, to them, to be irreconcilable with decision making, which to them must be based solely on law and facts. Everyone agrees that ideology should not guide a judge or a politician. The disagreement is about the role of empathy. For Dewey, and perhaps for Obama, strict impartiality or neutrality is impossible and in any case undesirable. When empathy is added to other important qualities, such as intellect, integrity, and respect for the law, those qualities broaden deliberation, and counteract narrow partiality to achieve justice.

6. CONCLUSION

Dewey's ethical-political thought is a resource worth considering as a guide to a postideological politics. A commitment, even a partisan commitment, to certain values and principles, while also being open and sensitive to the uniqueness and complexity of each problematic context, is a virtue for Dewey. Refusing to predefine "what works" ahead of problematic situations gives the ideal Pragmatist politician the flexibility that is not present in the ideologue.

It is true that there is always the danger that this flexibility could turn eventually into the undesirable flexibility of the self-serving "flip-flopper." Yet this "slippery slope" problem is not inevitable, and it is a danger worth taking in comparison to the alternatives, especially the rigidity of the ideological political leader. Moreover, the best way to prevent this danger is by making sure that virtues (such as good habits) are not turned into vices, and not by strict adherence to rules or absolute values. This is the importance of character in Dewey's ethics. For Dewey, good judgment and deliberation depend on the cultivation of virtuous habits. Encouraging in a community certain virtues is the best way to prepare for particular collective decision making, and the best way to counteract the seductions that politicians have to face (e.g., power, money, status, and wishful thinking). Instilling virtuous traits is the alternative to the imposition of proper rules or restrictions on public discourse , and the reason why Dewey puts so much faith in education.

The sort of intelligent and context-sensitive deliberation and communication that Dewey thought was needed in a democracy requires characters with certain dispositions. We have mentioned some of them here: sensitivity to context, open mindedness, tolerance, and empathy. These virtues, however, cannot be cultivated unless this last type of deliberation and communication is practiced, not just in the White House, but also within society as a whole. The obstacles needed to cultivate the virtues required for a postideological age in politics are too numerous to mention, but this is an inquiry worth having.

Pragmatists have been severe critics of abstract moral arguments, fixed or absolute values, and the quest for some ultimate criteria of all judgments. This has somehow been interpreted as implying the denial of the important role of values, principles, and morality. Dewey's normative view may still be considered too "thin" from the point of view of those that believe that the ideal politician must guide himself by absolute moral values. In other words, objectors may still insist that only adherence to absolute values would help us avoid moral anarchy or apathy. Under that assumption, it seems impossible to convince them that a Pragmatist has a strong enough "moral backbone" to make judgments and lead a country.

Do we need to worry about Obama being a Pragmatist in the philosophical sense? I have shown that these worries are based on misconceptions about the ethics of Pragmatism. A careful reading of this philosophical tradition, especially of Dewey, reveals an ethics that, while not centered on an ultimate criterion of right conduct, is substantive enough to offer normative moral guidance centered on democratic values and virtues. What we really need to worry about is putting too much hope on one single individual (e.g., Obama) to break the shared habits and the environment that continue to perpetuate ideological thinking and practical opportunism in politics. Dewey's ethics of democracy puts the emphasis not on particular politicians transcending ideology, but on having more communal inquiries and deliberations where people can rightfully and wisely choose from both sides of the political spectrum if the context calls for it. The recent brawls in town hall meetings about health care policy[29] are evidence that we are failing at all levels of society to have the sort of discussion about broad policy questions that democracy requires. We need to inquire into what it takes to break with the ideological ways of thinking that have dominated discourse at all levels. To leave things as they are will perpetuate pessimistic and cynical views about politicians *and* people. As we all know, losing faith in the people is the beginning of the end of a democracy.

ACKNOWLEDGMENT

An earlier version of this article appeared in *John Dewey at 150: Aesthetics, Ethics, Science, and Society* (Amsterdam and New York: Rodopi, forthcoming), ed. Larry A. Hickman, Matthew Caleb Flamm, Krzysztof Piotr, and Jennifer Anne Rea.

19.

DEWEYAN EXPERIMENTALISM AND LEADERSHIP

Eric Thomas Weber

The society of which the child is to be a member is, in the
United States, a democratic and progressive society. The
child must be educated for *leadership* as well as for obedience. He [or she] must have power of self-direction and
power of directing others, powers of administration,
ability to assume positions of responsibility. This necessity of educating for *leadership* is as great on the industrial as on the political side.
—John Dewey, "Ethical Principles Underlying Education"[1]

In this paper, I intend to lay out the various lessons that John Dewey has to
offer to scholars and teachers of leadership. It is odd that so few philosophers
today study the subject of leadership. It is even stranger for Pragmatists, who are
concerned with the practical application of philosophical ideas. For in the study
of leadership one finds necessarily the combined matters of intelligent judgment
and of practical application in important contemporary matters. To begin, I will
call attention to the place that the study of leadership held in past philosophical
discourse in order to offer my hypothesis regarding the reasons leadership as a
matter of study has receded from focus in philosophy. Next, I will describe the
growing movement of institutions of higher learning in America that are increasingly desirous of intelligent theorizing about leadership, particularly from
philosophers. Finally, I will describe the contributions that Dewey has to offer
the field that answer frequently raised challenges to the possibility of democratic
leadership theory, and I will present the positive content of the study which we
may draw from his theories of intelligence, ethics, and education.

Socratic criticisms of the Sophists are familiar. Plato told the stories of famous persons who proclaimed wisdom in various areas of public life and who charged fees for the wisdom they imparted. Socrates would visit with these Sophists and would question them about their areas of expertise so that he might test or confirm the notion he learned from the Delphic Oracle, that he was wisest of the Greeks. Time and time again, he learned that the persons famed for their wisdom in fact knew not what they claimed to, and revealed him to be wiser due to his awareness of his own ignorance. In this context, we see that in the Sophists there was a tradition of training the young in the arts of successful living and the achievement of power, but it was empty of the knowledge and ethics that would produce good and beneficial citizen leaders. Rather than avoid thinking of leadership, Plato's most famous work, the *Republic*, addresses leadership and the education thereof as a crucial political consideration. Plato warned, "the greatest punishment for being unwilling to rule is being ruled by someone worse than oneself."[2] With such warnings, Plato laid out his ideas about how best to organize societies, which included a stratification that is well known. Many other figures could be listed among those who have written philosophically about leadership. A few of them include Confucius, Lao Tzu, Aristotle, Cicero, Marcus Aurelius, Machiavelli, and Hobbes.

Scholars outside the field of philosophy have produced a significant literature on leadership in the last hundred years, but it has been dominated by authors who study business, the management of organizations, and education. The last of these is likely in some ways to have been influenced by Dewey, who spoke of leadership in the context of education in many writings. Also contributing to the scholarship on the subject of leadership are historians. Historians have long focused their studies on political power and dynasties. Today, historians have come to study leaders in a variety of areas, such as in the sciences. Still, few scholars focus on the philosophical demands of moral and democratic leadership, which I believe we can develop from a study of Dewey's work. I should mention a few scholars, however, who are philosophers of leadership. One example is Terry Price at the Jepson School of Leadership Studies at the University of Richmond. Price has authored several books on the general subject of ethical failures of leadership. He approaches the study from the Kantian perspective which criticizes the notion that as leaders, persons should have freedom to bend rules that ordinary citizens should not violate. Some of Price's colleagues study the subject of leadership from a philosophical perspective, but the very small number of such scholars in America is surprising at least.

Although I can only offer some initial conjecture here, I suspect there are a few reasons why philosophers have gotten away from studying leadership. The first and most fair reason is that traditional theories of leadership have in general *not* been democratic. That is, scholars historically have followed the sort of Machiavellian or Hobbesian reasoning that some associate with immorality. In times past, social stratification was taken for granted and went unchallenged, and thus the corresponding theories of leadership were considered outdated at best. In effect, scholars of leadership as recently as 2001 and 2003 titled papers such as Kathryn Riley's article, "'Democratic Leadership'—A Contradiction in Terms?" and Robert J. Starrat's article, "Democratic Leadership Theory in Late Modernity: An Oxymoron or Ironic Possibility?"[3] These and other articles are evidence of an apparent assumption that the theory of leadership must be considered elitist or undemocratic. Perhaps these scholars have been conditioned by authoritarian academic deans and department chairs, but more likely, they are revealing the baggage of theories of leadership that have yet to be sufficiently reconstructed in the contemporary world.

I have said that the philosophical study of leadership is a growth area for the future of philosophy. The following are some examples. In many states, private donors and retiring political leaders have been giving money to universities for the formation of institutes of public policy and leadership. The University of Mississippi, where I work and teach, has such an institute named after former Senator Trent Lott. Elsewhere, schools of leadership have been created, as at the Jepson School at the University of Richmond. More are in development, such as the Frank Batten School of Leadership and Public Policy at the University of Virginia. Still elsewhere, we find organizations growing, such as the Institute for Philosophy and Public Policy at the University of Maryland. Growth abounds too in the development of centers for ethical leadership. In short, there is great and increasing demand for practical philosophy, especially that which connects to the various responsibilities of leadership and ethics. In this area, Dewey has much to offer.

The first point I wish to make was evidenced in the quote that opens the present paper. Dewey was perfectly clear that he saw a fundamental goal of education in a democratic society as the preparation of students for leadership. As such, his work on judgment, inquiry, experimentalism, and education all can contribute to a Deweyan theory of leadership.

The next point is programmatic. Most, if not all, of the schools of leadership in the United States are tied to a particular or at least a general area of study and application. For instance, schools of public policy and leadership are growing, as are schools of ethics and leadership, business and leadership, etc. Although the Jepson School is called a school of leadership *tout court*, in fact the school has various trajectories of leadership studies, and thus does not fail at the point Dewey would make here. In "Individuality, Equality and Superiority," Dewey wrote, "The endeavor to discover abstract degrees of mental superiority which fit for 'leadership' in the abstract is evidence of the hold upon us still exercised by feudal arrangements." He continued to explain, "Our new feudalism of the industrial life which ranks from the great financier through the captain of industry down to the unskilled laborer, revives and reinforces the feudal disposition to ignore individual capacity displayed in free or individualized pursuits."[4] Dewey believed this effect of the lingering feudalistic outlook is pernicious and in this light, we can see in reverse what he valued in a democratic society's approach to leadership, namely, respect for individual capacity.

Fundamentally, this second lesson tells us that, unlike in Plato's writings, for Dewey leadership is not a class of persons. It is not a stratified notion focused on elites. Now, as a scholar and teacher in a program of public policy leadership, I must address the matter of my program's education of particularly strong students in the skills of leadership with knowledge of a field of practical inquiry—namely, public policy. A possible challenge could be that it does not make sense from a Deweyan point of view to run a program that selects the strongest students for special training. In fact, I believe that Dewey would object only if the training we offered were somehow exclusive in the sense that others not be trained for leadership. Programs such as ours and others around the country are perfectly consistent with the effort in education more widely to prepare all students in the abilities of leadership of their own lives and of others. Specialization in an area of concentration, with attention to students interested in public policy in particular, for example, is acceptable from a Deweyan point of view, I believe, so long as it is open to all who wish to apply for the study.

Elsewhere, Dewey wrote about the need for leadership in educational endeavors, though not a strongly authoritative and consolidated type of leadership. While some federal support for schools and direction were things he called for, Dewey also recognized that scattered American efforts in education appeared to yield results that foreign states admired. In his essay, "The Direction of Education," Dewey commented on the lack of government guidance in education:

Exemption of political government and officials from responsibilities that are elsewhere incumbent upon them places corresponding responsibilities upon individuals and institutions. With all our drifting, there must be leadership somewhere, or absence of governmental system will signify lack of all unified and cooperative educational movement. But leadership that is not official can only be intellectual and moral leadership. It is not merely leadership in education but it is leadership by education rather than by law and governmental authority. Indeed, it is a kind of leadership that gives a new meaning to the word. It is a process of guidance. It takes effect through inspiration, stimulation, communication of ideas, discovery and report of facts, rather than by decree. It is compelled to trust for the most part to the power of facts and ideas and to the willingness of the community at large to receive and act upon them.[5]

In this passage we see a number of concepts that help us to conceive of leadership in education, but in organizations generally as well. First among these is the commonly made distinction between authority and leadership. Dewey alludes to such a distinction when he differentiates the *de jure* leadership of government which is lacking. Government by definition is an authoritative body, but clearly in some circumstances it need not serve as a source of leadership in affairs that can be well advanced by other means. Even if government ought to take the lead in some matters, furthermore, groups of citizens can band together to fill leadership needs without the official or nominal titles of leadership which the government holds. Such forms of leadership he calls intellectual or moral. While he would hold these categories to be overlapping, he could mean by the idea of intellectual leadership the sort which is involved in laboratory work, versus the kind which Dr. Martin Luther King Jr. represented, or Gandhi before him, while holding no official, governmental offices in their movements.

Second, when there is leadership, either in the way of government or of groups of citizens acting in concert, Dewey explains that what that leadership offers is "unified and cooperative . . . movement" with regard to the problem in question. In combining these two developments in Dewey's thought about leadership we see first the attention to public inquiry as fundamental to intellectual leadership. Plus we see the component that leadership offers in inquiry, namely, the creative force of synthesis which takes place when an inquirer establishes order in an otherwise chaotic or inchoate problematic situation.

Finally, while Dewey understands leadership of the *de jure* sort to include the public decrees that governments issue, he fleshes out also the elements of intellectual and moral leadership that individual citizens or groups can exhibit in the form of "a process of guidance," which "takes effect through inspiration, stimulation, communication of ideas, discovery and report of facts." Each of these elements is worth examining in considering the dimensions of intellectual and moral leadership.

Dewey's psychological and educational theories center on the idea of interest. As early as in his essay, "The Reflex Arc Concept in Psychology," Dewey explained that a fundamental trait of human personality is its inclination to attend to particular things in their environment as stimuli. With this insight, Dewey overturned the still popular idea that stimuli come first in the "stimulus-response" model of behavioral psychology. What Dewey called selectivity underlies human attention and interest. In the case of the study of leadership, Dewey's insights about individuals' selectivity or interests can be seen to play a role in the clarification of those elements of a problematic situation to which a leader or group of leaders can draw a community's attention—the step Dewey called *inspiration*. We can understand the importance of selectivity in inspiration when we examine a particular case in which leadership is needed. Is a Mississippi community's problem to do with educational resources, economic development, racial relations, poor roads, lack of sidewalks, obesity, or illiteracy? Any leader who hopes to solve all problems at once will solve none. Some elements of a problematic situation can, if resolved, contribute to the resolution of other problems, but where to start is a matter that will depend both on the context in question and on the varied and ranked interests of the community.

Once leaders find inspiration with regard to a problematic situation, they must work on *stimulation*. Stimulation can take place in the form of raising awareness among fellow citizens of shared problems with a community that might wish to address them. Exercises in awareness raising can take the form of peaceful marches, the mailing of informational documents, advertisements on television, the reporting of stories in news outlets, and much more. Leadership must involve the process of public relations in whatever forms would be the most effective for the context involved. We can see clearly so far how students can be taught these skills of leadership—inasmuch as their interests can be made the forefront of their research projects in public policy, and they can be taught to communicate and transfer messages that they have learned to craft clearly and with strong moral arguments.

Once inspiration and stimulation have occurred, leaders may experience push-back from their communities. Leaders' efforts will nearly always be imperfect public experiments. Thus, the *communication of ideas* is crucial for communities to have a say in recasting the problems which leaders initially lay out for debate. At least one common cause of failure in leadership concerns those situations in which leaders formulate inspiration and stimulation for projects without the proper experimentalist attitudes that leave one open to adjusting one's conceptions of the community's problems. Thus, the unstated lesson we can learn from Dewey's experimentalism and the step of the communication of ideas is that leaders must be open to revising their conceptions when better ways of conceiving of problems arise. This fallibilist attitude and process of open communication and criticism is crucial in the public inquiry into refining the understanding of problems.

Finally, while communities can frame problems together and suggest avenues for addressing their problems, at some point concrete research about existential conditions and possible costs of carrying out plans and solutions must be collected and reported to community members. Whereas in traditional notions of leadership, these tasks might be labeled grunt work, we see in Dewey the identification of these elements of leadership with the democratic ideals of public inquiry. For, if research and reporting is done poorly or is falsified, the strongest of authorities might fail in the demands of leadership. In this sense, then, we can see that those who perform data entry or other collection in large industries play a crucial role in the tasks of leadership, even though they tend to feel inferior and disconnected from the chain of authority. Understood properly, however, and if properly valued by those in positions of official authority, the persons who serve as interns or assistants can see their roles as vital in this important task of leadership.

It would be disingenuous for me to end here on these positive notes about leadership in America, given Dewey's several instances of critiquing American culture for failures in intelligent thinking and democratic leadership. Two circumstances worried Dewey on separate occasions with regard to leadership in America. He puts several problems in a simple statement when he addresses deference to authority and the feeling of powerlessness in his book, *Construction and Criticism*. He writes that

> we in this country are too submissive to what are termed authorities in different fields, and too little given to questioning their right to speak with authority. It is a common complaint that we are too credulous a people and are only too ready to swallow any bunk if it is offered with the prestige of apparent authority.[6]

In a later essay from 1932, "The Economic Situation," Dewey writes scathingly:

> I cannot remember a time when collective thinking—the ideas that are organic
> to large numbers—was so stupid, so incredibly incompetent as it is today. It is
> a common remark that we have a surprising absence of effective leadership in
> this crisis, domestic and international, economic and political. Now leadership,
> like a bargain, has two sides. There can be leadership as there can be following
> only when human beings think together about a common theme with a shared
> purpose to a common result. Leadership is absent because this power of collec-
> tive thinking in connection with solidarity of emotion and desire is lacking
> today. We have in its stead attempts to whip up a seeming unity of idea and sen-
> timent by means of catch-words, slogans, and advertising devices.[7]

I am sad to say that if Dewey thought people were capable of limited thinking
and of overadherence to marketing terms and devices for persuasion, he might at
times in the last few years have been quite a bit more disappointed today than he
was in 1932.

Despite the great dearth of public intelligence that the United States
exhibits at times, Dewey was able to see the positive element in the mass of individuals who "may not be very wise. But there is one thing they are wiser about
than anybody else can be, and that is where the shoe pinches, the troubles they
suffer from." He continues, in an essay titled "Democracy and Educational
Administration," with his faith in democracy, despite the limits brought by the
forces of unreason, writing, "The foundation of democracy is faith in the capacities of human nature; faith in human intelligence, and in the power of pooled
and cooperative experience. It is not belief that these things are complete," he
qualifies, "but that if given a show they will grow and be able to generate progressively the knowledge and wisdom needed to guide collective action," the
public and communal process of leadership.[9]

Now, one could ask me whether the present paper constitutes just the kind
of abstraction of the principles of leadership that Dewey warned against. If my
goal were to divine the abstract content of leadership regardless of democratic
context and for no application besides seeking the mind-independent truth of
the matter, the challenge would in fact be problematic for me. In my current
work, however, I am charged with the education of students in matters of public
policy and leadership, in particular with students' ethical and communicative
training. In writing and in speech I undertake this charge in a democratic society.

Thus, the answers I find in Dewey inform my plans for educating and developing my students' leadership abilities. As an example of one of the efforts that I undertake given my Deweyan influences, consider my course in public speaking. Like Plato, I would not find a course in speech sufficient on its own. For as Sophocles has said, "It is terrible to speak well and be wrong."[10] Instead, my course is a combination, titled "Critical Thinking, Communication, and Public Policy." In it, students are trained in a variety of forms of communication, including a rarely practiced one—where students in class offer impromptu yet formal feedback to one another on the previous student's prepared presentations. I work with students on the ways in which feedback can be optimally constructive, which is quite different from feedback that is only critical in the negative sense. Students are expected to offer each other ways to consider enhancing the strengths of each others' speeches, something which inevitably consists in noting the positive elements of presentations. All along, too, students cannot get away with poor or unclear arguments, as those are the first areas of critique for improvement. In ways such as these and in possible future projects of civic engagement and moral leadership, I hope to work with my students on these many elements of democratic leadership, which we can find examined in germ in Dewey's writings.

Part Six

EDUCATION AND SOCIETY

20.

DEWEY'S IMPACT ON EDUCATION

Stephen M. Fishman
and Lucille McCarthy

PART ONE: THE DEWEY-BASED REVOLUTION
IN COMPOSITION INSTRUCTION,
BY STEVE FISHMAN

W hen Dewey scholars discuss his impact on pedagogy, what is most often mentioned is his influence on primary school education.[1] In particular, Dewey is credited, and rightly so, with encouraging teachers to help students engage in and study occupations and practices that are important in their communities, the sort of approach with which Dewey experimented in his Laboratory School at the University of Chicago. By contrast, our focus in this two-part paper is Dewey's influence on the revolution in the teaching of writing that began in the late 1960s. The main focus of this revolution, on the negative side, was criticism of the exclusive attention of modern rhetoricians and writing teachers on the modeling of correct written forms and error-free prose. On the positive side, the revolution urged a return to emphasis on the early stages of composing that were included in classical rhetoric. These are the stages of invention and discovery.[2]

An important catalyst for this revolution was a 1979 conference hosted by the Canadian Council of Teachers of English at Carleton University in Ottawa. The theme of the conference was "Learning to Write," and it attracted 1,250 delegates from the United States, Australia, England, and Canada.[3] Janet Emig, a professor of English Education at Rutgers University, presented a seminal paper at the conference titled, "The Tacit Tradition." In her address, she told the delegates that John Dewey is "everywhere in our work."[4] Emig's paper, along with the other conference papers, were published a year later by the Canadian Council of Teachers of English under the title, *Reinventing the Rhetorical Tradi-*

tion.[5] I purchased a copy of this book, and when I read Emig's paper and her remark about Dewey, I had no idea what lay behind her observation. However, three years later I had an experience that helped me appreciate Emig's claim, an experience that led me to change my pedagogical practice, the focus of my research, and, ultimately, my appreciation of the relevance of Dewey's work for both the revolution in composition instruction and my life.

1. Attending My First Writing Across the Curriculum Retreat

At the close of the spring semester, 1983, I saw notices on my university campus announcing a weekend Writing Across the Curriculum retreat sponsored by our English Department. "No way," I said to myself, "am I going to attend." However, four days before the retreat was to begin, I received a handwritten note from Sam Watson, one of the organizers, asking if there was any chance I could come. At that time we were a small school, and faculty members knew each other very well. I figured that Sam must be desperate for attendees if he was asking me to come since he was well aware that I enjoyed academic conferences even less than I enjoyed traveling. However, to be a good colleague and help Sam out, I decided to go, but I could not keep myself from complaining to some other faculty members that I would really be angry if this turned out, like many other academic conferences I had attended, to be a lot of theoretical talk "going nowhere." In response, they assured me that Sam said that this conference would be different.

About thirty-five faculty members attended the retreat, and, at the end of the first day's session, we were instructed to read an article before "calling it a night" and to then write for ten minutes about the article but without worry about grammar, punctuation, or anyone evaluating our written comments. Around 10 PM that evening I dutifully turned on the desk lamp in my small room and began reading. About halfway through I became discouraged and then angry about being tricked again. The piece that we were assigned to read was another instance of an academic author speaking about the intricacies of various theories of composition that, to me, seemed of interest only to those who were already familiar with detailed debates about the relative merits of these theories. As my feelings of disappointment built, I recalled the rest of our instructions: just respond quickly, writing for ten minutes without worry about grammar, correctness, or any evaluations of what you say. This recollection surprisingly changed my mood. I suddenly realized that I had something I wanted to say and had a chance to get down my thoughts and feelings without concern for how they happened to tumble out on the page. As a result, alongside my anger over what I was reading, an emotion of anticipation grew that I had never experienced before. Whereas previous writing assignments seemed a chore, I now was buoyed by the chance to write. I felt grateful for it and could not wait to finish the article so I could begin. Although at the moment I could not have expressed my feelings of anticipation in the following words, I was, for the first time, on the threshold of the discovery and invention stages of writing.

2. The Consequences of Attending My First Writing Conference

The retreat ended on a Sunday, and during my three-hour drive home I began to see how the revolution in composition instruction was indebted to Dewey's emphasis on integrating construction with criticism and distinguishing the actual exploration of new issues and thoughts from the subsequent mapping or recording of those discoveries.[6] Even more important, I felt a new appreciation for Dewey's remark in *How We Think* that there is a great difference between having to say something and having something to say.[7] Not only did my writing at the retreat open me to a deeper appreciation of Dewey, it also led me to recall how, as a student, I had often been put in the position of having to say something without really having anything to say. In addition, I began to feel guilty about how frequently I had put my own students in that same difficult position.

The day following my return from the retreat was the first day of my school's summer session. As I walked across campus from my office to the building where my class was to meet, I tossed away the copies of the course syllabus that I was carrying and had planned to give to my students. Instead, I decided I would write a new syllabus built around helping them use the various techniques I had practiced at the writing conference, techniques that might help them find that they had something to say when I asked them to say something. An important goal of my course would be to introduce them to focused free writing, double-entry notetaking, and journaling, plus any other techniques I could develop, to facilitate their discovering connections between their own interests and knowledge and the subject matter of my course.[8]

In short, on that summer morning I decided to abandon the Socratic questioning and minilectures that I had been using for almost fifteen years of university teaching and replace it with a teaching style that reflected my new appreciation of Dewey. Instead of questioning and lecturing, I would embrace, as my primary pedagogical approach, a commitment to teach indirectly.[9] Instead of focusing on questioning students and giving information, I would focus more self-consciously on shaping the class environment. I would organize my class activities so that students might more easily find ways in which their own interests could be satisfied and expanded by attending to my in-class discussions, course readings, and writings-for-discovery. In this way, I reasoned, I had a better chance of stimulating my students' attention and discipline than if I relied on their usual fear of receiving poor grades. I even dared hope that their interest and attention might help them—at least on an occasion or two—forget about grades altogether and, borrowing language from Dewey, "lose themselves" to "find themselves" in the reading, writing, and exchanging that they did in my course.[10]

3. Co-writing and Researching with Lucille McCarthy

After a few semesters of experimenting with my Dewey-inspired-revolution-in-composition-instruction pedagogy, I was eager to find out how my new classroom approach was working. So for several semesters I studied student papers from my Introduction to Philosophy classes and, on two occasions, wrote pieces about what I had learned regarding the effects on my students of my new pedagogy.[11] However, I was not satisfied with the data that I was able to collect on my own. As luck would have it, in the year following that first summer writing retreat, Sam Watson persuaded a number of UNCC faculty to join him in presenting our experiences with writing in our classes at the annual spring meeting of the Conference on College Composition and Communication (sponsored by the National Council of Teachers of English). Our presentations at these conferences continued for several years, and, at the 1989 CCCC meeting, we participated in a joint session with other writing-across-the-curriculum groups from universities in Virginia and Maryland.

It was at this 1989 conference that I met Lucille McCarthy, a professor of English at the University of Maryland, Baltimore County. After several conversations, we agreed to collaborate in researching my teaching and my students' learning, hoping that our different skills and concerns might complement one another. In particular, we hoped that Lucille's training as an educational ethnographer and experienced teacher of composition, when combined with my experience teaching philosophy, might yield fruitful results for both of us. Our hunch about our value to one another as researchers has, over the succeeding years, proven to be a good one. Regarding my own benefits, our classroom research has enabled me to experience one of the Deweyan ideals that I now hold most dear, namely, wholehearted interest.[12] It has frequently helped me integrate teaching and research, the study of classroom practice and of philosophic theory, and individual research and collaborative inquiry.

I now yield to Lucille McCarthy who, in the second part of our two-part essay, will describe the effects on my students of the Dewey-based revolution in composition instruction.

PART TWO: THE DEWEY-BASED REVOLUTION IN COMPOSITION INSTRUCTION AS SEEN IN ONE PHILOSOPHY CLASSROOM, BY LUCILLE MCCARTHY

As Steve Fishman has explained in Part One of our essay, the revolution in composition instruction in the 1960s and 1970s involved a shift from focus on students' finished products to a concern for their actual composing processes and their ability to make personally meaningful discoveries—what Dewey might call constructed knowing. In my part of our two-part presentation, I describe the effects of this Dewey-based revolution on an upper-division philosophy course that Steve taught and I observed in spring 2005. Fishman's class was titled "The Philosophy and Practice of Hope," and our study of it resulted in our coauthored 2007 book titled *John Dewey and the Philosophy and Practice of Hope*.[13] The course focused on four twentieth-century figures: three philosophers and one psychologist. The philosophers were John Dewey, Gabriel Marcel, and Paulo Friere. The psychologist was C. R. Snyder, a contemporary American who teaches at the University of Kansas and who has written extensively about hope. I observed Fishman's Hope class in person on seven occasions, and he had all class sessions videotaped for later analysis. In addition, I regularly interviewed the ten students who enrolled in the class, and I studied their writing across the semester. Throughout this project, Fishman and I collaborated on all aspects of data collection and analysis, and, although we wrote our research reports for our book under separate bylines—with Steve writing the first half of the book, the philosophy of hope, and me writing the second half, the practice of hope—across the several years we worked on this project, we read and commented on every line of each other's work.

My chief research questions going into this study were as follows: What were students' levels of hope at the start of the course? What discoveries, if any, did they make about hope during the semester? What literature and/or teaching techniques underlay such discoveries? As I describe my answers to these questions in our book, my challenge, as a composition researcher, was to straddle the line between what I call research validity and narrative validity. That is, I needed to gain credibility with my readers as a special kind of researcher, one who is never neutral or unbiased but one whose findings are, nevertheless, data based and trustworthy because I have employed well-accepted methods of qualitative inquiry. At the same time, my aim was to make my narrative accounts of this one teacher and his ten students as universal as I could so my readers had a chance to recognize themselves and their students and decide which of my findings they might transfer to their own lives and classrooms. Dewey himself supported this sort of qualitative classroom research. In a 1928 address to teachers, he said,

> [Research in education] requires judgment and art to select from the total circumstances of a case just what elements are the causal conditions of learning. . . . It requires candor and sincerity to keep track of failures as well as successes. . . . It requires trained and acute observation to note the indications of progress in learning . . . a much more highly skilled kind of observation than is needed to note the results of mechanically applied tests.[14]

I turn now to specific findings about Fishman's pedagogy and his students' experiences with it. These findings illustrate the impact of the Dewey-inspired revolution in writing instruction, a revolution that, as Steve has explained, fosters the integration of criticism and construction, the academic and personal, and the individual and group. As I will show, this revolution affects every aspect of Steve's classroom.

Fishman's teaching is shaped, as he has said, by his commitment to what Dewey might call constructed knowing, and this is unusual in his philosophy department and in the university generally. That is, Steve values thinking that requires students to construct personally meaningful knowledge by discovering how their academic work and their personal concerns might mutually inform one another. Thus, in all of his writing assignments, as well as in class discussion, Steve encourages students to apply concepts from the literature to their own lives. As he explained to me, he wants philosophy to "hit the ground." He fears, he said, being a philosopher who talks only to other philosophers while "the world is burning." In Fishman's commitment to having philosophy make a difference in the world, he echoes Dewey who inveighed against what he called "armchair philosophy." According to Dewey, philosophic thinking should begin and end in concrete problems; it should deal with the problems of people ("men") rather than with the problems of philosophers.[15]

In my interviews with the ten students in Fishman's Hope class, nine of whom were philosophy majors, I found they had had little or no experience in their college courses with constructed knowing, that is, with bringing their academic work and personal concerns together. Rather, they were much better acquainted with received knowing, where the knower receives and reproduces ideas and facts from outside authorities, and with critical knowing, where the knower steps back and critiques ideas and arguments. Although received and critical knowing are necessary if students are to master the concepts well enough to try them out in their own lives, I was aware from the beginning that Fishman, in making space in his classroom for constructed knowing, was inviting students to think, write, and speak in ways that were unusual for them.

For example, twenty-two-year-old, senior philosophy major Rebecca Hinson, in an April interview with me, contrasted the atmosphere in Fishman's class with the disputational climate in the other philosophy class in which she was enrolled that semester. Rebecca commented, "It's not so easy for me to speak up in my other philosophy class, because I know I'll be attacked by one or more classmates every time. However, in the Hope class, because we put so much of ourselves into it, we don't get into those objective conflicts. Instead, we're trying to come to an understanding about something, and we learn by hearing each other's different ways of responding to it." Another senior philosophy major, twenty-three-year-old Bob Glahn, agreed. In an interview at semester's end, Bob summed up Steve's teaching style with a term he had learned from Gabriel Marcel. Bob told me, "Dr. Fishman doesn't seem to feel that it's his automatic duty to argue with us or find holes in what we say. The best way to describe him is to say that he is 'present' to us."[16]

So how did Fishman's ten students fare in their efforts to integrate criticism and construction, individual and group, and academic and personal? In the end, six of the ten were able to balance academic and personal issues in their writing, and all but one of them said they appreciated Fishman's efforts to connect philosophy to their "real lives."

I will now tell you in some detail about one of these students who was able to apply philosophic concepts of hope to her personal concerns. Her name is Lindsey Weston, a twenty-one-year-old senior with a double major in philosophy and psychology. Lindsey entered the course saying that she needed to understand hope better. In mid-February, she told me, "I have a love-hate relationship with hope. Sometimes hope is good; sometimes it's not. I want to figure out when I should hope and when I shouldn't, when it's emotionally efficient and when it's not. I suspect this course won't help me figure it out, but maybe it will get me to think more."

Lindsey explained that she had been in Kuwait the previous summer with the Air National Guard, the only woman in her group of airplane mechanics, and she had been the victim of ugly rumors, with her friends not only failing to defend her but actually fanning the flames of the stories. Lindsey said that this, along with a cheating boyfriend back home, had caused her to lose her faith in humanity. She no longer trusted people and tended to see only the bad in them, which she hated, she said, and she wanted to get back to her pre-Kuwait openness and trust in others. She concluded our February interview by explaining that throughout her entire life she had done everything anyone asked of her. She had followed the rules. She had never harmed anyone. Yet the world had been cruel to her. She told me, "When I came back from overseas in September, I felt that the universe had screwed me, and it owed me some sort of compensation. I should get a break of some kind to restore the balance of good and bad in my life. . . . I'm hoping this course will make me look at my life differently. But that won't be easy because I can't accept truths that are handed to me by others. I have to make sense of things myself."

Although Lindsey said she didn't accept ideas handed her by others, in fact, she had been conditioned to be a received knower and was very concerned about grades since she wanted to go to graduate school in psychology. So for about half of the semester, in occasional conversations with Fishman after class, she tried to get him to tell her what he really wanted in her written work, that is, what she should do to get an "A." Steve told me that those conversations were difficult for him because, he said, "I can't tell Lindsey what these authors' ideas mean to her and her life." So he was gratified when Lindsey began to trust that he was serious about wanting students to explore new material by talking about how it applied to them.

As Lindsey gave up her received-knower, consumerist approach to learning, she moved to more of a co-investigator stance with Fishman and her classmates. Let me explain further. Lindsey started the semester by making rather loud and oversimple critical assertions in class about Dewey's work, declaring that he was "contradictory" and "inconsistent," seemingly trying, she said, to "have it both ways at once." Overall, she announced, Dewey's writing was very poor in comparison to the psychologists in her second major, who seemed "very precise." However, Lindsey worked hard on Fishman's reading and writing assignments, and in a class session in early March focusing on Dewey's book, *A Common Faith*,[17] Lindsey showed that she had become a more sensitive critical reader of Dewey's work. In fact, her comments show that she recognized a recurring pattern in Dewey's thinking, one in which, in ways he fully intends, he does indeed "have it both ways at once." But it is the question with which Lindsey concluded her contribution that day that Fishman later told me meant a great deal to him. The videotape shows Lindsey, after offering her interpretation of Dewey, turning to Fishman and asking, "Well, is that any help in our quest for the elusive Deweyan theory of hope?" Steve, who had told students all along that he was still trying to understand Dewey's ideas about hope, still working, that is, on what was to become Part 1 of our book, told me that it was as if, at that moment, Lindsey had become a different sort of learner, someone engaged in a collaborative project about which she was curious and in which she had a personal stake.

At semester's end, in Lindsey's final essay and in an interview with me, it was clear that the Dewey-inspired revolution in writing instruction had affected her learning. It was obvious that she had become comfortable connecting academic and personal concerns as she described the concepts from the hope literature that were most useful to her. These concepts came, ironically, not from the psychologist C. R. Snyder, whose book, *The Psychology of Hope*,[18] the class had read, but from Dewey. Most helpful to Lindsey, she said, was his idea that failure and success are intimately intertwined because they come from the same source. That is, all failures carry with them the possibility for new successes, and all successes carry with them the possibilities for new failures.[19] Lindsey told me that she had come to see that misfortune and disappointment—things we cannot control despite our best-laid plans—are to be expected. As a consequence, she began to reconstruct her experiences in Kuwait, and, she said, she had gradually let go of her anger. She came to see that she needed to change her view of the world, to understand that when things go badly it is neither a sign that the universe is punishing her nor a sign that she has been singled out for bad luck. She told me, "When I used to tell people about Kuwait, I would get all worked up because I felt a type of injustice that the good things I hoped for didn't turn out. I was like, I'm a good person, and I'm smart, and I can make things happen. So why didn't this or that materialize? . . . Now when bad things happen, I don't feel so much like I'm being picked on."

Lindsey said she also profited from a second idea she took from Dewey, namely, that "gratitude is the root of all virtue."[20] Lindsey's giving up her focus on the world's injustice and what the universe did not give her enabled her to be grateful for what the world *had* given her. This led her to feel some obligation, she said, to pay back. Instead of believing that the universe owed her a debt, Lindsey said, "if anything, I owe the world something."

This position, which Lindsey articulated in our May interview, had been tested and shaped outside the classroom during the semester. In late March, Lindsey learned that her parents, who had been married twenty-five years, had decided to divorce. Her father was devastated, and she told me that instead of feeling sorry for herself because of her parents' divorce, she was able to respond in a more productive way. She said she felt grateful that she was in college and could take courses in psychology and philosophy, and she wanted to pass along to her father some of the ideas she had learned in an effort to help him. She said that although she had faced many difficult situations in the past, this was the first time she actually had some useful tools with which to respond.

Bringing in a third Dewey idea, she said that one of the things she discussed with her father was that he might consider the divorce, despite the sadness associated with it, as an opportunity for growth. In effect, Lindsey was developing Dewey's corollary to the notion that misfortune and success are intimately intertwined, namely, it is *only* in a world where failure and despair exist that there are chances for recovery, new understanding, and growth.[21] Lindsey concluded, "I have tried to offer my dad some of what I've realized this semester, but like Dr. Fishman does with us, I've just provided him some ideas, and he'll have to decide for himself, which, if any, of these pieces of theory make sense to him."

In conclusion, Steve and I have, in this essay, sketched the influence of Dewey's theory on the revolution in writing instruction that began in the 1960s and continues to be important in the United States and elsewhere to the present day. In particular, this revolution is manifest in Fishman's classroom in his focus on the use of writing for discovery and his privileging of constructed knowing, that is, the integration of academic and personal concerns. Given the fact that discussion of Dewey's influence on education often focuses on progressive education, and child-centered education is still frequently roundly criticized, we believe that attention to this revolution in writing instruction is worthwhile. We hope that further examination of it, and its acceptance and success, will encourage people to look at Dewey's pedagogical theories in fresh light.

21.

AN EDUCATIONAL THEORY OF INQUIRY

Maura Striano

> While there still is, and probably always will be, a particular class having the special business of inquiry in hand, a distinctively learned class is henceforth out of the question. It is an anachronism. Knowledge is no longer an immobile solid; it has been liquefied. It is actively moving in all the currents of society itself.
>
> —John Dewey, *MW.* 1.17

This essay is grounded on the idea, widely diffused in Dewey's work, that any process of inquiry—from the simplest process to the more and more complex one—brings about growth and development for individuals, communities, and societies. This occurs as a more and more diffused mastery of methods, tools and forms of knowledge, which help us to develop a wider awareness and understanding of problems arising from human experience.

On the basis of this premise, it is very clear that, from a pedagogical point of view, inquiry develops into an *educational process* and can therefore be considered an *educational* device in itself. It thus becomes extremely significant to reflect on what *the principles for an educational theory of inquiry* could be according to a Deweyan perspective in today's educational scenarios, considering that education itself is the outcome of a continuous and reflective process of inquiry into educational situations and problems.

1. LOGIC, INQUIRY, AND EDUCATION: A PEDAGOGICAL PERSPECTIVE

Dewey's interest in *inquiry* is strictly connected with his interest in *thinking*, *logic*, and *education*. This interest makes more and more sense in connection with his pedagogical reflection, which started to be developed during the *Middle Works* period. In writings published between 1910 and 1911, including *How We Think*, the focus of Dewey's research was no longer on the physiological functions supporting thinking processes (in writings during the 1880s and 1890s such as "The Soul and Body" and *Psychology*), but rather on the *logical forms* of the ideas developed within inquiry operations.[1] These writings anticipate the analysis developed in the later *Essays on Experimental Logic* (1916), the second edition (1933) of *How We Think* (where we can see the structure of Dewey's *Logic*), and in *Logic: The Theory of Inquiry* (1938).[2]

In these first works, and in particular in *How We Think*, Dewey developed a "theory of thinking" which has deep educational implications. He wrote about an "educational theory of thinking" which focuses on the necessity for a discipline of cognitive processes according to a reflective pattern, and considers reflection to be a rigorous and consequential procedure, controlled by an inquiring and introspective rationality. This position is consistent with his ideas about education and its social implications developed in this period: *education* is intended as a *practice*, which can direct and facilitate activities leading to an organized and reflective use of inner forces and potentialities.

This conception (which would later be more precisely defined in *Democracy and Education*) is clearly visible in *The School and Society*, as Dewey writes:

> The statement so frequently made that education means "drawing out" is excellent, if we mean simply to contrast it with the process of pouring in. But, after all, it is difficult to connect the idea of drawing out with the ordinary doings of the child of three, four, seven, or eight years of age. He is already running over, spilling over, with activities of all kinds.
>
> He is not a purely latent being whom the adult has to approach with great caution and skill in order gradually to draw out some hidden germ of activity. The child is already intensely active, and the question of education is the question of taking hold of his activities, of giving them direction. Through direction, through organized use, they tend toward valuable results, instead of scattering or being left to merely impulsive expression.[3]

In this perspective, education can sustain growth, enhancing the "power of the mind," which comes out of a continuous mental discipline, through activity and reflection:

> In general, this growth is a natural process. But the proper recognition and use of it is perhaps the most serious problem in instruction upon the intellectual side. A person who has gained the power of reflective attention, the power to hold problems, questions, before the mind, is in so far, intellectually speaking, educated. He has mental discipline—power of the mind and for the mind. Without this the mind remains at the mercy of custom and external suggestions. Some of the difficulties may be barely indicated by referring to an error that almost dominates instruction of the usual type. Too often it is assumed that attention can be given directly to any subject-matter, if only the proper will or disposition be at hand, failure being regarded as a sign of unwillingness or indocility. Lessons in arithmetic, geography, and grammar are put before the child, and he is told to attend in order to learn. But excepting as there is some question, some doubt, present in the mind as a basis for this attention, reflective attention is impossible. If there is sufficient intrinsic interest in the material, there will be direct or spontaneous attention, which is excellent so far as it goes, but which merely of itself does not give power of thought or internal mental control. . . .
>
> True, reflective attention, on the other hand, always involves judging, reasoning, deliberation; it means that the child has a question of his own, and is actively engaged in seeking and selecting relevant material with which to answer it, considering the bearings and relations of this material—the kind of solution it calls for. The problem is one's own; hence also the impetus, the stimulus to attention, is one's own; hence also the training secured is one's own—it is discipline, or gain in power of control; that is, a habit of considering problems.[4]

The discipline of the mind is first of all a discipline of thinking, intended as a logical process which develops through different stages. For this reason it was very important, for Dewey, to understand *how thinking works* in order to see how it can be promoted and developed in educational contexts.

This issue then constituted the focus of a long process of clarification and exploration, beginning in the *Middle Works* and culminating in the *Later Works* with *Logic: The Theory of Inquiry*.[5] In the 1900 essay "Some Stages of Logical Thought"[6] Dewey anticipated the main issues which would then be developed both in *How We Think* and in *Logic: The Theory of Inquiry*.[7]

It is interesting to see that, in order to explain the development of the stages of logical thought, Dewey refers to the evolution of the *process of inquiry*, continuously arising from human activities and practices:

> It is within this evolution that we have to find our stages of thinking. The initial stage is where the doubt is hardly endured but not entertained; it is no welcome guest but an intruder, to be got rid of as speedily as possible. Development of alternative and competitive suggestions, the forming of suppositions (of ideas), goes but a little way. The mind seizes upon the nearest or most convenient instrument of dismissing doubt and re-attaining security. At the other end is the definitive and conscious search for problems, and the development of elaborate and systematized methods of investigation—the industry and technique of science.[8]

The investigation in the logical structure of thinking continues in "Studies in Logical Theory" (1903). Dewey's studies in this period anticipate some themes later treated in *Logic*, in which the theory of logic is intended as a "theory of inquiry."[9]

In "Studies in Logical Theory" Dewey is already starting to conceive of the "logical theory" as a "theory of inquiry" as he clearly states: "The antecedents of thought are our universe of life and love; of appreciation and struggle."[10] Sidney Hook explains that for Dewey, "thinking takes its point of departure from an experience of felt difficulty in a situation 'whose parts are actively at war with each other—so much so that they threaten to disrupt the situation, which accordingly for its own maintenance requires deliberate redefinition and relation of its tensional parts. This redefining and re-relating is the constructive process termed thinking.'"[11] In this formulation we can envisage a complex and strict connection between *logic* and *inquiry*, since the process of inquiry leads to an "existential reconstruction" of the situation and results in judgments, and these are not merely an outcome of inquiry, but also serve to direct future actions.[12]

In the Preface to *Logic: The Theory of Inquiry* Dewey identifies "reflective thinking" with "objective inquiry." If thinking is to be considered *a logical and methodological device*, whose task is to guide and sustain human explorations of reality, to accompany the growth of human knowledge, to head towards new discoveries and new goals, it is not possible to treat it as an abstract and decontextualized function, independent from people, environments, situations, individual and social experiences.

Logic as a "theory of inquiry" always implies *the presence of an individual or of many individuals* involved in a process of inquiry and *a context,* intended as a field of indeterminate and problematic experiences, which need to be explored and investigated. On this basis, logical forms are the by-products of thinking during the inquiry process and are therefore contextually determined and operationally directed. The objects of *Logic* conceived as a *Theory of Inquiry* are, thus, the inquiry processes produced in the exercise of reflective thinking (intended as the exploratory function of individual and collective life), which endlessly develop in all the fields of human experience, from commonsense experiences to scientifically controlled ones. Dewey's *theory of inquiry* is conceived as a scientific analysis of the inquiry procedures used within a determinate sociocultural context and in a particular historical moment, acknowledged and validated within a community and consolidated in a formalized structure.

This position would give to Logic—as a discipline—a historical and cultural status and situate it on an empirical rather than theoretical level. In these terms it can be read as the theoretical formulation of a reflection regarding *logos*, considered as a device to explore and understand human experience through logical procedures, which may be more or less complex. Moreover, the *Theory of Inquiry* can be understood as a response to the necessity to discover a *unified method* for commonsense experience and for science, on the basis of the acknowledgment of the principle of continuity of human experiences from the simplest to the more complex ones.[12]

Continuity is involved within the process of inquiry itself, as far as it is a developmental reality, evolving from simple forms, inferential "habits" which we are not always aware of, to more and more complex and sophisticated structures in a continuous process, deeply imbedded into our living experience.

2. THE EXPERIENTIAL AND EXISTENTIAL NATURE OF INQUIRY

In the description of the process of inquiry given by Dewey in *Logic: The Theory of Inquiry* the matrix of any kind of inquiry is both *experiential* and *existential.* Dewey's *Logic* is grounded on phenomenological and empirical assumptions: the condition of possibility for inquiry is the presence of indefinite and indeterminate situations, which individuals have to deal with, and they can do so by using a series of tools and devices, selected from individual and collective repertoires.

Within this framework, it is clear that the methods of inquiry can be applied only to *real problems* which stem from a situation, acknowledged as "problematic," when we find in it not only a state of confusion, but a state of doubt and perplexity. Inquiry always responds, therefore, to an existential necessity: to clarify indeterminate situations, reaching some clear statements which can guide us in our future experiences. "If inquiry begins in doubt, it terminates in the institution of conditions which remove need for doubt. The latter state of affairs may be designated by the words belief and knowledge."[13]

This point is further clarified when Dewey specifies how inquiry is deeply imbedded into the course of our lives as a pattern that governs its development:

> The structure and course of life-behavior has a definite pattern, spatial and temporal. This pattern definitely foreshadows the general pattern of inquiry. For inquiry grows out of an earlier state of settled adjustment, which, because of disturbance, is indeterminate or problematic (corresponding to the first phase of tensional activity), and then passes into inquiry proper, (corresponding to the searching and exploring activities of an organism); when the search is successful, belief or assertion is the counterpart, upon this level, of reintegration upon the organic level. There is no inquiry that does not involve the making of some change in environing conditions.[14]

Inquiry, as a process that is serially connected is therefore deeply involved in human life because "the basic importance of the serial relation in logic is rooted in the conditions of life itself."[15] Therefore "inquiry is a development out of organic-environmental integration and interaction"[16] which sheds a clear light on the empirical and experimental nature of the inquiry process in the sense pointed out by Dewey, who clarifies that

> the points that have been made may be gathered together by consideration of the current meaning of "experience," especially in connection with the intensified ambiguity, due to historical changes, that is attached to "empirical." [Logic is] experiential in the way any natural science is experiential, that is, as distinct from the merely speculative and from the a priori and intuitional.[17]

Later on, Dewey focuses on the situational conditions for the emergence of inquiry processes with these words:

The indeterminate situation comes into existence from existential causes, just as does, say, the organic imbalance of hunger. There is nothing intellectual or cognitive in the existence of such situations, although they are the necessary condition of cognitive operations or inquiry. In themselves they are precognitive. The first result of evocation of inquiry is that the situation is taken, adjudged, to be problematic. To see that a situation requires inquiry is the initial step in inquiry.[18]

According to this framework, in order to understand the development of the structure of human logic, Dewey's investigation requires a *biological-anthropological method* and presupposes a *functional model* for human reasoning processes, focusing on actions, beliefs, intentions, needs, and wants. This is very clear as Dewey specifies:

The existence of inquiries is not a matter of doubt. They enter into every area of life and into every aspect of every area. In everyday living, men examine; they turn things over intellectually; they infer and judge as "naturally" as they reap and sow, produce and exchange commodities. As a mode of conduct, inquiry is as accessible to objective study as are these other modes of behavior. Because of the intimate and decisive way in which inquiry and its conclusions enter into the management of all affairs of life, no study of the latter is adequate save as it is noted how they are affected by the methods and instruments of inquiry that currently obtains: Inquiry is the controlled or directed transformation of an indeterminate situation into one that is so determinate in its constituent distinctions and relations as to convert the elements of the original situation into a unified whole.[19]

For Dewey the connections felt in direct experience (existence) are what he defines as "existential involvements"; when these connections are further formulated into relations, they become "significances." So, as we come to envisage and to establish relations within our fields of experience,[20] when we come to use symbols, when we begin to construct meanings, we can experience the progressive *entrance of cognition in the process of inquiry* and we attain new relationships with our world.[21] Therefore, the outcome of the development of structures of logic on the basis of experience and learning is a generalizable way of thinking and conducting human inquiries, thus leading to a generalizable way of acting.[22]

Dewey clearly points this out in *How We Think* where, recalling "Some Stages of Logical Thought," he states:

Thoughts that result in belief have an importance attached to them which leads to reflective thought, to conscious inquiry into the nature, conditions, and bearings of the belief. To think of whales and camels in the clouds is to entertain ourselves with fancies, terminable at our pleasure, which do not lead to any belief in particular. But to think of the world as flat is to ascribe a quality to a real thing as its real property. This conclusion denotes a connection among things and hence is not, like imaginative thought, plastic to our mood. Belief in the world's flatness commits him who holds it to thinking in certain specific ways of other objects, such as the heavenly bodies, antipodes, the possibility of navigation. It prescribes to him actions in accordance with his conception of these objects.[23]

If structures of logic are constructed within a field of experience and emerge and develop through inquiry processes, which are produced by the problematic situations we encounter in everyday life, this implies that *every experiential field is potentially generative of new logical forms, new behavioural patterns, and new meanings*. There is, as Dewey points out, a *continuity in our cognitive experience*[24] and this continuity is fundamental in the construction of specific situations which generate new patterns of inquiry and new logical forms for the development of "reflective thinking." The process of the development of reflective thinking as an effective inquiry tool for human experience is, therefore, a *continuous process*, which goes through several existential and formative dimensions and is deeply imbedded in specific life situations, which we acknowledge as challenging and problematic.

For this reason, all experiences, even commonsense ones, can generate cognitive growth if within them reflective thinking is used and supported in a rigorous way. Therefore, in order to have a strong educational potential, these experiences should support the acquisition and development of conceptual tools and of inquiry methodologies, which can be helpful in the reconstruction of individual and collective experiences, giving them new sense and meanings.

3. INQUIRY AS A METHOD FOR LEARNING: EDUCATIONAL IMPLICATIONS

Dewey's focus on the empirical and existential matrix of logical and inquiry processes, from his first writings on logic to the masterpiece *Logic: The Theory of*

Inquiry, is the precondition to acknowledging logic and inquiry as *devices for learning and the construction of knowledge* and so to envisage their educational potential.[25] We should recall here that Dewey's educational perspective developed during the Chicago years (when he started and carried forward the challenging experiment of the laboratory school) and has, therefore, strong connections with this particular experience.

In *The School and Society* Dewey refers to the laboratory school as *the outcome of a process of inquiry* involving scholars, administrators, teachers, and students who came to focus on a specific set of *questions, or problems* and "attempted to find out by trying, by doing not alone by discussion and theorizing—whether these problems may be worked out, and how they may be worked out."[26]

It is very interesting to see that the inquiry process described by Dewey is not focused, however, only on problems of practical pedagogy, but also on broader and general educational issues as general frames of reference, which are to be clarified and explored in depth through the empirical and practical experience of schooling; at the same time, the practice of schooling itself will generate new educational issues, to be reflectively and thoroughly explored at a theoretical level, as Dewey started to do in his first educational writings and would later do extensively in works such as *Democracy and Education* and *Experience and Education*, elaborating a more defined *theory of education*.

Inquiry can be seen as the *matrix* of Dewey's pedagogical construction from several perspectives. We can see that *inquiry* is not only the method that Dewey and his colleagues used to explore educational issues and practices, but it was to become also *the method* used to support *learning and knowledge construction within educational contexts* according to the interests and the needs of the students, a *method* which must be developed by creating the conditions that enhance both the *attitude towards inquiry* and the *spirit of inquiry* at all levels.[27] Logic is neither abstract nor formal, but *experimental*, in the sense that logical patterns have meaning insofar as they can sustain the development of inquiry processes deeply imbedded in experiences which deal with concrete and real problems, leading to the production of new forms of knowledge.

Dewey's logical studies and his theory of inquiry are, therefore, strictly connected to an empirical and transactional epistemology.[28] As Dewey points out:

> The assumption of an educational laboratory is rather that enough is known of
> the conditions and modes of growth to make intelligent inquiry possible; and
> that it is only by acting upon what is already known that more can be found

out. The chief point is such experimentation as will add to our reasonable convictions. The demand is to secure arrangements that will permit and encourage freedom of investigation; that will give some assurance that important facts will not be forced out of sight; conditions that will enable the educational practice indicated by the inquiry to be sincerely acted upon, without the distortion and suppression arising from undue dependence upon tradition and preconceived notions. It is in this sense that the school would be an experimental station in education.[29]

Dewey is aware that:

the spirit of inquiry can be got only through and with the attitude of inquiry. The pupil must learn what has meaning, what enlarges his horizon, instead of mere trivialities. He must become acquainted with truths, instead of things that were regarded as such fifty years ago, or that are taken as interesting by the misunderstanding of a partially educated teacher. It is difficult to see how these ends can be reached except as the most advanced part of the educational system is in complete interaction with the most rudimentary.[30]

These pedagogical considerations are operationalized in *The Child and the Curriculum*, where Dewey's ideas regarding the role played by logic in education and its relation with knowledge and subject matter is effectively stated:

... the child's reasoning powers, the faculty of abstraction and generalization, are not adequately developed. So the subject-matter is evacuated of its logical value, and, though it is what it is only from the logical standpoint, is presented as stuff only for "memory." This is the contradiction: the child gets the advantage neither of the adult logical formulation, nor of his own native competencies of apprehension and response. Hence the logic of the child is hampered and mortified, and we are almost fortunate if he does not get actual nonscience, flat and commonplace residua of what was gaining scientific vitality a generation or two ago—degenerate reminiscence of what someone else once formulated on the basis of the experience that some further person had, once upon a time, experienced.[31]

Dewey's writings make a strong relation between subject matter and the processes of its construction; each subject matter and each content comes to have its meaning in individual and collective experience when it is understood as the product of a process of inquiry and when it is explored considering its potentiality to generate new inquiry processes and new forms of knowledge. The development of school *curricula* must therefore be oriented in the direction of the organization of experiences of inquiry within specific subject matters and must be oriented *both* towards the development of competences regarding inquiry as well as towards the acquisition and use of different forms of knowledge.

We acknowledge, here, two important educational goals which cannot be separated: the cultural focus on a subject matter (conceived as the social acknowledgment of a process of inquiry) gives meaning and sense to the experiences of inquiry within educational contexts; at the same time, the mastery of the process of inquiry is regarded as the condition of an effective and significant approach to subject matter, in connection and in continuity with individual life experiences, all of which are potentially educational.

4. INQUIRY AS A METHOD OF RECONSTRUCTION OF HUMAN EXPERIENCE: PEDAGOGICAL AND SOCIAL IMPLICATIONS

It is, at this point, very important to figure out what Dewey meant by *education* and *educational* and to see what the connections are between his *pedagogy* and his *theory of inquiry*.[32] The idea that education is a continuous process of "reconstruction" of human experiences based on a correct use of reflective thinking is clearly formulated in *Democracy and Education*, and further developed in *Logic: The Theory of Inquiry*, focusing on inquiry as both the method and the tool of this "reconstruction."

As a matter of fact, the *theory of inquiry* integrates both the propositions on the basis of the general principle of the *continuity of experience*, which becomes educational insofar as it generates new interpretative and reconstructive processes; it is thanks to these processes that we can situate human experiences within a universe of meaning and discourse and build up connections with past and future experiences.

It is important to say, at this point, that these processes come into being only within *regulated inquiry situations* where we can find the conditions of possibility to "reconstruct" our experiences in a more significant way, discovering connections, implications, and relations which make them more and more clear, understandable and meaningful. As soon as it becomes a matter of meaning making—insofar as it involves symbolic forms, insofar as organized forms of knowledge—inquiry is to be intended not only as an *organic process of accommodation*, but as *a cultural and social process of understanding*, which has its roots in a cultural context and is sustained by cultural and social frames, artefacts, tools.

From this perspective, inquiry comes out of social contexts and contributes to reconstructing them and to reorganizing them, insofar as a growing number of individuals and groups begin to explore the possibility to overcome and make sense of the problematic situations they live in, by using reflective tools and methodologies. Inquiry may become, therefore, a means to support and sustain social order, since it emerges from inside of society itself. Dewey explored this issue deeply in *The School and Society*, addressing two fundamental questions:

> How can a society be disciplined, organized, ruled in such a manner that all its members can be protected, satisfied, and sustained, while actively and responsibly participating in its development?

> How can a society develop and grow according to its intrinsic potential?

Social order is not a matter of general rules imposed on a society from the outside or from above. It is, instead, a matter of individual and collective awareness, reflectivity, and responsibility.

For these reasons, an effective social order can be achieved only *if and when* more and more individuals and groups become able to deal with social problems in a reasonable and reflective manner, using a disciplined method of inquiry into human experiences and relationships. The need for a social order (which is a *social need*) becomes an *educational need* if we focus on the *competences, the knowledge, and the tools* required to construct and maintain this order. This clarifies the connection in Dewey's thought between the conditions of possibility to build up inquiry competences on the basis of psychological/physiological maturational processes within educational contexts, and the achievement of a new social order based on the development of these competences and the dissemination of sound and rigorous inquiry practices in different social areas.[33]

It is, therefore, on the basis of the matrix of inquiry that individuals and social groups can acquire and develop competences useful in understanding human experience and in making sense of the problematic situations which compose the world of human life.

5. FOR AN EDUCATIONAL THEORY OF INQUIRY

Logic: The Theory of Inquiry may be, for many of its aspects, considered a definitive work, which Dewey felt the necessity to write in order to synthesize—in a complex argumentative framework—the two theoretical efforts which had characterized his entire speculation from the *Early Works* to the *Later Works*: a "theory of thinking" and a "theory of experience."

The first three chapters of the first part of *Logic* are extremely explicit in grounding this position, which becomes clearer when Dewey states that, wherever he has used the term "inquiry," he could as well have used the term "reflective thinking." The "theory of inquiry" could be intended as a "theory of reflective thinking" insofar as thinking is explored in its development, in its organization, in its coming to have specific forms and procedural rules within different fields of human experience, in its possibility to be educated according to socially acknowledged criteria and values. Still, it is a "theory of inquiry," as it focuses on the context, on the conditions, and on the process of the emergence and development of thinking, which are determinations and dimensions of inquiry.

The "theory of inquiry" was intended by Dewey to be—within a reflective pattern—an "inquiry into inquiry," which would shed light both on the *making of thinking* as well as on *its frames of reference, its norms, and its rules, as well as on best conditions for its development within human experience.* As it sheds light both on the relationship between thinking and experience within human formation processes, as well as on the educational conditions for human thinking, Dewey's *Logic* can be and should be read in *a pedagogical perspective.* The *theory of inquiry* can therefore be understood as an "educational" theory, grounded on three strong theoretical bases: (a) on an "educational theory of thinking"; (b) on an "educational theory of experience"; and (c) on a "theory of education" considered as a process of individual and social growth and development.

Since *inquiry* is explored both in its cognitive and logical structure as well as in its cultural and social implications, it can be seen (due to its origins, its conditions of possibility, and its structure) both as an *educational device* and as an *educational model,* thus supporting an *educational process* of growth and understanding, both at an individual and at a social level. If, in Dewey's terms, an educational process is a process of continuous and constant reconstruction of human experience in different contexts, *inquiry*—as it is described in *Logic*—is both the *tool* and the *model* for this process.

The acquisition, mastery, and dissemination of the method of inquiry through educational practices—which support the acquisition and development of inquiry attitudes and competences—can therefore support the reconstruction of human experiences in a wide range of contexts (formal, nonformal, informal), reflectively orienting and sustaining human living. *Inquiry* can be seen as the driving force for the development of educational (and therefore social) systems, for several reasons:

1. Inquiry is the method of scientific research and thinking, it contributes to developing and spreading innovation within the educational and social system, thus contributing to social advancement and growth;

2. Inquiry is the ground of the epistemic structure of each subject matter intended as a scientific outcome, and can be seen as the educational method which will allow a fruitful approach to knowledge contents, as they are presented not as finite products but as outcomes of an ongoing inquiry process whose social utility can be acknowledged and appreciated on an experiential basis;[34]

3. Inquiry is a regulated thinking procedure that can be seen as a model for logical thought (of reflective thinking, conceived as "the best" way to think things out and to explore every kind of human problem, even moral ones) whose structures and rules need to be clarified and introduced in each social context through appropriate educational practices;

4. Inquiry is the force which sustains professional practices, making them less and less routine and more and more innovative and productive of new forms of knowledge and understanding, which is particularly relevant for educational practices at all levels.[35]

But how can we organize effective educational practices to make this possible within contemporary educational scenarios?

Again, we can refer to a Deweyan suggestion. According to Dewey, education cannot occur outside experience; it is *a particular form of human experience*; on this basis, education should not be focused only on the development of inquiry attitudes and competences, but should support the organization and development of *inquiry experiences*, which are the only contexts where these attitudes and competences can be developed and fostered. How can we then construct and support true experiences of inquiry, which can be considered good educational models in a Deweyan perspective? We should first of all clarify what the constitutive characteristics of the *experience of inquiry* are, in Dewey's terms.

The experience of inquiry is always *an ongoing experience*: it stems from indetermination and uncertainty in real-life situations, it is governed by doubt, it is progressive and provisional, it is fallible, it requires constant verification and validation, and it produces outcomes which are constantly open to reconstruction. Inquiry is an experience of openness to multiple possibilities, of challenge and commitment, of responsible acknowledgment of our own failures, of reflective evaluation of our successes. Inquiry is contextually situated and is determined by the conditions of the contexts in which it is embedded, therefore involving aesthetic, cognitive, ethical, and practical dimensions.[36]

Insofar as inquiry is culturally and socially situated, it is also an experience of attentive listening, observation, interpretation, and understanding which helps us to discover new meanings and to construct new relationships in our experiences, building up new links and networks among concepts, ideas, symbols, etc. The experience of inquiry helps us to look at the multiple and different forms that the complex experience of human life can take, to understand its continuity and unity as well as its fragmentation, to make sense, within it, of the relationship parts/whole, to understand the relevance and significance of oppositions but also their definiteness and partiality, without being disoriented or stuck in a single perspective.

Inquiry helps us to overcome the limits of our single experience, to broaden our horizons, to master more and more perspectives, to become reflective and self-corrective. Inquiry provides us with the tool of reflective thinking, which it constantly improves and develops, helping us to master, attentively and responsibly, our life experiences.

What we can see, however, in today's educational scenarios is that many of the educational practices that are claimed to be "inquiry based" are not grounded on effective and real inquiry experiences. We know that a true inquiry experience should always start in an indeterminate situation, but very often the educational situations we encounter are predeterminate and oriented, therefore not calling for inquiry processes emerging from genuine puzzlement and interest; the inquiry processes are thus not authentic ones, since the problems are already posed and defined and not constructed starting from the situation; moreover, there is rarely a choice between different repertoires of methods and tools, which are instead already offered and organized.

Moreover, these so-called inquiry experiences are learning-oriented experiences, which lead to learning a particular content or subject matter as a definitive outcome of scientific inquiry, simulating some so-called experiment but not introducing individuals to an autonomous mastery of a scientific inquiry method within a discipline; the subject matter is therefore not approached in a participatory and consummatory way, but according to a "spectator" approach, which keeps it far and distant from human life experience. Learning is thus not a real learning, since it does not produce a real appropriation and mastery of knowledge and competences, but only a passive acquisition of information and facts.

What can we do in order to transform all this? The situation here considered is, for some reason, not very different from the one depicted by Dewey in his essay *The Educational Situation*. There he pointed out that, in order to understand the "educational situation" it is necessary to understand the underlying social situation. He saw the "educational situation" as the product of a dualistic society which had been developing, "drawing fixed lines between classes, and dualistic intellectually, with its rigid separation between the things of matter and of mind—between the affairs of the world and of the spirit."[37]

Surprisingly, 150 years after Dewey's birth, these dualisms seem not to be overcome yet. The inability of our educational system to provide real experiences of inquiry (even when it pretends to do so) is strictly connected to the idea that knowledge and inquiry are a business for few people and that cannot be approached through direct experience by everybody. In these terms, the contemporary "educational situation" is very challenging, since it calls for political and social consideration and leads us to pose some powerful educational questions focusing on issues of control, power, and the social order.

What will happen if everybody really attains a reflective mastery of inquiry practices in her/his everyday life? What if the information, the news, the knowledge that we approach in educational, and in general, in any formative context were considered to be partial, fallible, and were constantly revised and reconstructed through inquiry processes? What if people started to use and master reflective processes in their daily life, in their workplace, in the communities they live in? What if these communities began to treat themselves and their problems using a reflective approach?

An in-depth exploration of these issues (which cannot be a matter of analysis here) would imply a general reflective reconstruction of educational policies, which we consider to be—in a Deweyan perspective—the only means to reach a real and effective reconstruction of educational practices, leading towards a new social order, inspired to a true "social democracy." In order to be effective, this exploration must be conducted *from the inside* of educational and social systems, involve all the inner agents and forces operating within them, and be conducted—through sound and rigorous processes of inquiry—starting from real problems.

This process would lead to the construction of *inquiring communities*, whose understandings might come to have a more and more relevant impact on educational policies and educational systems. Within this framework, we would have the development of situated processes of *educational inquiry*, which would lead to an effective educational transformation affecting educational theories, and at the same time policies and practices. In these terms the transformative potential of inquiry could be used as a *true force for social change*.

This perspective leads us to a broader awareness and understanding of the power that the mastery of a sound and rigorous method of inquiry can give to individuals and groups in today's social and political scenarios, fulfilling Dewey's expectation for a real reform in education and in society.

ACKNOWLEDGMENTS

I thank James Downhour for his kind and careful support in the editing work; Jim Garrison, for his sound notes and suggestions, which have helped me in clarifying and developing some relevant issues, to be further explored in the future; Larry Hickman for his constant, precious encouragement and support to my research as well as for his comments to the present paper; and Stefano Oliverio for having discussed with me the different versions of the manuscript, from the original idea to its further developments; his criticism and his punctual remarks have been really determinant for the final outcome. Last, but not least, I thank Molly Rogers for her precise and thoughtful revision of the text.

22.

THE SOURCES OF A SCIENCE OF EDUCATION BY JOHN DEWEY AND THE ITALIAN INTERPRETATIONS

Giuseppe Spadafora

The complexity of John Dewey's thought is linked to a central aspect of theory of education: the possibility of defining a science of education. This problem was analyzed by Dewey in a short essay of 1929, *The Sources of a Science of Education*. This essay is not well known in American critical literature, with some important exceptions,[1] probably because the scientific attitude in American culture on educational issues has been more focused on experimental education.

The impact of this Deweyan theory has influenced the Italian philosophy of education, especially after World War II. The "paradigm of sciences of education" contributed to building the scientific quality of education through the concept of a science of education applied to teaching as well as to the politics of the school system. The text of *The Sources of a Science of Education* has been considered as an accurate philosophical theory still in progress. It is quite interesting to compare John Dewey's interpretation of *The Sources of a Science of Education*, which, in my opinion, is very meaningful in the context of Deweyan philosophy, to the Italian interpretations, which have played an important role in changing the concept of education and politics in the Italian school.[2]

Dewey's essay analyses the problem of a science foundation of education. It was published after the theoretical explanation of experience in *Experience and Nature* (1925) and the concept of "Public" in *The Public and Its Problems* (1927), and it was published before the political theory expressed in *Individualism, Old and New* (1930), *Liberalism and Social Action* (1935), and *Freedom and Culture* (1939). As I have already demonstrated in another essay,[3] the concept of the science of education in Dewey reveals a deeper meaning about the relationship between science and the development of democracy.

In fact, this text, seemingly isolated from the development of Dewey's theory, demonstrates that it is difficult to establish a science of education. At the beginning of Dewey's text there is a "prior question": "Can there be a science of education? Are the procedures and aims of education such that it is possible to reduce them to anything properly called a science?"[4] Dewey's reasoning develops through two central points.

First, education is a theory which is extremely difficult to control with a scientific method and to transform "into rules and standard of school-room practice."[5] But examining the meaning of science (in particular the physical sciences) Dewey affirms that science is a product of a connection amongst "various findings," linked up together to determine a "relatively coherent system." If so, it may not be possible to construct a science of education, primarily because the practical results are very different compared to scientific hypotheses in the physical sciences. Thus, second, the science of education can be defined only by borrowing from other sources that study, from their perspective, the educational issues. These sciences represent "the sources of a science of education." However, the question is: in what manner can these different "sources" can become a science of education? The philosopher states that they can be applied to the educational situations through the practical action of the teacher, who becomes an *investigator*, and who continuously researches the possibility of improving the learning of the student.[6] To better demonstrate this peculiarity of the science of education, Dewey compares this science to engineering. The engineer calculates the formulas which permit the construction of the bridges in particular situations. The same reasoning could be considered for the science of medicine. The doctor applies different sources of a science of health to the patient, and he becomes a doctor only when he applies these scientific sources to cure the illness.

Therefore two considerations are to be made. First, the science of education becomes a controlled science only when it is actually applied to an educational situation and its results (good or bad) are examined. Second, science is a progressive construction in the future, an "end in view" of other results, as Dewey clarifies in his 1939 *Theory of Valuation*. "Men built bridges before there was any science of mathematics and physics."[7] This means that Dewey, like Jean Piaget, considers the possibility of developing an experimental pedagogy. Another important aspect is that an "art of education" is connected to the possibility for creating a science of education, because only with a creative and aesthetic human action the sciences can be applied to any specific situation.

When Dewey refers to "special sources of a science of education"—particularly psychology, sociology, and philosophy of education—he intends to bring to light the close connection between scientific research and philosophical inquiry. In this way, *a science of education for Dewey is a metaphor to understand the real meaning of science*. Science can solve human problems, because it is connected to education. But, "Education is autonomous and should be free to determine its own ends, its own objectives."[8] Education is a "never ending circle," a "spiral" which "*includes*" (the italics is in the original text) science within itself.[9]

Dewey in *Democracy and Education* (1916) affirmed that philosophy is "the general theory of education." In *The Sources of a Science of Education* he similarly affirms that the sciences support a general theory of education.[10] Education can explain the mechanism of science, in the sense in which Dewey's *Logic* (1938) defines the scientific method as applying the method of intelligence, the social inquiry to solve human problems.[11]

A science of education must be applied to the individual, who is, according to Dewey, unique and different from all other individuals. This is the meaning of democracy: "a way of life" determined by the specificity of every individual. As Dewey demonstrates in "Mediocrity and Individuality" (1922), the difference between individuals is central to understand the meaning of democracy, because democracy makes it possible to understand the differences and not the uniformities, to limit the gaps between the better and the worse.[12]

A science of education could determine the variety of individuals in the world, and it could bring to further consequences the idea expressed in Dewey's manifesto of pragmatism, *The Reflex Arc Concept in Psychology* (1896). In this essay he demonstrates the focal meaning of pragmatism, that there are no mechanical responses of individuals to the environment, because the individual continuously determines his identity by fitting himself to the changes of the environment.[13]

This continuous changing of individuals can be expressed by a science of education. Science of education must study the ways individuals adapt themselves to the environment. This idea has been demonstrated by Larry Hickman, who considers Dewey's philosophy as a "pragmatic technology," that is, a poietic aptitude of the individual to change and adapt to reality.[14]

With this perspective it is fundamental to understand the meaning of science and technology in order to change reality and develop democracy. This is the main difference between pragmatism and European philosophy. Thus *The Sources of a Science of Education* could be considered an important part of Deweyan theory for demonstrating how the essence of science and technology can establish the possibility of a new democracy. Moreover, Dewey's interest in the sciences of education is linked to the possibility of reconstructing the epistemology of pragmatism.[15]

The sciences of education represent a metaphor of science, because science is inevitably constructed in network of different disciplines, and it must be considered not simply as an abstract theory far from practice and social problems, but rather as a project to guide human life toward future happiness. For Dewey, science is essential only if it can be applied with direct or indirect measurements to concrete reality for solving individual and social problems. In this way, only science can contribute to explore the possibility of human nature to express itself within human situations.

In Italy, the concept of a science of education was very successful, because it represented, for the Italian culture, the way to move beyond the fascist philosophy of education expressed by Giovanni Gentile's thought before World War II. Dewey's essay was translated twice, in 1951 and in 1967. The authors who promoted this aspect of Deweyan paradigm were Francesco De Bartolomeis and Aldo Visalberghi. Francesco De Bartolomeis wrote the book *La pedagogia come scienza* (The Pedagogy as Science) in 1953, inspired by Dewey's philosophy.[16] In this book, De Bartolomeis affirmed that pedagogy (which is a term more broadly used than "education" in Italian language and in European culture) is determined by the interdisciplinary cooperation of many sciences, particularly psychology, sociology, and philosophy of education.

As Giovanni Gentile theorized, pedagogy is not only linked to philosophy, but it is represented by a science network in an interdisciplinary context. The concept of the sciences of education is more advanced than the traditional idea of the experimental pedagogy from Jean-Marc-Gaspard Itard to Maria Montessori. The sciences of education are applied to different educational situations in order to solve the problems of learning and school organization.

Another relevant aspect is the importance of teachers' training through the sciences of education. In De Bartolomeis's opinion, the idea of the sciences of education is strictly connected with the training and the education of teachers, because a democratic school is based on the role of teachers. The other and more important interpretation of Aldo Visalberghi develops De Bartolomeis's theory further. Visalberghi has been considered as the most important Italian Deweyan scholar. He wrote several books about Dewey, and he translated Dewey's *Logic: The Theory of Inquiry* into Italian. He diffused this idea of the sciences of education in two books: *Problemi della ricerca pedagogica* (Problems of Educational Research) of 1965 and *Pedagogia e scienze dell'educazione* (Pedagogy and Sciences of Education) of 1978, with several new editions.[17] In this period of time, Visalberghi, along with many other philosophers and theorists of education, promoted John Dewey in the Italian culture as a philosopher of democracy and as the best expression of a secular culture opposed to Catholic thought and Marxist doctrine.

The concept of sciences of education was considered fundamental for changing the meaning of education in the school. Particularly, Visalberghi affirms that it was necessary to consider education from a scientific perspective, because it is necessary to control educational results in the school to improve the quality of schooling and to permit each individual to express his or her "embedded powers." Visalberghi attempted to link the Deweyan idea of the school as a "laboratory of democracy" with the idea of the sciences of education. The Italian school system after World War II was inspired by these principles. These ideas were also diffused in other European countries, where there has been an indirect influence of Deweyan educational ideas. An example is in France with the conception of "les sciences pédagogiques" by Maurice Debesse and Gaston Mialaret. The idea of science of education was linked to the idea of democracy in the school.

In Italy, the question of the sciences of education was related to the cultural and political role of teachers in order to understand the possibility of realizing democracy in the school. Giovanni Gentile (1875–1944), who was linked to fascism was also one of the most important European philosophers, was minister of education in Italy from 1922 to 1924. Gentile conceived and realized in that period the most important and organic Italian school reform.

This reform was associated with fascism; in fact, Mussolini in 1925 claimed that Gentile's reform is "the most important of all the fascist reforms. His reform was liberal (in a European sense) and very meritocratic.[18] Two principles represent the points of reference of this reform. First, the teacher must be a philosopher who transmits his knowledge ("He who knows is able to teach"). If the teacher knows the subject of his discipline, then he/she will be able to transmit this knowledge to students. Second, the real freedom of the student is to acknowledge the authority of the teacher. Gentile appeals to Kant's philosophy and the effort to develop the concept of "transcendental" to compare the relationship between the student and the teacher as an "a priori synthesis." Moreover, the "ethical State," derived from idealistic Hegelianism, is transformed into the concept of the "pedagogical State."

Going beyond Gentile, Visalberghi refers to the concept of the sciences of education to affirm that a genuinely democratic teacher must be an investigator, a gardener, who is a professional transmitter of knowledge, but at the same time a teacher who can understand the student's problems of learning and help to develop a unique personality. Democracy in the school depends on these two aspects which define the role of the teacher.

The idea of the sciences of education also influenced the politics of teachers' training. Teachers must be considered not only as role models, as the young Dewey theorized in *My Pedagogic Creed* of 1897, but as promoters of democracy. The school is, for Dewey, the local community of *The Public and Its Problems* of 1927, because the school is a *miniature society*, and it is not just a place for transmitting knowledge, but is also a place for creating a social and positive relationship between different individuals. In the school one must evaluate the talented individuals, but at the same time must also help every individual to orient himself towards better choices of life.

As I tried to demonstrate, the Italian interpretations of the Deweyan concept of a science of education is different from the authentic cultural message of Dewey.[19] It is easy to show that even Dewey himself had some perplexities about the scientific approach of learning (his dissents against Edward Thorndike are significant). However, the idea of a democratic school promoted by teachers has always been a fundamental idea in John Dewey's philosophy of education. The conception of promoting democracy in the world has always involved the school, the curriculum, and the education of teachers. In this regard, although Dewey's project was not successful, his suggestions for reforming Turkey's school system in the post-Islamic Atatürk era is significant.

We should probably continue to promote the Deweyan idea of a democratic school in a worldwide level. In this globalized world and media society, with such dramatic differences between advanced and underdeveloped countries, it is necessary to build a new citizenship which can link the needs of the little community to the universal language of the "Great Community."

Italian culture has been helped by Deweyan thought to change the social mentality. The challenge of our future is to diffuse this idea throughout the world, and to apply philosophy and education in order to create a new "promised land" for a new universal mentality. Deweyan democracy has been considered an experimental approach that can adapt institutions to the constant changes of society. The science of education could be the central pillar of this future democracy.

23.

THE ORIGINS OF THE ITALIAN MISUNDERSTANDING OF DEWEY'S PHILOSOPHY

Massimo Vittorio

I t is not an easy job to depict the meaning of Dewey's influence on the Italian culture, specifically philosophy. Difficulties do not lie in the lack of bibliographic references, nor in the quality of circumstantial studies. Moreover, Italian scholars have always tried to outline the main directions of Dewey's presence in Italy. Not many philosophers have achieved as much attention as Dewey had in Italy. The quantity of papers, reviews, and books that Italian academics have dedicated to Dewey is impressive. Besides the quantity, the quality of that literature is even more stunning. By quality I do not mean that all published studies are excellent, of course; I mean the peculiar kind of literature that has been produced about Dewey. Instead, it is not a hard job to have a look at the specific bibliography to realize that most of Italian academic literature examined a few points of Dewey's wide production. Just a few. Among them, one of the most analyzed issues does not concern "what Dewey says" or "let's try to better understand what Dewey says," but this main question: "Where does Dewey stay?" That is certainly an important question in philosophy.

When we try to approach a new philosophy or an unknown philosopher we usually try to bring that near to something or someone we know better. Comparative methodology would not be so successful in literature or in anthropology otherwise. The problem is different here, because the reason of the comparison is other. Basically, Italians canvassed Dewey by comparing him to what they already knew, as if their main concern was to establish whether or not Dewey was original. Why did they focus on that point? Because they could decide if Dewey was acceptable. As a stranger who knocks on our door and we need more information and further details before letting him enter or getting him out of the way. Such an attitude, advisable when an unwelcome guest comes to our door, does not often help in philosophy. From a synthesis of the Italian studies on this matter I could affirm that Italian philosophy has not been able to receive Dewey, so showing a sort of provincialism. It is not a provincialism from ignorance, but a provincialism from ideology. Therefore, much of the misunderstanding that affected Dewey's philosophy in Italy is not similar to the one that affected Croce in America.

In spite of Joel Spingarn's interest in Croce—the young scholar who published the first contributions to the journal *The Nation*—the Italian philosopher was never deeply understood in America. Croce and Dewey, who misunderstood themselves along the so-called "Croce-Dewey exchange," suffered a wide incomprehension. But Croce's situation was different: his philosophy underwent serious basic problems that Dewey's had not to face. First of all, not many American scholars could read Italian, while the first Italian readers of Dewey accessed his original works. Moreover, translations of Croce's works were few and poor. According to Frederic Simoni—author of one of the most important studies on Croce's penetration in America, *Benedetto Croce: A Case of International Misunderstanding*—one of the main reasons why Croce has been misunderstood in America was not the American ideological framework, which was anti-Hegelian, so anti-Croce; the main reason was a linguistic one. As Simoni affirms, "Since few Americans read Italian, those who are interested are forced to read translations, which are few and on the whole not too readable, or they are driven to read unreliable or sketchy secondary sources, thus perpetuating the misunderstandings with greater force. In aesthetics, the translation of the *Breviary*, originally published by the Rice Institute for its inauguration in 1912, was improved in the edition published by Heinaman in London, and the title was changed to *The Essence of Aesthetics*, but unfortunately it is now out of print. The short article in the fourteenth edition of the Encyclopedia Britannica, *Aesthetica in Nuce*, remains the only comparatively recent writing on aesthetics by Croce available to the English reader."[1] E. F. Carritt's translator's note in the book *My Philosophy*—Croce's pieces selected by R. Klibansky—sounds precautionary. Here is what he states: "The selection of these essays was not my own. Many of their metaphysical presuppositions and conclusions I am unable to accept. But my admiration for their author as a writer on aesthetics and politics and also as a man induced me to adventure their translation. Translations are notoriously frail; for, as the French proverb has it, when they are handsome, they are not faithful and when faithful not handsome. I have contented myself with plainness."[2] And, according to that French saying, *une traduction doit ressembler à une belle femme fidèle.* Certainly Simoni and other scholars did not reduce the explanation of that misunderstanding to a linguistic matter only. They also mentioned, as I did, the anti-Hegelian ambience that characterized American philosophy at the beginning of the last century.

If the ideological reference does not sound decisive in Croce's case, it surely does in Dewey's one. One of the most significant and recent studies on Dewey's impact in Italian philosophy was presented by Luciana Bellatalla in 1999, *John Dewey e la cultura italiana del Novecento.* In this book it is affirmed that one of the first Italian readers of Dewey was the Sicilian academician Antonio Aliotta, professor of philosophy at the University of Naples, whose department of philosophy is now named after him. In Aliotta's book *La reazione idealistica contro la scienza* (1917) it is possible to find several references to Dewey's books that had not been translated in Italian yet. Aliotta mentions Dewey's *Logical Conditions of Scientific Treatment of Morality* (1903), his review of James's *Pragmatism* (1902), and many other papers from several journals, included A. Schinz's *Professor Dewey's Pragmatism* (1908).

It is noteworthy to specify that Aliotta was not an isolated case. At the beginning of 1900 Dewey was known in the academic milieus, since a few works of his writings had been translated and the others were read in English. This scenario did not change until the end of World War II. The only limit, if one can be noted, is that Dewey's thought circulated for the first half of the last century through narrow circles, though those were the only chances Dewey had to be read and discussed. If the ambience is restricted, then the vista is often as narrow. Dewey's pragmatism was not seen on a unitary level; on the contrary, it was traced back to mere empiricism, whose main basis is antimetaphysical. As according to Bellatalla, Aliotta has been Dewey's first Italian critical reader, and as such, he began an unfortunate tradition of interpretation, as he did when he wrote the entry "pragmatism" in the dictionary of educational sciences in the 1912 and 1929 editions. Bellatalla affirms that "Dewey has been either appreciated, because he has been reduced to others, or he has been depreciated, because he was different: anyhow, he has never been considered *per se*, as a thinker who tried to give personal and original identities to his perspectives, though he never ignored the importance of certain masters or interlocutors."[3] Besides that fault, Aliotta has contributed towards creating a dichotomy that only in the last decades has been definitely refused: Dewey philosopher and Dewey pedagogue.

One of the traits that have typically marked the Italian approach to Dewey's philosophy has been the separation of its different aspects, the incapacity to gather them in order to grasp the unity of his thought. In particular, Italian philosophy has not been able to put on the same track both philosophy and education, as if there were two different authors called "Dewey," the one concerned with strictly or specifically philosophical theories and the other interested only in educational issues. Italian academicians have never caught the unity of the two sides, because they preferred to pay attention to "higher" philosophical issues— above all logical and epistemological ones—and they considered educational matters of a "lower" kind, not worthy of academia, but more of a schooling matter. I would not impute to Aliotta the origin of such a misinterpretation as Bellatalla does. What she ignores or does not like to mention is that, over Dewey and Aliotta, Italian philosophers have often shown the tendency to consider educational theories much more as mere didactics than as educational philosophy or pedagogy. The fault is not in Dewey, just as it is not in Aliotta; it is in the history of an academia whose main concern has simply been to understand different thoughts and thinkers, by establishing where to categorize them. Italian politicians do not act much differently. Their priority does not seem to regard the content of a proposal and its quality, but its color, that is, the membership of the proposer. So do the academicians: when they read Dewey they do not wonder about what he says; they only wonder whether he is acceptable. And if so, where to place him. Is he a Kantian, a Hegelian, an idealist, an empiricist? No, or maybe; for sure he is a pragmatist. But Italians did not know what pragmatism was at the beginning of 1900, and what they could do was to exchange a label they could not handle with other labels they liked much more. Then, as according to the reader and his school in turn, Dewey was all and nothing. He has been variously tagged and moved to several shelves or stands, the same way we do with goods or things whose use is not well known, moving them and placing them as according to the last use to which they were put.

In 1931, Giovanni Gentile entrusts Galvano Della Volpe with the writing of the entry on John Dewey for his *Enciclopedia Italiana*. Several inaccuracies mark the entry: Dewey is presented as a follower of neo-Kantian idealism; his philosophy is a development of James's; the reference to the relation between physical and spiritual aspects omits underlining the importance of the concepts of interaction and transaction; neither unity nor holism are taken into account. Idealists' fears concerned the lack of metaphysical instances of absolute and fixed elements in Dewey's philosophy. Idealism obtained its supremacy at the cost of silencing any other *Weltanschauung*. Italian idealism has been a sort of totalitarianism, whose hegemony has been strengthened either by publicly criticizing the supposed weak points of rivals or by "co-opting" them as members of idealism. The Croce-Dewey exchange is evidence of this strategy. In Dewey's case, idealists add up a strong scorn for didactics, which is considered to be merely empiric, nearly casuistic, as Gentile compares it to the prescriptions from a doctor. Dewey underwent what Bellatalla defines as *idealistic encircling*. The encircling is based on a sort of original sin, which marked out all Italian reading of Dewey's works: the dichotomy. Dewey is read in English, too; a critical apparatus is known, in English too. But no one made a qualitative leap of understanding Dewey's philosophy in a unified way, even though the presence and complexity of some components is noticed.

In 1938 we find the first Italian monograph on Dewey, by Maria Teresa Gillio-Tos. She drew the following conclusions. Dewey's pedagogical works are unrelated to the theoretical spirit of their author. The importance of his educational philosophy is reduced, since she affirms that Dewey has worked on it for a limited period (only from the 1890s until 1920). Finally, she claims that ethical and aesthetic issues do not belong together in a complex system of thought and they have no necessary connections with educational topics. In her opinion, Dewey's interest in pedagogy was basically limited to the period 1894–1904, relevant to Dewey's Chicago experience.

The first neutral reading of Dewey's philosophy is due to some Marxist approaches, specifically to Antonio Gramsci and Antonio Banfi. As the latter reminds us, to understand does not mean to necessarily agree with the author, but it means to attempt to read it in its integrity. Bellatalla specifies Banfi's thought, by saying that "Dewey must be read *iuxta propria principia*, in the unity of his thought, in respect of a complexity, which is the complexity of existence itself."[4] And I would add: that careful reading does not count for Dewey only; it is advisable when we read any author.

The separation between the two Deweys grew apparent in the 1950s and 1960s, when the newborn Italian Republic ran into organizational emergencies: public health system, transportation systems, infrastructures, military forces, bank system, social security benefits, and the school system. So, what happens after World War II is even worse for understanding Dewey. As a philosopher, a few academicians keep on analyzing some aspects of his political, ethical, or logical ideas; as pedagogue, he achieves wide success among teachers, becoming a sort of masters' master, a teachers' trainer. Dewey exits the strict aisles of the academy, but that aggravates the dichotomy. That separation will characterize Dewey's reading and comprehension in Italy—I should say miscomprehension—for decades, until the 1990s. This situation also leads scholars and teachers to ignore the common root of Dewey's political, ethical, and educational theories. I would say that a few academicians only never ignored it, but they never deeply understood that Dewey's educational philosophy was not a mere didactics. They set educational issues aside because they considered them as practical or technical problems, which theoretical philosophy had nothing to share with. They committed a sin of pride. Moreover, when it happened that an academician analyzed Dewey's educational philosophy—above all *The School and Society*—the judgment was that Dewey was not original, because the idea of changing schooling in connection with social changes had already been depicted in France by Faguet and in Italy by Fraccaroli, and "his proposals were widely put in practice by Montessori."[5] So, as Bellatalla summarizes, "Dewey's fortune is unhappy, since Aliotta reduces him to empiricists, Pironti to Montessori."[6]

In any case, for the new generations of teachers, who look at themselves as the pioneers of the new democracy and the new country, Dewey is a guide, now that he has been freed from the academicians. Dewey represents the lay pedagogy of republican Italy. What makes Dewey successful now, even though not fully understood, is his strong *faith* in mankind and its possibilities with no absolute frameworks. Italian teachers and the Italian school, freed from the ties of fascism and Gentile's reform, look to Dewey as a source of inspiration for an attitude of permanent doubt, of continuous opening to the world and the others. It is not wrong to affirm that Dewey develops a Socratic attitude, which is both educational and ethical (so political as well). Dewey's success is also due to the wider circulation of his works, thanks to the commitment of the publishing house La Nuova Italia in Florence.

The new class of teachers, lovers of liberalism, was opposed to Dewey's enemies, who did not understand his philosophy and rejected him because of different reasons: Marxists saw him as a Hegelian; idealists preferred to reduce him to empiricism, because they feared the lack of a metaphysical basis; Catholics could not agree with his general view of society and education. The role played by intelligence in Dewey's thought was the main reason why Catholicism opposed it, drawing the same conclusions as idealism: to hold that Dewey's educational philosophy was not holistic, and was not a reference to the complexity of life, helped Catholics to outline it as a kind of handbook or guidelines for some technical school procedures. Catholics ignored what Dewey means by intelligence, because they could not accept a dynamic view of existence.

Many Italian scholars put Dewey's renaissance in the 1980s, but I would not fully agree. I would be more cautious to say that we got a full view of the unity and complexity of Dewey's thought only during the past twenty years. Many articles and studies that have been published in the last ten years have taken a holistic view, even though a quick look through any Italian bibliography shows that most attention to Dewey regards education. When education is not conceived as merely didactics, then Dewey's Italian understanding will take a step forward compared to the past.

Dewey's holism is not a secondary point. We know, as according to what Dewey affirms in *The Quest for Certainty*, that

> ... what is known is seen to be a product in which the act of observation plays a necessary role. Knowing is seen to be a participant in what is finally known. Moreover, the metaphysics of existence as something fixed and therefore capable of literally exact mathematical description and prediction is undermined.... The quest for certainty by means of exact possession in mind of immutable reality is exchanged for search for security by means of active control of the changing course of events. Intelligence in operation, another name for method, becomes the thing most worth winning.[7]

And he writes on the previous page: "When we perceive an object by means of touch, the contact introduces a slight modification in the thing touched." When we touch a body, it reacts. The observer is part of what is observed. Observation changes what is observed. And the conditions of observation affect what is known. Knowing acts are operations that change, transform, and alter somehow the objects known. Heisenberg's uncertainty principle and Einstein's theory of relativity explain that the concept of absolute time has no sense. The way time changes perception and knowing is depicted very well by cubism and futurism. Umberto Boccioni, in his *Visioni simultanee* (1911), and Giacomo Balla, in his *Il dinamismo di un cane al guinzaglio* (1912) demonstrate this theory.

The way my situation, on the ontological level where I am, determines my observation and my knowing is well expressed by Bergson: "Though all the photographs of a city taken from all possible points of view indefinitely complete one another, they will never equal in value that dimensional object along whose streets one walks."[8] And so it is for a representation or a translation, as we comprehend from Bergson. The world as we know it is the world as we mold it. And the shape depends on the situation, on how and where we are situated. We are where we grew up, the people we met and the people we avoided, the books we read and those we just bought, the ideas we supported and those we set aside, the night thoughts and the daydreaming. We are our history. And we are our geography too. The Italian writer Italo Calvino once wrote: "It is clear that to describe the shape of the world the first thing is to establish the position I am in. I'm not saying where but how I am oriented."[9]

Intelligence is strictly connected with Darwinism, which is the key to understand Dewey's philosophy. Thanks to Darwin the *ordo geometricus* is replaced by evolutionism: the pretension to reduce everything within the schemes of the calculating reason is no longer sustainable. Evolutionism does not mean to drift onto *esprit de finesse* or a romantic idealism. Now *ordo* is change; the rule is evolution; the principle is changeable; no room for fixity, no discount is granted on hypostases. A remarkable consequence of such a reversal is the epistemological shift: knowledge is not acquirement of ultimate data, but possession of control tools, of methods and criteria of adaptation, of verification. If the reference is evolution, no goal can be considered as final. Each phase is an intermediate step between what is back and what is ahead. Knowledge moves to dynamic positions. Evolutionism changes the point of our knowledge, neither the quantity, nor the certainty. True knowledge refers to procedures, not to supposed essences. As one of the most recent Italian Dewey scholars, Mario Alcaro, writes, "Darwin passes the sponge over the central principle of traditional gnoseology: since there is no reality out of the law of change, the distinction between sensorial experience—as knowledge of changeable things, so imperfect and lower—and science—as rational knowledge, so certain and conclusive of the reign of immutable things—has not sense any longer."[10] The knowledge of changeable things is not of a lower kind, because the property of certainty is not an exclusive mark of the immutable reign. There can be knowledge of changeable things which can be certain without being conclusive.

The fact that I learn from the weather forecast that tomorrow it will rain is a certain fact, because I am sure of it and I certainly know it. But that knowledge is not conclusive, because the fact that I certainly know the forecast and that, as according to it, I plan my day somehow, does not exclude the chance to get a sunny day, making my umbrella of no use and convincing me to change my plans again. I had a certain knowledge about a probable rainy day and now I have a certain knowledge about the pointlessness of my raincoat. Neither of these two facts could be considered conclusive. As Einstein once wrote, "When a man sits with a pretty girl for an hour, it seems like a minute. But let him sit on a hot stove for a minute—then it's longer than any hour. That's relativity!"[11] And relativity and certainty do not necessarily conflict.

NOTES

CHAPTER 1: THE IMPORTANCE OF
DEWEY FOR PHILOSOPHY
(AND FOR MUCH ELSE BESIDES)

1. MW.9.338
2. Ibid.
3. Ibid.
4. William James, *Pragmatism* (New York: Henry Holt, 1907), p. 508.
5. William James, "The Sentiment of Rationality," in *The Writings of William James*, ed. John J. McDermott (Chicago: University of Chicago Press, 1977), p. 317.
6. MW.12.110.
7. LW.4.204.
8. LW.4.249
9. MW.12.164.
10. Ibid.
11. MW.14.74.
12. MW.14.19.
13. LW.2.327–8.
14. LW.2.320
15. LW.9.7.
16. LW.9.17.
17. LW.9.13.

CHAPTER 2: REFLECTIONS ON PRAGMATISM

1. For Brandom's interpretation of James, see his "Pragmatics and Pragmatisms" in *Hilary Putnam: Pragmatism and Realism*, ed. Urszula M. Zeglen and James Conant

(London: Routledge, 2002), pp. 40–58; and my "Comment on Robert Brandom's Paper" in the same volume, pp. 59–65. Rorty identifies his instrumentalist reading of James and Dewey with Brandom's reading in "Putnam, Parmenides and Pragmatism," in the forthcoming *The Philosophy of Hilary Putnam* (Chicago: Open Court, 2011).

2. William James, *Essays in Philosophy* (Cambridge, MA: Harvard University Press, 1978), pp. 21–22.

3. William James, *The Will to Believe* (Cambridge, MA: Harvard University Press, 1992), p. 66.

4. You will see that this is the case from the first lecture in Peirce's *Reasoning and the Logic of Things*, ed. Kenneth L. Ketner with expository matter by Hilary Putnam (Cambridge, MA: Harvard University Press, 1992).

5. The best account I know of the development of Peirce's views on truth is Christopher Hookway's *Truth, Rationality and Pragmatism* (Oxford: Oxford University Press, 2002).

6. See my "Pragmatism," *Proceedings of the Aristotelian Society* 95, pt. 3 (1995): 291–306.

7. In *The Analysis of Mind*, Russell wrote that the views of the American New Realists "are in large measure derived from William James, and before going further it will be well to consider the revolutionary doctrine [that] he advocated. I believe this doctrine contains important new truth, and what I shall have to say will be in considerable measure inspired by it." (Nottingham, UK: Spokesman, 2007), p. 22.

8. "The Need for a Recovery of Philosophy" (1917), LW.10.46.

9. Lionel Robbins, *On the Nature and Significance of Economic Science* (London: Macmillan, 1932), p. 132.

10. "Some Questions about Value" (1944), LW.15.106.

11. LW.15.101.

12. LW.15.440.

13. See, for example, James's "The Moral Philosopher and the Moral Life" in *Will to Believe* (see note 3).

14. Rudolf Carnap, *The Unity of Science* (London: Kegan Paul, Trench, Hubner, 1934), pp. 26–27.

15. Ibid., p. 22.

16. Carnap later loosened the verifiability criterion, but in a way that still left him open to Quine's famous criticisms. For an account, see my *The Collapse of the Fact/Value Dichotomy* (Cambridge, MA: Harvard University Press, 2002).

17. J. L. Mackie, *Ethics; Inventing Right and Wrong* (Harmondsworth, UK: Penguin Books, 1978).

18. Ibid., p. 41.

19. Thomas Scanlon, *What We Owe to Each Other* (Cambridge, MA: Harvard University Press, 1999).

20. Ibid., p. 155.

21. Rawls's "veil of ignorance" and "initial position" are what Scanlon is referring to.

22. Ibid., p. 191.

23. I discuss this claim in detail in the first chapter of *Collapse of the Fact/Value Dichotomy*.

24. Why this isn't the right way to think of ethics is something I argue in the opening and closing chapters of *Ethics without Ontology* (Cambridge, MA: Harvard University Press, 2004).

25. MW.5.272.

26. This is how I understand Dewey's answer to the noncognitivists in *Theory of Valuation*, vol. 2, no. 4 of *International Encyclopedia of Unified Science*, ed. Otto Neurath, Rudolf Carnap, and Charles W. Morris (Chicago: University of Chicago Press, 1939), reprinted in LW.13.191–252. For a discussion of the role of the notion of a "problematic situation" and the notion of an objective resolution of a problematic situation in both Dewey's theory of inquiry and his ethical theory, see Ruth Anna Putnam and Hilary Putnam, "Epistemology as Hypothesis" in *Transactions of the Charles S. Peirce Society* 26, no. 4 (Fall 1990): 407–33 (reprinted as "Dewey's *Logic*: Epistemology as Hypothesis" in my *Words and Life* [Cambridge, MA: Harvard University Press, 1994], pp. 198–220); and Ruth Anna Putnam and Hilary Putnam, "Education for Democracy," *Educational Theory* 43, no. 4 (Fall 1993): 361–76 (also reprinted in *Words and Life*, pp. 221–41).

27. *Collapse of the Fact-Value Dichotomy* and *Ethics without Ontology*.

28. Carnap, *Unity of Science*, p. 26.

29. This passage was recalled to me by reading Vivian Walsh's forthcoming "Facts, Values, Theories and Pragmatism."

30. Morton White, *Towards Reunion in Philosophy* (Cambridge, MA: Harvard University Press, 1956), p. 108.

31. I refer to Quine's celebrated article, "Two Dogmas of Empiricism" (1951), in W. V. Quine, *From a Logical Point of View* (1953; Cambridge, MA: Harvard University Press, 1961), with the following alterations: "The version printed here diverges from the original in footnotes and in other minor respects: §§1 and 6 have been abridged where they encroach on the preceding essay, and §§3–4 have been expanded at points. . . ."

32. W. V. Quine, "Carnap and Logical Truth," in his *Ways of Paradox and Other Essays*, 2nd ed. (Cambridge, MA: Harvard University Press, 1976), p. 132.

33. Vivian Walsh, "Philosophy and Economics," in *The New Palgrave: A Dictionary of Economics*, ed. J. Eatwell, M. Milgte, and P. Newman (London: Macmillan, 1987), 3:861–69.

34. I defend this claim in chapter 5 of *Collapse of the Fact/Value Dichotomy*, "The Philosophers of Science's Evasion of Values."

35. Iris Murdoch, *The Sovereignty of "Good" over Other Concepts* (Cambridge, UK: Cambridge University Press, 1967).

36. Bernard Williams reported that "the idea that it might be impossible to pick up an evaluative concept unless one shared its evaluative interest is basically a Wittgensteinian idea. I first heard it expressed by Philippa Foot and Iris Murdoch in a seminar in the 1950s." Bernard Williams, *Ethics and the Limits of Philosophy* (Cambridge, MA: Harvard University Press, 1985), p. 218.

37. See, for example, Ruth Anna Putnam, "Weaving Seamless Webs" in *Philosophy* 62, no. 240 (1987): 207–20 and "Perceiving Facts and Values," *Philosophy* 73, no. 283 (1998): 5–19; John McDowell, "Non-Cognitivism and Rule-Following," in *Mind, Value and Reality* (Cambridge, MA: Harvard University Press, 1998), pp. 198–218 (originally published in *Wittgenstein: To Follow a Rule*, ed. Steven H. Holtzman and Christopher M. Leich [London: Routledge, 1981], pp. 141–72); and my *Collapse of the Fact/Value Dichotomy* and *Ethics without Ontology*, plus "Capabilities and Two Ethical Theories," *Journal of Human Development* 9, no. 3 (November 2008): 377–88.

CHAPTER 3: LOOKING AHEAD: WHAT ARE THE PROSPECTS FOR DEWEY'S PHILOSOPHY IN THE FUTURE?

1. John Dewey, "Philosophy's Future in Our Scientific Age: Never Was Its Role More Crucial," *Commentary* 8 (October 1949): 388–94.

2. Paul Kurtz, *American Thought before 1900: From Puritanism to Pragmatism* (New York: Macmillan, 1966).

3. I also published a second sourcebook on American philosophy, and both were widely used: *American Philosophy in the Twentieth Century: From Pragmatism to Philosophical Analysis* (New York: Macmillan, 1966).

4. John Herman Randall Jr., "The Future of John Dewey's Philosophy," *Journal of Philosophy* 55 (1959): 1005–10.

5. Sidney Hook, "John Dewey—Philosopher of Growth," *Journal of Philosophy* 55 (1959): 1010–18.

6. Incidentally, this was republished in *The Influence of Darwin on Philosophy, and Other Essays* (Amherst, NY: Prometheus Books, 1997).

7. Charles Darwin, *The Descent of Man* (London: Charles Murray, 1871), 2:389.

8. The discovery of a fairly well preserved fossil of a 47-million-year-old primate indicates that it may be the link between humans and apes. Known as *Darwinius masillae*, it is a lemurlike creature; it had opposable thumbs and fingernails; and its hind legs suggest evolutionary changes that eventuated in the ability to stand upright.

9. Jerry Coyne, *Why Evolution Is True* (New York: Viking, 2009), p. 206.

10. See Carl Zimmer, *Evolution: The Triumph of an Idea* (New York: Harper, 2002).

11. Ibid.

12. Darwin, *Descent of Man*, 1:166.

13. Our knowledge of history demonstrates the rise and fall of civilizations in a way that earlier civilizations were not fully aware, and demonstrates that America, indeed Western civilization, will one day decline. All this of course is consonant with John Dewey's pragmatic instrumentalism. His theory of inquiry and valuation presupposes not only that existence is precarious, but that nature in general exhibits similar characteristics. New discoveries in astronomy dramatize the vastness of the universe (or multiverse) and the fact that our universe is expanding at a terrific pace. We observe in our telescopes the turbulence in outer space, the explosions and emergence of stars and the collision of galaxies.

14. George Santayana, "A General Confession," in *The Philosophy of George Santayana*, ed. Paul Arthur Schilpp (Evanston, IL: Northwestern University, 1940), p. 30.

15. See Roger-Maurice Bonnet and Lodewyk Woltjer, *Surviving 1,000 Centuries: Can We Do It?* (Berlin: Springer, 2008).

CHAPTER 4: DEWEY AND THE SUBJECT MATTER OF SCIENCE

1. For a summary, see Hans Reichenbach, *The Rise of Scientific Philosophy* (Berkeley: University of California Press, 1951).

2. Hans Reichenbach, "Dewey's Theory of Science," in *The Philosophy of John Dewey*, 3rd ed., ed. Paul A. Schilpp and Lewis Hahn (La Salle, IL: Open Court, 1989), 161, quoting *Quest for Certainty*, LW.4.85.

3. Ibid., p. 162.

4. Ibid., p. 169.

5. "Experience, Knowledge and Value: A Rejoinder" (1939), LW.14.20.

6. For relevant discussions of Aristotle's *Categories* and other works, see these *Stanford Encyclopedia of Philosophy* articles from Fall 2009, edited by Edward N. Zalta (available at http://plato.stanford.edu/archives/fall2009/): Jeffrey Brower, "Medieval Theories of Relations"; S. Marc Cohen, "Aristotle's Metaphysics"; and Paul Studtmann, "Aristotle's Categories." Brower discusses medieval responses to Aristotle's view. As he describes it, medieval philosophers were slowly forced by the Christian doctrine of the Trinity toward a more realist view of relational properties (God is the father, and that is a relational property), but they only moved away from Aristotle's framework of solely monadic properties with much reluctance.

7. All relations have "no other reality, but what they have in the Minds of Men." John Locke, *An Essay concerning Human Understanding*, ed. P. Nidditch (New York:

Oxford University Press, 1975), II, xxx, 4. Relations are nothing "but my way of considering, or comparing two Things together, and so also an Idea of my own making" (III, x, 33). Leibniz, who disagreed with Locke on many issues, had a similar view on this one.

8. Dewey freely used "the Greeks" as a category in his philosophical histories, sometimes paying little attention to the differences between different Greeks, such as (for example) Plato and Aristotle. When describing Dewey's analysis here, I will sometimes use the same blanket category.

9. See *Experience and Nature* (1925), LW.1.248–50; and *Quest for Certainty* (1929), LW.4.14–15.

10. LW.1.26.

11. LW.1.28.

12. See *Experience and Nature* (1925), LW.1.91–92, 201–202, 314–15.

13. For more careful formulations along the same lines, see Rae Langton, *Kantian Humility: Our Ignorance of Things in Themselves* (Oxford: Clarendon, 1998); David Lewis, "Ramseyan Humility," in *The Canberra Programme*, ed. D. Braddon-Mitchell and R. Nola (Oxford: Oxford University Press, 2009), pp. 203–22; and Brian Weatherson, "Intrinsic vs. Extrinsic Properties" in *Stanford Encyclopedia of Philosophy* (Fall 2008), http://plato.stanford.edu/archives/fall2008/.

14. In "Characteristics and Characters: Kinds and Classes" (1936), Dewey distinguishes between qualities and "attributes," noting that many unfortunately take these to be equivalent. A quality is something "existential," a real trait of some object and not merely a specification to which an object *may* conform—an attribute (LW.11.97). As far as I can tell, this complication does not affect the issues discussed in this paper, as here we are always dealing with real traits of objects.

15. See *Experience and Nature* (1925), LW.1.74, 114–15; and for "tropes" see D. M. Armstrong, *Universals: An Opinionated Introduction* (Boulder, CO: Westview, 1989).

16. LW.1.198–99.

17. LW.1.106, see also 201–202.

18. For a survey, see James Ladyman, "Structural Realism" in *Stanford Encyclopedia of Philosophy* (Summer 2009), http://plato.stanford.edu/archives/sum2009/. See Langton, *Kantian Humility*, for the connection to Kant.

19. John Worrall, "Structural Realism: The Best of Both Worlds?" *Dialectica* 43 (1989): 99–124.

20. Larry Laudan, "A Confutation of Convergent Realism," *Philosophy of Science* 48 (1981): 19–49.

21. See, for example, Stathis Psillos, "Is Structural Realism Possible?" *Philosophy of Science* 68 (2001): S13–S24.

22. "[A]ll structure is structure *of* something." LW.1.64. See also *Quest for Certainty* (1929), LW.4.153–55.

23. LW.1.74–75. See also LW.1.119 for a similar passage.

24. *Quest for Certainty* (1929), LW.4.105.

25. LW.14.22.

26. Ibid.

27. From here I will contrast the intrinsic with the extrinsic, not with the relational. This is because of cases in which a property is both intrinsic and, in some sense, relational. Weatherson's "Intrinsic vs. Extrinsic Properties" uses the example of *having longer legs than arms*.

28. In "Ramseyan Humility," David Lewis argues that ignorance of the intrinsic properties of fundamental entities undermines knowledge of the intrinsic properties of higher-level entities (such as samples of carbon), using a Ramsey-sentence interpretation of physical theories.

29. *Quest for Certainty* (1929), LW.4.105.

30. Ibid. See also Peter Godfrey-Smith, "Dewey on Naturalism, Realism, and Science," *Philosophy of Science* 69 (2002): S25–S35.

CHAPTER 5: DEWEY AND DARWIN ON EVOLUTION AND NATURAL KINDS: A PRAGMATIC PERSPECTIVE

1. R. W. Sellars, *Evolutionary Naturalism* (La Salle, IL: Open Court, 1922).

2. Charles Darwin, *The Origin of Species* (New York: Mentor Books, 1859/1958); John Dewey, *The Influence of Darwin on Philosophy* (Bloomington: Indiana University Press, 1910/1965).

3. Dewey, *The Quest for Certainty* (New York: Capricorn Books, 1929/1960).

4. John Herman Randall, Jr., *Philosophy After Darwin* (New York: Columbia University Press, 1977).

5. Jaegwon Kim, "The American Origins of Philosophical Naturalism," *Journal of Philosophical Research* 28 supplement (2003): 83–98; See Sellars, *Evolutionary Naturalism*.

6. Morris R. Cohen, *Reason and Nature* (New York: Dover Press, 1931/1959); George Santayana, *Scepticism and Animal Faith* (New York: Dover Press, 1923/1955).

7. Dewey, *The Influence of Darwin on Philosophy*, LW 4: 11.

8. Hilary Putnam, *Realism with a Human Face* (Cambridge, MA: Harvard University Press, 1990).

9. Chauncey Wright, *Philosophical Writings* (New York: Liberal Arts Press, 1958); Edward H. Madden, *Civil Disobedience and Moral Law in 19th Century American Philosophy* (Seattle: University of Washington Press, 1968); William James, *The Principles of*

Psychology (New York: Dover Press, 1890/1952); James, *Pragmatism* (Cleveland: World Publishing, 1907/1969); Madden, *Chauncey Wright* (New York: Washington Square Press, 1964); Philip P. Wiener, *Evolution and the Founders of Pragmatism* (Philadelphia: University of Pennsylvania Press, 1972).

10. Ralph B. Perry, *In the Spirit of William James* (Bloomington: Indiana University Press, 1938/1958); see also Madden, *Civil Disobedience and Moral Law in 19th Century American Philosophy*.

11. Reinhold Niebuhr, *The Irony of American History* (New York: Charles Scribner's Sons, 1952); A. O. Lovejoy, *Essays on the History of Ideas* (New York: George Braziller, 1955).

12. LW 4: 134.

13. Philip Kitcher, *The Advancement of Science* (Oxford: Oxford University Press, 1993).

14. Peter Godfrey-Smith, "Dewey on Naturalism, Realism, and Science," *Philosophy of Science* 69 (2002): S1–S11.

15. Gerd Gigerenzer, *Adaptive Thinking* (Oxford: Oxford University Press, 2000); see also the books by Kitcher and Godfrey-Smith cited above.

16. R. Boyd, "Homeostasis, Species, and Higher Taxa," in *Species: New Interdisciplinary Essays*, ed. R. A. Wilson (Cambridge, MA: MIT Press, 1999).

17. C. S. Peirce, "Questions Concerning Certain Faculties Claimed for Man," *The Essential Pierce*, vol. 1 (Bloomington: Indiana University Press, 1992); C. S. Peirce, "Deduction, Induction, and Hypothesis," *Popular Science and Monthly* 13 (1878): 470–82; Larry Laudan, *Progress and its Problems* (Berkeley: University of California Press, 1977).

18. Ernest Nagel, *Sovereign Reason* (New York: Free Press, 1954); Michael Williams, *Unnatural Doubts* (Princeton, NJ: Princeton University Press, 1996).

19. C. S. Peirce, *Reasoning and the Logic of Things*, ed. K. L. Ketner and H. Putnam (Cambridge, MA: Harvard University Press, 1992); D. L. Hull, *Science as a Process* (Chicago: University of Chicago Press, 1988).

20. E. Mayr, *Animal Species and Evolution* (Cambridge, MA: Harvard University Press, 1963); P. Rozin, "The Evolution of Intelligence and Access to the Cognitive Unconscious," in *Progress in Psychobiology and Physiological Psychology*, ed. J. Sprague and A. N. Epstein (New York: Academic Press, 1976); P. Rozin, "Evolution and Development of Brains and Cultures: Some Basic Principles and Interactions," in *Brain and Mind: Evolutionary Perspectives*, ed. M. S. Gazzaniga and J. S. Altman (Strassbourg: Human Frontiers Science Program, 1998).

21. T. R. Malthus, *An Essay on the Principle of Population* (Baltimore: Penguin Books, 1798/1970).

22. P. Mellars, "Why Did Modern Human Populations Disperse from Africa ca. 60,000 Years Ago?" *PNAS* 103 (2006): 9381–86; R. Boyd and P. Richerson, *Culture and Evolutionary Process* (Chicago, University of Chicago Press, 1985).

23. R. Foley, "The Emergence of Culture in the Context of Hominin Evolutionary Patterns," in *Evolution and Culture*, ed. C. Levinson and P. Jaisson (Cambridge, MA: MIT Press, 2006); S. Mithen, *The Prehistory of the Mind* (London: Thames and Hudson, 1996); R. Foley and M. M. Lahr, "Human Evolution Writ Small," *Nature* 431 (2004): 1043–44.

24. D. Premack and A. J. Premack, "Moral Belief: Form versus Content," in *Mapping the Mind: Domain Specificity in Cognition and Culture*, ed. L. A. Hirschfeld and S. A. Gelman (Cambridge: Cambridge University Press, 1994); D. Premack and A. J. Premack, "Origins of Human Social Competence," in *The Cognitive Neurosciences*, ed. M. S. Gazzaniga (Cambridge, MA: MIT Press, 1995); M. D. Hauser, *The Evolution of Communication* (Cambridge, MA: MIT Press, 1997); M. C. Corballis, *From Hand to Mouth* (Princeton, NJ: Princeton University Press, 2002); R. I. M. Dunbar, *Grooming, Gossip, and the Evolution of Language* (Cambridge, MA: Harvard University Press, 1996).

25. M. Donald, "Hominid Enculturation and Cognitive Evolution," in *The Development of the Mediated Mind*, ed. J. M. Luraciello et al. (Mawah, NJ: Erlbaum Press, 2004).

26. E. Grant, *A History of Natural Philosophy* (Cambridge: Cambridge University Press, 2007); R. G. Collingwood, *The Idea of Nature* (Oxford: Oxford University Press, 1945/1976); J. Schulkin, *The Delicate Balance* (Lanham, MD: University Press of America, 1996). A. N. Whitehead, *An Enquiry Concerning the Principles of Natural Knowledge* (New York: Dover Press, 1919/1982); J. Schulkin, *Cognitive Adaptation: A Pragmatist Perspective* (Cambridge: Cambridge University Press, 2009).

27. M. Oelschlaeger, *The Idea of the Wilderness* (New Haven, CT: Yale University Press, 1991); Ralph Waldo Emerson, *Nature, Addresses, and Lectures* (Cambridge, MA: The Riverside Press, 1855/1883); R. Nash, *Wilderness and the American Mind* (New Haven, CT: Yale University Press, 1967); B. Wilshire, *The Primal Roots of American Philosophy* (University Park: Penn State University, 2000); Henry David Thoreau, *Great Short Works* (New York: Harper and Row, 1971). D. Worster, *Nature's Economy* (Cambridge: Cambridge University Press, 1977/1991); M. Midgley, *Beast and Man* (London: Routledge, 1979/1995); E. O. Wilson, *The Diversity of Life* (Cambridge, MA: Harvard University Press, 1992).

28. J. B. Bury, *The Idea of Progress* (New York: Dover Press, 1933/1960); T. H. Huxley, *Man's Place in Nature* (London: Macmillan, 1863).

29. S. J. Gould, *Ontogeny and Phylogeny* (Cambridge, MA: Harvard University Press, 1977); R. Goldsmith, *The Material Basis of Evolution* (New Haven, CT: Yale University Press, 1940/1982); S. J. Gould and N. Eldridge, "Punctuated Equilibria: The Tempo and Mode of Evolution Reconsidered," *Paleobiology* 3 (1977): 115–51. W. Von Humbolt, *Linguistic and Intellectual Development* (Philadelphia: University of Pennsylvania Press, 1836/1971). S. J. Gould, *The Structure of Evolutionary Theory* (Cambridge,

MA: Harvard University Press, 2002); H. M. McHenry, "Tempo and Mode in Human Evolution," *Proceedings of the National Academy of Sciences* 97 (1994): 6780–86.

30. N. Chomsky, *Language and Mind* (New York: Harcourt, 1972); S. Pinker, *The Language Instinct* (New York: William Morrow, 1994).

31. K. R. Gibson and T. Ingold, ed., *Tools, Language, and Cognition in Human Evolution* (Cambridge, MA: Cambridge University Press, 1993).

32. M. Donald, *Origins of Modern Man* (Cambridge, MA: Harvard University Press, 1991); M. D. Hauser, *The Evolution of Communication* (Cambridge, MA: MIT Press, 1996/1997); J. H. Jackson, "Evolution and Dissolution of the Nervous System," in *Selected Writing of John Hughlings Jackson* (London: Staples Press, 1884/1958); N. Geschwind, *Selected Papers on Language and the Brain* (Boston: Reidel, 1974).

33. S. Levison, "Cognition at the Heart of Human Interaction," *Discourse Studies* 8 (2006): 85–93; M. Tomasello, *Why We Cooperate* (Cambridge, MA: MIT Press, 2009); J. Schulkin, *Rethinking Homeostasis* (Cambridge, MA: MIT Press, 2003); J. Schulkin, *Roots of Social Sensibility and Neural Function* (Cambridge, MA: MIT Press, 2000).

34. K. Sterelny, *The Evolution of Agency and Other Essays* (Cambridge, UK: Cambridge University Press, 2000); C. R. Gallistel, *The Organization of Learning* (Cambridge, MA: MIT Press, 1990).

35. J. Sabini and J. Schulkin, "Biological Realism and Social Constructivism," *J for the Theory of Social Behavior* 224 (1994): 207–17: J. D. Moreno, *Deciding Together* (Oxford: Oxford University Press, 1995); G. H. Mead, "Evolution Becomes a General Idea," in *Selected Papers* (Chicago: University of Chicago Press, 1934/1964); J. Dewey, "The Reflex Arc Concept in Psychology," *Psychological Review* 3 (1896): 357–70; P. A. Heelan and J. Schulkin, "Hermeneutical Philosophy and Pragmatism: A Philosophy of Science," *Synthese* 115 (1998): 269–302; M. Johnson, *The Meaning of the Body* (Chicago: University of Chicago Press, 2007); J. Dewey, *Experience and Nature* (La Salle, IL: Open Court, 1925/1989).

36. C. R. Gallistel, *The Organization of Action: A New Synthesis* (Hillsdale, NJ: Lawrence Erlbaum, 1980); J. Schulkin, *Bodily Sensibility: Intelligent Action* (Oxford: Oxford University Press, 2004); J. Schulkin, *Effort: A Neurobiological Perspective on the Will* (Mahwah, NJ: Erlbaum Press, 2007); R. A. Barton, "Binocularity and Brain Evolution in Primates," *PNAS* 101 (2004): 10113–15; R. A. Barton, "Primate Brain Evolution: Integrating Comparative Neurophysiological and Ethological Data," *Evolutionary Anthropology* 15 (2006): 224–36; R. I. M. Dunbar, "Neocortex Size as a Constraint on Group Size in Primates," *Journal of Human Evolution* 22 (1992): 469–93.

37. J. Diamond, *Guns, Germs, and Steel* (New York: Norton, 1998).

38. A. Martin, "The Representation of Object Concepts in the Brain," *Annual Review of Psychology* 58 (2007): 25–45; See also Schulkin, *Bodily Sensibility*; M. T. Ullman, "A Neurocognitive Perspective on Language: The Declarative Procedural Model," *Nature Neuroscience* 9 (2001): 266–86.

39. M. Tomasello and J. Call, *Primate Cognition* (Oxford: Oxford University Press, 1997).

40. F. C. Keil, *Concepts, Kinds, and Cognitive Development* (Cambridge, MA: MIT Press, 1989); Keil, *Semantic and Conceptual Development: An Ontological Perspective* (Cambridge, MA: Harvard University Press, 1979); S. Levinson, "Cognition at the Heart of Human Interaction," *Discourse Studies* 8 (2006): 85–93; E. S. Spelke, A. Phillips, and A. L. Woodward, "Infants' Knowledge of Object Motion and Human Action," in *Causal Cognition: A Multidisciplinary Debate*, ed. D. Sperber, D. Premack, and A. J. Premack (Oxford: Clarendon Press, 1995).

41. G. Lakoff and M. Johnson, *Philosophy in the Flesh* (New York: Basic Books, 1999); Ernst Cassirer, *An Essay on Man* (New Haven, CT: Yale University Press, 1944/1978); Cassirer, *The Philosophy of the Enlightenment* (Princeton, NJ: Princeton University Press, 1951).

42. See Keil, *Concepts, Kinds, and Cognitive Development*; S. Carey, *Conceptual Change in Childhood* (Cambridge, MA: MIT Press, 1987); Carey, "Bootstrapping and the Origins of Concepts," *Dedalus* 133 (Winter 2004): 59–68; Carey, *On the Origins of Concepts* (Oxford: Oxford University Press, 2009); A. Atran, D. L. Medin, and N. O Ross, "The Cultural Mind," *Psychological Review* 112 (2005): 744–66; J. J. Gibson, *The Senses Considered as Perceptual Systems* (New York: Houghton Mifflin, 1966); A. Clark, *Being There* (Cambridge, MA: MIT Press, 1997).

43. P. Wolff and D. L. Medin, "Measuring the Evolution and Devolution of Folk-Biological Knowledge," in *On Biocultural Diversity: Linking Language, Knowledge, and the Environment*, ed. L. Maffi (Washington, DC: Smithsonian Institute, 2001).

44. A. Atran et al., "The Cultural Mind."

45. C. R. Gallistel, *The Organization of Learning* (Cambridge, MA: MIT Press, 1990); see also Lakoff and Johnson, *Philosophy in the Flesh*.

46. C. S. Peirce, "The Architecture of Theories," *The Monist* 1 (1892): 61–76; N. R. Hanson, *Patterns of Discovery* (Cambridge: Cambridge University Press, 1958); W. V. Quine, *From a Logical Point of View* (New York: Harper Torchbooks, 1961); Quine, "Epistemology Naturalized," in *Ontological Relativity and Other Essays* (New York: Columbia University Press, 1969); J. E. Smith, *Themes in American Philosophy* (New York: Harper & Row, 1970); J. E. Smith, "Experience in Pierce, James, and Dewey," *Monist* 68 (1985): 538–54. See also references to works by Peirce and Dewey in previous endnotes.

47. N. Goodman, *Fact, Fiction, and Forecast* (New York: Bobbs-Merrill, 1978).

48. P. L. Farber, *Finding Order in Nature* (Baltimore: Johns Hopkins University Press, 2000).

49. Peirce, "On a New Class of Observations, Suggested by the Principles of Logic," *The Essential Pierce*, vol. 1 (Bloomington: Indiana University Press, 1992), p. 107; "Questions Concerning Certain Faculties Claimed for Man," p. 30.

50. See also P. Dear, *Discipline and Experience* (Chicago: University of Chicago Press, 1995); Dear, *The Intelligibility of Nature* (Chicago: University of Chicago Press, 2006).

51. Dewey, *Experience and Nature*, LW 1: 22

52. Quine, "Epistemology Naturalized," p. 43.

53. Quine, *From a Logical Point of View*, p. 123.

54. Ibid., p. 125.

55. Hanson, *Patterns of Discovery*, p. 16.

56. D. Premack, "The Infant's Theory of Self-Propelled Objects," *Cognition* 36 (1990): 1–16.

57. Hanson, *Patterns of Discovery*, p. 59.

58. Ibid., p. 72.

59. Wilfrid Sellars, *Science and Metaphysics* (London: Routledge and Kegan Paul, 1968); Sellars, *Empiricism and the Philosophy of Mind* (Cambridge, MA: Harvard University Press, 1997), p. 3.

60. R. N. Giere, *Scientific Perspectivism* (Chicago: University of Chicago Press, 2006).

61. Ian Hacking, *Logic of Statistical Inference* (Cambridge: Cambridge University Press, 1979); Hacking, *The Taming of Chance* (Cambridge: Cambridge University Press, 1990). G. H. Mead, *Evolution Becomes a General Idea* (Chicago: University of Chicago Press, 1934/1964).

62. R. Boyd, "Homeostasis, Species, and Higher Taxa."

63. R. A. Wilson, *Species: New Interdisciplinary Essays* (Cambridge: Cambridge University Press, 1999), p. 147; C. L. Elder, "Biological Species are Natural Kinds," *Southern Journal of Philosophy* 46 (2008): 339–62; C. F. Craver, "Mechanisms and Natural Kinds," *Philosophical Psychology* 22 (2009): 575–94; J. Dupré, "Natural Kinds and Biological Taxa," *Philosophical Review* 90 (1981): 66–90.

64. J. Dupré, *The Disorder of Things* (Cambridge, MA: Harvard University Press, 1993); H. Kornblith, *Knowledge and its Place in Nature* (Oxford: Oxford University Press, 2003).

65. J. Dupré, *Humans and Other Animals* (Oxford: Oxford University Press, 2002).

66. R. A. Wilson, *Genes and the Agents of Life* (Cambridge: Cambridge University Press, 2005).

67. P. E. Griffiths, "Squaring the Circle: Natural Kinds with Historical Essences," in *Species: New Interdisciplinary Essays*, ed. R. A. Wilson (Cambridge, MA: MIT Press, 1999), pp. 209–28.

68. Dewey, *Art as Experience* (1934), LW 10: 34

69. LW 10: 139.

70. Larry A. Hickman, *John Dewey's Pragmatic Technology* (Bloomington: Indiana University Press, 1980/1992); Hickman, *Pragmatism as Post-Modernism* (New York: Forham University Press, 2007).

71. In addition to previously cited studies, see S. J. Shettleworth, *Cognition, Evolution and Behavior* (Oxford: Oxford University Press, 1998); S. Levinson, "Cognition at the Heart of Human Interaction," *Discourse Studies 8* (2006): 85–93; E. Mayr, *One Long Argument* (Cambridge, MA: Harvard University Press, 1991).

72. Martin Heidegger, *The Question concerning Technology*, trans. W. Lovitt (New York: Harper and Row, 1962).

73. C. S. Peirce, "Evolutionary Love" (1893) in *The Essential Peirce*, vol. 1, ed. N. Houser and C. Kloesel (Bloomington: Indiana University Press, 1992), pp. 352–62.

74. Dewey, *A Theory of Valuation* (Chicago: University of Chicago Press, 1939).

75. M. Sagoff, *The Economy of the Earth* (Cambridge: Cambridge University Press, 1988).

76. See B. Wilshire, *The Primal Roots of American Philosophy*; D. Sarokin and J. Schulkin, "Co-evolution of Rights and Environmental Justice," *The Environmentalist* 14 (1994): 121–29; S. L. Pratt, *Native Pragmatism* (Bloomington: Indiana University Press, 2002).

CHAPTER 6: RECLAIMING THE PRAGMATIST LEGACY: EVOLUTION AND ITS DISCONTENTS

1. *Journal of Mind and Behavior* 29 no.1–2 (2008): 1–216, ed. David Livingstone Smith.

2. Robin L. Zebrowski, "Continuous Sticktogetherations and Somethingelseifications: How Evolutionary Biology Rewrote the Story of Mind." *Journal of Mind and Behavior* 29 (2008): 87–97.

3. John Dewey, "The Influence of Darwinism on Philosophy" in *The Influence of Darwin on Philosophy and Other Essays in Contemporary Thought* (Bloomington: Indiana University Press, 1965), pp. 1–19.

4. Larry L. Hickman, *John Dewey's Pragmatic Technology* (Bloomington: Indiana University Press, 1990), pp. 181–83.

5. Dewey, "The Influence of Darwinism on Philosophy," pp. 2–3.

6. Ibid., p. 8.

7. Ibid.

8. Ibid., p. 9.

9. Ibid., pp. 12–13.

10. Ibid., p. 2.

11. Ibid., p. 18.

12. Ibid., p. 19.

13. Ibid., p. 18.

14. Zebrowski, "Continuous Sticktogetherations," p. 87.

15. Philip P. Wiener, *Evolution and the Founders of Pragmatism* (Cambridge, MA: Harvard University Press, 1949).

16. Louis Menand, *The Metaphysical Club: A Story of Ideas in America* (New York: Farrar, Straus & Giroux, 2001).

17. Mark Pallen, *The Rough Guide to Evolution* (London and New York: Rough Guides, 2009).

18. Karl Popper, *Objective Knowledge: An Evolutionary Approach* (Oxford: Clarendon Press, 1972).

19. William James, as quoted in Pallen, *The Rough Guide to Evolution*, p. 238.

20. Dewey, "The Influence of Darwinism on Philosophy," p. 19, quoted in Pallen, *The Rough Guide to Evolution*, p. 238.

21. Henri Bergson, *Creative Evolution*, trans. Arthur Mitchell. (New York: Henry Holt, 1949).

22. Pierre Teilhard de Chardin, *Christianity and Evolution*, trans. René Haque. (New York: Harcourt Brace Jovanovich, 1971).

23. Nicole Winfield, "Vatican Convenes Event on Darwin," *Buffalo News* (March 4, 2009).

24. Suzanne Cunningham, *Philosophy and the Darwinian Legacy* (Rochester, NY: Rochester University Press, 1996).

25. Ibid.

26. Stephen Jay Gould, *The Structure of Evolutionary Theory* (Cambridge, MA: Harvard University Press, 2002).

27. David Depew, "Darwin's Multiple Ontologies," in *Darwinism and Philosophy*, ed. Vittorio Hösle and Christian Illies (Notre Dame, IN: University of Notre Dame Press, 2005), pp. 106–8.

28. Bill Harrell, email communication on October 2, 2009.

29. Jerry A. Coyne, *Why Evolution Is True* (New York: Viking, 2009).

30. Winfield, "Vatican Convenes Event on Darwin."

31. John Dewey, "The Intellectualist Criterion for Truth," in *The Influence of Darwin on Philosophy*, pp. 112–53.

32. Coyne, *Why Evolution Is True*, pp. 17–18.

33. Ibid.

34. James Campbell, *Understanding John Dewey* (Chicago: Open Court, 1995).

35. *Darwinism and Philosophy*, ed. Hösle and Illies.

36. Depew, "Darwin's Multiple Ontologies," p. 106.

37. John Dewey, *Human Nature and Conduct*, LW 14.

38. David Depew, "Darwin's Multiple Ontologies," p. 106.

39. Thomas C. Dalton, *Becoming John Dewey: Dilemmas of a Philosopher and Naturalist* (Bloomington: Indiana University Press, 2002).

40. *Darwinism and Philosophy*, ed. Hösle and Illies. See especially Michael Ruse, "Darwinism and Naturalism: Identical Twins or Just Good Friends?" pp. 83–91.

41. Stephen C. Pepper, *World Hypotheses: A Study in Evidence* (Berkeley: University of California Press, 1943). See also Pepper's sizeable treatment of evolution in the scale of human values in *The Sources of Value* (Berkeley: University of California Press, 1970), pp. 612–61.

42. Richard Dawkins, *The Selfish Gene* (Oxford: Oxford University Press, 1976).

43. Depew, "Darwin's Multiple Ontologies," p. 106.

44. Pepper, *World Hypotheses: A Study in Evidence*, pp. 256–60, 279.

45. John Dewey, *The Quest for Certainty* (New York: Capricorn Books, 1960), pp. 254–86.

46. David Sloan Wilson, *Evolution for Everyone: How Darwin's Theory Can Change the Way We Think About Our Lives* (New York: Bantam Dell, 2007), p. 105.

47. Ibid.

48. David Sloan Wilson, "Evolution for Everyone: How to Increase Acceptance of, Interest In, and Knowledge About Evolution." *Public Library of Science, Biology* 3 (2005): 1001–1008.

49. Gerald M. Edelman, *Neural Darwinism: The Theory of Neuronal Group Selection* (New York: Basic Books, 1987).

50. Pallen, *Rough Guide*, p. 113.

51. Bill Harrell, e-mail communication, October 2, 2009.

52. Elliot Sober and David Sloan Wilson, *Unto Others: The Evolution and Psychology of Unselfish Behavior* (Cambridge, MA: Harvard University Press, 1998).

53. Philip Kitcher, *Living With Darwin: Evolution, Design and the Future of Faith* (Oxford: Oxford University Press, 2008).

54. Denis Dutton, *The Art Instinct: Beauty, Pleasure, and Human Evolution.* (New York: Bloomsbury, 2009). Note the review article by Mara Miller in *Journal of Aesthetics and Art Criticism* 67 (2009): 333–36.

55. See however Jay Appleton, *The Experience of Landscape* (New York: Wiley, 1975). This work, based on Dewey's aesthetics, is praised by Dutton. But no mention is made of Dewey.

56. Dalton, *Becoming John Dewey: Dilemmas of a Philosopher and Naturalist*, pp. 78–80.

57. Ibid., p. 78.

58. Charles Darwin, "The Biographical Sketch of an Infant," *Mind* 2 (1877): 288.

59. Arthur Efron, *The Sexual Body: An Interdisciplinary Perspective.* Published as an issue of *Journal of Mind and Behavior* 6 no. 1–2 (1985): 1–314.

60. Efron, *The Sexual Body*, pp. 89–126.

61. Ibid., p. 126.

62. Dewey, *Human Nature and Conduct*, p. 114.

63. Geoffrey F. Miller, *The Mating Mind: How Sexual Choice Shaped the Evolution of Human Nature* (New York: Doubleday, 2000).

64. Charles Darwin, *The Descent of Man and Selection in Relation to Sex* (London: John Murray, 1871).

65. Geoffrey F. Miller, *The Mating Mind*, p. 36.

66. Dalton, *Becoming John Dewey*, pp. 233–51.

67. Charles Darwin, *The Expression of Emotions in Animals and Man* (London: John Murray, 1872).

68. Dalton, *Becoming John Dewey*, pp. 77–80.

69. John Dewey, "The Evolutionary Method as Applied to Morality" (1902), MW 2: 1–38. See also Dewey, "The Theory of Emotion" (1894), EW 4: 152–58; and Dewey, "Evolution and Ethics" (1898), EW 5: 34–53.

70. Dalton, *Becoming John Dewey*, p. 78.

71. Ibid., p. 79.

72. Ibid., p. 80.

73. John Dewey, "Evolution: The Philosophical Concepts" (1911), MW 6: 443–45.

CHAPTER 7: TWO TYPES OF PRAGMATISM: DEWEY AND ROYCE

1. This is why he rewrote the methodological part of the book almost immediately—compare the differences between the 1925 and 1929 versions of the book in *Later Works of John Dewey*, ed. Jo Ann Boydston, vol. 1 (Carbondale: Southern Illinois University Press, 1981); and note that Dewey was still trying to rewrite the same parts shortly before his death. The book simply did not accomplish what Dewey wanted to accomplish in his own judgment, an opinion with which I concur.

2. To be clearer about this, I should note that the Harvard philosophy department continued the work of pragmatism during this time, although they rarely used the name "pragmatism" to describe their efforts. There is little question that the giants of the Harvard department in the second half of the 20th century were mostly pragmatists, and carried on in the tradition of C. I. Lewis, who had been the brilliant student of Royce, and who worked Royce's logical ideas into the first systems of modal logic. Thus, W. V. Quine, Nelson Goodman, Stanley Cavell, and Hilary Putnam have all been pragmatists of one sort or another, and it is not quite correct to date the end of "pragmatism" with

the death of Dewey. But there certainly was a change in emphasis. I have treated this question, in part, in "The Decline of Evolutionary Naturalism in Later Pragmatism," in *Pragmatism: From Progressivism to Postmodernism*, eds. David DePew and Robert Hollinger (New York: Praeger Books, 1995), pp. 180–207.

3. There is no reason here to make the historical case that Royce was a pragmatist. This case has been made many times, and is now definitively documented beyond any disputing in Frank M. Oppenheim's most recent historical study, *Reverence for the Relations of Life: Re-imagining Pragmatism via Josiah Royce's Interactions with Peirce, James and Dewey* (Notre Dame, IN: University of Notre Dame Press, 2005). Anyone who at this point persists in saying "Royce was not a pragmatist" is being willful and showing a narrowness of thinking and historical grasp both of the term "pragmatism" and of Royce's thought.

4. Important essays in this debate over nomenclature and the pragmatic movement include John Elof Boodin's "What Pragmatism Is and Is Not," *Journal of Philosophy* 6 (1909): 627–35.

5. See Arthur O. Lovejoy, "Thirteen Pragmatisms," *Journal of Philosophy* 5 (1908): 5–12, 29–39.

6. John Elof Boodin, "What Pragmatism Is and Is Not," pp. 627–35. Boodin was a student of both James and Royce. He spent his career running a middle course between them and wrote some excellent and unduly neglected books in the pragmatic tradition.

7. For a summary of Boodin's thought and a working bibliography, see my "John Elof Boodin," in *The Dictionary of Modern American Philosophers*, ed. John R. Shook (Bristol, UK: Thoemmes Press, 2005), vol. 1, pp. 283–88.

8. See Oppenheim, *Reverence for the Relations of Life*, cited above. Oppenheim's study comes close to exhausting what documented history can teach us in terms of the relations among these four important thinkers. Obviously the term "prophetic pragmatism" is Cornel West's self-description of his own version of pragmatism, but Oppenheim's sense of the term is more thoroughly historical, as opposed to historicist, which is more West's sense of the idea.

9. I should make clear here that in my view, possibilities *are* immediately given— indeed, it is actuality that is always thoroughly mediated, and possibility that is experienced immediately. Possibilities are transformed into the actual world of a conscious or sentient being by a process of semiotic and symbolic mediation. This is not, however, the view of Royce or of any other philosopher I know of, apart from Whitehead. I have pressed Royce's thought gently in the direction of recognizing that immediacy is possibility in my book (cited below), and I have argued that the mode of existence possibility has is indeed the place where existence and experience coincide, and that understanding "time" is the key to this relation. In my view, Royce was on the threshold of seeing this immediate experience of the possible, but he did not quite get to it.

10. I have addressed in detail the structure of Royce's ontology in chapter two of my

forthcoming book, *Time, Will, and Purpose: Living Ideas from the Philosophy of Josiah Royce* (Chicago: Open Court, 2011). The issue of immediacy is also addressed in detail in chapter three of this book. The current essay is adapted from chapter four of the same book. In brief, Royce never claims that philosophy can deliver certainty about the necessary structure of being, nor about the necessary relations of knowing and being. Royce is commonly misunderstood by pragmatists as being a necessitarian and doing the old style of metaphysics, but this is wholly incorrect and unsupportable in the text. Rather, Royce adopts from the start all of the restrictions upon philosophy required by Peirce's 1868 analysis of the four incapacities, and the consequences of these incapacities, and also adopts Peirce's critique of necessity. Royce's metaphysics is entirely hypothetical, or as he calls it in places, "fictional." We create fictional models of how the wider universe of the "possible" *might be*, and we use the tools of logic, thoroughly normative tools, to assess our models. For Royce, no single model suffices to address all philosophical problems. The essential problem with Douglas Anderson's work on Royce lies here. Not having grasped the character of Royce's ontology, Anderson attributes to Royce a necessitarian viewpoint, which he says Peirce backs away from. This is incorrect, and it distorts the rest of Anderson's argument about whom and how to count the pragmatists. See Anderson, "Who's a Pragmatist: Royce and Peirce at the Turn of the Century," *Transactions of the Charles S. Peirce Society* 41 (2005): 467–81. On the other side, this interpretation of Royce is defended also by Dwayne Tunstall in his "Concerning the God that Is Only a Concept: A Marcellian Critique of Royce's God," *Transactions of the Charles S. Peirce Society* 42 (2006): 394–416. But Tunstall finds the thesis unsatisfying, while I think it is a good view to have.

11. Josiah Royce, *Basic Writings*, 2 vols., ed. John J. McDermott (New York: Fordham University, Press, 2005), vol. 1, pp. 363–64.

12. For a further elucidation of the role of feeling and immediacy in the development of this type of pragmatism, see my chapter on "Mysticism and Immediacy" in the forthcoming book cited above, in which I trace William Ernest Hocking's contributions to these themes.

13. I have come to appreciate how good a psychologist Royce was reading chapter two of Jacquelyn Kegley's most recent book, *Josiah Royce in Focus* (Bloomington, IN: Indiana University Press, 2008), pp. 21–43.

14. It is gratifying to see contemporary logicians return to the serious study of the relations of parts and wholes, now called mereotopology. See for instance, Roberto Casati and Achille C. Varzi, *Parts and Places: The Structures of Spatial Representation* (Cambridge, MA: MIT Press, 1999). It is unfortunate that many contemporary pragmatists do not think they need to study such matters.

15. Peirce's review of Dewey's *Studies in Logical Theory* (Chicago: University of Chicago Decennial Publications, 1903), appeared in *The Nation* in 1904 and is reprinted in *Collected Papers of Charles Sanders Peirce*, ed. Arthur W. Burks (Cambridge, MA: Har-

vard University Press, 1958), pp. 145–47 (*CP* 8.188–90). There Peirce says that what Dewey is doing simply is not "logic," and that Dewey's collection of inquirers "are not making any studies which anybody in his senses can expect, directly or indirectly, in any considerable degree, to influence twentieth century science." (*CP* 8.190) Peirce is correct. This is not logic and it had no considerable effect on anything. In a letter to Dewey (although it is not entirely clear whether he actually sent it) Peirce is even more critical of Dewey's project, although he expresses warm personal and philosophical respect. (*CP* 8.239–44) Larry A. Hickman has nicely analyzed these issues in "Why Peirce Didn't Like Dewey's Logic," *Southwest Philosophy Review* 3 (1986): 178–89. Royce echoes Peirce's exact criticism of Dewey and James in his 1915–1916 course; see Royce, *Metaphysics*, ed. W. E. Hocking et al (Albany: State University of New York Press, 1999), p. 47. By contrast, there actually is some logic in Dewey's *Logic: The Theory of Inquiry* (1938), which was written after Dewey had awakened to the import of Peirce's criticisms. Most Deweyans, however, treat that work as though it were a natural history of thought rather than a theory of inquiry (i.e., a meta-inquiry into logical structures of inquiry). Dewey invites this misunderstanding by beginning the treatise with an epistemological argument grounding the biological and cultural matrices of inquiry, which are indeed more relevant to the genetic situatedness of logical activity than to formal structures of thinking and the norms and limits governing them. However, in his theory of propositions and judgment, and especially in his account of the relation between mathematics and logic, Dewey demonstrates that he finally did grasp the difference between genetic and formal thought, for pragmatism, that is, between logic and the natural history of thought. As a result, his handling of the issue of possibility greatly improved in 1938 and he came to understand the import of the theory of signs for connecting logic to life (even if his subsequent efforts in this domain, the 1949 book with Arthur Bentley entitled *Knowing and the Known*, were quite disappointing and have been justly ignored).

16. James is so bad at metaphysics (and logic) that it is no wonder many of his followers have forsaken metaphysics altogether. Most notable among the detractors of metaphysics is Charlene Haddock Seigfried, who, even when she admits James tried his hand at metaphysics, insists ardently that this only proves what a mistake it is even to attempt it. If one's hero is inept at some important undertaking, it seems natural to attempt to minimize the importance of that activity. I think it is safe to assume that metaphysics will always be a part of philosophy, no matter how vehemently it is rejected by some. See Haddock Seigfried, *William James' Radical Reconstruction of Philosophy* (Albany: State University of New York Press, 1990).

17. See Richard Rorty, "Dewey's Metaphysics," in *Consequences of Pragmatism* (Minneapolis: University of Minnesota Press, 1982), pp. 72–89.

18. Royce, *The Philosophy of Loyalty*, in *The Basic Writings of Josiah Royce*, ed. John J. McDermott (New York: Fordham University Press, 2005), vol. 2, p. 858.

19. Royce, "The Nature and Use of Absolute Truth," Lecture I of The Harrison Lectures in Response to John Dewey, presented February 6–8, 1911, typescript, p. 17. These lectures are in the Harvard University Archives, HUG 1755.5, vol. 85, items 3, 4, and 5.

20. See Thomas M. Alexander, "Dewey's Denotative-Empirical Method: A Thread through the Labyrinth," *Journal of Speculative Philosophy* 18 (2004): 248–56.

21. Royce addresses the issue of the nature and scope of philosophy in many places. The most extended treatment is in the Preface and first chapter of *The Spirit of Modern Philosophy* (1892). This is probably one of the finest essays ever written on the nature and scope of philosophy and the character of the philosopher. I challenge any student of philosophy to read it without reaching for a pencil to mark phrases, jewels of thought and expression so beautifully arranged as to make the reader sigh.

22. The blending of the Peircean and Roycean accounts is best explained by John E. Smith in *Royce's Social Infinite: The Community of Interpretation*, (New York: Liberal Arts Press, 1950), chaps. 1–3. The history of their philosophical relationship in Smith's book is incorrect, superseded by later, documented history that was unavailable to Smith in 1950. The relationship between Peirce and Royce was far more extensive than Smith suspected. But Smith's philosophical analysis of the relationship between Peirce's semiotics and Royce's theory of interpretation is excellent.

23. See Gabriel Marcel, *Royce's Metaphysics*, trans. Virginia Ringer and Gordon Ringer (Westport, CT: Greenwood Press, 1975).

24. See for example, Bruce Wilshire, *William James and Phenomenology* (Bloomington: Indiana University Press, 1968).

25. See for example, Victor Kestenbaum, *The Phenomenological Sense of John Dewey* (Atlantic Highlands, NJ: Humanities Press, 1977).

26. See Eddie S. Glaude, Jr.'s "Tragedy and Moral Experience: John Dewey and Toni Morrison's *Beloved*," in *Pragmatism and the Problem of Race*, ed. Bill E. Lawson and Donald F. Koch (Bloomington: Indiana University Press, 2004), pp. 89–121.

27. Cornel West told David Lionel Smith in an interview conducted on October 12, 1998, that he was in the process of writing a book on Royce (West, *Cornel West Reader* [New York: Basic Civitas Books, 1999], p. 561). West has yet to publish this book, but his address at the 2007 Harvard conference on James and Royce made very clear that he has devoted extensive study to Royce in recent years.

28. See John E. Smith's discussion of truth in Royce in *Royce's Social Infinite*, pp. 48–59, esp. pp. 56–57 on the "long run."

CHAPTER 8: DEWEY'S UNFINISHED
CULTURAL PROJECT

1. John Herman Randall, Jr., "Dewey's Interpretation of the History of Philosophy," in *The Philosophy of John Dewey*, ed. P. A. Schilpp (New York: Tudor, 1951), pp. 75–102, at 101–102.

2. "John Dewey and Ancient Philosophies," *Philosophy and Phenomenological Research* 25 (1965): 477–99.

3. LW 8: 29–30.

4. LW 15: 164.

5. LW 6: 60.

6. LW 3: 10.

7. LW 3: 9.

8. LW 2: 20.

9. "The 'Socratic Dialogues' of Plato" (1925), LW 2: 124–40.

10. LW 13: 286.

11. Ibid.

12. LW 13: 287.

13. LW 13: 291.

14. LW 13: 293.

CHAPTER 9: DEWEY AND THE MORAL RESOURCES
OF HUMANISTIC NATURALISM

1. This includes Richard Dawkins, Sam Harris, Christopher Hitchens, and Daniel Dennett. See Ronald Aronson's article "The New Atheists" *The Nation* (June 25, 2007).

2. Among their contributions, they are largely responsible for having helped forge a cultural space where discussion about the positive merits of unbelief—once considered off limits—can take place frankly and honestly in the marketplace of ideas. Moreover, they have helped to raise public consciousness about the terrible dangers associated with blind faith, especially in its dogmatic and fanatical manifestations.

3. Ronald Aronson, "Faith No More" *Bookforum* (October/November 2005). Philip Kitcher avers similarly in his *Living with Darwin* (New York: Oxford University Press, 2007), especially pp. 154–66.

4. Mark Johnson offers a sensitive and innovative discussion about the narrative context of moral growth in his wonderful book *Moral Imagination* (Chicago: University of Chicago Press, 1993). See especially chap. seven. See also Judy Walker's chapter in this volume.

5. George Santayana, *Persons and Places* (Cambridge, MA: MIT Press, 1986), p. 170.

6. Lionel Trilling, *Sincerity and Authenticity* (New York: Harcourt, Brace, Jovanovich, 1972), p. 92.

7. John Dewey, *Experience and Nature*, LW 1: 41.

8. *The Philosophy of John Dewey*, ed. John J. McDermott (Chicago: University of Chicago Press, 1973).

9. This is true of Dewey's psychology, if not his ethics.

10. LW 7: 198.

11. LW 1: 43.

12. M. Scott Peck, *The Road Less Traveled* (New York: Simon & Schuster, 1978) pp. 15–16.

13. LW 10: 20–21.

14. Peck, *The Road Less Traveled*, pp. 16, 30.

15. LW 10: 23.

16. Paul Kurtz, *Forbidden Fruit: The Ethics of Secularism* (Amherst, NY: Prometheus Books, 2008). See pp. 113–31, 143–69.

17. MW 10: 10.

18. LW 1: 268–69.

19. LW 1: 270.

20. Michael Eldridge, *Transforming Experience* (Nashville, TN: Vanderbilt University Press, 1998), p. 33.

21. Ibid., pp. 32–33.

22. LW 16: 376, 379.

23. LW 9: 18.

24. Dewey defined meliorism as "the belief that the specific conditions which exist at one moment, be they comparatively bad or comparatively good, in any event may be bettered." Hilary Putnam has termed this healthy-minded approach "strategic optimism," noting that it "is something we badly need at the present time." See his "Ethics without Ontology" (Cambridge, MA: Harvard University Press, 2004).

CHAPTER 11: DEWEY'S FAITH

1. An analogous argument was worked out in great detail by William James in "The Dilemma of Determinism" in his *The Will to Believe* (New York: Longmans, Green, and Co., 1897)

2. John Dewey, *A Common Faith* (New Haven, CT: Yale University Press, 1934), p. 84.

3. *A Common Faith*, p. 8.

4. William James, *The Varieties of Religious Experience* (Cambridge, MA: Harvard University Press, 1985).

5. *A Common Faith*, p. 12.

6. Ibid.

7. Steven Rockefeller, *John Dewey: Religious Faith and Democratic Humanism* (New York: Columbia University Press, 1991), p. 67.

8. Ibid., p. 68.

9. *A Common Faith*, p. 22.

10. Ibid., p. 23.

11. Ibid., p. 42.

12. Ibid.

13. Ibid., p. 43.

14. Ibid., p. 44.

15. Ibid., p. 45.

16. Ibid., p. 48.

17. "Experience, Knowledge and Value: A Rejoinder" in *The Philosophy of John Dewey*, ed. Paul A. Schilpp (Evanston, IL: Northwestern University, 1939), pp. 517–608. LW 14: 8–91.

18. John Dewey, *The Quest for Certainty* (1929), LW 4: 241.

19. LW 4: 242.

20. Ibid.

21. William James, *Pragmatism* (New York: Longmans, Green, and Co., 1907), p. 298.

22. LW 4: 242.

23. LW 5: 267.

24. LW 5: 271.

25. LW 5: 272.

26. *A Common Faith*, p. 84.

27. LW 14: 226.

28. Nevertheless, I have made an attempt at this in my "Democracy as a Way of Life" in *John Dewey's Educational Philosophy in International Perspective: A New Democracy for the Twenty-first Century*, ed. Larry Hickman and Guiseppe Spadafora (Carbondale: Southern Illinois University Press, 2009), pp. 36–47.

29. *A Common Faith*, p. 87.

CHAPTER 12: JOHN DEWEY'S SPIRITUAL VALUES

1. *The Correspondence of John Dewey*, John Dewey to Max C. Otto, 1935.01.14 (08049).

2. LW 9: xxx.

3. *A Common Faith*, LW 9: 36.

4. Ibid.

5. Max C. Otto, *The Human Enterprise: An Attempt to Relate Philosophy to Daily Life* (New York: F. S. Crofts and Co., 1940).

6. See Dewey's review in LW 14: 291.

7. See *Ethics*, MW 5: 337.

8. Shailer Matthews, *The Growth of the Idea of God* (New York: Macmillan Company, 1931), p. 226.

9. Dwight Welch, Term Paper, Spring 2004, Philosophy 577, Seminar on George Herbert Mead at Southern Illinois University, Carbondale.

10. Unfinished introduction to a revised edition of *Experience and Nature*.

11. *Individualism Old and New*, LW 5: 117.

12. "The Scholastic and the Speculator," EW 3: 152.

13. "America by Formula," LW 5: 50.

14. See C. B. Macpherson, "Pluralism, Individualism, and Participation," in *The Rise and Fall of Economic Justice and Other Essays* (Oxford: Oxford University Press, 1987), pp. 92–101. Thanks to Maciej Kassner for this reference.

15. "Body and Mind," LW 3: 29.

16. Jean-Luc Marion, "Mihi magna quaestion factus sum: The Privilege of Unknowing," *Journal of Religion* 85 (January 2005): 11.

17. Ibid., p. 17.

18. *Ethics*, MW 5: 377.

19. "Body and Mind," LW 3: 30.

20. "Antinaturalism in Extremis," LW 15: 50.

21. W. H. Sheldon, "Critique of Naturalism," *Journal of Philosophy* 42 (1945): 255.

22. Ibid., p. 256.

23. "Are Naturalists Materialists?" LW 15: 116.

24. Peter Steinfels, "The New Atheism, and Something More," *New York Times* (February 14, 2009).

25. Ronald Aronson, *Living Without God: New Directions for Atheists, Agnostics, Secularists, and the Undecided* (Berkeley, CA: Counterpoint Press, 2008).

26. Reinhold Niebuhr, *Faith and History: A Comparison of Christian and Modern Views of History* (New York: Charles Scribner's Sons, 1949), p. 156.

27. See Mortimer J. Adler, "God and the Professors," in *Vital Speeches of the Day* 7 (December 1, 1940): 100, 102.

28. *Human Nature and Conduct*, MW 14: 228.

29. James Campbell, *A Thoughtful Profession: The Early Years of the American Philosophical Association* (Chicago: Open Court, 2006), p. 209.

30. Charles Franklin Thwing, *American Colleges and Universities in the Great War, 1914–1918: A History* (New York: Macmillan, 1920). Quoted in Campbell, *A Thoughtful Profession*, pp. 209–10.

31. See Steven C. Rockefeller, *John Dewey: Religious Faith and Democratic Humanism* (New York: Columbia University Press, 1991), p. 302.

32. From "Will Secularism Survive?" *Free Inquiry* (October/November 2005): 44.

CHAPTER 13: REREADING DEWEY'S *ART AS EXPERIENCE*

1. I explore the idea in "The Definition of the Human," in *The Arts and the Definition of the Human: Towards a Philosophical Anthropology* (Stanford: Stanford University Press, 2009).

2. Here, I recommend the felicity of Marjorie Grene's phrasing, which she shares with Helmuth Plessner: conceiving the human self as a "natural artifact," which I take to combine the principal themes of Hegel and Darwin. See Marjorie Grene, "People and Other Animals," *The Understanding of Nature: Essays in the Philosophy of Biology* (Dordrecht: D. Reidel, 1974), p. 358. I favor the thesis in a radical way, which Grene does not seem drawn to, which (to my mind) answers Dewey's question very nicely and in a way that extends the power of classic pragmatism beyond its characteristic limitations: that is, urges a full adoption of the master themes of Hegelian and Darwinian thought just mentioned. For some unexplained reason, the classic pragmatists never captured the full force of their own discoveries. I should also add that I don't find it at all implausible to favor a deep affinity between Dewey's emphasis on consummatory experience and Darwin's emphasis on the innate and involuntary aspects of bodily expression in man and animals. On the contrary, it serves to mark something of Dewey's innovation, at the same time it goes some distance in explaining Dewey's tolerance of what I regard as an uncharacteristic tendency toward dualism. See, here, Charles Darwin, *The Expression of the Emotions in Man and Animals* (Breinngsville, PA: Filiquarian Publishing, 2009).

3. Monroe C. Beardsley, *Aesthetics from Classical Greece to the Present: A Short History* (New York: Macmillan, 1966), p. 329.

4. George Santayana, *The Sense of Beauty; Being the Outlines of Aesthetic Theory* (New York: Charles Scribner's, 1907), pp. 44–45. (This is the edition Beardsley cites.)

5. Beardsley, *Aesthetics from Classical Greece to the Present*, p. 330.

6. See George Santayana, "The Mutability of Aesthetic Categories," *Philosophical Review* 34 (1925): 284n.

7. Dewey, *Experience and Nature*, 2nd ed. (Chicago: Open Court, 1929), p. 389 (in the edition cited by Beardsley).

8. Dewey makes no more than a minor appearance in Beardsley's own aesthetics. See Monroe C. Beardsley, *Aesthetics: Problems in the Philosophy of Criticism* (New York: Harcourt Brace, 1958).

9. See, further, my *On Aesthetics: An Unforgiving Introduction* (Belmont, CA: Wadsworth, 2009).

10. See Dewey, *Art as Experience*, chap. 1, for instance p. 8.

11. See, for instance, Richard Shusterman, *Pragmatist Aesthetics: Living Beauty, Rethinking Art* (Malden, MA: Blackwell, 1992), chap. 1–3.

12. Dewey, *Art as Experience*, pp. 18–19.

13. Ibid., p. 28.

14. See, particularly, ibid., chap. 5.

15. Ibid., pp. 18–19.

16. Ibid., p. 137.

17. See, for instance, ibid., p. 292, for Dewey's most explicit acceptance of Santayana's original paradox.

18. See Shusterman, *Pragmatist Aesthetics*, pp. 236–38. Dewey may well have encouraged such a reading; but if so, it helps to explain the decline of any pointed interest in "pragmatist" aesthetics. Santayana's paradox would have been a better spur.

19. Beardsley, *Aesthetics from Classical Greece to the Present*, p. 333.

20. If this is indeed Dewey's meaning, then, surprising as it may seem, Dewey anticipated the main strategy of an influential group of philosophers of art I call "piecemeal reductionists"—including, prominently, Arthur Danto, Richard Wollheim, Kendall Walton, Jerrold Levinson, and others. The "piecemeal" strategy fails utterly—forces us to consider an entirely different approach to the emergent novelty of the cultural world. See, further, my *The Cultural Space of the Arts and the Infelicities of Reductionism* (New York: Columbia University Press, 2010).

21. This is a very complex matter, of course. I'm persuaded that the "self" or "person" is not a natural-kind kind of any sort but, rather, a socially constructed artifactual "product" of external and internal *Bildung* answering to the internalized ability of human infants to master a true language and to function thereupon as new members of one or another society of apt selves. I have been honing this conception for a good many years. The model of internal *Bildung* (without reference to external *Bildung*) has been recently rather boldly revived by John McDowell, attempting to bring together Aristotle's notion of the "second-natured" rearing of children according to some favored form of *paideia* and something close to Hegel's and Gadamer's accounts of ("internal") *Bildung*. The notion is all but inchoate in McDowell, though its proposal startled both analytic and pragmatist philosophers. The pragmatists should be able to do much better.

(McDowell's argument attempts to reconcile Aristotle and Kant!) See John McDowell, *Mind and World*, 2nd ed. (Cambridge, MA: Harvard University Press, 1996); and Nicholas H. Smith, ed., *Reading McDowell: On Mind and World* (London: Routledge, 2002). On the issue of the relationship between biological and cultural evolution, see Richard Dawkins, *The Selfish Gene*, rev. ed. (New York: Oxford University Press, 1989); Phillip Kitcher, *Vaulting Ambition* (Cambridge, MA: MIT Press, 1985); and Steven Mithen, *The Singing Neanderthals: The Origins of Music, Language, Mind and Body* (Cambridge, MA: Harvard University Press, 2006). I provide some recent versions of my own treatment of the artifactual nature of a "person," in "Constructing a Person: A Clue to the New Unity of the Arts and Sciences," *European Journal of Pragmatism and American Philosophy* 1.1 (2009) online at http://www.journalofpragmatism.eu, and "An Ounce of Prophecy," forthcoming.

22. I've been inclined to read George Herbert Mead as the one pragmatist who got these matters right. But it's not really true. Mead's dialectic of the "I" and the "me" is terribly abstract and finally circular (in the same way internal *Bildung* is), and his discussion of the historical process is essentially formulaic, too far removed from any robust analysis of the specificity, say, of Hegel and Marx. We must make a fresh start.

23. See my "The Point of Hegel's Dissatisfaction with Kant," in *Hegel and Analytic Philosophy*, ed. Angelica Nuzzo (London and New York: Continuum, 2010).

24. Richard Rorty christened John McDowell and Robert Brandom the "Pittsburgh Hegelians" of our day. Thus far, I judge, they've both failed (for different reasons) to reconcile Hegel with either analytic philosophy or pragmatism. But that's not the essential issue: what must be weighed, precisely, is what's *possible* in the way or a rapprochement between Hegel and the strongest movements of Anglo-American philosophy and what advantage may be gained or lost in the bargain. The turn of events toward the end of the last century and the first decade of the present century, including the weak responses of the Pittsburgh Hegelians, obliges would-be pragmatists to distinguish carefully between pragmatism's own best prospects and a merely lockstep loyalty to Dewey's particular doctrines (or those of Peirce or James). I see no reason why the proposals and findings of the classic pragmatists should not be reexamined at the same time we consider reinterpreting the Kantian/Hegelian confrontation in a way that addresses our currently perceived needs. McDowell, I would say, precisely in his improbable effort to bring into some sort of conceptual harmony (involving *Bildung*) the strikingly disparate systematic views of Aristotle, Hume, Kant, Hegel, and Gadamer at least, finds himself obliged to urge the need to ground "experience" (in a sense rejected by Rorty, who favors the linguistic turn over "experience") in some "reality external to thought . . . if experience is to be a source of knowledge," *Mind and World*, 5. But this violates the contingent and thoroughly constructivist cast of what to count as knowledge in both Hegel and (perhaps more daringly in) Dewey. It also does not address the evident dilemma of how to estab-

lish any such grounding. There is, it needs to be conceded, a certain lack of precision in Dewey regarding the use of "experience"—which affects (I believe) Dewey's reliance on "consummatory experience" in *Art as Experience*: Dewey *may* at times allow some vestige of realist (animal) reliability in immediate or direct experience, though it's clear that he typically opposes any such confidence; Hegel's *Phenomenology*, of course, provides a sense in which (which Dewey may have adapted to his Darwinian themes) "experience" (very broadly conceived) is said to be "given" phenomenologically, but not in any way in which it could be made "foundational." There's a helpful summary of this sort of to-and-fro in Colin Koopman, *Pragmatism as Transition: Historicity and Hope in James, Dewey, and Rorty* (New York: Columbia University Press, 2009), chap. 3. My only hesitation about Koopman's account is that he does not discuss the importance of Hegel's alternative to McDowell's disjunctive choice—or the right way to construe Hegel's language. By contrast, Brandom's discussion of Hegel seems to me to miss nearly everything that is generally admitted to bear on the formation of Dewey's instrumentalism or, for that matter, on the point of Hegel's critique of Kant. See, further, Robert Brandom, *Between Saying and Doing: Towards an Analytic Pragmatism*, (New York: Oxford University Press, 2008); and my "A Pragmatist among Disputed Pragmatists: A Review of Robert Brandom's *Between Saying and Doing: Towards an Analytic Pragmatism*," *Contemporary Pragmatism* 6, no. 1 (June 2009): 183–95; and "The Greening of Hegel's Dialectical Logic," in *The Dimensions of Hegels' Dialectic*, ed. Nectarios Limnatis (London and New York: Continuum, 2010), pp. 193–215.

CHAPTER 14: JOHN DEWEY AND THE ONTOLOGY OF ART

1. The Happening was a late 1950s and early 1960s avant-garde art form, usually held outdoors, where spectators interacted with a variety of "materials" including colors, smoke, sounds, odors, household trinkets, and other manners of everyday objects. See Allan Kaprow. "Happenings in the New York Scene" in *Essays on the Blurring of Art and Life*, ed. Jeff Kelley (Berkeley: University of California Press, 1993), pp. 15–26.

2. The Institutional theory of art is the view that something is a work of art if it is (1) an artifact and (2) presented to the "art world" as a candidate for appreciation. Kaprow's *Yard* presents a challenge to both these criteria as (1) there is no "object" which can be correctly identified as *Yard* and (2) even though *Yard* was installed in a Manhattan art gallery, as an exemplar of a Happening it represents an avant-garde challenge to the predominance of the museum and gallery system that (still) dominates art. For the classic statement of the Institutional theory of art see George Dickie, *Art and the Aesthetic: An Institutional Analysis* (Ithaca, NY: Cornell University Press, 1974).

3. Allan Kaprow, *Essays on the Blurring of Art and Life*, ed. Jeff Kelley (Berkeley: University of California Press, 1993), xi.

4. Ibid., p. xii.

5. Ibid.

6. Dewey, *Art as Experience*, LW 10: 84.

7. See Richard Rorty, "Dewey's Metaphysics" in *Consequences of Pragmatism* (Minneapolis: University of Minnesota Press, 1982), pp. 72–89.

8. Richard Bernstein, "John Dewey's Metaphysics of Experience," *Journal of Philosophy* 58 (1961): 6–7.

9. Dewey, Experience and Nature, LW 1: 361.

10. LW 1: 363.

11. LW 10: 42

12. LW 10: 113.

13. Philip W. Jackson, *John Dewey and the Lessons of Art* (New Haven, CT: Yale University Press, 1998), pp. 5–6.

14. LW 10: 218.

15. Joseph Margolis, *The Arts and the Definition of the Human* (Stanford, CA: Stanford University Press, 2009), p. 46.

16. Ibid., p. 92.

17. Joseph Margolis, "The Deviant Ontology of Artworks" in *Theories of Art Today*, ed. Noel Carroll (Madison: University of Wisconsin Press, 2000), p. 120. See also Joseph Margolis, *What, After All, is a Work of Art?* (University Park: Pennsylvania State University Press, 1999), chap. 3.

18. LW 10: 151.

CHAPTER 15: NARRATIVE NATURALISM

1. Richard Rorty, *Contingency, Irony, and Solidarity* (Cambridge: Cambridge University Press, 1989), p. 7.

2. Aristotle, *Aristotle's Poetics*, trans. S. H. Butcher (New York: Hill and Wang, 1961), pp. 65, 105.

3. See, e.g., John Dewey, *How We Think*, LW 8: 200–209.

4. Robert C. Solomon, *The Passions: Emotions and the Meaning of Life* (Indianapolis: Hackett, 1993), p. ix.

5. See Antonio Damasio, *Descartes' Error: Emotion, Reason, and the Human Brain* (New York: Penguin Books, 2005); *The Feeling of What Happens: Body and Emotion in the Making of Consciousness* (San Diego: Harcourt, 1999); *Looking for Spinoza: Joy, Sorrow, and the Feeling Brain* (Orlando, FL: Harcourt, 2003).

6. Damasio, *The Feeling of What Happens*, p. 172.

7. Ibid., p. 313.

8. See, e.g., Christine A. Courtois, Julian D. Ford, and Marylene Cloitre, "Best Practices in Psychotherapy for Adults," in *Treating Complex Traumatic Stress Disorders: An Evidence-Based Guide*, ed. Christine A. Courtois and Julian D. Ford (New York: Guilford Press, 2009), pp. 93–95; Jim Duvall and Laura Béres, "Movement of Identities: A Map for Therapeutic Conversations About Trauma," in *Narrative Therapy: Making Meaning, Making Lives*, ed. Catrina Brown and Tod Augusta-Scott (Thousand Oaks, CA: Sage Publications, 2007), pp. 229–50; Robert A. Neimeyer and Finn Tschudi, "Community and Coherence: Narrative Contributions to the Psychology of Conflict and Loss," in *Narrative and Consciousness: Literature, Psychology, and the Brain*, ed. Gary D. Fireman, Ted E. McVay, Jr., and Owen J. Flanagan (Oxford: Oxford University Press, 2003), pp. 166–91; Derek Boulton, "Meaning and Causal Explanations in the Behavioural Sciences," in *Nature and Narrative: An Introduction to the New Philosophy of Psychiatry*, ed. Bill Fulford, et al. (Oxford: Oxford University Press, 2003), p. 122; Kitty Klein, "Narrative Construction, Cognitive Processing, and Health," in *Narrative Theory and the Cognitive Sciences*, ed. David Herman (Stanford, CA: CSLI Publications, 2003), pp. 56–84; Bronna D. Romanoff, "Research as Therapy: The Power of Narrative to Effect Change," in *Meaning Reconstruction and the Experience of Loss*, ed. Robert A. Neimeyer (Washington, DC: American Psychological Association, 2001), pp. 245–57. See also Judith Lewis Herman, *Trauma and Recovery* (New York: Basic Books, 1992); Daniel B. Carr, John D. Loeser, and David B. Morris, eds., *Narrative, Pain, and Suffering* (Seattle: IASP Press, 2005); and Richard G. Tedeschi, Crystal L. Park, and Lawrence G. Calhoun, eds., *Posttraumatic Growth: Positive Changes in the Aftermath of Crisis* (Mahwah, NJ: Lawrence Erlbaum, 1998).

9. Damasio, *Descartes' Error*, p. 264.

10. Dewey, *A Common Faith*, LW 9: 14.

11. Dewey, Art as Experience, LW 10: 272.

12. Susan Haack, *Defending Science, within Reason: Between Scientism and Cynicism* (Amherst, NY: Prometheus Books, 2003), p. 266.

13. Ruth Anna Putnam, "The Moral Impulse," in *The Revival of Pragmatism: New Essays on Social Thought, Law, and Culture*, ed. Morris Dickstein (Durham, NC: Duke University Press, 1998), p. 63.

14. Damasio, *Descartes' Error*, p. xiv.

15. Mark Johnson, *Moral Imagination: Implications of Cognitive Science for Ethics* (Chicago: University of Chicago Press, 1993), pp. 166–70.

16. Ibid., p. 77.

17. Thomas M. Alexander, *John Dewey's Theory of Art, Experience, and Nature: The Horizons of Feeling* (Albany: State University of New York Press, 1987), p. 52.

18. Owen Flanagan, *Self Expressions: Mind, Morals, and the Meaning of Life* (New York: Oxford University Press, 1996), pp. 67, 68.

19. Daniel C. Dennett, "Why Everyone is a Novelist," *Times Literary Supplement* (September 16–22, 1988), pp. 1016–22. See also Dennett, *Consciousness Explained* (Boston: Little, Brown, 1991).

20. Pascal Boyer, *Religion Explained: The Evolutionary Origins of Religious Thought* (New York: Basic Books, 2001), p. 204.

21. John Tooby and Leda Cosmides, "Does Beauty Build Adapted Minds? Toward an Evolutionary Theory of Aesthetics, Fiction and the Arts," *SubStance: A Review of Theory and Literary Criticism* 30 (2001): 24.

22. Manfred Jahn, "Cognitive Narratology," in *Routledge Encyclopedia of Narrative Theory*, ed. David Herman, Manfred Jahn, and Marie-Laure Ryan (London: Routledge, 2005), p. 67.

23. Kristin Sommer and Roy Baumeister, "The Construction of Meaning from Life Events: Empirical Studies of Personal Narratives," in *The Human Quest for Meaning: A Handbook of Psychological Research and Clinical Applications*, ed. Paul T. P. Wong and Prem S. Fry (Mahwah, NJ: Lawrence Erlbaum, 1998), p. 157.

24. Steven Pinker, *The Stuff of Thought: Language as a Window into Human Nature* (New York: Viking, 2007), p. 222.

25. Johnson, *Moral Imagination*, pp. 168–70.

26. See, e.g., John P. Anton, *American Naturalism and Greek Philosophy* (Amherst, NY: Prometheus Books, Humanity Books, 2005), p. 268.

27. Larry A. Hickman, *Pragmatism as Post-Postmodernism: Lessons from John Dewey* (New York: Fordham University Press, 2007), pp. 182–84, 187–88.

28. Kim Díaz, "Process Philosophy," in *American Philosophy: An Encyclopedia*, ed. John Lachs and Robert Talisse (New York: Routledge, 2008), p. 619.

29. Irving Singer, "A Reply to My Critics and Friendly Commentators," in *The Nature and Pursuit of Love: The Philosophy of Irving Singer*, ed. David Goicoechea (Amherst, NY: Prometheus Books, 1995), p. 345.

30. Alexander Nehamas, *Nietzsche: Life as Literature* (Cambridge, MA: Harvard University Press, 1985), p. 3.

31. LW 10: 22.

32. Agnes Martin, *Writings*, ed. Herausgegeben von Dieter Schwarz (Stuttgart: Cantz, 1992), p. 93.

CHAPTER 16: JOHN DEWEY AND THE EARLY NAACP: DEVELOPING A PROGRESSIVE DISCOURSE ON RACIAL INJUSTICE, 1909–1921

1. Some of the critiques I find most thoughtful include Eddie S. Glaude, Jr., *In A Shade of Blue* (Chicago: University of Chicago Press, 2007), pp. 1, 18 (noting that classical pragmatists, including Dewey, "rarely took up the issue of white supremacy in their philosophical writings," but that Dewey's philosophy does offer "unique insights that can help us address" problems of racism in the United States today); Frank Margonis, "John Dewey, W. E. B. Du Bois, and Alain Locke," in *Race and Epistemologies of Ignorance*, ed. Shannon Sullivan and Nancy Tuana (Albany: State University of New York Press, 2007), pp. 173, 175–77 (noting that Dewey tended to neglect the problem of race in foreign and domestic policy and erased racial violence from his narratives about the American frontier); Michael Eldridge, "Dewey on Race and Social Change," in *Pragmatism and the Problem of Race* (Bloomington: Indiana University Press, 2004), pp. 11, 13–14 (noting that Dewey was active at times on issues affecting African Americans but arguing that he should have done more); "Afterword: A Conversation between Cornel West and Bill E. Lawson, in ibid., pp. 225, 226, where Cornel West echoes his earlier critiques that "Dewey never saw white supremacy as a major priority in his wrestling with philosophy and democracy."

2. *Proceedings of the National Negro Conference* (1909; repr. New York: Arno Press, 1969), p. 94.

3. Oswald Garrison Villard to Joel E. Spingarn (1910.10.17), in *The Correspondence of John Dewey, 1871–1952*, ed. Larry A. Hickman (Charlottesville, VA: InteLex Corp., 1999–2005).

4. Harvey Amani Whitfield, "African Americans in Burlington, Vermont, 1880–1890," *Vermont History* 75 (2007): 101–23.

5. Ibid., p. 111.

6. Ibid., pp. 113–15.

7. W. E. B Du Bois, *The Souls of Black Folks* (New York: Random House, 1996), p. 4.

8. Dewey served on the Board of Trustees of Hull House and delivered a several-months-long series of weekly lectures there. Dewey's correspondence reflects the intensity of his association. See, e.g., *Correspondence*, 1894.07.04, 05 (Dewey wrote to Alice about his visit to Hull House).

9. See Alma Herbst, *The Negro in the Slaughtering and Meat-Packing Industry in Chicago* (New York: Arno Press and New York Times, 1971), pp. 17–18.

10. Ibid., pp. 18–27.

11. Ibid., pp. 18–19 (quoting variety of newspaper accounts).

12. *Correspondence*, 1894.07.14, 16 (John Dewey to Alice Dewey).

13. See Reverdy S. Ransom, *The Pilgrimage of Harriet Ransom's Son* (Nashville, TN: Sunday School Union, n.d.), pp. 1112–14. Ransom describes his efforts to mediate turn-of-the-century labor-related racial violence.

14. W. E. B. Du Bois, "The Conservation of Races," *Occasional Papers No. 2* (Washington, DC: The American Negro Academy, 1897).

15. Ibid., p. 9.

16. "Christianity and Democracy," EW 4: 3.

17. Dewey, "What Education Is," EW 5: 84.

18. Ibid., p. 87.

19. As Dewey warns, a child's early interest during the "agricultural" phase does not call for lessons about agricultural implements but instead suggests the value of involving the child in planting seeds, while the "nomadic" stage suggests reasons for a child's interests in modern modes of transportation such as trucks. Similarly, a child's later developing interest in ideas and in reading and writing should be stimulated with ideas of his own modern society, and only later with historical ideas corresponding to this stage in the dawning of Western civilization. EW 5: 250–53.

20. See Joe R. Burnett, "Introduction to Dewey's Middle Works," MW 1: ix, xi–xii. Burnett notes that Dewey's waning interest in physiological psychology corresponded with his developing concentration on social psychology.

21. "The School as the Social Centre," MW 2.85.

22. Ibid.

23. See *Correspondence* 1914.10.26 (a letter from Lillian Wald to John Dewey mentioning plans to see the Deweys socially); ibid., 1914.10.27 (#04548) (a polite but noncommittal reply from Dewey).

24. See William Twining, *Karl Llewellyn and the Realist Movement* (London: Weidenfeld & Nicolson, 1973), pp. 110, 371.

25. See Susan D. Carle, "Theorizing Agency," *American University Law Review* 55 (2005): 351–52, and notes 208 and 212.

26. Charles Flint Kellogg, *NAACP: A History of the National Association for the Advancement of Colored People, 1909–1920* (Baltimore: Johns Hopkins University Press, 1967), pp. 297–99.

27. Ibid., pp. 300–301.

28. Such precursor organizations, whose platforms provided much of the substantive content for the platform of the early NAACP, included the Afro-American League, the first national civil rights organization dedicated in part to the bringing of national legal "test cases," founded by T. Thomas Fortune in 1889 and later revived as the Afro American Council; and the Niagara Movement, founded by W. E. B. Du Bois and others in 1905. See Susan D. Carle, "Debunking the Myth of Civil Rights Liberalism: Visions

of Racial Justice in the Thought of T. Thomas Fortune, 1880–1890," *Fordham Law Review* 77 (2009): 1517–30.

29. James Boylan, *Revolutionary Lives: Anna Strunsky and William English Walling* (Amherst: University of Massachusetts Press, 1998), p. 173 (Walling confessed after swimming with Du Bois that he felt "he was 'swimming with a monkey'"); Michael Wreszin, *Oswald Garrison Villard: Pacifist at War* (Bloomington: Indiana University Press, 1965), p. 34 (Villard's wife refused to engage in racially mixed dining).

30. Elisabeth Lasch-Quinn discusses examples revealing Addams's racial attitudes in *Black Neighbors: Race and the Limits of Reform in the American Settlement House Movement, 1890–1945* (Chapel Hill: University of North Carolina Press, 1993), p. 14.

31. *Proceedings of the National Negro Conference, 1909* (New York: Arnos Press, 1969), pp. 79–82, 98, 164–65, 203.

32. Ibid., p. 21.

33. Ibid., p. 54.

34. Ibid., p. 68.

35. Ibid., p. 69.

36. Ibid., p. 71.

37. Ibid., p. 72.

38. Ibid.

39. Papers of the NAACP, Box IC-292, Folder titled "Federal Aid to Education, 1913–1914," Letter from John Dewey to Florence Kelley, April 6, 1914 (Dewey agreeing to attend a meeting of the committee if it fits his schedule); unsigned letter to F. M. Marshall, April 13, 1914 (listing Dewey as member of NAACP Committee to Aid Federal Education).

40. "Federal Aid to Education," a speech delivered before conference of National Child Labor Committee, MW 10: 125, 129.

41. See Papers of the NAACP, Box IC-292, Folder titled "Federal Aid to Education, 1913–1914," Letter from John E. Milholland to Oswald G. Villard, May 29, 1914. This letter discusses disputes between Milholland and Villard about strategy for the NAACP's federal aid to education work and other matters.

42. "Essays in German Philosophy and Politics," MW 8: 188.

43. Dewey wrote, "An attempt has been made to define nationality upon the basis of race, but this racial definition is founded upon a precarious foundation; it works fairly well some cases, but in others it breaks down. The concept of a nation of one race and one blood has mainly been invented after the event to account for certain unclear ideas of nationality, rather than to state the presence of a physiological fact." "The Principle of Nationality," MW 10: 285.

44. Alan Ryan, *John Dewey and the High Tide of American Liberalism* (New York: W. W. Norton, 1995), p. 153.

45. MW 9: 25–26.

46. "Race Prejudice and Friction," MW 13: 242.

47. Ibid., p. 245.

48. Ibid., p. 246.

49. Ibid., p. 248.

50. Ibid., p. 253.

51. Ibid., p. 254. Dewey repeated similar themes in a number of other essays from the same period including "Individuality, Equality and Superiority," MW 13: 295. There Dewey noted the socially constructed nature of measures of merit and worth, raising as a thought exercise how estimations of value would be if different social classes were in power, as for example, if investigators or artists were socially dominant. How different, Dewey noted, are the standards of superior judgment and ability held by professors than by "captains of industry." Ibid. Dewey in this essay further pushes his thinking on the social construction of race (though still not quite escaping race essentialism), when he argues that "[a]t present superior races are superior on the basis of their own conspicuous achievements. Inferior races are inferior because their successes lie in different directions, though possibly more artistic and civilized than our own." Ibid.

52. LW 6: 224.

53. *Correspondence*, 1932.11.23 (#04305) (John Dewey to Albert Barnes).

54. *Correspondence*, 1942.05.18 (copy of letter mailed to Frank P. Graham).

55. *Correspondence*, 1950.02.02 (Madison S. Jones Jr. to John Dewey).

56. *Correspondence*, 1949.10.19 (Roy Wilkins to John Dewey).

57. *Correspondence*, 1952.06.02 (Walter White to Roberta Dewey).

CHAPTER 17: PUBLIC REASON VS. DEMOCRATIC INTELLIGENCE: RAWLS *AND* DEWEY

1. Rawls, "The Ideal of Public Reason Revisited" in *Collected Papers*, ed. Samuel Freeman (Cambridge, MA: Harvard University Press, 1999), p. 574.

2. Ibid., p. 131.

3, Rawls, *Political Liberalism* (New York: Columbia University Press, 1996), pp. li–lii.

4. Ibid., p. liii.

CHAPTER 18: DEWEY'S ETHICAL-POLITICAL PHILOSOPHY AS A PRESENT RESOURCE

1. I agree with Michael Eldridge when he writes, "It is not necessary that Obama knows this intellectual movement and considers himself to be a part of it. It is sufficient that he practices what they recommended. He exemplifies the pragmatism they articulated and defended. By placing Obama in this context we are able to make use of the resources of this tradition to explain and justify his practice. Some of these charges are that his pragmatism is a matter of mere expediency or that he is anti-ideological and thus devoid of principle." Online at http://www.obamaspragmatism .info/MEonOP.htm

2. LW 2: 361.

3. John Gray, "Utopia Falls" *Harpers Magazine* (December 2008): 17.

4. Richard W. Stevenson "Obamanomics: Capitalism after the Fall" New York Times (April 19, 2009).

5. MW 12: 137.

6. LW 7: 336.

7. John Gray, "Utopia Falls," p. 17.

8. See http://www.obamaspragmatism.info/LandS.htm for links to the online contributions of Mitchel Aboufalia and others in blogs.

9. Richard Posner *Law, Pragmatism, and Democracy* (Cambridge, MA: Harvard University Press, 2003), p. 50.

10. Ibid., p. 166.

11. Ibid., p. 130.

12. Jacob Bronsther "The Emptiness of Obama's Pragmatism" from the May 26, 2009 edition, online at http://www.csmonitor.com/2009/0526/p09s02-coop.html.

13. Chris Hayes, "The Pragmatist" in December 29, 2008 edition of *The Nation*, http://www.thenation.com/doc/20081229/hayes/single.

14. See Robert B. Talisse, *A Pragmatist Philosophy of Democracy* (New York and London: Routledge, 2007) and Cheryl Misak, *Truth, Politics, and Morality: Pragmatism and Deliberation* (New York: Routledge, 2000).

15. Chris Hayes, "The Pragmatist."

16. See, for example, Robert Reich, "Obama and Pragmatism: Thinking Through Values" (5 May 2009), online at http://robertreich.org/post/257310346/.

17. Jacob Bronsther, "The Emptiness of Obama's Pragmatism."

18. In ethical theory, consequentialism is a view about the ultimate or universal criterion of correct judgment.

19. Jacob Bronsther, "The Emptiness of Obama's Pragmatism."

20. See Gregory Pappas, "Openmindedness and Courage: The Virtues of the Prag-

matist Ideal Believer," *Transactions of the Charles Peirce Society* 32. 2 (Spring 1996): 316–35.

21. LW 6: 14–15, emphasis added.

22. LW 6: 14–15, my emphasis.

23. LW 7: 187.

24. MW 14: 144.

25. LW 7: 270.

26. MW 5: 303.

27. LW 7: 270, emphasis added.

28. LW 7: 251.

29. See http://www.nytimes.com/2009/08/09/weekinreview/09stolberg.html?hpw.

CHAPTER 19: DEWEYAN EXPERIMENTALISM AND LEADERSHIP

1. EW 5: 59, emphasis added.

2. Plato's *Republic*, 347c.

3. Kathryn Riley, "'Democratic Leadership'—A Contradiction in Terms?" *Leadership and Policy in Schools* 2 (2003): 125–40; Robert J. Starrat, "Democratic Leadership Theory in Late Modernity: An Oxymoron or Ironic Possibility?" *International Journal of Leadership in Education* 4 (2001): 333–52.

4. MW 13: 296–97.

5. LW 3: 252–53.

6. LW 5: 135.

7. LW 6: 128.

9. LW 11: 219.

10. In Sophocles' *Electra* (written 410 BCE). The passage translated by R. C. Jebb reads, "Sad, that one who speaks so well should speak amiss!" This version is available on The Internet Classics Archive, Daniel C. Stevenson (Web Atomics 1994–2009), at http://classics.mit.edu/Sophocles/electra.html.

CHAPTER 20: DEWEY'S IMPACT ON EDUCATION

1. For historical and sympathetic accounts of Dewey's theory of education, see Lawrence Cremin, *The Transformation of the School* (New York: Vintage, 1964), and Robert Westbrook, *John Dewey and American Democracy* (Ithaca, NY: Cornell University Press, 1991), pp. 93–113. For a highly negative assessment of Dewey, one that is rep-

resentative of those who attack his theory of education, see Albert Lynd, "Who Wants Progressive Education? The Influence of John Dewey on the Public Schools," in *Dewey On Education: Appraisals*, ed. Reginald D. Archambault (New York: Random House, 1966), pp. 191–208.

2. See Aviva Freedman and Ian Pringle, "Learning to Write" in *Reinventing the Rhetorical Tradition*, ed. Aviva Freedman and Ian Pringle (Conway, AR: L&S Books, 1980), pp. 173–85.

3. Freedman and Pringle, "Preface," in *Reinventing the Rhetorical Tradition*, pp. vii–ix.

4. Janet Emig, "The Tacit Tradition," in *Reinventing the Rhetorical Tradition*, p. 12.

5. *Reinventing the Rhetorical Tradition*, ed. Freedman and Pringle.

6. John Dewey, "Construction and Criticism," LW 5:125–43; "The Child and The Curriculum," MW 2: 283–84.

7. Inasmuch as I see this observation of Dewey's as a major element in the "tacit tradition" of the revolution in composition instruction, I quote at length the passage from the 1933 edition of *How We Think* in which he expands on his observation. "Children who begin with something to say and with intellectual eagerness to say it are sometimes made so conscious of minor errors in substance and form that the energy that should go into constructive thinking is diverted into anxiety not to make mistakes, and even, in extreme cases, into passive quiescence as the best method of minimizing error. This tendency is especially marked in connection with the writing of compositions, essays, and themes. It has even been gravely recommended that little children should always write on trivial subjects and in short sentences because in that way they are less likely to make mistakes. The teaching of high-school and college students occasionally reduces itself to a technique for detecting and designating mistakes. Self-consciousness and constraint follow. Students lose zest for writing. Instead of being interested in what they have to say and in how it is said as a means of adequate formulation and expression of their own thought, interest is drained off. Having to say something is a very different matter from having something to say" (LW 8: 314).

8. For discussion of these techniques by one of the most respected leaders of the revolution in composition studies, see Peter Elbow, *Writing Without Teachers* (New York: Oxford University Press, 1973).

9. Dewey, "Education, Direct and Indirect," MW 3: 240–48.

10. Dewey, *Democracy and Education*, MW 9:133.

11. Stephen M. Fishman, "Writing-To-Learn in Philosophy," *Teaching Philosophy* 8 (October 1985): 331–34; "Writing and Philosophy," *Teaching Philosophy* 12 (December 1989): 361–74.

12. Dewey, *Ethics* (1932), LW 7: 256.

13. Stephen M. Fishman and Lucille McCarthy, *John Dewey and the Philosophy and Practice of Hope* (Urbana: University of Illinois Press, 2007).

14. Dewey, "Progressive Education and the Science of Education," LW 3: 268.

15. Dewey, "The Need for A Recovery of Philosophy," MW 10: 46.

16. Bob Glahn took this notion of "presence" from the Hope course's reading and discussion of Gabriel Marcel's essay "On The Ontological Mystery" in *The Philosophy of Existentialism: An Exposition of The Character of Existential Philosophy*, trans. Manya Harari (New York: Citadel Press, 1970), pp. 9–46.

17. Dewey, *A Common Faith*, LW 9: 1–58.

18. C. R. Snyder, *The Psychology of Hope* (New York: Free Press, 1994).

19. Dewey's approach to failure and achievement that helped Lindsey Weston is found in chapter one, "Existence As Precarious and As Stable," of *Experience and Nature*. Dewey writes, "We live in a world which is an impressive and irresistible mixture of sufficiencies, tight completenesses, order, singularities, ambiguities, uncertain possibilities, processes going on to consequences as yet indeterminate. They are mixed not mechanically but vitally like the wheat and tares of the parable. We may recognize them separately but we cannot divide them, for unlike wheat and tares they grow from the same root" (LW 1: 47).

20. Dewey, *Human Nature and Conduct*, MW 14: 19.

21. The third Deweyan idea that helped Lindsey Weston is well expressed by Dewey in several of his works. It is found in the same passage in *Experience and Nature* from which I quote in note 19 above. Dewey writes, "Qualities have defects as necessary conditions of their excellencies; the instrumentalities of truth are the causes of error; change gives meaning to permanence and recurrence makes novelty possible. A world that was wholly risky would be a world in which adventure is impossible, and only a living world can include death" (LW 1: 47). This idea is also expressed in Dewey's essay, "What I Believe," published in 1930, five years after *Experience and Nature*. In "What I Believe," he writes, "Faith in the varied possibilities of diversified experience is attended with the joy of constant discovery and of constant growing. Such a joy is possible even in the midst of trouble and defeat, whenever life-experiences are treated as potential disclosures of meanings and values that are to be used as means to a fuller and more significant future experience" (LW 5: 272).

CHAPTER 21: AN EDUCATIONAL THEORY OF INQUIRY

1. See *How We Think* (1910), and H. S. Thayer and V. T. Thayer, "Introduction," MW 6: 10.

2. MW 10 (*Essays on Experimental Logic*), LW 8 (*How We Think*), and LW 12 (*Logic: The Theory of Inquiry*). If we look at the writings on education starting from the

first volume of the *Middle Works* (with particular attention to *The School and Society* and *The Educational Situation*) we can see that, as Burnett notes in this volume's introduction, educational problems are addressed from two perspectives: "how to coordinate aspects of logical inquiry with physiological/psychological maturation" and "the need for a rich, dynamic, and viable social order," which are strictly interconnected and "separate except by a distinction of reason." It is within this context, as Burnett points out, that Dewey takes the first steps in "the construction of a logic . . . which would apply without abrupt breach of continuity" to both "science" and "morals," a *logic* thus deeply connected to education. Joe R. Burnett, "Introduction," MW 1: xviii, ix.

3. MW 1: 25.

4. MW 1: 104.

5. MW 1: xv.

6. As Burnett notes, this essay is "the first extensive, albeit schematic, attempt by Dewey to formulate the pattern of inquiry;" therefore its importance "stems from several points: it is, first, a very concise theory of inquiry;" second, it is a theory of "developmental logic" as much as a theory of developmental psychology; third, it is almost a "cultural epoch" or "recapitulation theory of thought." Burnett, "Introduction," MW 1: xv.

7. This essay was very much appreciated by William James, who noticed that the strong interconnection between Dewey's logical studies and the experiment of the laboratory school would bear a "wonderful" result: "a real school and real Thought. Important thought, too!" James, letter to Mrs. Henry Whitman (Oct. 29, 1903), in *The Letters of William James*, ed. Henry James (Boston: Little, Brown, 1926).

8. MW 1: 152.

9. Sidney Hook writes, "At this stage of his thinking about thinking, Dewey was moving toward greater clarity, not yet aware of formidable counter movements emerging in philosophy that would seek to relegate all of his inquiries to the field of psychology, and whose mathematical-formal approach would set the tone and style for future work in logic. The kind of questions and criticisms that naturally arise among traditional logicians, who regard logic as a theory of proof rather than of inquiry, were issues that Dewey was to grapple with later." Hook, "Introduction," MW 2: xvi.

10. MW 2: 299.

11. Hook, "Introduction," MW 2: xvi.

12. This is clearly pointed out by Kennedy, who observes that "in this way too an existential transformation of the situation will occur." For this reason, inquiry is instrumental. It is a "means of control" that produces a higher degree of understanding and mastery of human experiences. Inquiry is a continuum, and "a body of funded knowledge and skills is gradually built up. Wherever there is a persistence of interest new problems grow out of funded knowledge that is established. Many communities may be identified in this way." Therefore, to engage in the process of inquiry is "the exercise of an art" and

"corresponding to this art there is a science." Thus, logical forms are "products of thought constructed during the process of inquiry as means of carrying out an inquiry" and "are therefore funded results of prior inquiries" which come to have a universally acknowledged codification, since they are the by-products of a process of thinking sustained and regulated by a rigorous method. On this basis a logical theory comes to be no more than "a detailed critical analysis of the actual procedures utilized wherever inquiries are successful; in this respect logic is itself an empirical science." Gail Kennedy, "Dewey's Logic and Theory of Knowledge," in *Guide to the Works of John Dewey*, ed. Jo Ann Boydston (Carbondale: Southern Illinois University Press, 1970), pp. 61–98.

13. Which, as Morris notes, is a "naturalistic postulate," since for Dewey "there is a line of continuity from the less complex to the more complex forms and functions of life. It is not arbitrary: it functions in experience and is tested in experience. It becomes a means by which many things in experience and nature may be understood;" it "lies at the base of any constructed history, whether it be the story of an individual life, the life of a nation, or the life of a geological world." S. Morris Eames, "Experience and Philosophical Method in John Dewey," *Midwestern Journal of Philosophy* 4 (Spring 1976): 15–29.

14. LW 12: 15.

15. LW 12: 41.

16. LW 12: 42. As Joseph Margolis points out, to formulate his logical theory Dewey used a new language, a "peculiar idiom designed to link ordinary cognitive distinctions continuously with whatever more fundamental forces are at work, below the level of cognition, in the life of human beings as biologically sensitive and culturally formed creatures." In these terms, as Margolis notes, inquiry is to be seen as "an interaction of a special sort between a certain biologically organized creature and the organized environment which itself depends on certain *precognitive interactions*" considered as "situations" which are "whatever in the precognitive phase of man's interaction with his natural and cultural environment generates inquiry." Situations are thus intended by Dewey as "ecological systems" or "the fragments of such systems as, in context, generate particular inquiries." These are, essentially, functional systems characterized in terms, precisely, of modifiable ranges of normal forms of human response to environmental stimuli; that is why Dewey insists that situations are "existential"; therefore, "inquiry develops as the cognitive emergent way in which organisms, already functioning precognitively at least in terms of survival, enlarge the range of interaction with the environing world." Margolis, "The Relevance of Dewey's Epistemology," in *New Studies in the Philosophy of John Dewey*, ed. Steven M. Cahn (Hanover, NH: University Press of New England, 1977), pp. 129–30.

17. LW 12: 43, 45.

18. LW 12: 111.

19. LW 12: 108.

20. As Gail Kennedy points out, for Dewey there are, then, four basic *kinds of rela-*

tions which mark the development of the process of inquiry: (a) "involvement," a deep existential relationship with an object/situation; (b) "inference," what was originally identified as an object is now treated as a datum; (c) "implication," which comes with the introduction of a discourse on an object/situation and brings about the relation symbol-meanings as well as the possibility to investigate the possible relations among symbol/meanings with a view to their eventual and possible application to the solution of existential problems; and (d) "reference," the actual relation of these symbol-meanings to existence. Kennedy, "Dewey's Logic and Theory of Knowledge."

21. Marvin Farber describes how Dewey's concept of "antecedent existential material" is very close to Husserl's conception of "life world," intended as something similar to socially, culturally, or evolutionarily established (but nevertheless abstract) sense or meaning, such as the system of senses (or meanings) constituting the common understanding and the common symbolic structure of meanings shared within a society. Farber, "The Idea of a Naturalistic Logic," *Philosophy and Phenomenological Research* 29 (1969): 598–601.

22. As Carroll Guen Hart notes, "the existential basis of logic is the ecological structure of meaning. In Dewey's terms, meaning is an emergent quality of organic association, a tripartite relation involving at least two persons and a common object. The meaning relation is constituted by a genuine 'participation in intent' between the two persons with regard to the object." In these terms "meaning is firstly a 'property of behaviour,' a matter of 'intent' that is not primarily personal in a private and exclusive sense" and it is "an inherently generalizable way of acting with respect to objects." Hart, "Power in the Service of Love: John Dewey's Logic and the Dream of a Common Language," *Hypatia* 8 (Spring 1993): 190–214.

23. MW 6: 185.

24. The theme of continuity of experience is very well clarified and developed in *Experience and Education* (1938), where Dewey points out the necessity for education to be designed on the basis of a theory of experience which rests on two central tenets—continuity and interaction. Within this framework, the concept of "continuity" refers to the notion that each experience is stored and carried on into the future: humans learn something from every experience—whether positive or negative—and each accumulated learned experience will influence all the potential future experiences of individuals, communities, societies; on the other hand, the concept of "interaction" explains how past experience interacts with the present situation, thus creating one's present experiences.

25. It is very interesting to look at the development of these themes in Dewey's writings. In particular, in *The Middle Works of John Dewey*, vol. 6, we find in the "Syllabus of Six Lectures on Aspects of the Pragmatic Movement of Modern Philosophy" (1910) two lectures which clearly anticipate the structure of *Logic: The Theory of Inquiry*. Lecture 4, "The Biological Foundations," follows a structure involving the following passages: The problem of control of the environment. The function of sense-organs; of the

central organs. Adjustment (habit) and adjusting (attention); reflection as readjusting. The novel, prospective, and precarious factor. Needs, experiments and success (satisfaction). Lecture 5, "Equivalents in Logical Theory," has the following structure: The experimental character of reflective knowing. The sensory factor and the ideal (meaning). The Kantian problem of the percept and concept in knowledge, and its solution. A priori and "empirical" aspects. The place of ends (or conceived results) and of means (given data). MW 6: 176.

26. MW 1: 62.

27. As James Kern Feibleman points out, Dewey's logic is strictly involved with a subject "since a subject is always implied in practice, and with history, since practice is always an historical occurrence." Feibleman, "The Influence of Peirce on Dewey's Logic," *Journal of Philosophy* 36 (1939): 682.

28. Which, as Jeanne Connell explains, has deep educational implications as it "undercuts the basic division between culture and nature, and thereby could transform the nature of subject matter of schools by rejecting the fundamental division between science and humanities." Connell, "Reconstructing a Modern Definition of Knowledge," *Philosophy of Education* (1995): 225–34.

29. MW 1: 69.

30. MW 1: 49.

31. MW 2: 288.

32. Henry C. Lu notes how Dewey's conception of education implies two propositions, one *existential*, valid as a function of continuity of inquiry (education is what meets the need of the individual and the society); the other *universal*, valid by definition (education is a reconstruction of experience, with no end beyond itself). Lu, "Dewey's Logical Theory and His Conception of Education," *Educational Theory* 18 (1968): 388–95.

33. The method of inquiry intended as a model for human reflective thinking—as Schön notes—is, therefore, Dewey's most important legacy to education, intended as that dimension of human experience where processes of growth are produced, new meanings are constructed, new knowledge is developed. Donald Alan Schön, "The Theory of Inquiry: Dewey's Legacy to Education," *Curriculum Inquiry* 22 (Summer 1992): 119–39. Schön has developed a powerful framework of understanding for Dewey's theory of inquiry as an educational model, in order to support the construction and development of a reflective epistemology of practice in the professions. Schön, *The Reflective Practitioner: How Professionals Think in Action* (London: Temple Smith, 1983), and *Educating the Reflective Practitioner* (San Francisco: Jossey-Bass, 1987).

34. Dewey describes how the premise of an effective learning process is a "true, reflective attention" which "always involves judging, reasoning, deliberation; it means that the child has a question of his own, and is actively engaged in seeking and selecting relevant material with which to answer it, considering the bearings and relations of this

material—the kind of solution it calls for. The problem is one's own; hence also the impetus, the stimulus to attention, is one's own; hence also the training secured is one's own—it is discipline, or gain in power of control; that is, a habit of considering problems" (MW 1: 103). From this perspective, "at the maximum appeal, and the full meaning in the life of the child, could be secured only when the studies were presented not as bare external studies, but from the standpoint of the relation they bear to the life of society" (MW 1: 70).

35. Dewey points out this issue clearly in *The Educational Situation* where he writes: "I have already referred to the fact that we are living in a period of applied science. What this means for present purposes is that the professions, the practical occupations of men, are becoming less and less empirical routines, or technical facilities acquired through unintelligent apprenticeship. They are more and more infused with reason; more and more illuminated by the spirit of inquiry and reason. They are dependent upon science, in a word. To decline to recognize this intimate connection of professions in modern life with the discipline and culture that come from the pursuit of truth for its own sake, is to be at least one century behind the times" (MW 1: 310).

36. The process of inquiry, as Jim Garrison points out, cannot be explored outside its context which is a whole with aesthetic and emotional implications. Therefore inquiry has an affective dimension and involves emotions, imagination, intuition. Garrison, "The Aesthetic Context of Inquiry and the Teachable Moment" in his *Dewey and Eros: Wisdom and Desire in the Art of Teaching* (New York: Teachers College Press, 1997).

37. MW 1: 310.

CHAPTER 22: *THE SOURCES OF A SCIENCE OF EDUCATION* BY JOHN DEWEY AND THE ITALIAN INTERPRETATIONS

1. Paul Kurtz, "Introduction" to *The Later Works of John Dewey*, vol. 5, LW 5: xi–xxxii.

2. Giuseppe Spadafora, *Studi deweyani* (Cosenza, Italy: Fondazione Italiana John Dewey, 2006).

3. Larry Hickman and Giuseppe Spadafora, ed., *John Dewey's Educational Philosophy in International Perspective: A New Democracy for the Twenty-First Century* (Carbondale: Southern Illinois University Press, 2009).

4. LW 5: 3.

5. LW 5: 8.

6. LW 5: 23.

7. LW 5: 17.

8. LW 5: 38.

9. LW 5: 40.

10. Giuseppe Spadafora and Colonnello Pio, ed., *Croce e Dewey* (Naples: Bibliopoli, 2002).

11. LW 12: 481–505.

12. MW 13: 290.

13. Teodora Pezzano, *Il giovane Dewey. Individuo, Educazione, Assoluto* (Rome: Armando, 2007).

14. Larry Hickman, *John Dewey's Pragmatic Technology* (Bloomington: Indiana University Press, 1990).

15. John R. Shook, *Dewey's Empirical Theory of Knowledge and Reality* (Nashville, TN: Vanderbilt University Press, 2000).

16. Francesco De Bartolomeis, *La pedagogia come scienza* (Florence: La Nuova Italia, 1953/1972).

17. Aldo Visalberghi, *Problemi della ricerca pedagogica* (Florence: La Nuova Italia, 1964); Aldo Visalberghi, Roberto Maragliano, and Benedetto Vertecchi, *Pedagogia e scienze dell'educazione* (Milan: Mondadori, 1978).

18. Giuseppe Spadafora, *Interpretazioni pedagogiche deweyane in America e in Italia* (Catania, Italy: Facoltà di Lettere e Filosofia, 1997); Spadafora, ed., *Giovanni Gentile. La pedagogia, la scuola* (Rome: Armando, 1997); Spadafora, "Genesi e struttura della società, ovvero l'attualismo incompiuto," *Topologik* 4 (2008): 123–35; Spadafora, "Giovanni Gentile. Ipotesi di una biografia filosofica," in *Rileggere Gentile*, ed. Franco Cambi and Epifania Giambalvo (Florence: Fondazione Nazionale "Vito Fazio Allmayer," 2009).

19. Spadafora, *Interpretazioni pedagogiche deweyane in America e in Italia*.

CHAPTER 23: THE ORIGINS OF THE ITALIAN MISUNDERSTANDING OF DEWEY'S PHILOSOPHY

1. F. Simoni, "Benedetto Croce: A Case of International Misunderstanding," *JAAC* 11 (1952): 7.

2. E. F. Carritt, "Translator's Note," in B. Croce, *My Philosophy* (London: Allen & Unwin, 1949), p. 5.

3. L. Bellatalla, *John Dewey e la cultura italiana del Novecento* (Pisa, Italy: ETS, 1999), pp. 36–37.

4. Ibid., p. 73.

5. Quoted in C. Pironti, "La scuola e la società in John Dewey," *Rivista Pedagogica* 2 (1911): 193–203.

6. Bellatalla, *John Dewey*, p. 43.

7. *The Quest for Certainty*, LW 4: 163.

8. H. Bergson, *La pensée et le mouvant* (Paris: PUF, 1969), pp. 99–100.

9. I. Calvino, "Dall'opaco," in I. Calvino, *Romanzi e racconti*, vol. 3 (Milan: Mondadori 1994), pp. 89–91.

10. M. Alcaro, "La riflessione di Dewey sulla scienza," in *Croce e Dewey. Cinquanta anni dopo*, ed. P. Colonnello and G. Spadafora (Naples: Bibliopolis, 2002), p. 201.

11. A. Einstein, "On the Effects of External Sensory Input on Time Dilation," in *Journal of Exothermic Science and Technology* 1, no. 9 (1938).

About the Contributors

JOHN PETER ANTON is Distinguished Professor of Greek Philosophy and Culture at the University of South Florida in Tampa.

RANDALL E. AUXIER is Professor of Philosophy at Southern Illinois University, Carbondale.

NATHAN BUPP is Director of Communications at the Center for Inquiry in Amherst, New York.

SUSAN D. CARLE is Professor of Law at American University in Washington, DC.

ARTHUR EFRON is Professor Emeritus of English at the University at Buffalo, New York.

STEPHEN M. FISHMAN is Professor of Philosophy at the University of North Carolina, Charlotte.

PETER GODFREY-SMITH is Professor of Philosophy at Harvard University in Cambridge, Massachusetts.

JAMES GOUINLOCK is Professor Emeritus of Philosophy at Emory University in Atlanta, Georgia.

JUDITH M. GREEN is Professor of Philosophy at Fordham University in New York City.

LARRY A. HICKMAN is Professor of Philosophy and the Director of the Center for Dewey Studies at Southern Illinois University, Carbondale.

PHILIP KITCHER is John Dewey Professor of Philosophy and James R. Barker Professor of Contemporary Civilization at Columbia University in New York City.

PAUL KURTZ is Professor Emeritus of Philosophy at the University at Buffalo, New York, and founder and former chairman of the Center for Inquiry in Amherst, New York.

JOSEPH MARGOLIS is Laura H. Carnell Professor of Philosophy at Temple University in Philadelphia, Pennsylvania.

LUCILLE MCCARTHY is Professor of English at the University of Maryland, Baltimore County.

GREGORY FERNANDO PAPPAS is Professor of Philosophy at Texas A&M University in College Station, Texas.

RUSSELL PRYBA is a doctoral candidate in the philosophy department of the University at Buffalo, New York.

HILARY PUTNAM is Cogan University Professor Emeritus of Philosophy at Harvard University in Cambridge, Massachusetts.

RUTH ANNA PUTNAM is Professor Emerita of Philosophy at Wellesley College in Wellesley, Massachusetts.

JAY SCHULKIN is Research Professor of Physiology, Biophysics, and Neuroscience in the Center for the Brain Basis of Cognition at Georgetown University in Washington, D.C.

JOHN R. SHOOK is Research Associate in Philosophy at the University at Buffalo, New York, and Senior Research Fellow at the Center for Inquiry in Amherst, New York.

GIUSEPPE SPADAFORA is Professor of the Science of Education at the University of Calabria, Italy.

MAURA STRIANO is Associate Professor in the Department of Relational Sciences, University of Naples Federico II, Italy.

MASSIMO VITTORIO is Professor of Social Ethics at the University of Catania, Italy.

JUDY WALKER is a Fellow of the Center for Inquiry in Amherst, New York, and an independent author living in Colorado.

ERIC THOMAS WEBER is Assistant Professor in the department of Public Policy Leadership at the University of Mississippi in Oxford, Mississippi.